500
Small Houses
of the Twenties

500
Small Houses
of the Twenties

Compiled by

Henry Atterbury Smith

DOVER PUBLICATIONS, INC.
New York

Published in Canada by General Publishing Company, Ltd., 30 Lesmill Road, Don Mills, Toronto, Ontario.
Published in the United Kingdom by Constable and Company, Ltd.

This Dover edition, first published in 1990, is an unabridged republication of the work first published by Home Owners Service Institute, New York, 1923, under the title *The Books of a Thousand Homes: Volume I containing 500 plans of Moderate Cost 3 to 8 Room Houses: Working Drawings & Specifications Available*. The original title page carried the date of 1921, an obvious error. Pages 1–24, 281–85, and 287, printed in black, white, and blue in the original, are here reproduced in black and white. The text and illustrations on page 4, "The Most Talked-of House in America," originally faced the title page. The Publisher's Note has been specially prepared for this edition.

Manufactured in the United States of America
Dover Publications, Inc.
31 East 2nd Street
Mineola, N.Y. 11501

Library of Congress Cataloging-in-Publication Data

Smith, Henry Atterbury, b. 1872.
    [Books of a thousand homes. Volume 1]
    500 small houses of the twenties / compiled by Henry Atterbury Smith.
        p.   cm.
    Reprint, with new introd. Originally published as v. 1 of: The books of a thousand homes. New York : Home Owners Service Institute, 1923.
    ISBN 0-486-26300-2
    1. Architecture, Domestic—United States—Designs and plans. 2. Small houses—United States—Designs and plans. I. Title. II. Title: Five hundred small houses of the twenties.
NA7205.S6525   1990
728'.37'0222—dc20   90-2845
                                        CIP

Publisher's Note

THE PROSPEROUS YEARS following the First World War saw an increased demand for middle-class housing in the United States. For some decades prior to the War, a set of ideals for such housing had been evolving, in part owing to the influence of the American Arts and Crafts movement. It was felt that a dwelling should be owned by the family that occupies it and should be occupied by just one family. The house should be aesthetically pleasing but not overornate and should be well integrated with its surroundings. It should be soundly constructed and comfortable but also practical and economical to live in.

The five hundred houses in this book represent almost every type of design for a small or midsized single-family dwelling that had been conceived up to that time and could be made to fit the prevalent ideals. With floor plans and photographs or perspective drawings, as well as descriptions of the distinctive features of each house, these designs form an invaluable record of middle-class single-family housing in America around 1923. Most of these houses were intended for suburban sites, but a few were suitable for the country or the less congested parts of cities.

All of the material following the descriptions of the houses, including the practical advice on construction and decoration, has been retained here, primarily for its historical value, although some of it may still be of use to current home owners. Naturally, the costs specified and mail-order offers made in these pages have been long out-of-date and no longer hold good. Dover Publications has no connection with the Home Owners Service Institute and cannot provide the working drawings mentioned herein or any further information on the houses described in this book. Offers of this kind printed herein are retained solely for their value as historical documents.

The Most Talked-of House in America

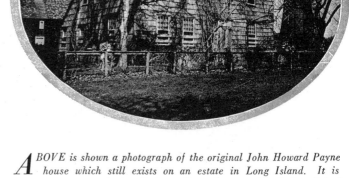

THIS house was built in the Spring of 1923 as a modernized replica of the home of John Howard Payne to commemorate the one hundredth anniversary of the writing of his immortal song, "Home Sweet Home." It also represents the official demonstration house in the National Capitol for the "Better Homes in America" movement. The house was built in the shadow of the White House and officially opened by President Harding, after which it was presented to the General Federation of Women's Clubs as a permanent demonstration point for home economics. The funds which paid for its construction were provided by the Home Owners Service Institute through contributions of materials and money from the various nationally known manufacturers who are co-operating members of the Institute. Complete plans are available for this attractive home as described on Page 24, where floor plans are shown. The architect for the house as built in Washington is Donn Barber but the interior arrangement has been changed for general use as shown in the floor plans after redesigning by the Home Owners Service Institute.

ABOVE is shown a photograph of the original John Howard Payne house which still exists on an estate in Long Island. It is interesting to note how well the architect has maintained the original lines, making only changes necessitated by modern homeowning requirements.

Photographs of the completed house shown on Page 41.

See Page 24 for Floor Plans as Redesigned by the Home Owners Service Institute

ACKNOWLEDGMENT

IT is perhaps difficult to conceive the vast amount of human effort and time involved in a preparation of a service book as this Volume I of the Books of a Thousand Homes. This has been not merely an editorial problem, complex in its nature, and requiring comprehensive knowledge of all elements of dwelling house construction, but each plan in itself represents the original expenditure of much careful thought and time in its execution. When it is understood that for each plan shown in this book there is now ready a complete set of working drawings, details and specifications, some visualization of the extent of this enterprise may be possible.

At this time the Home Owners Service Institute is glad of the opportunity of acknowledging the invaluable co-operation of a number of individuals and organizations without whom the provision of this book and the service behind would have been impossible.

Our first acknowledgment, therefore, is to Henry Atterbury Smith, member of the American Institute of Architects and of the American Society of Civil Engineers, an architect of high standing and long experience in the housing field. Henry Atterbury Smith has become internationally known for his unusual and successful work in the development of practical forms of multi-family housing, being the originator and designer of the open-stair type of apartment and tenement housing the masses at low rental. The East River Homes designed for Mrs. William K. Vanderbilt, Sr., at a cost of over $2,000,000 to house originally 400 tubercular families, are a monument to his efforts. Several thousand families of wage earners live in other open-stair dwellings designed and several of them built by him. At present he is constructing an open-stair apartment near Columbia University, New York, to shelter university, musical and other students at rentals within their frequently limited means.

Graduating from the School of Architecture, Columbia University, in 1892, he has practiced the architectural profession for over thirty years, in the small house field exclusively, until 1909, when he designed the first open-stair dwellings for Mrs. Vanderbilt. As the demand for moderate cost dwellings developed rapidly during the last few years and with nearly one million such homes now needed throughout the United States, his interest has in a large measure returned to this field. He has been a strong power in the development of the Home Owners Service Institute, an organization primarily devoted to the provision of a practical educational service for the prospective home builder. This book and the plan service which it represents is but one of the divisions of activities of the Institute in which the co-operation of Henry Atterbury Smith has been found invaluable.

Our next expression of appreciation is directed to the large number of architects whose work is represented in this volume. Among these will be noted the names of many of the foremost small house architects of America and in all cases the plans are representative of skill and experience which has been directed toward the solution of almost every type of small house problem with which a designer may be confronted. Because of the limitation of space it is impossible to list here the names of the architects, to all of whom our gratitude is expressed, but with each plan will be found the name of the architect who has been responsible for its development. The total of 500 plans which are shown in this book represent an original expenditure of well over a quarter of a million dollars which, of course, would have been impossible from the viewpoint of the Institute if the architects and organizations by whom the plans were developed had not given their consent to co-operate in this effort to provide a dependable plan service for the building public.

In developing this collection of plans an intensive study was made not only of the work of individual architects in the small house field but of groups of plans developed by various individuals and organizations as a form of service to home builders. A large proportion of these plans are the work of individual architects which has never before been made available to the general public. Other plans represent a careful selection of the best material of this nature which has been developed through architectural competitions organized by the service departments of building material manufacturers and manufacturers' organizations.

Organizations which have co-operated in supplying plans include: American Face Brick Association, Portland Cement Association, Common Brick Industries of America, The Curtis Companies, Hollow Building Tile Manufacturers Association, National Lumber Manufacturers Association and Associated Metal Lath Manufacturers.

To these it is also a pleasure to extend the assurance of our appreciation and our acknowledgment of the great value of their co-operation in the difficult task which is now completed as this book reaches its final form.

President, Home Owners Service Institute

America's Most Popular Small House Plan

THIS charming and picturesque six-room house has probably been built more times throughout the country than any other ever designed. In October, 1919, John Floyd Yewell was awarded second prize in the competition conducted by the American Face Brick Association, with the co-operation of the Architectural Forum, among architects and draftsmen nationally for the best designs of small brick homes.

Practicability of the plan is proven by a photograph of this house shown on the page opposite. Every graceful line and angle conceived by Mr. Yewell, its designer, has been brought out in the house as built at Atlanta, Georgia.

Comparing the photograph with the architect's perspective sketch will indicate how easy it is for a good builder to perfectly reproduce the design of a house from architect's working drawings and specifications, if the plans are properly prepared to begin with.

The interior of this brick house of English suburban type is just as distinctive as its exterior. Living room is nicely proportioned and well lighted with attractive groups of windows. It has an open fireplace, and cozy window seat.

There is a breakfast nook as well as the dining room. The kitchen is conveniently planned. The rear is so arranged that the garden development can be enjoyed from both dining room and living porch, which could be glassed in as a continuation of the living room.

There are three bedrooms and bath on the second floor. A fireplace also can be built in one of the upstairs bedrooms, as indicated. There is ample clothes closet space. A trap door overhead in the hall permits of access to storage space in the attic.

The dimensions of the house are 27 feet by 34 feet. The height of the first floor ceiling is 8 feet, and of the second, 7 feet 6 inches.

The house is fitted to either an inside or a corner lot location. It can face the street as shown in the illustration, or the long side of the living room and the porch may be toward the street.

As built in Atlanta, Ga.
Burge, Stevens & Condlin, Supervising Architects

America's Most Popular Small House Plan

First Floor—*Living room with fireplace and built-in window seat, living porch or glassed-in sun parlor, vestibule hall with coat closet, dining room, separate breakfast nook, kitchen with built-in cabinets, 2 closets, service vestibule with ice box recess.*

Second Floor—*3 bedrooms, fireplace in master bedroom as shown, 6 closets, tiled bathroom, trap door in ceiling providing access to storage space above.*

A detailed description of this plan will be found on the opposite page.

As designed by John Floyd Yewell, Architect

An Unusual 6-Room Colonial Frame House

THERE are a number of points about this plan which make it one of the most unusual and interesting plans presented in the entire volume.

The elevation of the house has been designed in the simple, dignified Colonial style, using siding and roof in wood, masonry or patented shingles, with chimney of brick or stone.

The interior arrangement of the house is well worth careful study. A small entry is provided with convenient coat closet, and passing into the living room the distinguishing feature is the large fireplace with ingle nook and built-in seats. This room is lighted at one side by a five-section casement window, and a French door is provided at the other end of the room opening on to the living porch. Flanking this door are built-in book closets. From the living room small arched doors lead to the service section of the house and to the dining space which is arranged with built-in seats and a refectory type table. A small cold room is provided off the kitchen with refrigerator located so that ice may be provided from the entry porch. The subdivision of the service section allows also space for an extra lavatory, while a linen closet with a laundry chute is conveniently located on the first floor.

In this plan the dining space is provided on a temporary basis and provision is made for a future dining room, at which time the present dining space may be a breakfast room.

One of the three bedrooms upstairs is provided with an open fireplace, and all have ample closet room. It will be noted on the plan that provision is also made for a bedroom extension above the future dining room.

An Unusual 6-Room Colonial Frame House

With plan for future wing to contain a dining room and bedroom

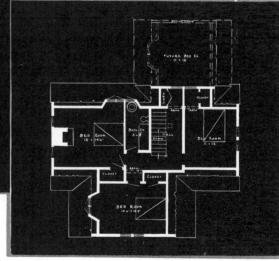

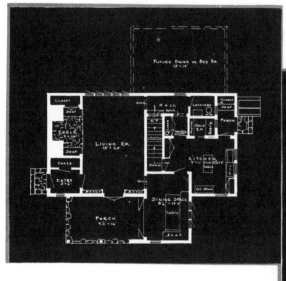

CHARLES E. CUTLER, *Architect*

An 8-Room House of Unusual Architectural Merit

IT is perhaps impossible to offer a better example than this design indicating the practical application of good architecture in the small house field. The architect who designed this house, James Dwight Baum, is the winner of the 1923 Gold Medal of the Architectural League of New York, awarded for meritorious contribution to the architecture of the Country. In the awarding of this medal, domestic architecture played no small part and the excellence of small house design as developed by Mr. Baum has contributed strongly to his success.

In common with many other leading architects whose work appears in this volume, this is the first time that any of Mr. Baum's designs have been made available to the public through a service organization such as the Home Owners Service Institute. It is gratifying that this form of co-operation should be forthcoming as a recognition of the service which this volume represents to the prospective builder of a moderate cost home.

In developing the exterior of this design the combination of simplicity and correct architectural detail results in a pleasing, dignified effect. A study of the main entrance indicates the importance of this feature and the attractive result which may be gained where careful designing provides correct proportions. All window openings are also carefully proportioned and arranged, while the selection of brick in color and texture contributes strongly to the finished effect.

The roofing and columns of the porte-cochere and the open porch greatly increase the visual impression of size and well balanced proportion.

A square house of this type lends itself to a clean-cut subdivision of the floor areas and consequently the plan is an excellent example of a central hall and staircase layout. The kitchen facilities are increased by the desirable feature of a pantry. An extra lavatory is provided on the first floor and various service features connected with the kitchen are well arranged. The living room is thrown open to a large porch and to the sun room, creating a maximum of comfort and utility in the living section of the house.

The bedrooms are well lighted and well proportioned, with ample wall space.

An 8-Room House
of Unusual Architectural Merit

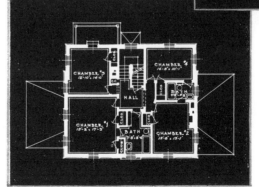

DETAIL OF ENTRANCE DOOR

Porte-cochere and p o r c h
wings add to mass and proportion, greatly increasing
visual impression of size.

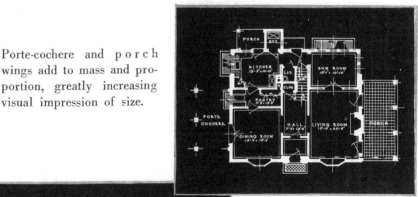

The architect of this house is
the winner of the 1923 Gold
Medal awarded by the Architectural League of New York.

JAMES DWIGHT BAUM, *Architect*

Plan No. 221   45,484 *Cubic Feet*

A Popular 6-Room Colonial Residence

(Brick or Stucco on Hollow Tile)

IN gathering together various house plans illustrated in this volume, the endeavor was made to select the best from among many designs that had proven most popular and generally desired by home builders. This two-story Colonial residence is an adaptation of the plan so generally followed by our English Colonist forefathers, both in exterior architectural lines and interior room arrangement, with the opportunity for utility and space conservation.

In a survey conducted among many owners of hollow-tile houses it was found that this house design was the most popular among the plans of homes built of this material. Consequently the plan is presented here. The exterior walls are hollow tile with either stucco finish or with brick veneer. The front perspective drawing shows how the house would appear if brick veneering was used over the tile. The rear view shows the exterior finish of stucco.

A simple grandeur is achieved by the terraced lawn, which completely surrounds the house, according to the architect's suggestion. It is not necessary, however, to so locate or terrace the house. It would be most pleasing on any fairly level lot, either inside or corner.

The slightly severe lines are effectively softened by the graceful Colonial entrance details, the open porch across the end supported by handsome Colonial pillars, adding to the impression of spaciousness, with the projecting end chimneys and wooden shutters giving the home a most pleasing and inviting air. The end porch, of course, could be glassed in to be used as a sun room.

FRONT VIEW IN HOLLOW TILE
AND BRICK CONSTRUCTION

REAR VIEW IN HOLLOW TILE AND STUCCO CONSTRUCTION

A Popular 6-Room Colonial Residence

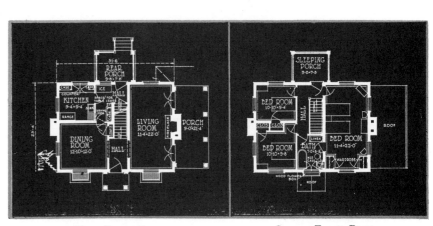

FIRST FLOOR PLAN   SECOND FLOOR PLAN

An Interesting 8-Room House in Four Exteriors

THERE is no better nor more convincing illustration of the fact that totally different architectural exterior designs are applicable to one and the same floor plan than is shown on the opposite page. For practically every plan in this volume an entirely different architectural elevation could be designed, to suit the taste of the owner or as one possibly more in keeping with traditions of the section in which it is to be built.

Similarly, different structural materials can be used in the erection of side walls, for roofing, in interior construction and fixtures, with almost any plan. The accompanying four elevations show clearly the possible diversity of exterior architecture and structural materials.

Plan No. 318 is a splendid example of Colonial type, carried out in stucco, with composition roofing on the flat hip roof. The strictly symmetrical placing of chimneys and shuttered windows focuses the attention on the beautiful entrance portico. Mahogany and ivory hall stair, along with the mantels and corner dining room china closet emphasize the Colonial atmosphere.

Plan No. 117 is a pure Colonial design for frame construction. This gives you an idea of the difference produced by changing materials of construction and form of roof. Specifications call for 10-inch siding with a slightly overhanging second story and gable roof. Casements in the gable ends ventilate the attic and make it possible to finish off rooms there later, if desired.

Plan No. 319 shows a half-timbered and stucco design of English architectural influence. Overhanging second story, windows of dormer type with triple casements breaking through the eaves, and a quaint vestibule entrance, all contribute to the distinctiveness of the exterior. The living room of this design has wood-paneled walls and beamed ceiling. Woodwork is specified of oak, stained dark, in English fashion. It is possible to get correct English designs of interior millwork and built-in features from stock.

Plan No. 118 is of the so-called American Western type of architecture. A combination of stucco and eight-inch wood siding is shown, but brick could be used equally effectively for the lower portion. Twin gables and chimneys are strictly symmetrical. Central motif of formal entrance and grouped casements above is attractive. Notice the well-chosen brackets supporting the overhanging second story. Batten shutters at the symmetrically placed windows add to the exterior appearance. Paneled wainscot and beamed ceiling are specified for living room.

STUCCO WITH LOW-PITCHED TILE ROOF
(Plan No. 318)

COLONIAL SIDING WITH HIGH SHINGLE ROOF
(Plan No. 117)

An Interesting 8-Room House in Four Exteriors

A demonstration of the adaptability of varied architecture to the same
floor plan—an indication of the logical use of exterior wall materials.

STUCCO AND TIMBER WITH SLATE ROOF
(Plan No. 319)

STUCCO WITH SHINGLED GABLES AND SIDING
(Plan No. 118)

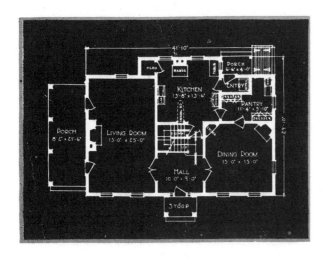

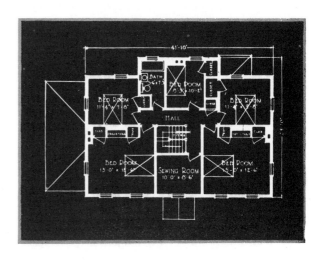

FREDERICK L. ACKERMAN, *Architect*

Plans 318, 117, 319, 118   *Average* 37,000 *Cubic Feet*

A Square Dutch Colonial 6-Room House

(With Sleeping Porch)

IT has been well said that the character of a people may be determined by the homes they live in, and that the best monument a man can erect for future generations is a home of permanent construction. The pioneers in America, being dependent upon the materials at hand, built log cabins, and from these evolved the American home of our fathers.

Materials obtainable in Colonial days are often unsuited to the congested areas of large cities. Attention, therefore, is being concentrated much on permanent, fire-resistive types of construction. Concrete block and tile go long toward meeting these requirements. Cement stucco is pleasing and artistic in appearance. A roof of fireproof shingles or tile completes the requirements for a type of fire-resistive home such as the one illustrated on the opposite page.

The outside elevations are an adaptation of the Dutch Colonial design which is generally popular. White stucco on concrete block with green blinds and trim and red brick sills, course and steps, will be very pleasing, while the trellis-covered front porches when overgrown with vines will add greatly to the artistic charm of the dwelling.

This is a six-room, square, two-story house; a model of compact and commodious planning. The living porch and sleeping porch above in reality add two more rooms.

Only 28 feet wide, it could, if necessary, be placed on a 35-foot lot, though a 40-foot lot would be better.

From a tile vestibule with double doors one enters a convenient hallway and passes through an arch into a finely proportioned living room. The central fireplace has deep openings on each side and in the recesses of the openings, bookshelves and cupboards have been artfully contrived. Another opening leads into a fine sun porch with casement windows on three sides. The dining room and kitchen occupy the rear of the house. Both rooms have windows on both sides. The kitchen is a model of good arrangement, with an opening for the icebox so it may be filled from the entryway. The upstairs contains one small room and two larger bedrooms; a sleeping porch above the sun porch is entered from the front bedrooms. The bathroom has a tile floor.

A Square Dutch Colonial House (*with Sleeping Porch*)

A six-room, square two-story house of white
stucco on concrete block, red brick sills and steps.

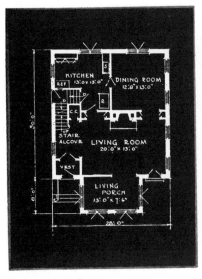

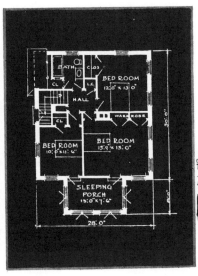

J. T. POMEROY, *Architect*

Two Attractive 7-Room Brick Bungalows

THE upper house shown on the opposite page is a brick bungalow of southern type.

Large rooms with high ceilings and plenty of porches characterize this plan, features especially popular in the South. In addition to an open terrace, two main porches, and two sleeping porches, there is a patio in the rear for flowers, which serves as an entrance to the garden. It would require a lot with a hundred foot frontage at least, and would look best if placed upon a slight elevation. It may be faced in any direction and yet obtain good exposure for all rooms.

As only a part of the space is excavated for a cellar, there is plenty of room for a garage under the house, if it is desired, and the conditions of the lot permit. The basement contains space for heating plant, coal bins, laundry, and fruit cellar.

Garden Wall Bond and raked joints are suggested for the brickwork. Spanish or shingle tile, or thick slates of variegated color, are recommended for the roof. Brick floors on the porches and terraces, as well as brick walks, will harmonize best with the walls of the house. The ceiling height is nine feet, except in the dining and living rooms, which are ten and twelve respectively.

The lower house is an English bungalow design. It is one of the most interesting bungalow designs shown in this book. It provides the casual rambling type of home which is found desirable by many, and its plan offers unusual opportunities for attractive interior decoration, and for the establishment of interesting vistas both outside and inside.

The two well-balanced and proportioned gables, connected by the central living room, with its fine bay, form a delightfully charming composition. The arched entrance leads to a reception hall which directly opens into the living room. The detail gives a good idea of this large, fine room, out of which one may go directly to the flower court, breakfast room, dining room, or main porch.

The dining room is of good size and has a fireplace at one end flanked by built-in china cases. The breakfast room, with its built-in sideboard, looks out on the flower garden court. The kitchen, pantry, and porch complete that wing. In the other wing are located the bedrooms, two of which have a bathroom between them, while the third has a private bath, with a shower instead of a tub. There are two good sleeping porches opening from two of the rooms, one with a small fireplace.

Besides ample closets in the bedrooms, there are good linen and coat closets in the hall. The basement is arranged as in No. 715. The ceiling height is nine feet, except in the dining and living rooms, which are ten and eleven feet respectively.

The construction of these houses is of face brick, and the working drawings include three wall sections which show the complete wall construction for face brick over solid brick on hollow tile backing and brick veneering, in which face brick is used instead of siding over the frame of the house.

GARDEN VISTA

LIVING-ROOM
PERSPECTIVE

Two Attractive Bungalows of Face Brick Construction

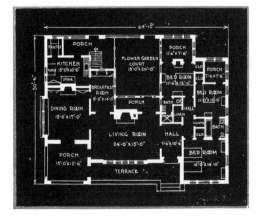

(Floor plan for upper house is shown at the left.)

These floor plans indicate alternative arrangements suitable to either elevation.

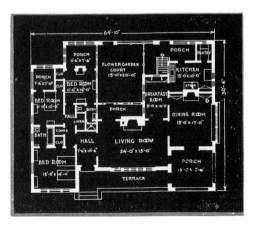

Plan No. 217

Plan No. 218

WARREN & KNIGHT, *Architects*

GEORGE W. REPP, *Architect*

Plan 217 *contains* 45,600 *Cubic Feet*

Plan 218 *contains* 42,235 *Cubic Feet*

A 6-Room Spanish Colonial Tile and Stucco House

THIS house has been very carefully designed for erection in southern climates. In addition to architectural attractiveness the designer has provided good ventilation, unusually ample living accommodations for a small house, and structural integrity which will insure a low factor of depreciation under severe climatic conditions.

Analyzing the floor plans we find that one enters the first floor through an oak and iron door into a small vestibule. The living room, which is of ample size, is well lighted, and contains an attractive fireplace. From the living room French doors open to a large porch. The dining room also contains a fireplace; this provision being made because ordinarily the house will contain no heating plant.

The kitchen is conveniently arranged with a separate entry containing refrigerator. The additional feature of the kitchen is the breakfast nook.

The second floor plan is interesting not only because of its convenient layout, but because of the ample sleeping accommodations achieved through the use of door-beds. In addition to three chambers there are two sleeping porches with special closets built to hold three door-beds. This arrangement provides an alternative for sleeping outdoors, or may accommodate a number of additional guests.

The construction of the house is of masonry and metal throughout, with the exception of the second floor, which is of wood. All rooms on the first floor have floors of tile, interior walls being finished with rough plaster with mosaic tile ornamentation. Windows throughout are of metal. The roof is of clay or cement tile, the exterior color combination being selected by the owner.

This house has recently been built in St. Petersburg, Florida, and has met with unusual favor.

6-Room Spanish Colonial Tile and Stucco Dwelling

(Designed particularly for Southern requirements)

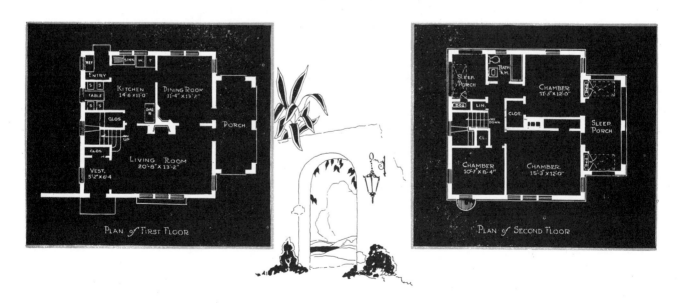

PHILIP RESNYK, *Architect*

A 6-Room House—Modified Georgian Design

(With Common Brick Exterior)

THIS interesting six-room brick house with alternative floor plans, as shown on the opposite page, has received considerable favor in many sections of the country.

An examination of the exterior floors, as shown on the photograph will indicate the possibility of using common brick to obtain a good finished architectural effect. The exterior walls are of solid brick, and for the roof the use of slate or asbestos shingles are suggested.

A choice is offered between two floor plans, in one the opportunity of providing a very large master's bedroom and two small bedrooms, while in the second plan the upper floor is subdivided to provide two fairly large bedrooms and one small bedroom.

The living room in this house offers an opportunity for a particularly attractive interior, casement windows being provided at both ends with small windows flanking the fireplace. A large sun porch is directly connected with the dining room, opening through a wide doorway. This is an attractive arrangement which serves to enlarge the size of the room, and extends an unusual opportunity for attractive decorating and furnishing.

In one plan a large kitchen is provided while the alternative is a smaller kitchen with a pantry, which is a feature desired by many.

6-Room Dwelling of Modified Georgian Design
(Exterior of Common Brick)

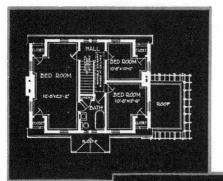

Alternative floor plans are
indicated offering large master's bedroom or space distributed throughout smaller
rooms.

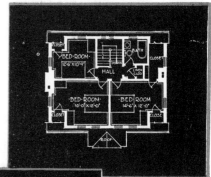

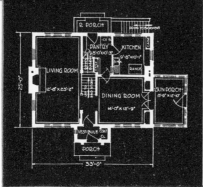

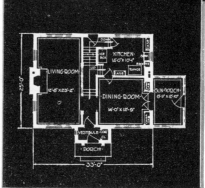

GROSVENOR ATTERBURY, *Architect*

The Most Talked of House in America

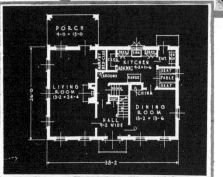

*P*HOTOGRAPHS show (left) Secretary of Commerce Herbert Hoover, Chairman, Advisory Council, National Better Homes Week Committee, breaking ground for the 1923 demonstration "model" house at Washington, D. C.; and (right) Mrs. Frederick G. Winters, President, General Federation of Women's Clubs, laying the cornerstone.

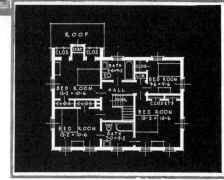

(Perspective Drawing is Shown on Page 4 and Photograph on Opposite Page)

*S*YMBOLIZING the spirit of home ownership and better built homes, on June 4, 1923, President Warren G. Harding officially opened at Washington, D. C., a modernized adaptation of John Howard Payne's birthplace, the "Home, Sweet Home," which inspired that wandering playwright and actor to write the immortal song first sung on May 8, 1823, one hundred years ago.

Constructed of concrete block and white Portland cement stucco, on Sherman Monument Plaza, opposite the White House grounds and the Treasury Building, on Pennsylvania avenue, in the heart of official Washington, it served as the demonstration "model" house for 1923 "Better Homes Week," June 4 to 10.

The house was presented as a

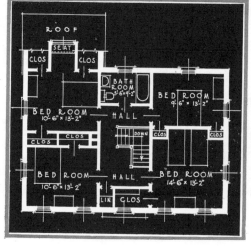

gift to the General Federation of Women's Clubs by a group of nationally known manufacturers of building materials, and associations of such manufacturers, the funds, materials, equipment and labor, and this co-operative action having been received by the Home Owners Service Institute, Inc., L. Porter Moore, President.

Floor plans shown herewith are not those used in the construction of the Washington house, but have been developed from the Payne house to meet requirements in various sections of the country.

Plan No. 316 (above) shows the house with two bathrooms on the second floor (right), while Plan No. 316A (below) shows the second floor with only one bathroom. The first floor plan is identical for both plans.

Plan No. 316 *(and 316A below)*　　　　　　　　　　　　29,500 *Cubic Feet*

The *"Home, Sweet Home"* at *Washington, D. C.*

The completed "Home, Sweet Home."

WITH the permission of Donn Barber, F.A.I.A., of New York, designer of the "Home, Sweet Home," the floor plans for a modernized replica of the birthplace of John Howard Payne (as shown on page 24, opposite) have been redesigned by Whitman S. Wick, architect. The rear elevation has been altered, allowing for a living porch, and a dormer window breaks through the roof to permit of cross ventilation in one rear bedroom.

The house at Washington was planned inside to accommodate the crowds of thousands of visitors who inspected it. A few of the additional door openings cut through for this purpose have been eliminated by Mr. Wick. Dining alcove and kitchen and front entrance hall are of different dimensions.

Specifications call for construction of concrete block or tile, stuccoed with white Portland cement, as the "Home, Sweet Home" house was built at Washington. Plans in frame also are now available through the Home Owners Service Institute.

The living room is developed across the entire end of the house, with light on three sides, a fireplace and French doors opening onto rear living porch. Following the design of the Payne home, the main entrance is directly into the central hall. The square dining room to the right has ample side wall space for placing furnishings. The kitchen, unusually complete, has pantry facilities, breakfast nook and entry.

As the floor plans indicate, two designs are provided for second floor arrangement. In Plan "A" there is only one bath. Two bathrooms are indicated on the other plan. All four bedrooms are ample in size, with

*P*RESIDENT HARDING, *dedicating the "Better Homes Week" demonstration house at Washington, June 4, 1923, received the key from Miss Lida Hafford, Director, General Federation of Women's Clubs. Mrs. Harding and Secretary of War Weeks are on the steps.*

good closet space and linen closet off the upstairs hall. A ceiling trap in the hall gives access to storage space above. Emergency guest accommodation is provided by the installation of a bed-closet off the living room, or this may be made into a book alcove if desired.

Plans of the "Home, Sweet Home" at Washington, as designed by Mr. Barber, modifying and modernizing the plans of the original Payne homestead at Easthampton, are the property of the General Federation of Women's Clubs. Only the redesigned plans of the original Payne homestead, by Mr. Wick, are available through the Home Owners Service Institute.

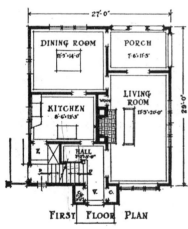

FIRST FLOOR PLAN

A Popular Plan for Stucco Exterior

Six-room house of English cottage type

OSCAR T. LANG, *Architect*

Plan No. 309   *19,858 Cubic Feet*

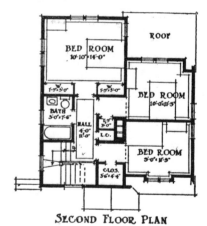

SECOND FLOOR PLAN

THIS attractive English type of six-room stucco house has proven to be an exceedingly popular plan and has been built several times to our knowledge in the suburban districts of New York City. It is a house which, when completed, is quite impressive in character and particularly well suited for location on a fairly large lot in suburban districts. The specifications call for the construction of the house in stucco on back-plastered metal lath or stucco on wood.

The most successful coloring for the stucco exterior seems to be a cream-yellow, which is obtained by mixing the required color with the cement before ap-plication. The finish which seems desirable is a rough-trowelled or hand-plastered effect. For the roof, shingles of copper, slate or asbestos-cement will be found preferable. The color scheme should be a general blending of reds, blues and yellows; or brown, green and blue. The exterior trim may be painted to match or may be painted in some complementary color which will provide sufficient contrast to stress the well-located exterior openings.

The arrangement of the floor plans is practical and seems to meet the requirements of the average small family without any change from the layouts indicated.

Full directions for obtaining complete working drawings and specifications will be found on page 281

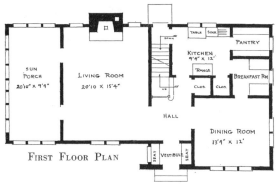

FIRST FLOOR PLAN

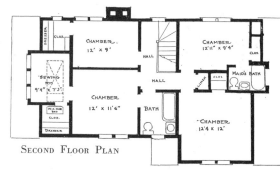

SECOND FLOOR PLAN

Plan No. 720   GLENN PHELPS, *Architect*   28,860 *Cubic Feet*

A 7-Room House of English Character

THIS attractive seven-room dwelling has an exterior of stucco with some half-timbered work in the gables. This house was published originally in the Small House Page of the *New York Tribune* in 1923, and received extremely favorable comment. Many persons indicated their interest in building the house because of its impressive but practical character for a dwelling of such limited size.

In designing the exterior the architect has very cleverly utilized long sweeping roof lines, but has provided a sufficient number of breaks and details to eliminate any possible monotony. By the selection of proper stucco color and roof shingles, it is possible to develop a most pleasing architectural effect.

The house is entered through a small vestibule into a central hall, which has a wide inter-room opening into commodious living quarters. These include a large living room, with open fireplace, the size of which is augmented by a sun porch running across the entire end of the house and connected through the living room by two doors, or wide French doors may be used.

Full directions for obtaining complete working drawings and specifications will be found on page 281

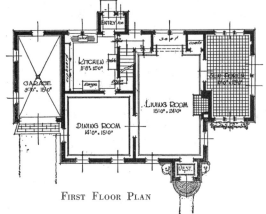

FIRST FLOOR PLAN

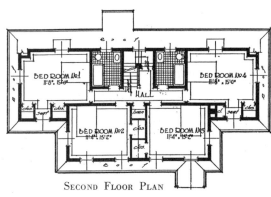

SECOND FLOOR PLAN

Plan No. 131   R. C. HUNTER & BRO., *Architects*   34,490 *Cubic Feet*

A 7-Room Colonial Home—Shingled Exterior

HERE is a type of home made familiar by the good taste and common sense of the domestic architecture developed in past years throughout the New England and North Atlantic states. This is an English Colonial house, having an exterior of shingles or wide siding and a roof of shingle type with large chimney of brick. The plan has been excellently developed and cleverly provides space for a built-in garage as indicated on the first floor. The entrance is directly into a large living room which has the attractive features of window seat and open fireplace, together with wide entrance into a large sun room. The second floor arrangement is excellent. Each bedroom has ventilation and lighting from two or three sides and ample closet space is provided. It would be difficult to imagine a more attractive or convenient arrangement for a house of this character.

For those who desire a variation of exterior building materials it will be noted that the exterior walls of the first story may be in red or red-toned face brick, while the upper section and gables may be in white or cream colored shingles or wide Colonial siding.

Full directions for obtaining complete working drawings and specifications will be found on page 281

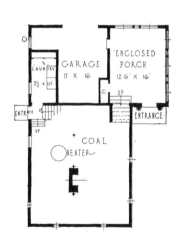

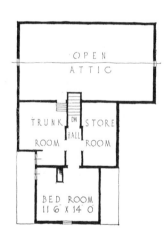

Plan No. 721   J. T. TUBBY, *Architect*   23,100 *Cubic Feet*

An Interesting Innovation in Dwelling Design

THIS unusual design may in a sense be termed an innovation by an architect who has long specialized in moderate cost domestic architecture. Owing to lack of space we have not been able to show a section through this house, but it will be noted by a study of the floor plans and the perspective that the house is arranged in unusual floor levels. There is a cellar space excavated only under the main section of the house which contains a living room, dining room and kitchen. The rear section of the house which contains garage and an enclosed porch, has a first floor level slightly below grade and a second floor level which is only a few steps up from the floor level of the living room section (which is located considerably above grade). This provides two bedrooms above the garage and enclosed porch, while another short flight of stairs leads up to bedroom and store rooms above the living room.

The architect's theory, which seems to be thoroughly practical, is that this type of house is more economical to build than the ordinary cellar and two-floor design to which we are accustomed by long use.

Full directions for obtaining complete working drawings and specifications will be found on page 281

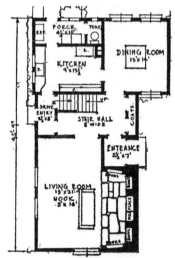

FIRST FLOOR PLAN

Three Interesting Homes of Spanish Character

The houses on this and the opposite page are designed for construction of stucco on back-plastered metal lath.

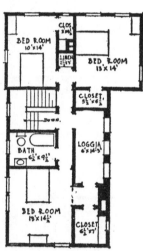

SECOND FLOOR PLAN

Plan No. 303   MONTGOMERY & NIBECKER   26,507 *Cubic Feet*
Architects

ON this and the opposite page there will be found three particularly interesting designs of houses which have the characteristics of Spanish architecture. While these are the types which are often built on the Pacific Coast and are sometimes known as the California Mission type, they are quite practical and acceptable for building in any section of the country.

The house shown on this page is a six-room residence having a large living room, the feature of which is an unusual ingle-nook floored with stone flagging and containing bookcases, seats and a large fireplace. The usual kitchen and dining room facilities are provided in an attractive layout, and in addition there is an extra lavatory located off the service porch. A feature of the second floor is the loggia, which might easily be used as a sleeping porch or as an enclosed porch. The closet at one end could be arranged to contain a door bed, adding a bedroom.

Full directions for obtaining complete working drawings and specifications will be found on page 281

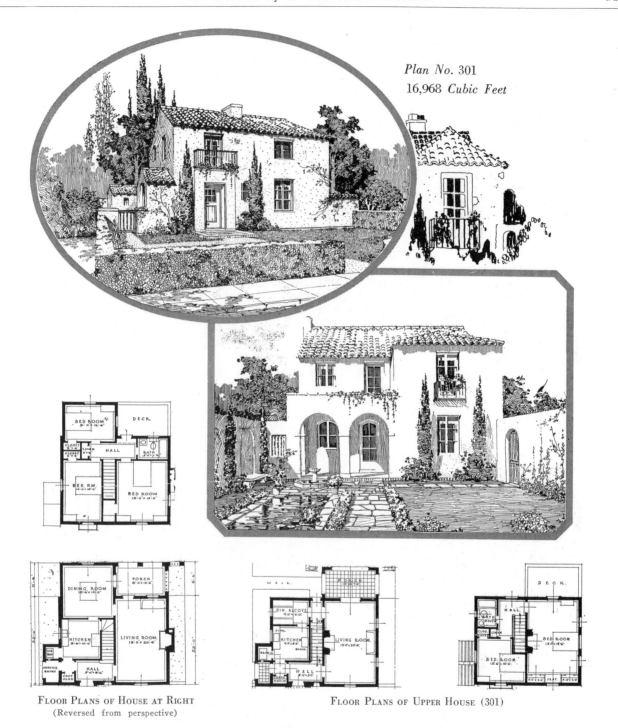

Plan No. 301
16,968 Cubic Feet

FLOOR PLANS OF HOUSE AT RIGHT
(Reversed from perspective)

FLOOR PLANS OF UPPER HOUSE (301)

Plan No. 308 (lower) LOUIS JUSTEMENT, *Architect* *17,562 Cubic Feet*

The 4-Room House

THE upper plan shown on this page indicates the exterior appearance of Plan No. 301 which is for a four-room house. The construction of the houses shown on this page is specified as stucco on back-plastered metal lath. The stucco color will probably be cream or a brilliant yellow, and the roof would normally be of cement tile or clay tile in red.

The 6-Room House

THIS Plan, No. 308, indicates a dwelling somewhat like the four-room house presented on this page, but provides considerably more living space. Exterior construction is similar, and the use of Spanish type garden walls is indicated as adding considerably to the size and architectural effect of the house. On the first floor there is a dining room instead of alcove.

Full directions for obtaining complete working drawings and specifications will be found on page 281

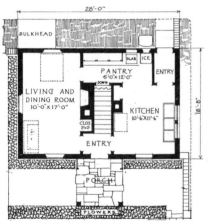

FIRST FLOOR PLAN

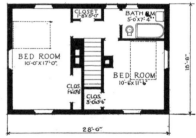

SECOND FLOOR PLAN

RICHARD M. POWERS

Architect

Plan No. 207   14,122 *Cubic Feet*

A Brick House of New England Type Containing Four Rooms

HERE is an interesting New England Colonial type of brick residence, designed by an architect who has designed a number of popular types of homes for readers of monthly publications of interest to women. This small house plan has been very carefully studied to provide all possible features of comfort combined with practical economy and without neglecting the element of attractiveness which can be provided through well-proportioned architecture.

The architect suggests that the exterior walls of this house be of face brick, with brick jambs of window and door openings coated with cement; and jambs and wood staff beads painted a deep warm brown. The exterior of sash and doors, the porch finish and lattice should be painted cream white; roofing to be of clay or cement tiles.

The first floor is arranged with a large living room, occupying approximately one half of the area, and a large kitchen and pantry. It is suggested that one end of the living room be used for dining purposes, as indicated by the dotted line table location on the plan. On the second floor there are two large bedrooms and bath, providing in all a very livable type of house for a comparatively small investment.

Full directions for obtaining complete working drawings and specifications will be found on page 281

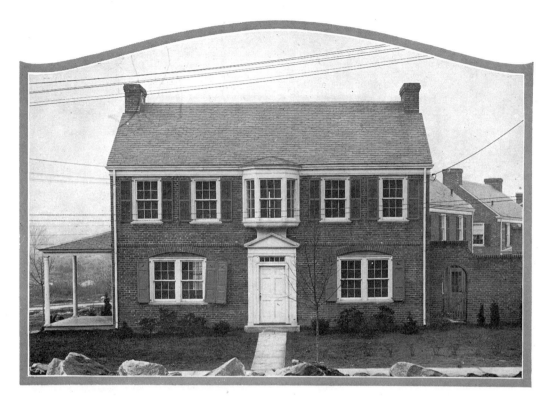

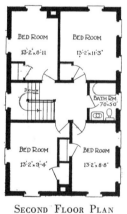

SECOND FLOOR PLAN

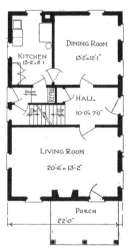

FIRST FLOOR PLAN

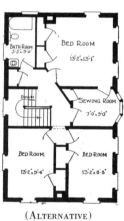

(ALTERNATIVE)

Plan No. 825

23,760 *Cubic Feet*

ELECTUS D. LITCHFIELD & ROGERS, *Architects*

A Dignified Colonial Home of Brick

THIS plan for a Colonial brick residence of seven rooms has been developed by a firm of architects well known in the housing field in connection with the design of residences for government housing work, such as Yorkship Village, located at Camden, N. J., where 1,687 small houses were constructed at one time. This is the *New York Tribune* House No. 37, recently built in the Pelham District of New York City.

Alternative second floor plans are provided, in one of which there is an attractive sewing room and two bedrooms and bath; and in the other four bedrooms are provided, with bathroom.

The architectural design of the house is simple but has been rendered particularly attractive by the use of well proportioned exterior openings and an attractive entrance doorway with small bay above.

Full directions for obtaining complete working drawings and specifications will be found on page 281

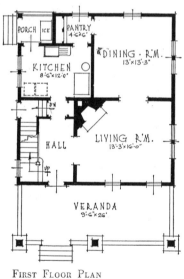

FIRST FLOOR PLAN

Two Excellent Plans for Dutch Colonial Homes

Frame construction throughout, with exteriors of wide siding

This house and that on the opposite page are well-planned for economy of construction

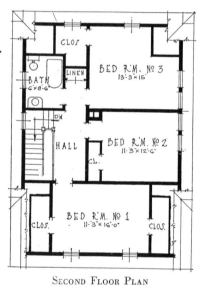

SECOND FLOOR PLAN

Plan No. 655   WHITMAN S. WICK, *Architect*   21,840 *Cubic Feet*

ON these pages there are shown two well-selected plans for Dutch Colonial frame houses having roofs of shingle type. The plan shown on this page is that of a very comfortable six-room house. A large living room extends across the entire front of the house and may easily be glassed in for sun porch if desired. The entrance is into a side entrance hall where the stairs are located and a large inter-room opening provides access to a living room with brick fireplace located in one corner. This location of the chimney allows a flue for the kitchen range. The dining room is square and well lighted, and between kitchen and dining room there is located a convenient pantry. A small rear entry porch with a place for the ice box completes the first floor plan. On the second floor are three well-planned bedrooms.

Full directions for obtaining complete working drawings and specifications will be found on page 281

SECOND FLOOR PLAN

FIRST FLOOR · PLAN

*In the upper photograph this house is shown as actually
built. The only change from the architect's perspective
(below) is the enclosed porch.*

W. W. WEFFERLING, *Architect*

Plan No. 109   19,859 *Cubic Feet*

THE practical phase of the plan service represented
by this book can be no better demonstrated than
by a comparison of the above actual photograph and
the architect's perspective drawing for this house as
indicated in the lower plan. Here it will be found
that the house as actually constructed deviates in no
detail from the architect's perspective except that the
living porch has been built in as a sun porch.

A feature of the exterior is the simple but unusually
attractive entrance selected from a stock design. The
entrance leads directly into a small hall in which the
stairs are located. From this hall a door opens directly into a living room connected with the sun porch
by a wide opening. The living room has a brick fireplace with tiled hearth. The dining room connects
directly with the kitchen and a service entry is provided at the side of the house. On the second floor
there is a central hall with a large linen closet and
openings into three bedrooms, each of which is provided with unusually ample closet space. These bedrooms are all of good size and well arranged for light,
ventilation, and the placing of furniture.

Full directions for obtaining complete working drawings and specifications will be found on page 281

A 5-Room Bungalow of Southern Type

THIS flexible type of bungalow was originally designed for use in the South where, as heating is unnecessary, it is not customary to excavate for cellars. The construction of this house is of frame throughout, where exterior of wide siding is indicated. The architectural design of this house is good and its simple lines are relieved by the two well-designed dormers which serve to break the extensive roof plane.

While this house is planned for the finishing of the first floor only, it would be possible to alter the plan slightly and provide two bedrooms and bath upstairs without destroying the architectural effect.

The first floor is subdivided by simple partition work and chimney is located to allow two open fireplaces.

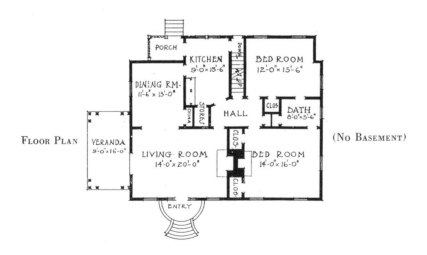

Plan No. 656   **MILLER & MARTIN,** *Architects*   18,200 *Cubic Feet*

Full directions for obtaining complete working drawings and specifications will be found on page 281

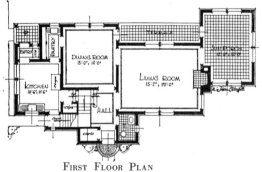

FIRST FLOOR PLAN

SECOND FLOOR PLAN

Plan No. 722   R. C. HUNTER & BRO., *Architects*   36,240 *Cubic Feet*

A Small Country Home — Stucco and Half-Timbered Exterior

(Six rooms and sun room arranged in an elongated plan)

HERE is a type of high-gabled stucco house which has proven particularly appealing in the attractive suburban districts of the eastern states of this country. The design is of English character accentuated by the half-timbered work in the large gable. The exterior is of stucco and the roofing is of copper, slate or asbestos-cement shingles in varying colors. The large brick chimney is capped by clay chimney pots, adding a touch of color. The windows through-out are of casement type, and flashings, gutters and leaders for this type of house will presumably be of copper with ornamental heads in stock designs.

The plan is of elongated shape, offering an unusual opportunity for attractive interiors, and the architects have not failed to take advantage of these possibilities. The central hall provides access to the dining room and living room, from which French doors lead to a long tiled terrace and a large sun porch.

Full directions for obtaining complete working drawings and specifications will be found on page 281

FIRST FLOOR PLAN

A Dignified Colonial Home of Six Rooms

Frame construction throughout, with exterior of wide siding.

SECOND FLOOR PLAN

Plan No. 102   J. IVAN DISE & E. J. MAIER, *Architects*   23,717 *Cubic Feet*

THE perspective of this six-room house is proof positive that it is quite possible to achieve considerable dignity in the impression value of the small house. An analysis of the exterior shows that this has been done by the careful planning of exterior openings and by the use of large chimneys at either end of the house. The construction is of frame throughout with exterior of shingles or of wide siding and roof of shingle type.

The detail of the main entrance has been carefully studied and the impression of size has been augmented by the dormer break directly above the entrance door. On the first floor there is a small vestibule which contains a well-designed Colonial stairway, for which de-

tails are supplied with the working drawings. From this hall wide inter-room openings provide access to the living room and to the dining room. The living room is a very practical and attractive feature, being large in size and having an open fireplace flanked by French doors leading to a large enclosed porch. A special feature of the living room is the provision of a door bed located in a small dressing closet. This installation provides for the unexpected guest without adding materially to the first investment. The kitchen is large and light and has a well arranged pantry.

On the upper floor there are three bedrooms, one extending entirely across the end of the house. Two linen closets are provided in the hall.

Full directions for obtaining complete working drawings and specifications will be found on page 281

FIRST FLOOR PLAN

SECOND FLOOR PLAN

A Popular 6-Room Colonial Home

Plan No. 401   *18,675 Cubic Feet*

JOHN FLOYD YEWELL
Architect

This was the official "Better Homes Week" house built in New York City for 1922.

THIS is the six-room frame house which was built in Larchmont Gardens, New York, by the *New York Tribune* and Home Owners Service Institute as the model demonstration house for "Better Homes Week" in 1922.

The construction of this house is frame throughout and has roofing of asbestos-cement shingles. Flashing, leaders and gutters are of copper, which weathers to an attractive color and adds materially to the architectural effect.

The house as originally built and shown in this photograph contains only five rooms, but plans shown here have been enlarged on a more practical basis to provide three bedrooms and bath upstairs instead of two bedrooms as in the original house. The living room extends across the entire end of the house, and the porch may easily be glassed in to form a sun porch if desired.

There is an attractive brick fireplace in the living room. The main entrance to the house is into a small hall from which stairs lead directly up and doors communicate with living room and dining room. A living porch is provided at the rear of the house and this, too, may be enclosed if desired, and connected with dining room by French doors.

On the second floor there are three bedrooms and bath. The principal bedroom is attractive because of its large size and the arrangement of windows. While providing ample light and ventilation, these windows do not interfere with the placing of furniture.

Full directions for obtaining complete working drawings and specifications will be found on page 281

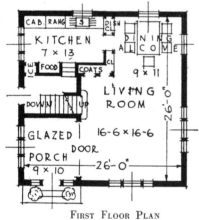

FIRST FLOOR PLAN

The "Bob and Betty" House

Stucco on concrete blocks

This house (as shown in photograph at the right) was built on the floor of the New York "Own Your Home Exposition," 1923.

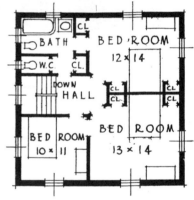

SECOND FLOOR PLAN

Plan No. 723   MILTON DANA MORRILL, *Architect*   20,280 *Cubic Feet*

THIS is the attractive stucco dwelling which was designed as a feature of the New York Own Your Home Exposition for 1923. As indicated in the photograph above, the front section of this house was built in full size on the floor of the exposition as a demonstration feature.

The construction of this house is of stucco on concrete blocks. Copper shingles were used for the roofing and for the hood over the entrance porch. Flashing, leaders and gutters are of weathered copper.

Entrance is directly into an enclosed porch which forms part of a large living room. The living room extends the entire depth of the house but at the rear there is located a dining alcove as indicated on the plans shown herewith. The kitchen is well arranged for service in a small house of this type, containing various closets and a recess for refrigerator.

On the second floor there are three ample bedrooms, a bath and an extra lavatory as an additional convenience.

Full directions for obtaining complete working drawings and specifications will be found on page 281

The Plans of Five Hundred Homes

First Section—6-Room Houses

THE following pages, 42 to 280, are devoted to the presentation of d w e l l i n g plans covering a range of from three to eight rooms and every type of American domestic architecture.

In analyzing these plans it will be found that practically all forms of exterior wall construction are included, as detailed in the panel below.

A large proportion of the plans presented in this volume are for six-room houses, which are indicated as the more popular size in the moderate cost dwelling field. The following section, beginning on page 42, presents a large number of six-room houses of two-story and of bungalow types. Here will be found almost every plan arrangement which is possible of practical development. A study of these plans will indicate many special features of æsthetic and utility value and will also provide valuable suggestions as to space-saving and developing efficiency in home-planning.

Beginning on page 281 will be found a simple and practical outline of the methods by which a home-builder may carry his project through the various stages from planning to completion. For all plans presented in this book the complete working drawings and specifications are available, as explained in the

Night view of the model house built recently at Washington, D. C. (See Page 24)

section beginning on page 281, together with an advisory service which renders this plan book the most complete and practical service medium which has ever been presented to the American homebuilding public.

Following the section in which plans for six-room houses are presented, there will be found a division page e x p l a i n i n g briefly various practical points in relation to the selection of plans for three-, four- and five-room houses. A large number of plans for houses of these sizes are then presented, and finally a division of seven- and eight-room houses for those who are interested in larger types of residences.

No attempt has been made to segregate plans according to building materials used, but with each house there is a brief description which covers interesting points, including exterior materials provided for in specifications. Every effort has been made to select only plans which are thoroughly practical from the viewpoints of domestic efficiency and economy of construction and maintenance. The working drawings and specifications available for each plan are unusually complete, and full details are given so that the homebuilder is ready to arrange his contracts.

Arrangement of Plans on Following Pages, 42 to 280

A large proportion of the plans which have been selected for presentation in this book are for houses of six rooms and bath, which represent a standard in the field of moderate cost dwellings. For those who are interested in smaller and larger houses there are also presented a number of plans of three-, four- and five-room houses and plans for seven- and eight-room houses. The first section of the plan pages (beginning on page 42) contains six-room houses. Following these will be found a division page indicating the presentation of three-, four- and five-room houses. The last section of the plan pages contains seven- and eight-room houses, also indicated by a division page.

NUMBER OF ROOMS AND TYPES OF CONSTRUCTION

The 500 house plans presented in this book cover a range of from three to eight rooms. Every type of American domestic architecture is represented, as well as all types of construction. Included in the types of exterior wall construction will be found **face brick**; **common brick**; **brick veneers** *on hollow tile, common brick or frame;* **stucco** *on cement blocks, hollow clay tile, back-plastered metal lath, frame and various patented bases; and* **frame** *with wide siding or shingle finish.*

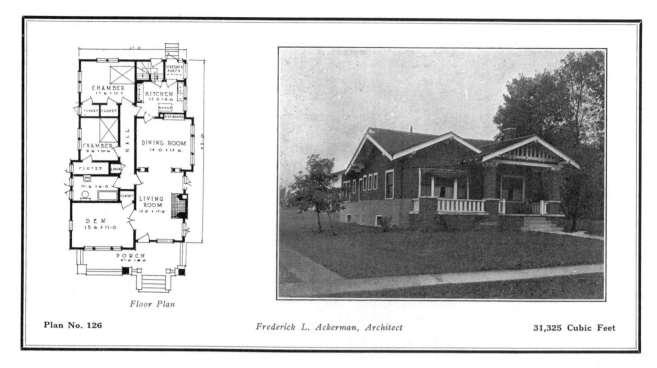

Floor Plan

Plan No. 126   *Frederick L. Ackerman, Architect*   **31,325 Cubic Feet**

(Description of house shown in above plans)

(Description of house shown in plans below)

THIS cozy-looking bungalow owes its low-lying effect to the use of four-inch siding up to the sill line, and above that shingles laid in alternate course two and one-half inches and four and one-half inches to the weather. The porch balusters are interesting, as is the gable with its exposed timbers painted in contrasting colors. The house is very roomy. Advantage is taken of the length rather than the width of the lot. The fireplace is on the long outside wall and there are splendid spaces for furniture.

THE charmingly simple lines of this six-room bungalow may be enhanced by some attention to the choice of the brick color tones and bond pattern. For example, a bond such as French Cross or Garden Wall would make a pleasing pattern throughout. To reduce the initial cost of building, the rear bedroom of this bungalow may be omitted at first with but little change in the plan, and easily added when convenience suggests. This is an ideal house for a corner lot, and should be set well back.

Full directions for obtaining complete working drawings and specifications for these plans will be found on page 281

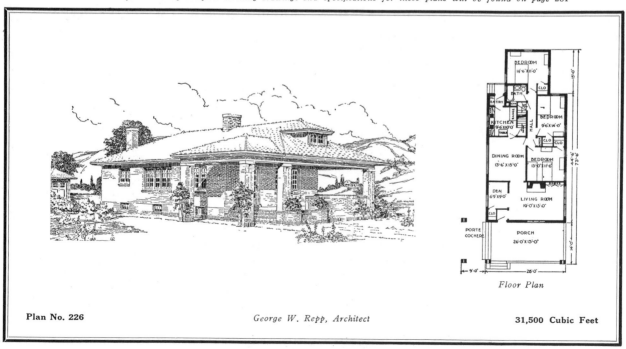

Floor Plan

Plan No. 226   *George W. Repp, Architect*   **31,500 Cubic Feet**

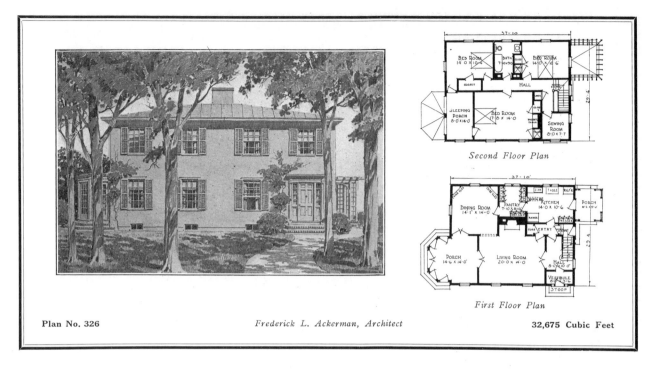

Second Floor Plan

First Floor Plan

Plan No. 326   *Frederick L. Ackerman, Architect*   **32,675 Cubic Feet**

(Description of house shown in above plans)

AT first glance this house would appear to have more than six rooms. As a matter of fact the glazed sun porch, hall, vestibule, generous pantry, sleeping porch, and sewing room are not included in counting the six principal rooms. This house demonstrates the use of stucco in Colonial homes, but any desired material may be used. The vestibule receives ample light from the sidelights of the entrance. To the rear is a small hall with French doors opening into the living room.

(Description of house shown in plans below)

HERE is a fine English type of house with a floor plan that is especially well arranged. Entering through the porch and vestibule, one finds himself in a large hall from which the stairs ascend to a well-lighted landing. On one side is the living room with its fireplace, bookcases, and window seat; on the other is the dining room with its group of casement windows and a built-in sideboard. Special attention is called to the kitchen which is compact and conveniently arranged. Face brick exterior.

Full directions for obtaining complete working drawings and specifications for these plans will be found on page 281

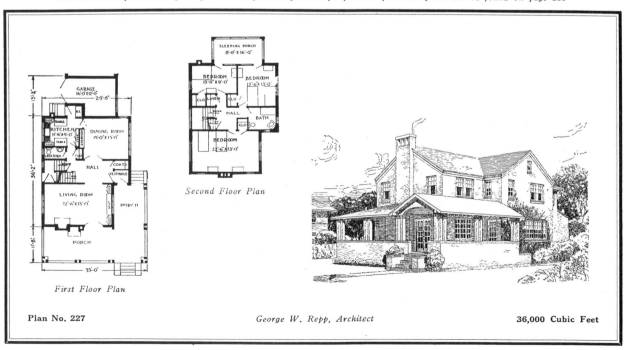

First Floor Plan

Second Floor Plan

Plan No. 227   *George W. Repp, Architect*   **36,000 Cubic Feet**

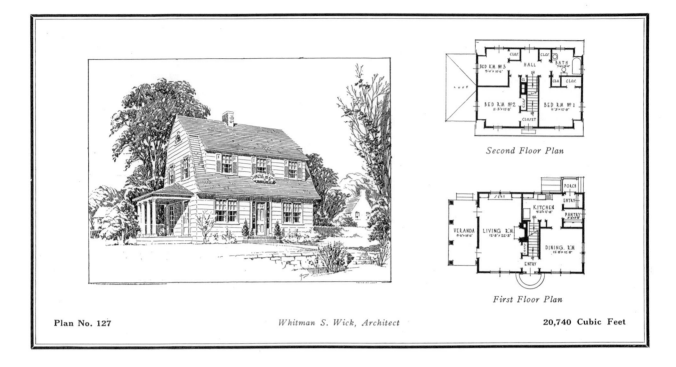

Plan No. 127   *Whitman S. Wick, Architect*   **20,740 Cubic Feet**

(Description of house shown in above plans)

THE Dutch Colonial type of house is becoming increasingly popular as the homebuilder realizes its beauty and adaptability to both country and city building sites. Here is one of uncommon attractiveness from the exterior and well planned on the interior. The finish is shingles with wide exposure or, if you will, wide siding. The roof should be shingled. The entrance hall is cut down to the minimum and there is little waste space elsewhere in the house.

(Description of house shown in plans below)

DIGNITY and formality characterize this design, making it suitable for a suburban or small city house. A grass or brick terrace across the front bounded by a hedge, would give the house a splendid setting. The front of the house is given over to living and dining rooms with a vestibule at the entrance. The stairs are located separately at the rear and there is a bedroom on the first floor which could be used for a study. Two of the rooms have fireplaces.

Full directions for obtaining complete working drawings and specifications for these plans will be found on page 281

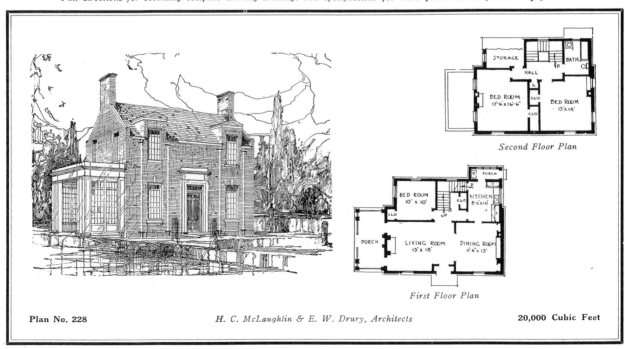

Plan No. 228   *H. C. McLaughlin & E. W. Drury, Architects*   **20,000 Cubic Feet**

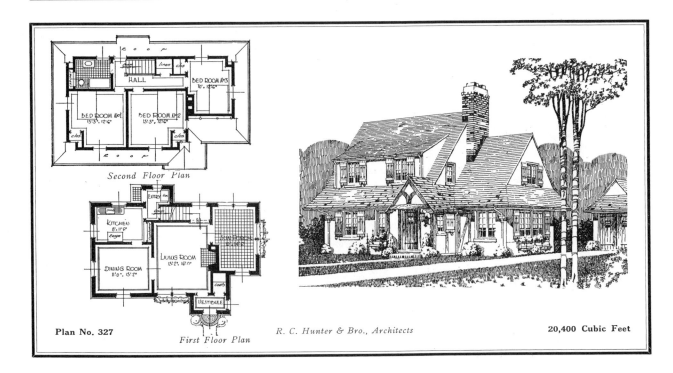

Second Floor Plan

First Floor Plan

Plan No. 327   *R. C. Hunter & Bro., Architects*   **20,400 Cubic Feet**

(Description of house shown in above plans)

THE decided irregularity of the exterior of this house makes it uncommonly attractive and interesting. The finish is stucco and the roof of shingles, either wood or of fire-resisting materials. The arrangement of rooms on both floors is convenient. The stairs are especially well placed to insure economy of space and to reduce the size of the second floor hall to the minimum. Plenty of closet room is a feature that will appeal to all.

(Description of house shown in plans below)

THIS house could be built on practically any site that had a level space at the rear to afford a lawn on the dining room and porch side. It is of picturesque design with suggestions of the English cottage. All its sides are interesting and any one of them could face the street, the entrance facing northwest. It is conveniently planned and has a fine living room with light on three sides. The illustration shows the entrance side of the house.

Full directions for obtaining complete working drawings and specifications for these plans will be found on page 281

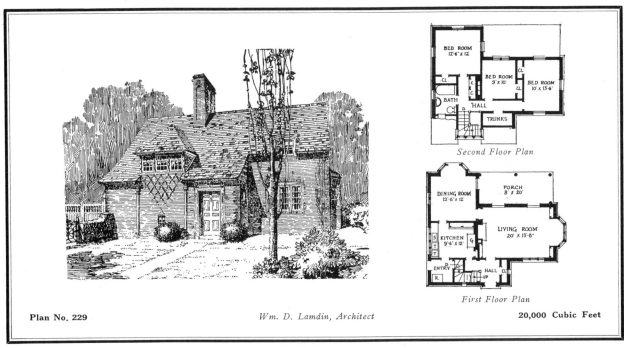

Second Floor Plan

First Floor Plan

Plan No. 229   *Wm. D. Lamdin, Architect*   **20,000 Cubic Feet**

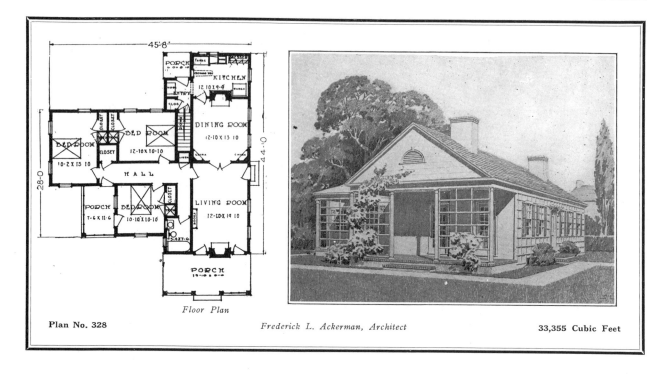

Floor Plan

Plan No. 328   *Frederick L. Ackerman, Architect*   **33,355 Cubic Feet**

(Description of house shown in above plans)

THIS attractive bungalow of the Colonial type is an excellent plan for a corner lot. The long side of the house, with its formal entrance, would be most attractive facing the street, with the living porch at the side. The sleeping quarters have been well isolated from the living rooms, and all rooms have ample ventilation. Each bedroom has a built-in tray case as well as a good clothes closet, so that a minimum of furniture is needed. Frame and stucco.

(Description of house shown in plans below)

HERE is a six-room bungalow the very simplicity of which tends to give it distinction. The living and dining rooms in this bungalow are very large and comfortable. There is a cozy brick fireplace at one end of the living room, while French doors at the opposite end open to a fine large porch. The bedrooms are well lighted, have good closets, and are connected with the bath by a convenient hall. The kitchen is exceptionally complete and convenient.

Full directions for obtaining complete working drawings and specifications for these plans will be found on page 281

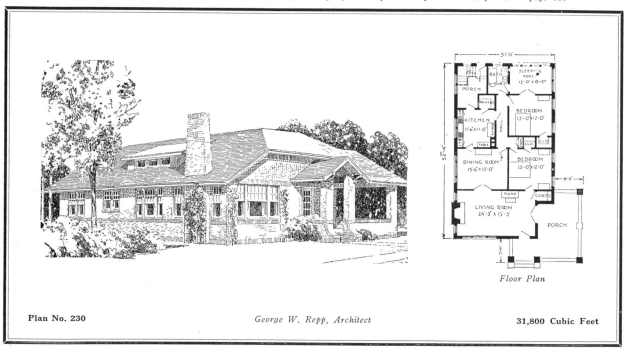

Floor Plan

Plan No. 230   *George W. Repp, Architect*   **31,800 Cubic Feet**

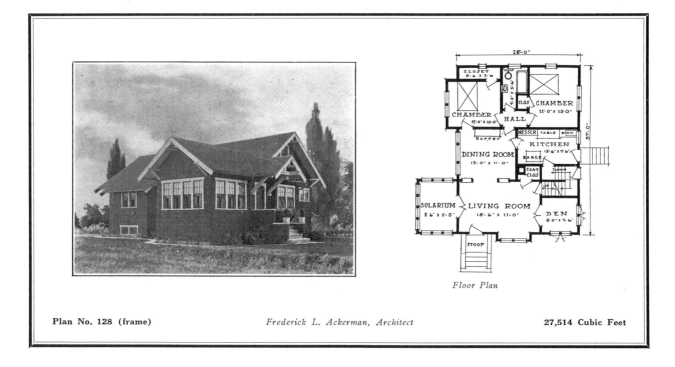

Plan No. 128 (frame)   *Frederick L. Ackerman, Architect*   **27,514 Cubic Feet**

Floor Plan

(Description of house shown in above plans)

HERE is another house having a solarium adjoining the living room by means of French doors. Another pair of French doors at the opposite end of the living room leads to a small den, a cosy room with high casements on two sides, that will find many uses. There is a little alcove on the outside wall of the living room forming an interesting little nook. The attic, reached by a boxed stair, has windows on three sides, so is a light storage place.

(Description of house shown in plans below)

THE exterior treatment of this six-room bungalow is along modern lines. The ornamental frieze under the cornice could be treated in many different ways by using different colors and textures of brick. The breakfast room in this plan is a most attractive spot. It is located on the rear of the house overlooking the garden, and is convenient to the kitchen and bedrooms. The light and airy kitchen has cupboards at both sides of the sink, in addition to a large pantry.

Full directions for obtaining complete working drawings and specifications for these plans will be found on page 281

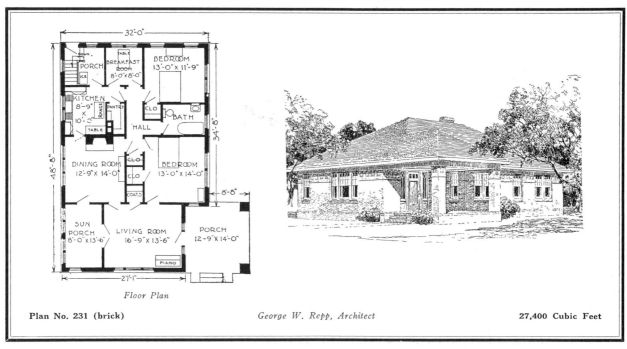

Floor Plan

Plan No. 231 (brick)   *George W. Repp, Architect*   **27,400 Cubic Feet**

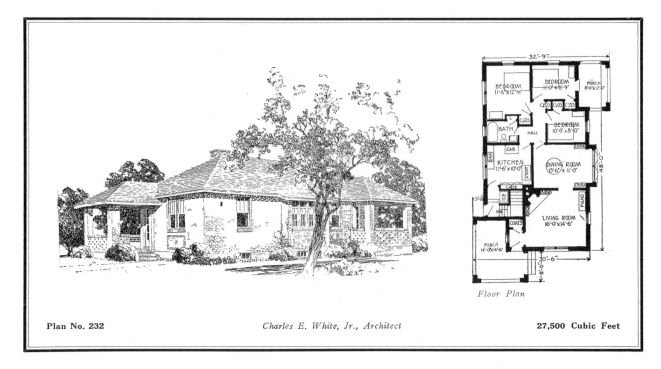

Plan No. 232   *Charles E. White, Jr., Architect*   **27,500 Cubic Feet**

Floor Plan

(Description of house shown in above plans)

WITH porches on two opposite corners of the house, one is sure to have a shady spot no matter which way the house faces. This arrangement has the advantage also of a porch with a view to the street and one overlooking the garden. The exterior treatment is very simple and as the design is English, the brickwork could appropriately be laid up in an English bond with tooled mortar joints of harmonious but contrasting color. The floor plan is well arranged with the sleeping quarters isolated at the rear.

(Description of house shown in plans below)

THIS house shows the use of siding in alternate wide and narrow courses which makes a very attractive exterior wall. The porch and terrace in this house are especially attractive. The living room has direct light from two sides and through French doors and an inter-room opening on the other two sides. There is a beautiful fireplace on the narrow outside wall with a built-in bookcase at one side and a window seat at the other with plastered arches above. The den is the lightest room in the house.

Full directions for obtaining complete working drawings and specifications for these plans will be found on page 281

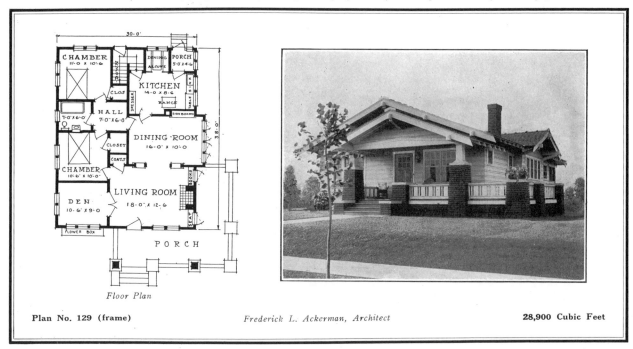

Floor Plan

Plan No. 129 (frame)   *Frederick L. Ackerman, Architect*   **28,900 Cubic Feet**

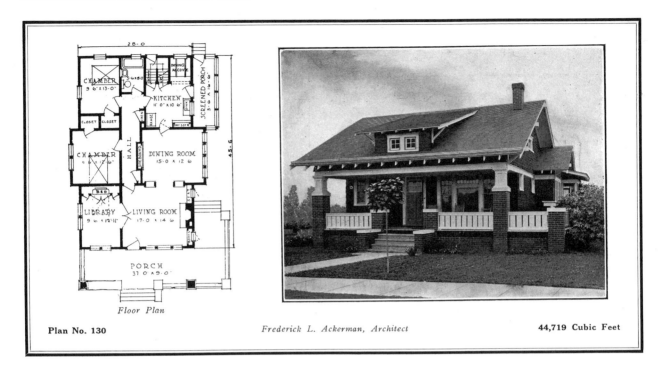

Floor Plan

Plan No. 130   *Frederick L. Ackerman, Architect*   **44,719 Cubic Feet**

(Description of house shown in above plans)

A WHITE-painted balustrade about the porch and terrace, and other exterior details, attract attention to this six-room house. Ten-inch siding and shingles with brick piers, are the materials of which it is built. The library is separated from the living room by French doors so that it may readily become a part of that room. The living room is provided with a hearth, built-in bookcase and window seat, which make it a very delightful room. A group of four windows fills one side of the dining room.

(Description of house shown in plans below)

THE combination here of a gambrel with two flanking bays on the side and a gable toward the front makes exceedingly attractive roof lines and surfaces. The wide brick-paved front porch extends around the side to the bay. The living room, occupying the entire front of the house is accessible from the porch either on the front or side, and the fine brick hearth is flanked by bookcases. The dining room is entered through folding doors from the living room or through the hall, and opens to the kitchen.

Full directions for obtaining complete working drawings and specifications for these plans will be found on page 281

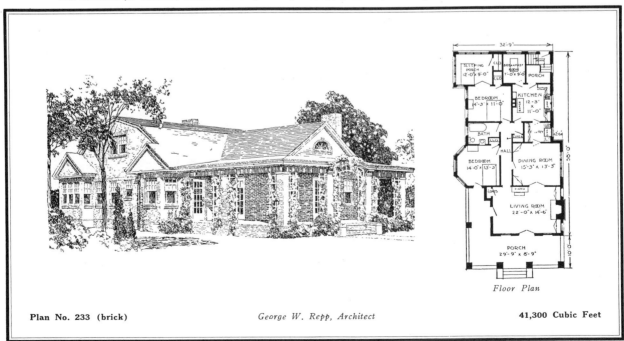

Floor Plan

Plan No. 233 (brick)   *George W. Repp, Architect*   **41,300 Cubic Feet**

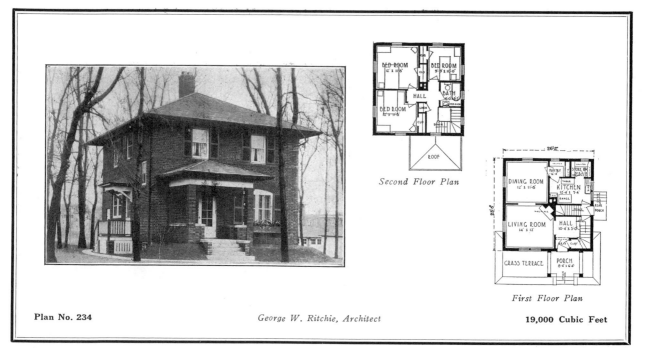

Second Floor Plan

First Floor Plan

Plan No. 234   *George W. Ritchie, Architect*   **19,000 Cubic Feet**

(Description of house shown in above plans)

A CHARMING little house" would correctly describe this house of brick. It is very well proportioned, especially the roofs, all of which have the same pitch. The roofs are all slate covered, and this, together with the brick exterior walls, reduces the fire hazard to the minimum. The living room contains a corner fireplace and connects with the hall and dining room through wide cased openings. Three bedrooms and good closet space as well as a bath are found on the second floor.

(Description of house shown in plans below)

NOTHING more suitable for a village or country home could be had than this informal cottage. Its low sloping roofs create at once an atmosphere of home; there is, however, ample room in the second story gained by long dormers on the side and rear. The living room is of good size and connected directly with the porch and overlooking the space that should be developed as a garden. The house could be placed close to the road, and a hedge will afford privacy as shown in the illustration. Brick exterior.

Full directions for obtaining complete working drawings and specifications for these plans will be found on page 281

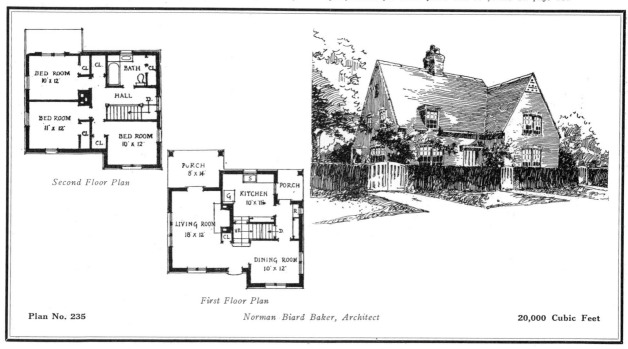

Second Floor Plan

First Floor Plan

Plan No. 235   *Norman Biard Baker, Architect*   **20,000 Cubic Feet**

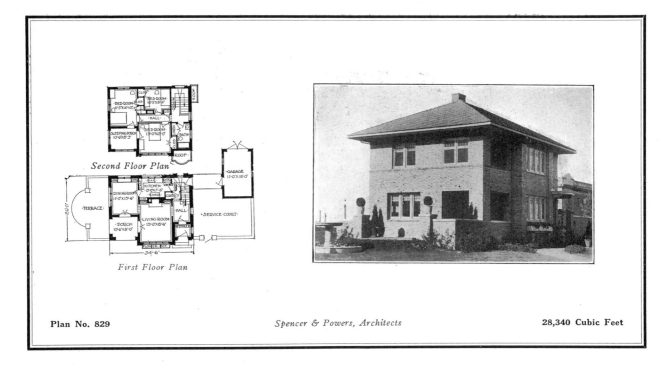

Plan No. 829   *Spencer & Powers, Architects*   **28,340 Cubic Feet**

(Description of house shown in above plans)   *(Description of house shown in plans below)*

THIS square, well-planned six-room house is constructed with common brick exterior and roof of shingle type. An attractive feature is the brick terrace laid out as shown on the plan. Casement windows are indicated for the living room and principal bedroom. The stairway is located at the back of the house and provides easy access from the service section. The dining room has built-in window seat flanked by china closets. On the second floor a built-in sleeping porch virtually adds another room.

THIS is an interesting six-room dwelling designed for stucco construction. The planning of each floor has been carefully carried out to give maximum utility and attractiveness. The large entrance porch lends an important note to the architectural design. The living room is well lighted and has a large open fireplace. The square dining room is connected with living room by wide arched entrance. Kitchen service is through a large pantry, and rear entry is provided. There is a double approach to the stairs.

Full directions for obtaining complete working drawings and specifications for these plans will be found on page 281

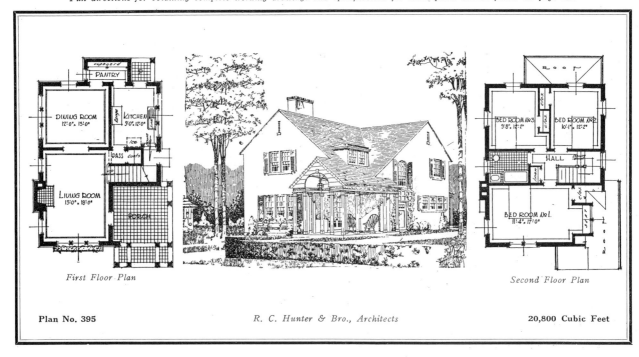

Plan No. 395   *R. C. Hunter & Bro., Architects*   **20,800 Cubic Feet**

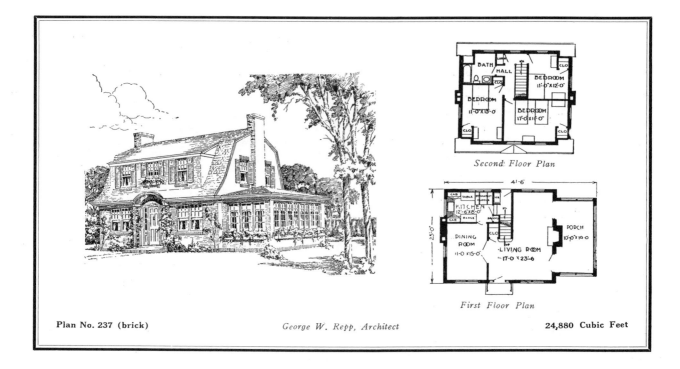

Plan No. 237 (brick)   *George W. Repp, Architect*   24,880 Cubic Feet

Second Floor Plan

First Floor Plan

(Description of house shown in above plans)

HERE is another of the popular Dutch Colonial type of six-room houses. The customary central hall has been omitted and the space thrown into the living room, but it would be an easy matter to restore the partition, if a hall is desired. On the broad side of the living room is the fireplace, flanked by double French doors which open to the porch. There are three good rooms on the second floor all with exposure on two sides, and well supplied with closets.

(Description of house shown in plans below)

THIS six-room bungalow boasts a den which is connected with the living room by French doors. The living room is very bright and is separated from the dining room only by an inter-room opening so that it receives light from that side also. There is a cased opening setting off the bay in the dining room, and centered on the rear wall is a combination sideboard and kitchen dresser. Two small but adequate bedrooms are reached by way of a hall.

Full directions for obtaining complete working drawings and specifications for these plans will be found on page 281

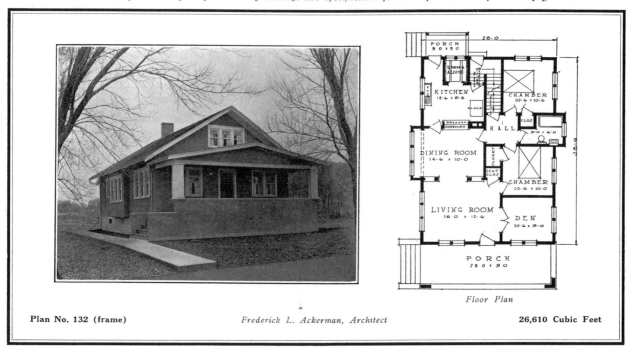

Floor Plan

Plan No. 132 (frame)   *Frederick L. Ackerman, Architect*   26,610 Cubic Feet

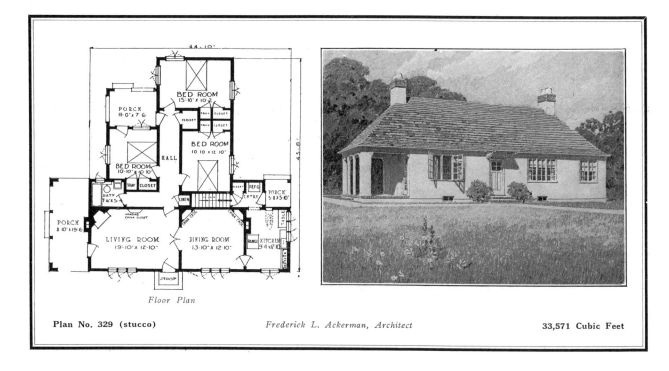

Floor Plan

Plan No. 329 (stucco)   *Frederick L. Ackerman, Architect*   **33,571 Cubic Feet**

(Description of house shown in above plans)

HERE is a house that is characteristically English, though it is small and therefore would be perfectly at home in the most exclusive neighborhood. One enters the living room directly. In the far corner there is a fireplace; near it, a glazed door leading to the porch. A hanging china closet on the wall is decorative and useful. There is a long inside wall space desirable for piano or other large piece of furniture. At the right are French doors.

(Description of house shown in plans below)

THE proportion and treatment of the roof of this bungalow seem to recall the old thatched cottages of England. The dormers in front and rear give the necessary ventilation to the attic space. The color combination is very important. The brick below may be different from those above, or the mortar may be of different colors. That is, with lighter mortar above and darker below, the bricks will stand out in contrast, giving the desired effect.

Full directions for obtaining complete working drawings and specifications for these plans will be found on page 281

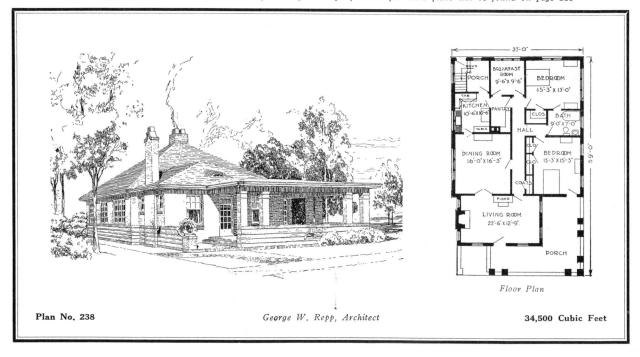

Floor Plan

Plan No. 238   *George W. Repp, Architect*   **34,500 Cubic Feet**

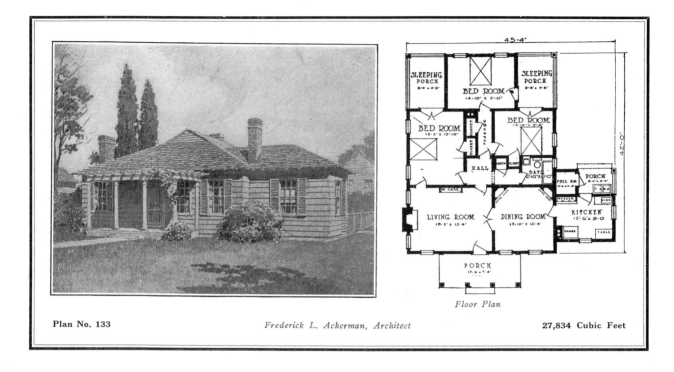

Floor Plan

Plan No. 133   *Frederick L. Ackerman, Architect*   **27,834 Cubic Feet**

(Description of house shown in above plans)

THOUGH this bungalow appears to be quite small it offers accommodations for a large family, since it has three bedrooms and two sleeping porches. The living room has a comfortable rectangular shape, with the fireplace in the center of the outside narrow wall, flanked by windows. There are two long wall spaces for the bookcase and the piano. The bedrooms have been well separated from the living quarters and are of good size. Frame construction.

(Description of house shown in plans below)

HERE is a six-room bungalow that would be a gem in any setting. The gabled arch of the porch entrance and the hipped and tiled roof present very pleasing lines and surfaces to the eye. The arrangement of the rooms has been planned with a view to avoiding any waste space, and the result is a very compact layout. The basement is also conveniently arranged and provided with laundry, heater, coal bins, and a vegetable cellar, besides general storage spaces.

Full directions for obtaining complete working drawings and specifications for these plans will be found on page 281

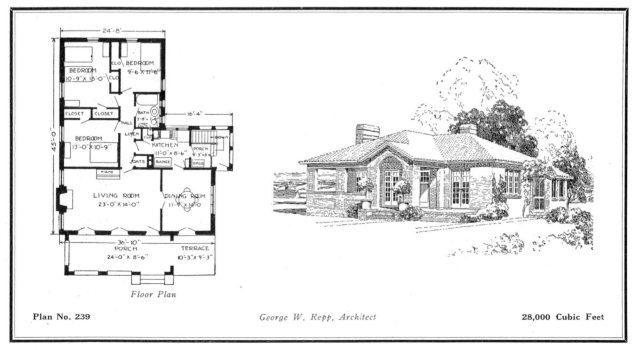

Floor Plan

Plan No. 239   *George W. Repp, Architect*   **28,000 Cubic Feet**

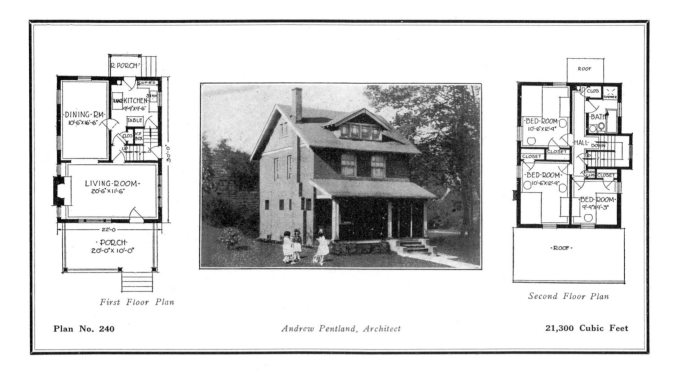

First Floor Plan

Second Floor Plan

Plan No. 240   *Andrew Pentland, Architect*   **21,300 Cubic Feet**

(Description of house shown in above plans)

THIS simple rectangular house of brick could easily be constructed on a two-rod lot with plenty of space for a driveway on the side. It has six well lighted and ventilated rooms, economically arranged and of good size. There is an abundance of closet space on the second floor, besides a large light attic easily reached from the upper hall. A grade entrance and ten-foot wide front porch are other features of this house not to be overlooked. Common brick.

(Description of house shown in plans below)

A SIMPLE house that would look equally well on a level lot or one sloping toward the street. If the lot is narrow the living room end could be turned toward the street, and if the frontage is 60 feet or more it could be placed as shown in the illustration. In either case the end of the living room should face south or southwest. The principal rooms are arranged to make the interior look as large as possible, and the kitchen is most convenient. Face brick exterior.

Full directions for obtaining complete working drawings and specifications for these plans will be found on page 281

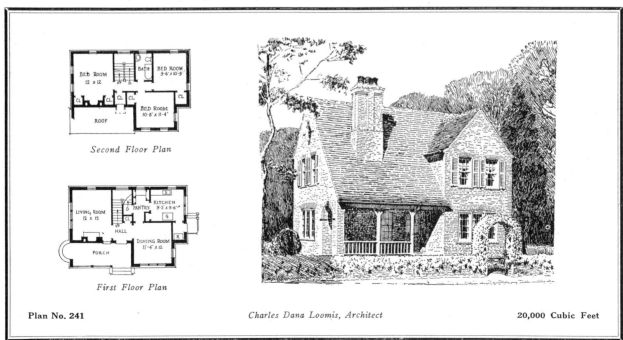

Second Floor Plan

First Floor Plan

Plan No. 241   *Charles Dana Loomis, Architect*   **20,000 Cubic Feet**

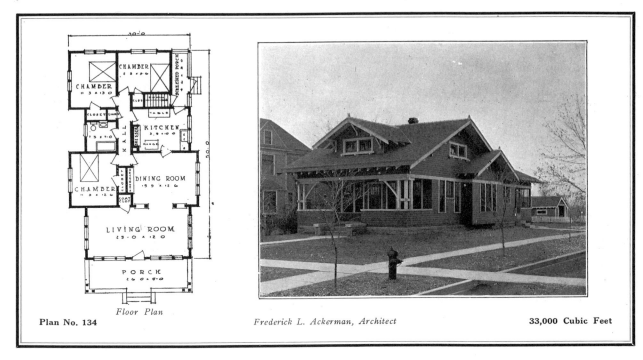

Floor Plan

Plan No. 134   *Frederick L. Ackerman, Architect*   **33,000 Cubic Feet**

(Description of house shown in above plans)

THE treatment of the roof is an interesting feature of this house. The main gable roof includes the porch and the front part of the house, with supplementary gables over the projections at each side. Another gable, at right angles, covers the rear part. The dormer, and windows at each side, light the attic. One feature of this plan which is seldom found in bungalows is a long living room with windows on three sides. A group of three windows at each side of the front entrance, and at each side a group of two windows make it a delightful place.

(Description of house shown in plans below)

HERE is a cool, shady porch with a fine gable and balustrade treatment that gives dignity to the design. Access to one bedroom is had from the porch. The breakfast room, in case it is not wanted as such, may be converted into a bedroom, playroom, office or den. The living and dining rooms are of good size and are connected by French doors. A convenient feature is the sideboard in the dining room arranged with an opening to the kitchen for the passage of dishes. A good-sized rear porch is included under the main roof. Face brick exterior.

Full directions for obtaining complete working drawings and specifications for these plans will be found on page 281

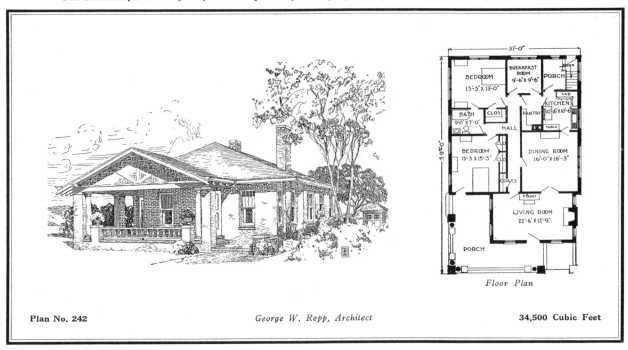

Floor Plan

Plan No. 242   *George W. Repp, Architect*   **34,500 Cubic Feet**

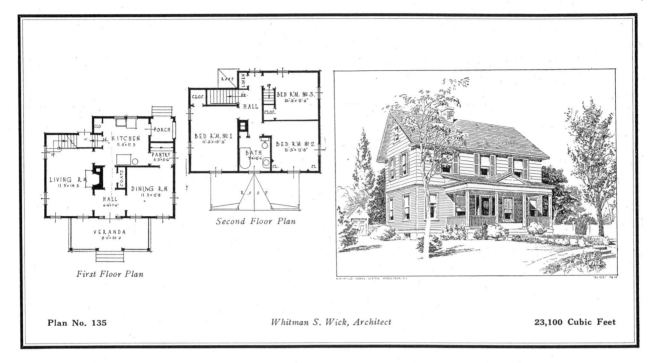

Second Floor Plan

First Floor Plan

Plan No. 135   *Whitman S. Wick, Architect*   **23,100 Cubic Feet**

(Description of house shown in above plans)

HERE is a six-room Colonial house with first story of six-inch siding, upper story and gables of wide siding (or shingles), roof of special shingles or slate. This house is carefully designed for economy of construction and an examination of floor plans will show that all posible waste space has been eliminated. The living room is arranged with entrance through the hall and into the kitchen. Stairs are not placed in the central hall as usual, but located at the back of the living room providing an architectural feature which helps in interior decorating.

(Description of house shown in plans below)

WITH the cool, recessed porch, shown in the picture, and all corner rooms, this cottage should be delightfully comfortable. The large, well-lighted living room has an attractive fireplace set in a slight recess, which adds to the apparent width of the room. The end of the living room, used for dining, is convenient to the kitchen, so placed as not to be seen from the living room. The kitchen is compact, well arranged and has cupboards in place of a pantry. The bedrooms and bath are secluded in the rear portion of the house. Face brick exterior.

Full directions for obtaining complete working drawings and specifications for these plans will be found on page 281.

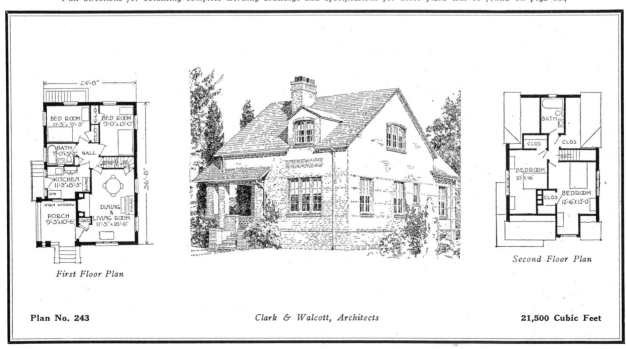

First Floor Plan

Second Floor Plan

Plan No. 243   *Clark & Walcott, Architects*   **21,500 Cubic Feet**

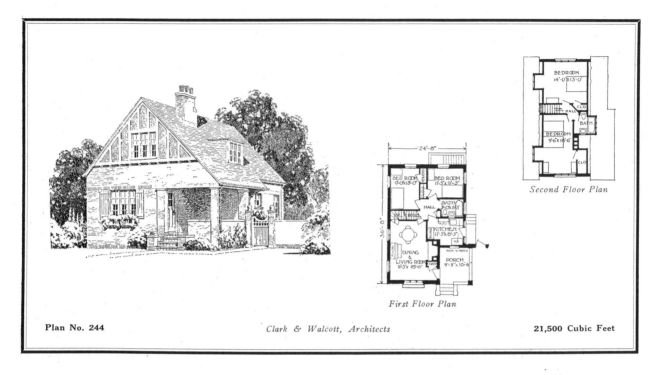

Second Floor Plan

First Floor Plan

Plan No. 244   *Clark & Walcott, Architects*   **21,500 Cubic Feet**

(Description of house shown in above plans)

THIS attractive exterior is a successfully striking example of the English type. The half-timbered gable with its herring-bone pattern brickwork will make this house stand out among its neighbors. This plan is adaptable to a narrow lot as the kitchen has been placed on the side of the house, leaving an unobstructed rear view to be enjoyed from the two bedrooms. The attractive fireplace set in a recess adds to the apparent width of the room. The end of the living room is used for dining purposes.

(Description of house shown in plans below)

HERE is a distinctive six-room residence which could be carried out successfully with exterior walls of stucco, relieved by a simple brick trim around the upper edge of the porch, the window sills, and the top of the flue. There is a good-sized living room across the front of the house, from which a stairway leads to the second floor. The dining room and kitchen are back of it, the kitchen being separated from the living room by the side entrance hall. The three bedrooms upstairs all have clothes closets.

Full directions for obtaining complete working drawings and specifications for these plans will be found on page 281

First Floor Plan

Second Floor Plan

Plan No. 330 (stucco on hollow tile)   *Olsen & Urbain, Architects*   **17,800 Cubic Feet**

First Floor Plan

Second Floor Plan

Plan No. 245   *George H. Schwan, Architect*   **20,624 Cubic Feet**

(*Description of house shown in above plans*)

THE exterior of this house is particularly attractive. Long roof lines have been obtained with very little sacrifice of usable space. The exterior walls are of common brick laid with wide joints, and the gables are of stucco and timber. The roof is of slate or other type of flat shingle. The entrance is from a large covered porch directly into the living room or into a small hall which provides access to living room, stairs and kitchen. The second floor plan provides three well arranged bedrooms and a large linen closet.

(*Description of house shown in plans below*)

THERE are very pleasing proportions and attractive roof lines in this design. The house is extremely simple and would for that reason be inexpensive to build. All the rooms are well lighted from the sides and in omitting the windows on the front, except for two small ones either side of the door, an individual character has been given the house. The house could be placed close to the street and the rear of the lot reserved for garden and lawn. The second floor is well supplied with closets.

Full directions for obtaining complete working drawings and specifications for these plans will be found on page 281

First Floor Plan

Second Floor Plan

Plan No. 246   *George H. Van Anda, Architect*   **20,000 Cubic Feet**

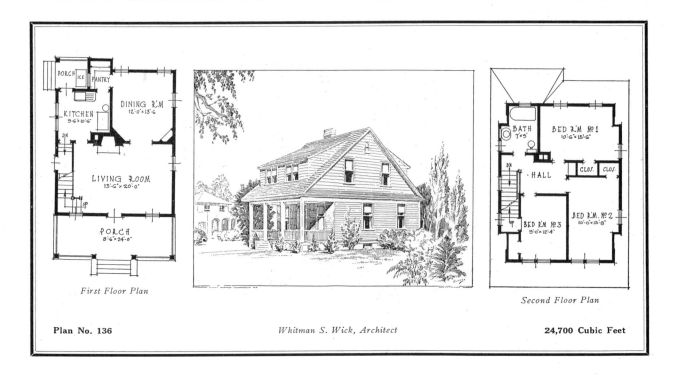

First Floor Plan

Second Floor Plan

Plan No. 136   *Whitman S. Wick, Architect*   **24,700 Cubic Feet**

(Description of house shown in above plans)

A SIMPLE type of Colonial frame six-room house, showing efficiency of space as developed through the architect's design. This house is simple and economical in construction and represents the maximum of utility for the necessary investment. The entrance hall is entirely eliminated, as the stairs are thrown into the living room, providing an architectural feature in addition to the open fireplace. The dining room has a built-in china closet.

(Description of house shown in plans below)

HERE is a design that will stand out among any group of houses as an example of fine architectural composition. As shown below, broad-side to the street, it would require a frontage of fifty feet, in order to give ample room on the sides. If, however, it is desired to turn the house endwise, with the living room and porch toward the street, it may be placed upon a forty-foot lot, leaving sufficient room for a driveway. If desired, the fireplace may open on the porch side.

Full directions for obtaining complete working drawings and specifications for these plans will be found on page 281

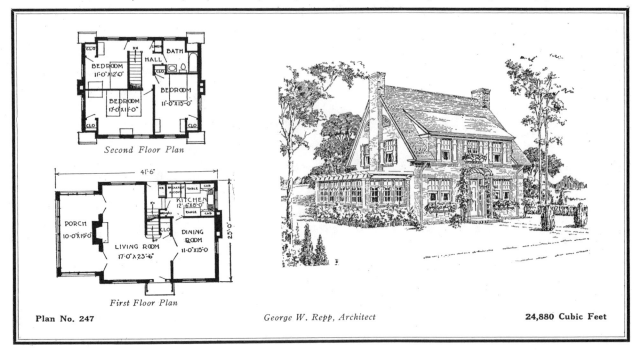

Second Floor Plan

First Floor Plan

Plan No. 247   *George W. Repp, Architect*   **24,880 Cubic Feet**

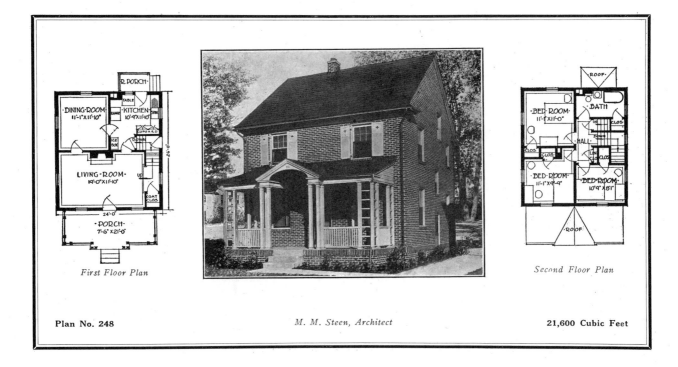

First Floor Plan

Second Floor Plan

Plan No. 248   *M. M. Steen, Architect*   **21,600 Cubic Feet**

(Description of house shown in above plans)

HERE is a simple type of modified English Colonial house having exterior walls and foundations of common brick with soldier course of brick around the base. Roofing is of the flat shingle type. Entrance from the large front porch is directly into the living room. Stairs lead up from an alcoved hall in which coat closet is located. The open fireplace is flanked by two doors, one leading into the dining room and the other directly into the kitchen.

(Description of house shown in plans below)

THIS design shows a dignified handling of the Colonial style and is a good type of house for a suburban location. It can be placed near the street. The outlook for the principal rooms is from the front, and to obtain the best exposure it should face north; this gives morning sun in the dining room and sun all day in the living room. The house would best fit a corner lot with the long side the principal frontage. The exterior wall construction is of rough-textured face brick.

Full directions for obtaining complete working drawings and specifications for these plans will be found on page 281

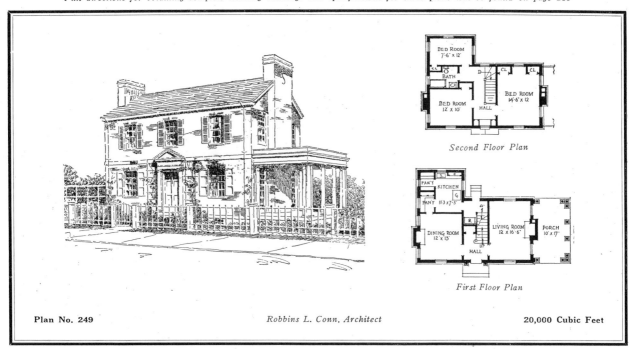

Second Floor Plan

First Floor Plan

Plan No. 249   *Robbins L. Conn, Architect*   **20,000 Cubic Feet**

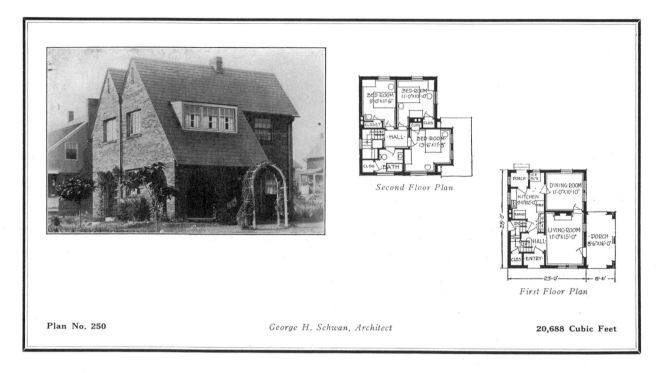

Second Floor Plan

First Floor Plan

Plan No. 250   *George H. Schwan, Architect*   **20,688 Cubic Feet**

(Description of house shown in above plans)

THIS six-room house is carefully designed for economy of construction and full utility of space. The exterior is of common brick with roof of slate shingles. A small entrance hall is provided with coat closet off the first stair landing and direct access to the living room and service section of the house. The kitchen is well arranged with ice box located for icing directly from the service porch without entering the house. The living room is augmented in size by a large living porch with French doors.

(Description of house shown in plans below)

THIS simple cottage gives the impression of a bungalow because of the low sloping roof. It has a full second story, however, with windows in a gable and generous dormers on the sides and rear. The first floor has an attractive entrance hall, reached from the kitchen through the pantry. The sitting porch opens directly from the living room. The house should preferably face northeast, thereby providing morning sun in the dining room and a pleasant exposure for the living room and garden.

Full directions for obtaining complete working drawings and specifications for these plans will be found on page 281

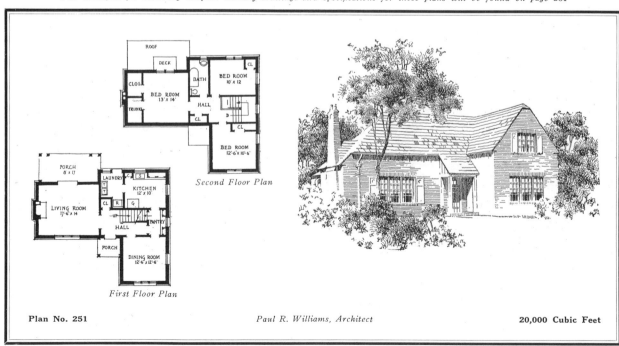

Second Floor Plan

First Floor Plan

Plan No. 251   *Paul R. Williams, Architect*   **20,000 Cubic Feet**

Second Floor Plan

First Floor Plan

Plan No. 252   *George H. Schwan, Architect*   **20,736 Cubic Feet**

(Description of house shown in above plans)

THIS six-room brick cottage has an interesting stucco dormer. A sweeping roof line is provided by carrying the main roof directly out over the entrance porch. There is a combined entry and stair hall with doors leading to the living room and to the kitchen. A service entrance is provided at the rear. On the second floor there will be found two large and one small bedroom. The arrangement of the plan has made it possible to work in a number of closets. A very large living porch is provided, running across one end.

(Description of house shown in plans below)

DUTCH Colonial, which always gives a homelike character, is used to advantage in the design of this house. The lower story of the front is especially charming because of the nice relation between the bay windows and the fan-light doorway. The interior is planned to give the appearance of a large house with the principal rooms on either side of the hall. The kitchen is conveniently arranged and connected with the dining room by a pantry. The space at the left of the kitchen would serve for a breakfast nook.

Full directions for obtaining complete working drawings and specifications for these plans will be found on page 281

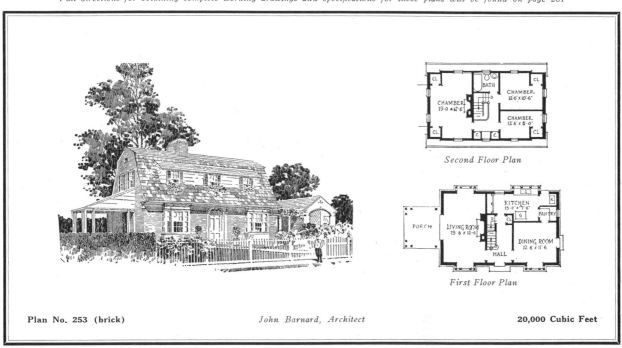

Second Floor Plan

First Floor Plan

Plan No. 253 (brick)   *John Barnard, Architect*   **20,000 Cubic Feet**

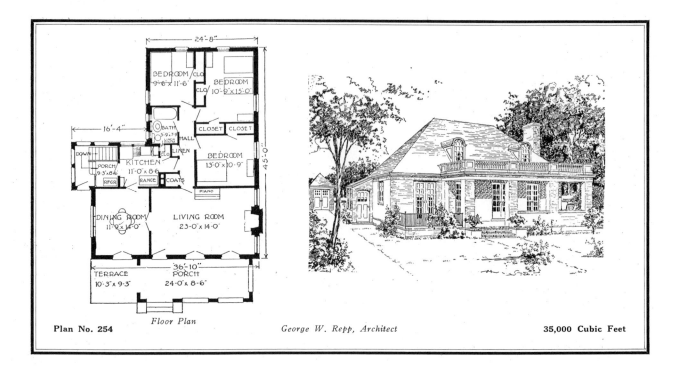

Floor Plan

Plan No. 254   *George W. Repp, Architect*   **35,000 Cubic Feet**

(Description of house shown in above plans)

AT first glance this house would seem to be very small but it contains three good-sized bedrooms with closets, dining room and a spacious living room, besides the bathroom, kitchen and hall with linen and coat closets. The compact arrangement of the plan leaves not an inch of waste space. The attic is so designed that it permits of various arrangements, such as two nice bedrooms with bath or a large billiard room or den. Exterior walls of face brick.

(Description of house shown in plans below)

THE generous breadth of this design allows half of its rooms to have a front position. No pleasanter rooms could be imagined than the living room and dining room with their many casements. On chill evenings, the fireplace is the logical center of the family group. Another charm of this room is its paneled walls. One room-end of the dining room is composed of a pair of casements, flanked by corner china cupboards. Frame and stucco construction.

Full directions for obtaining complete working drawings and specifications for these plans will be found on page 281

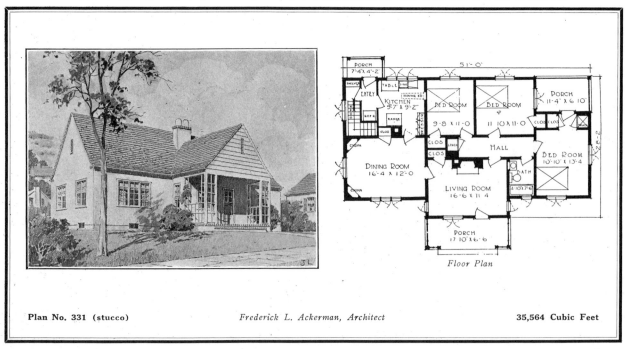

Floor Plan

Plan No. 331 (stucco)   *Frederick L. Ackerman, Architect*   **35,564 Cubic Feet**

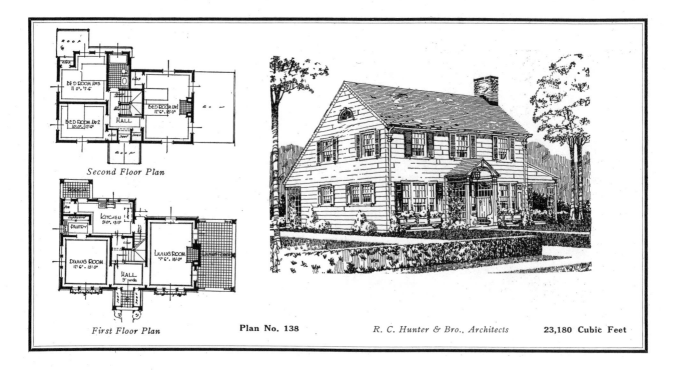

Second Floor Plan

First Floor Plan   **Plan No. 138**   *R. C. Hunter & Bro., Architects*   **23,180 Cubic Feet**

(Description of house shown in above plans)

IT is difficult to imagine a more beautiful home than this one of Colonial design. The trellised entrance porch with seats surely would invite one to come in. The living room is lighted from three sides and opens onto a large porch through French doors. The arrangement of dining room, kitchen and pantry tends to make the preparation and serving of a meal a pleasure rather than drudgery. The exterior finish of side walls is shingles or wide Colonial siding.

(Description of house shown in plans below)

HERE is another of the popular Colonial type of homes. On the exterior ten-inch siding is used, with brick for the well-balanced chimneys. Notice, too, the excellent proportions of the well-shaped dormers that break the gentle slope of the shingle roof. Slender porch columns and six-panel doors are also true to type. Although there are two stories, the impression is of a cottage. The central-hall type of floor plan is used. Frame construction throughout.

Full directions for obtaining complete working drawings and specifications for these plans will be found on page 281

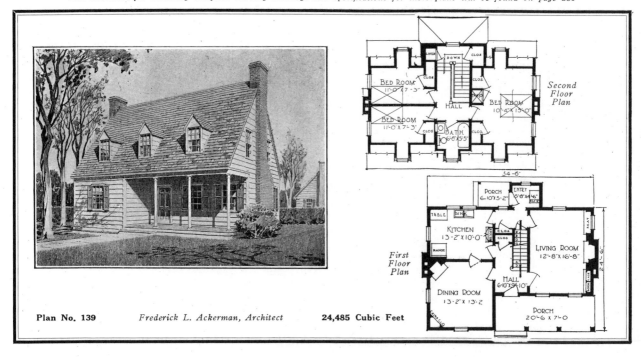

Plan No. 139   *Frederick L. Ackerman, Architect*   **24,485 Cubic Feet**

Second Floor Plan

First Floor Plan

Plan No. 255   *M. M. Steen, Architect*   **22,800 Cubic Feet**

(Description of house shown in above plans)

AN interesting arrangement for a six-room brick house of Colonial type. The main entrance is at the side of the house into a hall equipped with coat closet from which stairs lead up. There is another entrance from the porch flanking the fireplace. The living room is of ample size with good wall spaces for the arrangement of furniture. The kitchen and dining room are compactly arranged and a valuable feature is a separate entry to the service quarters.

(Description of house shown in plans below)

PLACED endwise or broadside to the road, this charming six-room bungalow will be equally attractive. The simplicity of its design suggests a simple treatment of the brickwork, relieved by just a touch of ornament in the pattern on the living room bay. Only a portion of the area is excavated for a cellar, which is arranged for heating plant and fuel bins, laundry, and vegetable cellar. This house is well planned with entrance and kitchen in the middle.

Full directions for obtaining complete working drawings and specifications for these plans will be found on page 281

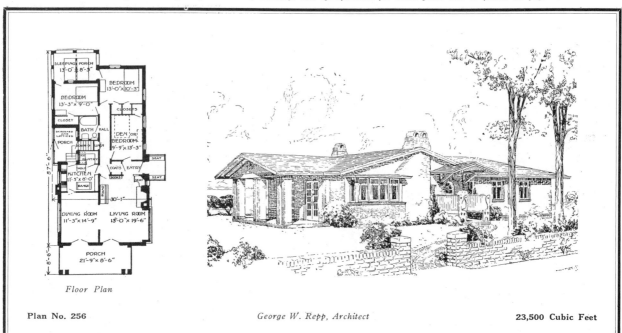

Floor Plan

Plan No. 256   *George W. Repp, Architect*   **23,500 Cubic Feet**

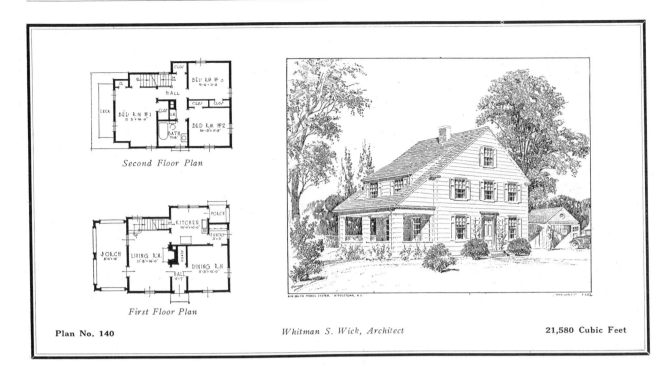

Second Floor Plan

First Floor Plan

Plan No. 140   *Whitman S. Wick, Architect*   **21,580 Cubic Feet**

(Description of house shown in above plans)

ANOTHER carefully planned six-room Colonial frame house. No little attractiveness is added to this design by the long roof slope broken by a dormer section. Here again a small amount of space is used for the entrance hall and the stairs become an architectural feature of the living room. French doors give access to a large porch off the living room and a pantry is a valuable additional service feature. Three sizeable bedrooms and bath are well arranged.

(Description of house shown in plans below)

IN this Western design, the plan approximates a square, and includes the porch within the body of the house. The low, rakish slant of the roof sweeping down over the porch gives a distinctive and pleasing effect to the exterior. An interesting feature is the open fireplace with built-in bookcases. The kitchen is well arranged with built-in cabinets and large pantry. There is a well lighted basement, complete with laundry, heater, fuel room and vegetable cellar.

Full directions for obtaining complete working drawings and specifications for these plans will be found on page 281

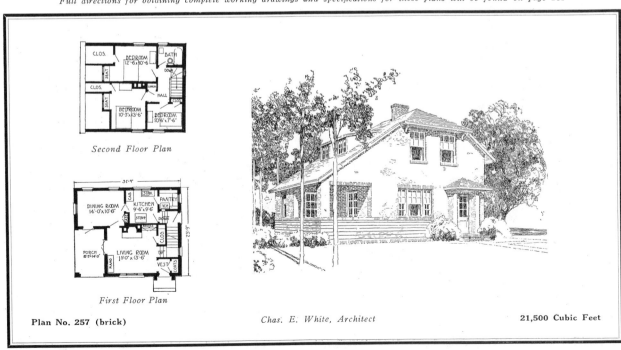

Second Floor Plan

First Floor Plan

Plan No. 257 (brick)   *Chas. E. White, Architect*   **21,500 Cubic Feet**

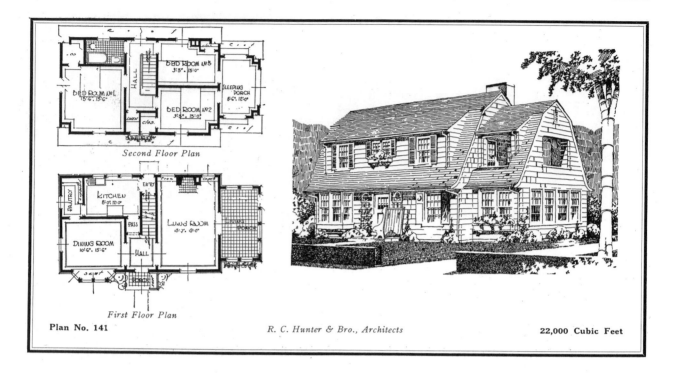

Second Floor Plan

First Floor Plan

Plan No. 141   *R. C. Hunter & Bro., Architects*   **22,000 Cubic Feet**

(Description of house shown in above plans)

HERE is a Dutch Colonial home containing many interesting features both in interior arrangement and exterior treatment. The entrance hall is in the center of the house, opening into the living and dining rooms on opposite sides. There is a large living porch on one end and over this is an airy sleeping porch accessible from two bedrooms. The position of the bathroom over the kitchen brings the plumbing all in one line—an economy which is desirable.

(Description of house shown in plans below)

THIS house is extremely simple in its design and would make an attractive and practical home. The porch extends across the front with the assumption that the best outlook would be toward the street. For this reason, the house should set back a good distance from the street and a hedge would be advisable at the property line to afford privacy. The plan shows a generous entrance hall, a good sized living room, with the dining room opening from it.

Full directions for obtaining complete working drawings and specifications for these plans will be found on page 281

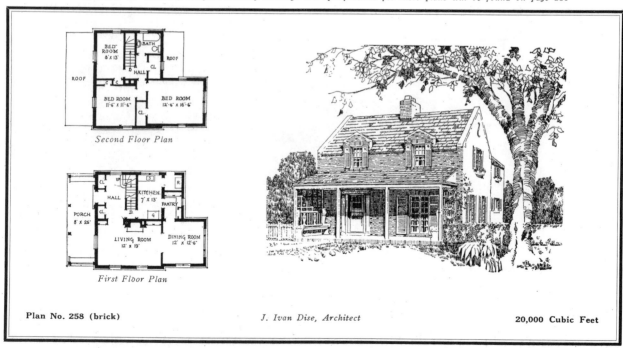

Second Floor Plan

First Floor Plan

Plan No. 258 (brick)   *J. Ivan Dise, Architect*   **20,000 Cubic Feet**

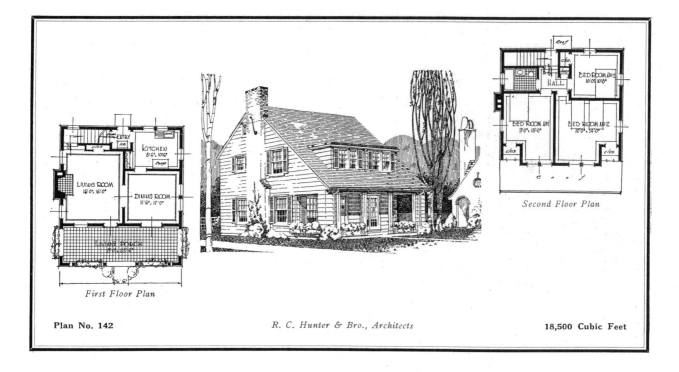

First Floor Plan

Second Floor Plan

Plan No. 142   *R. C. Hunter & Bro., Architects*   **18,500 Cubic Feet**

(Description of house shown in above plans)

FOR every variety of personal taste will be found in this book a design to satisfy it. To one partial to a spacious front porch this Colonial home should appeal very strongly. It extends the entire width of the house and is eight feet wide in the clear. The living and dining rooms both open on to it and combine to form an excellent place for entertaining friends. The massive brick chimney on one side serves to contrast and accentuate the other more refined details.

(Description of house shown in plans below)

THIS attractive house has a plan which insures pleasant, sunny rooms at any time of the day, and the best of light and air, since most of the rooms have windows on three sides. It is conveniently planned, the rooms are comfortably large, the kitchen is compact and well located with respect to the dining room and entrance hall. A space for the sewing machine off the upstairs hall and a clothes chute (marked X on the plan) are special features. Frame throughout.

Full directions for obtaining complete working drawings and specifications for these plans will be found on page 281

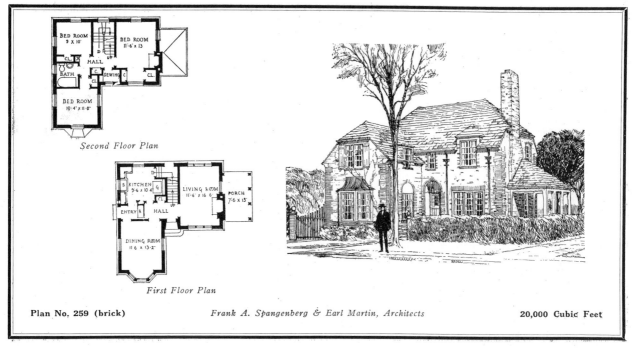

Second Floor Plan

First Floor Plan

Plan No. 259 (brick)   *Frank A. Spangenberg & Earl Martin, Architects*   **20,000 Cubic Feet**

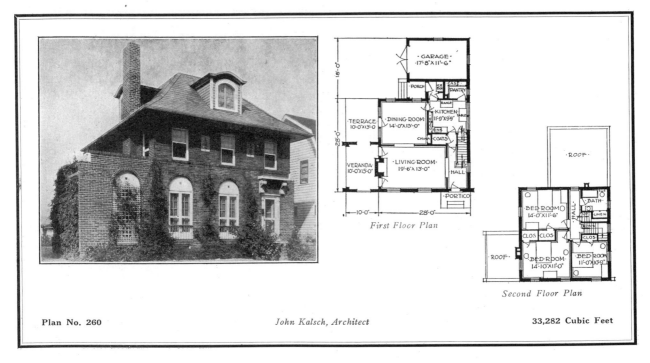

First Floor Plan

Second Floor Plan

Plan No. 260   *John Kalsch, Architect*   33,282 Cubic Feet

(Description of house shown in above plans)

THIS house demonstrates the possibilities of a common brick exterior in which the architectural effect is gained by the shape and placing of openings, particularly arched window openings of the living room and verandah. This verandah and the terrace behind it add considerably to the visual impression without a great addition in structural cost. A special feature of this house is the arrangement of the garage built in a unit of the main building. The dining room and living room are well arranged, with ample light, and interesting communication with terrace.

(Description of house shown in plans below)

THE porch on this house is the principal external feature. Although it extends along two sides of the living room, it does not darken that room, which has a fine group of windows at the uncovered side. The front part of the porch may be glassed in, if desired, and made into a sun parlor, as French doors connect it with the living room. The open fireplace on the porch will make it a delightful spot on autumn days. The kitchen is particularly well arranged, and the provision of a lavatory on the first floor is a convenient feature. Face brick exterior.

Full directions for obtaining complete working drawings and specifications for these plans will be found on page 281

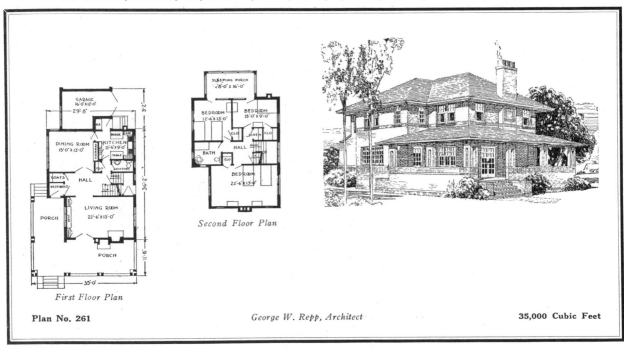

First Floor Plan

Second Floor Plan

Plan No. 261   *George W. Repp, Architect*   35,000 Cubic Feet

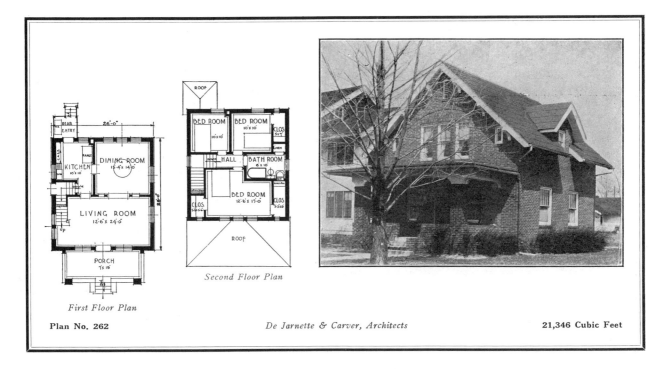

First Floor Plan

Second Floor Plan

Plan No. 262   *De Jarnette & Carver, Architects*   **21,346 Cubic Feet**

(Description of house shown in above plans)

HERE is a favored type of house for closely built suburban residential districts. It is a house which can be built on a comparatively small lot and at the same time standing out distinctly when compared with neighboring buildings. The exterior of the house is of selected common brick laid with wide mortar joints. Roofing can be of any shingle type laid double at intervals to provide shadow lines as indicated in photograph. Entrance hall is eliminated, stairs being located directly in the living room.

(Description of house shown in plans below)

HERE is a house which would be appropriate for a suburban or small city location. It could be placed near the street or set back some distance, depending upon the location of adjoining houses. The principal rooms face the street and the front should be toward the southeast to obtain the best exposure. The exterior is designed for two tones of brick with the darker shade used for the corners and the pattern on the walls. The interior is arranged with the principal rooms either side of the entrance hall.

Full directions for obtaining complete working drawings and specifications for these plans will be found on page 281

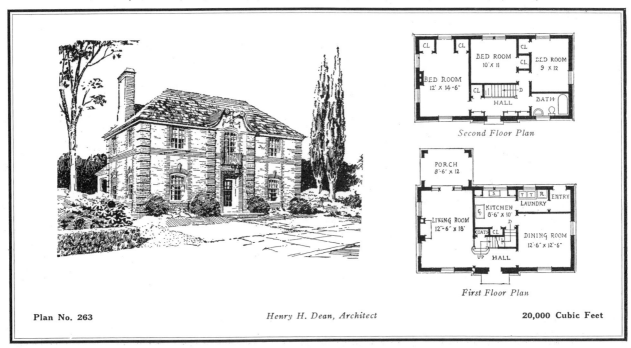

Second Floor Plan

First Floor Plan

Plan No. 263   *Henry H. Dean, Architect*   **20,000 Cubic Feet**

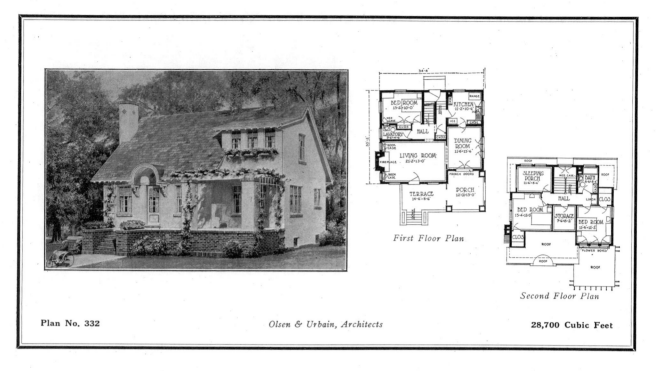

First Floor Plan

Second Floor Plan

Plan No. 332   *Olsen & Urbain, Architects*   **28,700 Cubic Feet**

(Description of house shown in above plans)

THE plans of this attractive bungalow, which call for a complete hollow tile structure with an exterior finish of stucco and brick, are exceptionally well worked out. This home would look well with walls of exposed tile or with tile walls faced with brick. There are six large rooms and a sleeping porch; also a terrace and porch running across the front of the house. The bedroom and lavatory on the first floor are convenient features, especially in a home where there are children or aged people.

(Description of house shown in plans below)

THE construction of this house calls for a stuccoed first story and wood siding above. The roof is of shingles. Special features of the first floor plan include a fireplace in the living room and a pantry conveniently located as a service point between kitchen and dining room. Instead of rising from the hall the stairs become a feature of the living room interior design, allowing a better arrangement of the second floor. Here the principal bedroom occupies a space equal to that of the living room.

Full directions for obtaining complete working drawings and specifications for these plans will be found on page 281

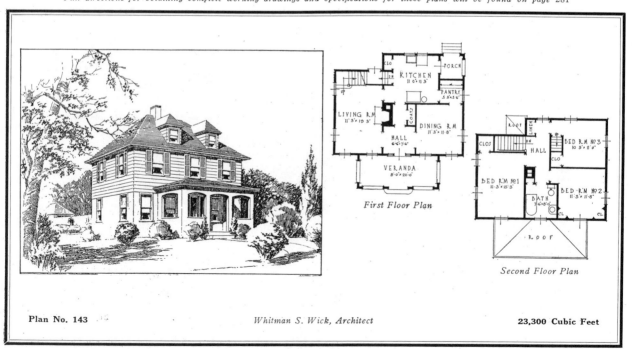

First Floor Plan

Second Floor Plan

Plan No. 143   *Whitman S. Wick, Architect*   **23,300 Cubic Feet**

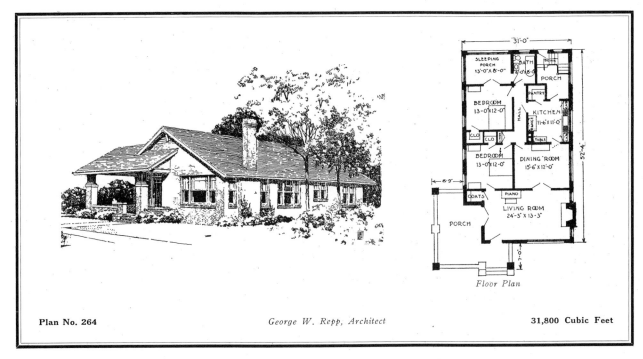

Plan No. 264   *George W. Repp, Architect*   31,800 Cubic Feet

(Description of house shown in above plans)   *(Description of house shown in plans below)*

WITH this type of house, simple in outline and detail, much thought should be given the type of brick to be used and how it should be handled in the wall. The color of the mortar, the treatment of the joint, and the kind of bond are things often overlooked, but which, if given careful consideration, will greatly enhance the beauty of the brickwork, much to the advantage of the whole house. Although the illustration shows this house built on a level, it could be built on a sloping site by slight changes in the front or rear steps. Face brick exterior.

A TOUCH of color in brick copings is part of the attractiveness of this stucco bungalow. The solarium at the right of the porch is a year round living room. The living room is separated from the solarium and the den by two pairs of French doors. There is a fireplace in the living room with a simple mantel, and an inter-room opening with bookcases on each side. The den is a small but useful room. It has a coat closet with mirror door so that it may serve as an emergency bedroom. In line of view from the living room is a built-in sideboard.

Full directions for obtaining complete working-drawings and specifications for these plans will be found on page 281

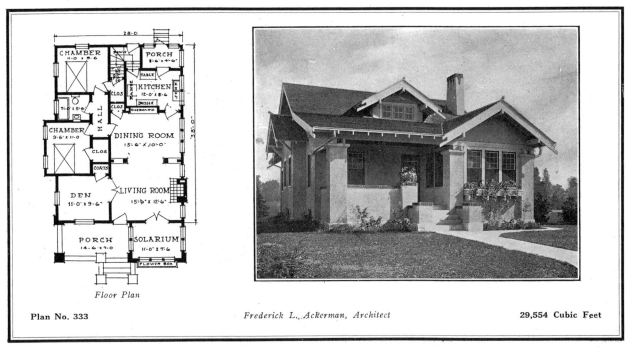

Floor Plan

Plan No. 333   *Frederick L. Ackerman, Architect*   29,554 Cubic Feet

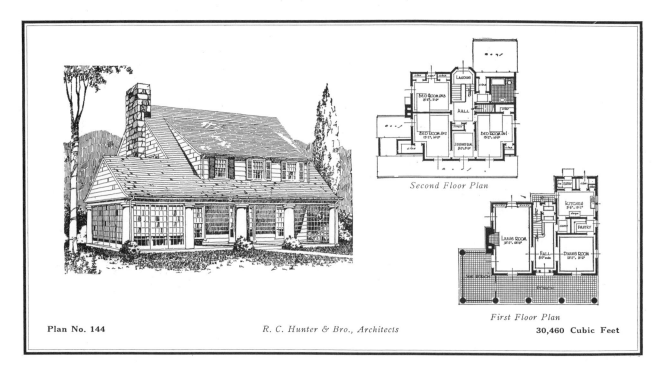

Second Floor Plan

First Floor Plan

Plan No. 144   *R. C. Hunter & Bro., Architects*   **30,460 Cubic Feet**

(Description of house shown in above plans)

THE proper position for this house should be facing the east. That would give sunlight in the living room and sun parlor all day long the year around. In like manner the kitchen, being to the north, would have more uniform light and be cooler in summer. The exterior walls are of shingles with wide exposure, and the roof also shingled. There is a large stone chimney on the living room end. There is a roomy attic in which one or two additional bedrooms could be finished if desired.

(Description of house shown in plans below)

A SKILLFUL adaptation of the hip roof is a feature of this six-room house. A service wing on one side and a porch wing balancing it on the other give the house a distinctive appearance. There is no useless ornamentation. The symmetrical placing of windows with green shutters against clapboard walls is one of the chief factors in the appearance of the house. The quaint formal entrance is accented by the little hood. French doors open from the hall to the living room and the dining room.

Full directions for obtaining complete working drawings and specifications for these plans will be found on page 281

Second Floor Plan

First Floor Plan

Plan No. 145   *Frederick L. Ackerman, Architect*   **29,363 Cubic Feet**

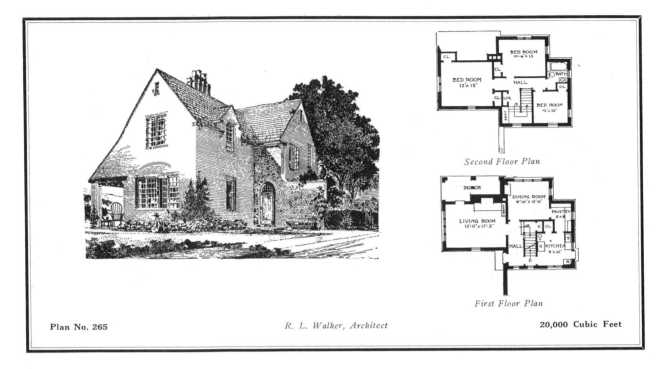

Second Floor Plan

First Floor Plan

Plan No. 265   *R. L. Walker, Architect*   **20,000 Cubic Feet**

(Description of house shown in above plans)

HERE is an attractive house based on modern English designs. It could readily be adapted to a hilly or level site and could be placed in a number of different positions depending upon the shape of the lot and the exposure. If the lot is narrow the living room end could be turned toward the street as shown in the illustration. With a wide frontage and a good view at the rear, the kitchen and long side of the living room should face the street. The floor plan is attractive; the rooms are comfortably large.

(Description of house shown in plans below)

IF well set back from the road this house could face as shown in the illustration, with the garden in front and the entrance on the side. Otherwise it would be better to turn the narrow end to the street with the garden in the rear, reached from the porch. This house has comfortable rooms with square ceilings. The circular stairs are a very attractive feature of the interior. Exterior of house is of face brick on hollow tile and the roof is of clay tile. This has proven to be a very popular type.

Full directions for obtaining complete working drawings and specifications for these plans will be found on page 281

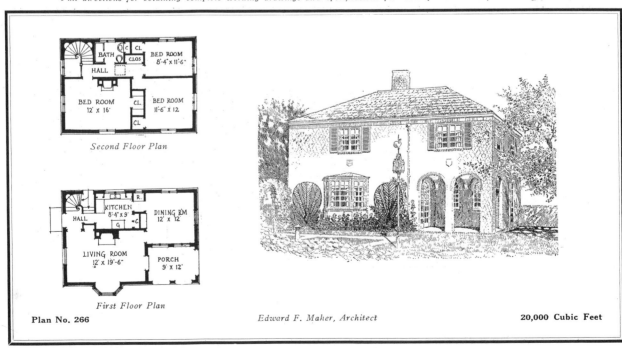

Second Floor Plan

First Floor Plan

Plan No. 266   *Edward F. Maher, Architect*   **20,000 Cubic Feet**

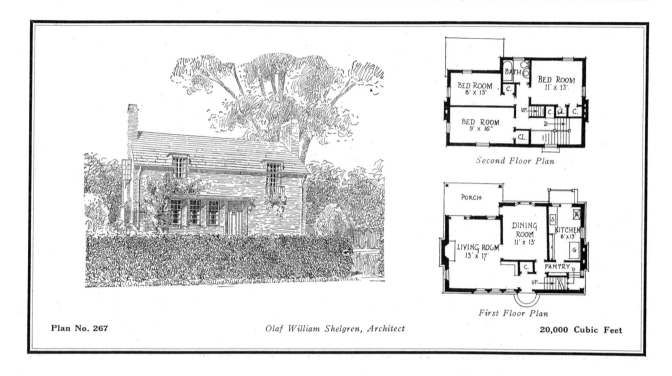

Plan No. 267   *Olaf William Shelgren, Architect*   **20,000 Cubic Feet**

(Description of house shown in above plans)

THIS house could be placed close to the street with a boundary hedge as suggested in the illustration, and the rear reserved for garden and lawn. The porch and dining room would thus have a pleasant outlook. The floor plan is well arranged and though only the minimum space is given to the entrance hall, it is directly connected with every room on the first floor. The stairs are attractive, with the large window toward the street. Exterior is of face brick.

(Description of house shown in plans below)

THIS house occupies a small ground space, and the square layout and two stories give it a maximum of space with a minimum construction and up-keep cost. The living room extends across the front of the house, and its most impressive feature is the stair across one side with balustrade. An inter-room opening with bookcase pedestals forms the entrance to the dining room, affording a glimpse of the built-in sideboard at the back. Frame construction throughout.

Full directions for obtaining complete working drawings and specifications for these plans will be found on page 281

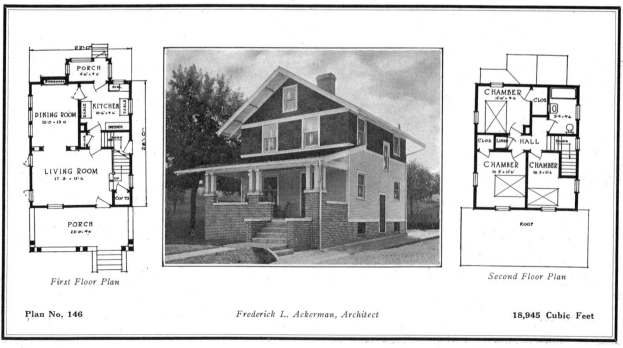

Plan No. 146   *Frederick L. Ackerman, Architect*   **18,945 Cubic Feet**

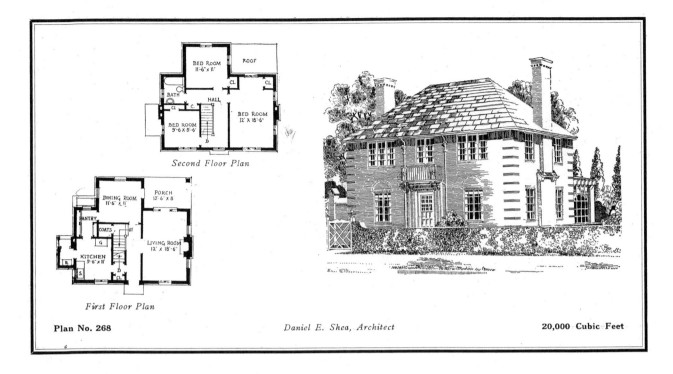

Second Floor Plan

First Floor Plan

Plan No. 268   *Daniel E. Shea, Architect*   **20,000 Cubic Feet**

(Description of house shown in above plans)

HERE is a good type of house for a closely built up suburban community. It can be placed near the street with the rear reserved for garden and lawn. The drive to a garage could be at the left and a wall or fence with gate would close off the kitchen yard from the street. The kitchen is conveniently arranged with refrigerator room and large pantry, and affords a pleasant view of the street. The porch is on the rear and reached from both living and dining rooms.

(Description of house shown in plans below)

HERE is a house combining all the convenience of the popular 24 by 26 floor plan with a distinctive architectural exterior. Its chief feature is the half-timbered second story, with bracketed overhang. Batten shutters are an excellent touch, as is the lattice work of the front porch. The central front entrance admits directly to the living room, which extends across the front of the house, and a handsome open stair at the left of the room predominates.

Full directions for obtaining complete working drawings and specifications for these plans will be found on page 281

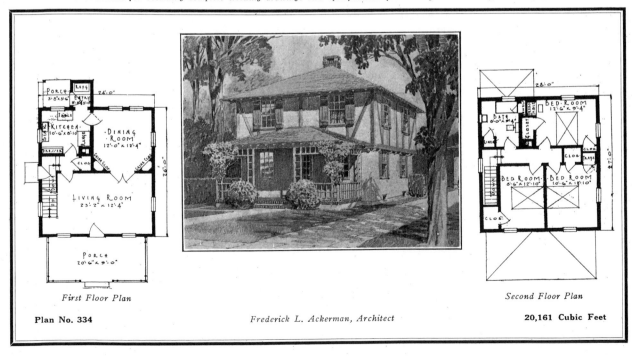

First Floor Plan

Second Floor Plan

Plan No. 334   *Frederick L. Ackerman, Architect*   **20,161 Cubic Feet**

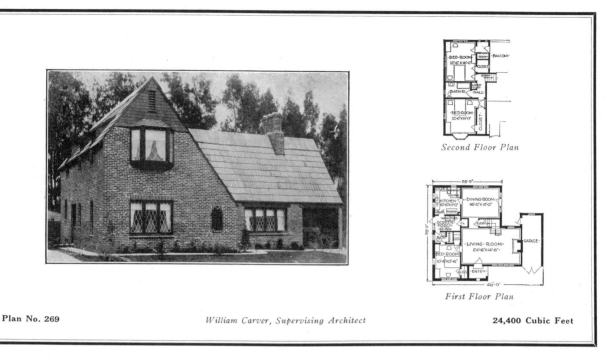

Second Floor Plan

First Floor Plan

Plan No. 269   *William Carver, Supervising Architect*   24,400 Cubic Feet

---

(Description of house shown in above plans)

HERE is an unusually interesting English cottage type of house. Common brick with wide mortar joints, irregular spacing, is used for the exterior walls with upper gable of shingles. Roof is of irregular slate laid in an unusual pattern. The design calls for casement windows and a good architectural feature is the small bay window in the second floor bedroom. This is a six-room house with one bedroom on the main floor. The living room is built almost as a separate unit with no second floor.

(Description of house shown in plans below)

RECTANGULAR in outline, with low walls and simple roof, this plan should appeal to those who wish to profit by a simple arrangement. Occupying the entire front of the house are the living and dining rooms, with French doors opening upon the porch, which extends the full width of the house. An open brick fireplace, flanked by a seat and a shallow bay, gives a charming aspect to the living room. Across the entrance hall is a den, or library, which may be used as a bedroom if desired. Face brick exterior.

Full directions for obtaining complete working drawings and specifications for these plans will be found on page 281

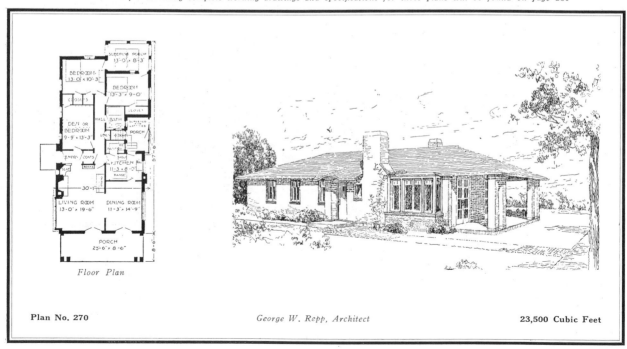

Floor Plan

Plan No. 270   *George W. Repp, Architect*   23,500 Cubic Feet

Floor Plan

Plan No. 271   *Chas. E. White, Jr., Architect*   **29,000 Cubic Feet**

(Description of house shown in above plans)

A RAMBLING, rustic type of Western bungalow fitting well almost any setting. The front porch, while sheltering the entrance, is placed at one side so that its use is not interrupted by passage to or from the house. The living room is lighted by windows on two sides and has an unusual arrangement of fireplace and bookcases. Note the china cabinets in connection with the dining room. The kitchen has been so placed as to allow the bedrooms to occupy the rear corners, where they will get cross draft.

(Description of house shown in plans below)

HERE is a delightful bungalow of the Southern type, which would be very attractive with exterior of stucco or a brick veneer over hollow tile. There are six rooms and two sleeping porches, all on the ground floor, and all rooms have casement windows. The living room, dining room and kitchen run across the front of the house, while the sleeping quarters are well isolated from the living rooms of the house. The kitchen is semi-detached and well arranged with the range and case just off the dining room.

Full directions for obtaining complete working drawings and specifications for these plans will be found on page 281

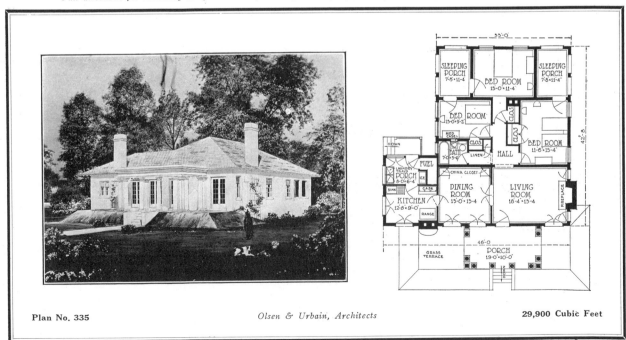

Plan No. 335   *Olsen & Urbain, Architects*   **29,900 Cubic Feet**

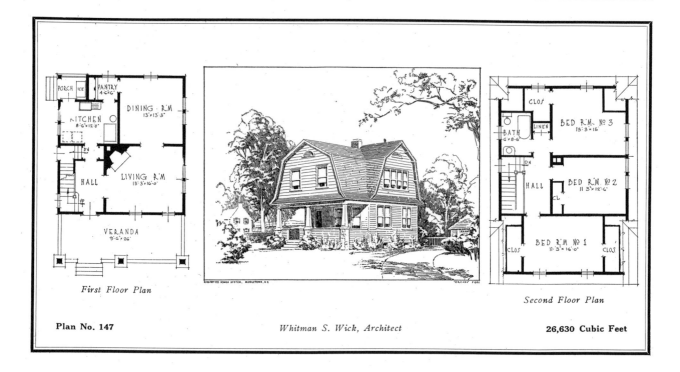

First Floor Plan

Second Floor Plan

Plan No. 147   *Whitman S. Wick, Architect*   **26,630 Cubic Feet**

(Description of house shown in above plans)

THIS six-room frame house of modified Dutch Colonial type is designed for standardized economy in construction. The use of this type of roof provides ample headroom in bedrooms and allows a greater usable cubic footage than in steep slopes. The exterior of this house is of white siding, while the roof is of wood or patented shingles. A large porch is arranged across the entire front and the subdivision of the first floor provides a splendid arrangement.

(Description of house shown in plans below)

THIS is a popular type of six-room house, having exterior of warm colored face brick in rough texture. A large enclosed porch is an architectural feature as well as one of convenience. Stairs lead up from the living room and a special feature is a small side service entrance. The dining room is of ample size and has in addition a large glass enclosed dining porch. There are three bedrooms upstairs, each of which is a corner room, and contains ample closets.

Full directions for obtaining complete working drawings and specifications for these plans will be found on page 281

First Floor Plan

Second Floor Plan

Plan No. 272   *George W. Repp, Architect*   **27,000 Cubic Feet**

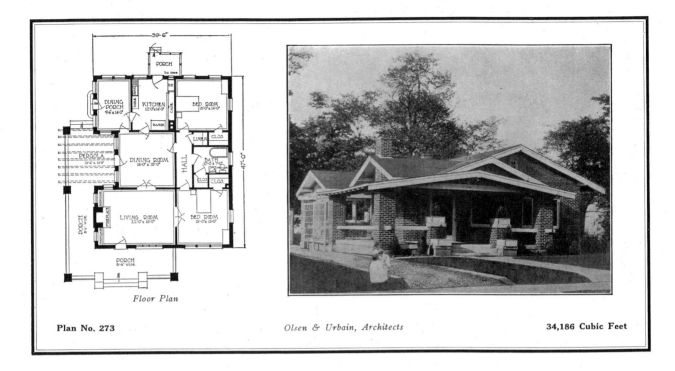

Floor Plan

Plan No. 273   *Olsen & Urbain, Architects*   **34,186 Cubic Feet**

(Description of house shown in above plans)

COMMON brick is used for the exterior of this five-room bungalow. An attractive pattern is provided by the use of wide white mortar joints and a soldier course of brick used as a belt course. The exterior trimming is of white wood and white cement caps. A special feature of the plan is the provision of a built-in dining porch which virtually adds another room. Another attractive feature is the pergola and porch which forms the outlook from the dining room.

(Description of house shown in plans below)

THIS house has been designed especially for the narrow city lot. It may be placed on as small a frontage as thirty-five feet. As the entrance is at the side of the house half way from the front, it allows uninterrupted space in the front for living quarters, and makes possible a small hall with direct connection to the bedrooms. There is a fine, well-lighted and ventilated basement with laundry, drying space, fruit cellar, and heating plant with coal bins provided.

Full directions for obtaining complete working drawings and specifications for these plans will be found on page 281

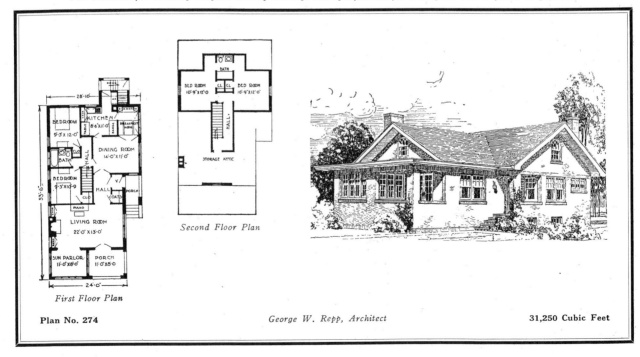

First Floor Plan

Second Floor Plan

Plan No. 274   *George W. Repp, Architect*   **31,250 Cubic Feet**

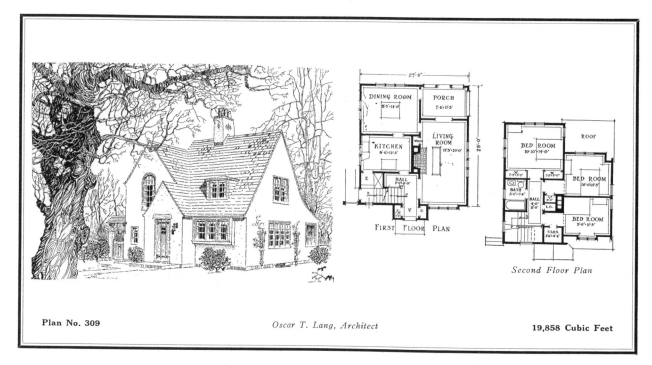

Plan No. 309   *Oscar T. Lang, Architect*   **19,858 Cubic Feet**

(Description of house shown in above plans)   *(Description of house shown in plans below)*

THIS popular design for a six-room house has been used a number of times with unvarying success. The construction of the exterior walls is of Portland cement stucco on metal lath and roofing of flat shingle type. A very successful color combination for the exterior may be had by introducing a yellow mortar color in the stucco and using slate or asbestos cement shingles of varying colors. The use of casement windows adds to the attractiveness of the exterior. The layout of the first floor provides a large living room with enclosed porch.

A CHARMING design, lending itself to a variety of effects. It could be built of two shades of brick, using one for the quoins and base and the other for the body of the house. A similar effect could be obtained with different colored mortars. This house has been designed to reduce to a minimum the number of steps necessary for the operation of the household. Both front and rear doors and stairs are conveniently near the kitchen, and just a step from the living room. The basement stairs are so located, with outside door at grade, to eliminate outside basement entrance.

Full directions for obtaining complete working drawings and specifications for these plans will be found on page 281

First Floor Plan   *Second Floor Plan*

Plan No. 275   *Clark & Walcott, Architects*   **20,000 Cubic Feet**

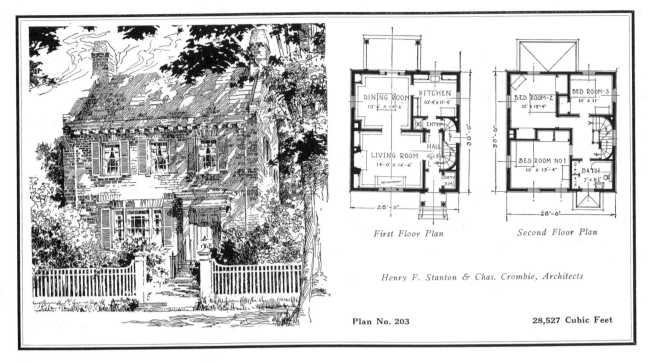

First Floor Plan   *Second Floor Plan*

Henry F. Stanton & Chas. Crombie, Architects

Plan No. 203   **28,527 Cubic Feet**

(Description of house shown in above plans)

THE plan of this charming Colonial house is very compact, the minimum of space being given to stairs and halls. The living room and dining room open from each other pleasantly on the first floor with a view from the living room through the rear porch to the garden. Access from the kitchen to the hall is conveniently had, and on the right hand side an entrance at grade line provides access to both cellar and kitchen. The second floor has two large and one small bedroom, together with a good-sized bath and ample closet space. Exterior of face brick.

(Description of house shown in plans below)

ALTHOUGH the roof of this six-room English cottage has a low effect, it attains sufficient height for two fine bedrooms on the second floor. To gain the best effect this house should be built close to the ground in front, with the grade sloping to the rear, where basement windows are located. As there is a bath and bedroom on the first floor, only the four lower rooms need be finished at first, leaving the second floor until later. If, however, the rooms upstairs are also finished when the house is built, the bedroom and bath on the main floor may be re-planned.

Full directions for obtaining complete working drawings and specifications for these plans will be found on page 281

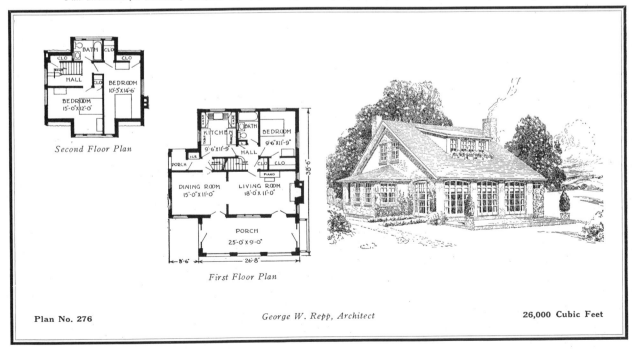

Second Floor Plan

First Floor Plan

Plan No. 276   *George W. Repp, Architect*   **26,000 Cubic Feet**

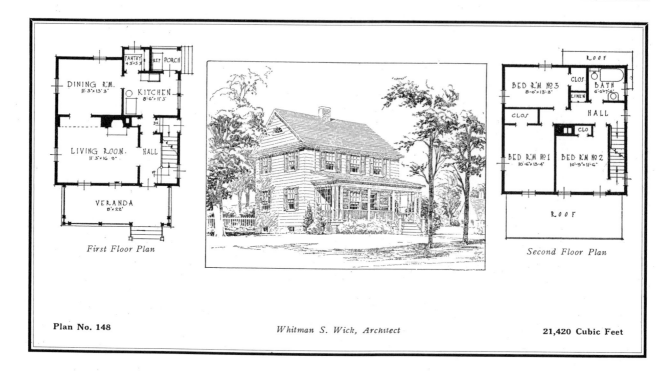

DINING R'M. 11'-3"x13'-3"
PANTRY 4'-5"x5'-3"
KITCHEN 8'-6"x11'-3"
LIVING ROOM 11'-3"x16'-0"
HALL
VERANDA 8'x22'

First Floor Plan

BED R'M N° 3 8'-0"x13'-8"
CLOS
BATH 6'-6"x7'-6"
LINEN
HALL
CLO
BED R'M N° 1 10'-6"x13'-4"
BED R'M N° 2 10'-3"x11'-6"
ROOF

Second Floor Plan

Plan No. 148   *Whitman S. Wick, Architect*   **21,420 Cubic Feet**

(Description of house shown in above plans)

A TYPICAL white Colonial house of frame construction with shingle roof. This house contains six rooms of ample size and is well planned with entrance hall at the side from which stairs lead directly to the upper floor. The living room contains an open fireplace located off-center, an interesting interior feature. Access to the dining room is through an arched entrance. A pantry is provided as an additional kitchen feature.

(Description of house shown in plans below)

A STUDY of this plan will reveal a great amount of livable space and little waste, within a very small area. The house is rectangular in form and easily framed and roofed—thus lowering costs. The living room occupies the front portion of the house and opens to the front porch by a pair of French doors. There is a fine, well-lighted basement, containing heating plant, fuel bins, fruit cellar, garbage incinerator, laundry and storage space.

Full directions for obtaining complete working drawings and specifications for these plans will be found on page 281

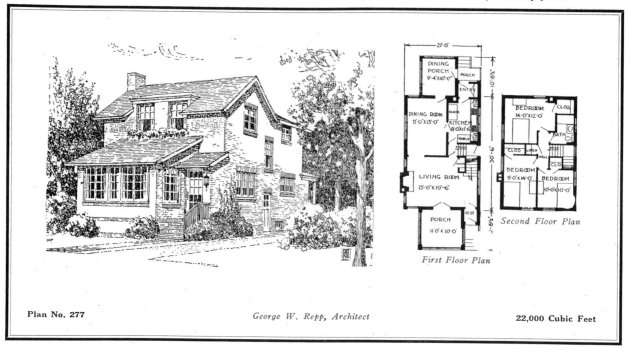

DINING PORCH 9'-4"x10'-0"
PORCH
ENTRY
DINING ROOM 11'-0"x15'-0"
KITCHEN 8'-0"x11'-6"
RANGE
TABLE
LIVING ROOM 13'-0"x19'-6"
PORCH 11'-0"x10'-0"

First Floor Plan

BEDROOM 14'-0"x12'-0"
CLOS
BATH
CLOS
LINEN
HALL
BEDROOM 9'-0"x14'-0"
CLO
BEDROOM 10'-6"x10'-0"

Second Floor Plan

Plan No. 277   *George W. Repp, Architect*   **22,000 Cubic Feet**

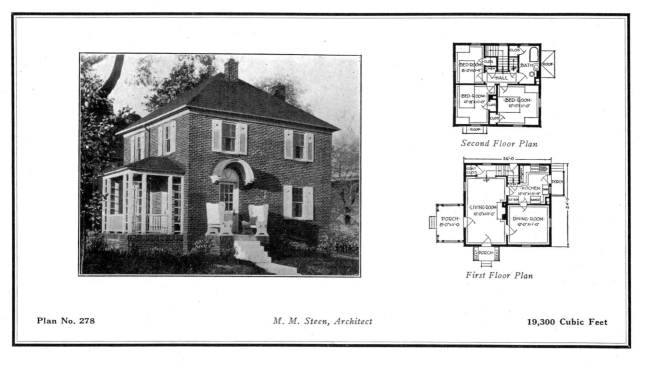

Second Floor Plan

First Floor Plan

Plan No. 278   *M. M. Steen, Architect*   **19,300 Cubic Feet**

(Description of house shown in above plans)

A SIX-ROOM house having exterior of common brick with shingle roof. Two entrance porches are provided, both leading into the living room. Stairs and coat closet are located at the rear. The second floor arrangement is of conventional type providing three bedrooms of comparatively small size but well arranged for the limited area occupied by the house. To obtain the right architectural effect the first floor level should be high, as indicated in the photograph.

(Description of house shown in plans below)

THIS house has a dignity in its design that would make it prominent even among houses of much larger size. The principal rooms are across the front and the exposure should be southeast to insure their being sunny and pleasant. A terrace across the front connects the side porch with the entrance, and French windows in living and dining rooms give access to the terrace. The roof of the porch is flat and is reached by a French window from bedroom.

Full directions for obtaining complete working drawings and specifications for these plans will be found on page 281

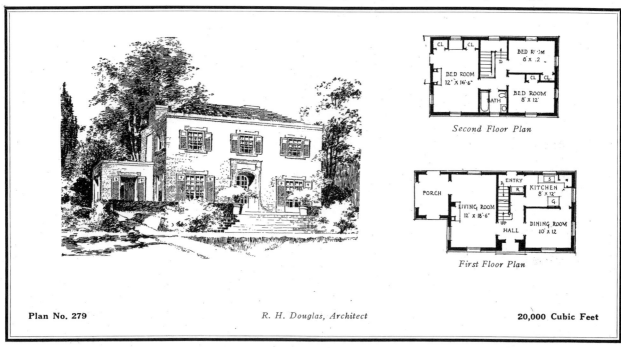

Second Floor Plan

First Floor Plan

Plan No. 279   *R. H. Douglas, Architect*   **20,000 Cubic Feet**

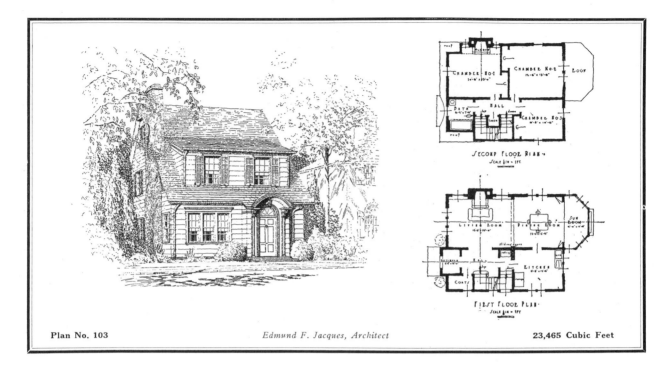

Plan No. 103   *Edmund F. Jacques, Architect*   **23,465 Cubic Feet**

(Description of house shown in above plans)

THIS house, which is designed for exterior walls of wide siding or shingles, would be particularly suitable for a closely built-up suburban section because of the narrow side being toward the street. The first floor is planned so that living room, dining room and sun room can open into one another, giving a large, well-lighted space when wanted. The entrance to the kitchen is through a door at the grade line, which gives access to the cellar as well.

(Description of house shown in plans below)

HERE is a home which typifies the ideals of our early pioneers—economy, usefulness, charm. Its design and construction allow of a roominess which is a delight to the occupants. On the ground floor is a spacious living room with a sun parlor extending from it and an open fireplace directly opposite. The dining room opens on to the living room, giving a maximum of air and light. The kitchen is well equipped and arranged with a view to saving steps.

Full directions for obtaining complete working drawings and specifications for these plans will be found on page 281

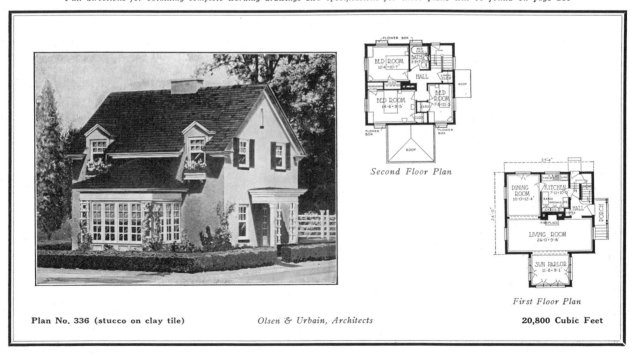

Plan No. 336 (stucco on clay tile)   *Olsen & Urbain, Architects*   **20,800 Cubic Feet**

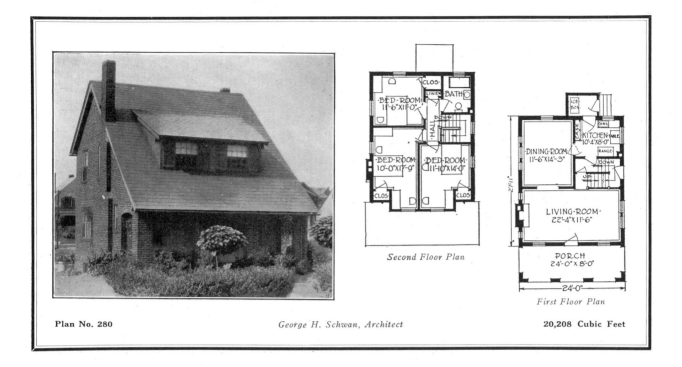

Plan No. 280   *George H. Schwan, Architect*   20,208 Cubic Feet

(Description of house shown in above plans)

(Description of house shown in plans below)

AN attractively planned brick house of English cottage type. Materials used for the house in photograph are common brick and slate roof. The large living room is an attractive feature and the stair arrangement is somewhat unusual, but quite practical, as it occupies the least valuable space of the floor plan. The second floor arrangement of this six-room house provides three bedrooms of ample size, having good light and ventilation.

ALL sides of this house are interesting, and it could face the street as shown in the illustration, or the dining room could face the street. The house is of English Tudor design and could be carried out nicely in brick with suggestions of half timber work in weathered oak or chestnut around the porch. The plan is compact and presents a very livable arrangement with especially good bedrooms. The dimensions are twenty-eight feet by twenty-nine feet deep.

Full directions for obtaining complete working drawings and specifications for these plans will be found on page 281

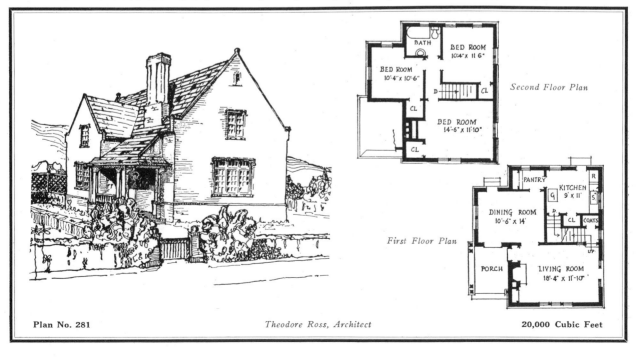

Plan No. 281   *Theodore Ross, Architect*   20,000 Cubic Feet

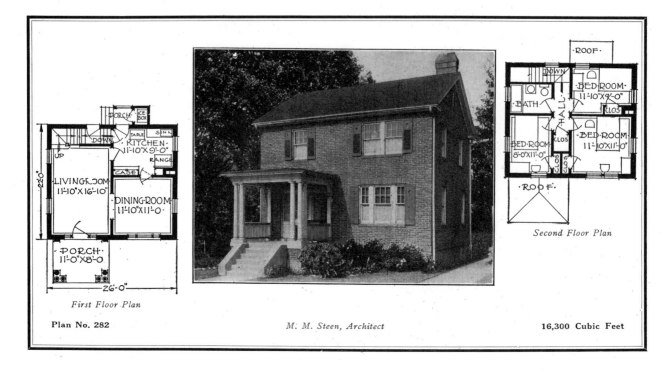

First Floor Plan

Plan No. 282   M. M. Steen, Architect   16,300 Cubic Feet

(Description of house shown in above plans)

THIS plan shows a very practical and economical arrangement of a nearly square house. The rooms are of such size as to permit the use of standard lengths of joists without cutting. A suggestion for the exterior color scheme might be dark red bricks, moss green blinds, white trim and sash, and variegated slate roof. Where practicable this house should be built lower on the ground than the one illustrated, to give the most pleasing effect.

(Description of house shown in plans below)

THE design of this house is based on no special style and it would therefore harmonize with the houses of any community. It would be best located on a corner lot with the front parallel with the long frontage. In this arrangement a garage could be placed at the right end of the lot opposite the porch, and with a short drive from the street. The front of the house should preferably face the southwest; this will give good exposure to the principal rooms.

Full directions for obtaining complete working drawings and specifications for these plans will be found on page 281

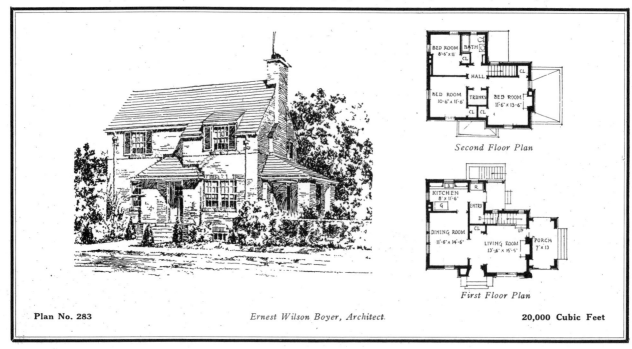

Plan No. 283   Ernest Wilson Boyer, Architect.   20,000 Cubic Feet

Floor Plan

Plan No. 501   *George W. Repp, Architect*   **38,000 Cubic Feet**

(Description of house shown in above plans)   *(Description of house shown in plans below)*

THE wide-spread gables, the dormer, the overhanging eaves, the low broad porch suggest the origin of this type in the Southwest, where protection from the summer sun is always grateful. The roof line is very pleasing with its low, rambling sweep, and the porch is made somewhat secluded by the pleasing brick parapet which would lend itself to very artistic treatment. The floor plan is very carefully arranged for the maximum utility of space and the basement is provided with laundry, heating apparatus, vegetable cellar and storage rooms. Face brick exterior.

HERE is an attractive bungalow with an excellently planned interior arrangement. A pleasing color effect would be obtained by using a gray or cream colored stucco with white sash against a red roof. A small vestibule with clothes closet leads to the living room. This room is of splendid size, extending across the front of the house. Some may prefer to transpose the kitchen and front bedroom, thus bringing the kitchen entrance nearer the front. There will also be some economy in plumbing by this arrangement. Exterior walls of stucco on concrete blocks.

Full directions for obtaining complete working drawings and specifications for these plans will be found on page 281

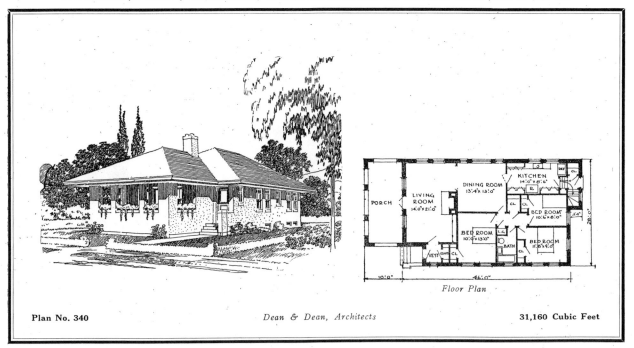

Floor Plan

Plan No. 340   *Dean & Dean, Architects*   **31,160 Cubic Feet**

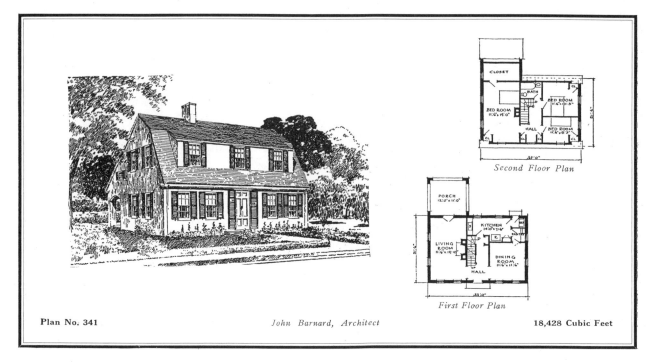

Plan No. 341   *John Barnard, Architect*   **18,428 Cubic Feet**

(Description of house shown in above plans)

THIS is a delightful example of the old New England Colonial type of house, and although the illustration shows the use of stucco, it would appear to good advantage in other building material. In this plan the living room runs the full depth of the house, giving a splendid room nearly twenty feet long, and containing four windows. The porch off this room makes a splendid addition for the summer months. The dining room is at the right of the hall, and pantry and kitchen beyond. The largest closet could be changed into a sleeping porch without much difficulty.

(Description of house shown in plans below)

THE steeply pitched roof and gables of this charming house are reminiscent of northern France, and illustrates a style that is rapidly coming to vogue in this country. A fine living room with fireplace occupies the center of the frontage with recessed entrance porch and hall on one side and a large open porch with arched entrances on the other. Behind this is a dining room and kitchen with a convenient back porch. On the second floor there are three bedrooms of good size; all have commodious closets, and plenty of windows insure light and a good circulation of air.

Full directions for obtaining complete working drawings and specifications for these plans will be found on page 281

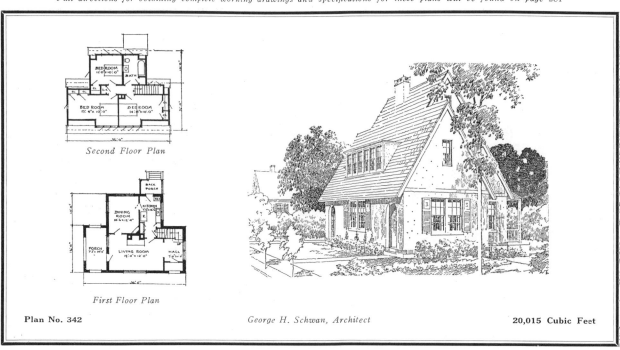

Plan No. 342   *George H. Schwan, Architect*   **20,015 Cubic Feet**

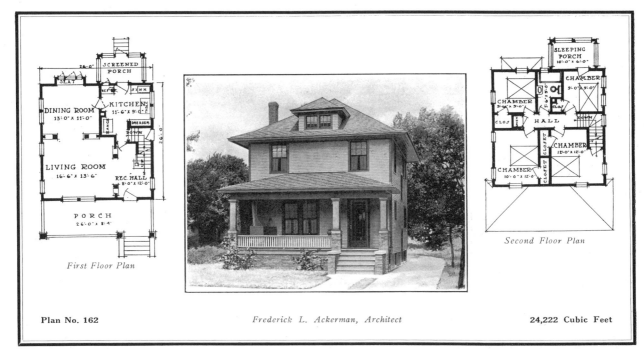

Plan No. 162   *Frederick L. Ackerman, Architect*   24,222 Cubic Feet

(Description of house shown in above plans)   *(Description of house shown in plans below)*

HERE is an example of the square type of house. The downstairs is spacious and arranged in a step-saving manner. From the large front porch one enters the reception hall. At the rear is a mirror door which leads directly to the kitchen, so the front door and upstairs can be reached from the kitchen without going through any other room. The plan also provides four bedrooms with ample closets, bathroom, sleeping porch, a usable attic, and splendid basement. Although the illustration shows the use of clapboards, this house could be built attractively with shingled exterior.

THIS is another design in which the porch is made part of the house with the roof running over it and supported by four columns. The floor plan has been well worked out and in addition to the living room, large dining room and kitchen there is a room on the first floor which may be used for an office or a bedroom on occasion; or, if desired, this room can be thrown into the living room, giving a fine room the width of the house. Upstairs there are three bedrooms, cross-ventilated, and all containing large-sized closets. Exterior walls stucco on concrete blocks.

Full directions for obtaining complete working drawings and specifications for these plans will be found on page 281

Plan No. 343   *College of Architecture, Ohio State University*   22,732 Cubic Feet

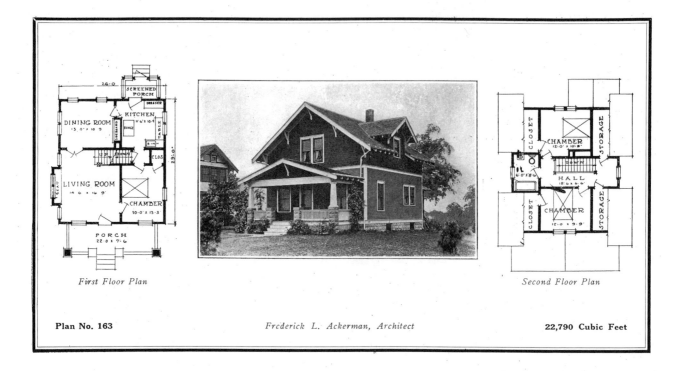

First Floor Plan

Second Floor Plan

Plan No. 163   *Frederick L. Ackerman, Architect*   **22,790 Cubic Feet**

(Description of house shown in above plans)

HERE is a plan which includes a downstairs bedroom, a convenient feature, and in some families considered indispensable. It is cross-ventilated and has a good closet. It opens directly upon the kitchen and the basement steps so that it would be an excellent maid's room. The living room has an abundance of windows, two of them being in the bay, with a window seat beneath. In a rear corner is a decorative open stair with turned balusters.

(Description of house shown in plans below)

THIS house is very economical to build, due to the fact that it is perfectly square with only the porches projecting. The exterior of the house is of brick and the main roof of slate. The arrangement of the kitchen is unique. The various fixtures are so arranged as to make housework easy. Another convenience is the grade entrance in connection with the cellar stairs. Three bedrooms and bath with many convenient closets are contained on the second floor.

Full directions for obtaining complete working drawings and specifications for these plans will be found on page 281

First Floor Plan

Second Floor Plan

Plan No. 502   *George H. Schwan, Architect*   **22,650 Cubic Feet**

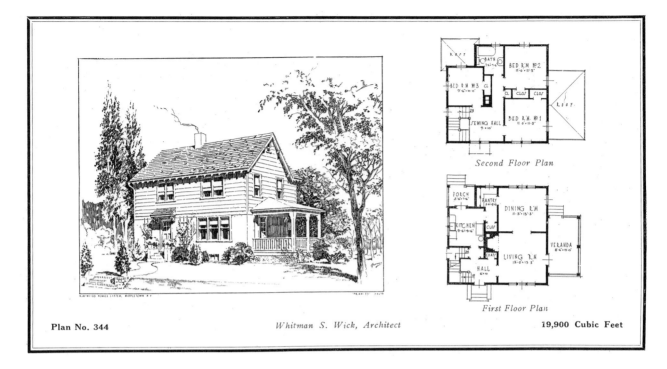

Plan No. 344   *Whitman S. Wick, Architect*   **19,900 Cubic Feet**

(Description of house shown in above plans)

SIMPLICITY of exterior design is the most striking characteristic of this house. It is built of frame, the lower portion being stuccoed, and above finished in siding. A very simple hood over the entrance door with wood trellis on either side gives an expression of hominess which one finds upon entering. A feature of the living room is the fireplace, built in an inglenook. Good sized rooms and an abundance of closet space make the interior very complete and livable.

(Description of house shown in plans below)

HERE is a simple house derived from the style of the English cottage, that could be placed close to the street with good effect. It would be placed to the best advantage facing west, giving morning sun in the dining room and a southern exposure to the porch. Because of its simple composition this house could be built inexpensively. The arrangement of the rooms is compact and convenient. All the bedrooms have cross-ventilation and good closets. Face brick exterior.

Full directions for obtaining complete working drawings and specifications for these plans will be found on page 281

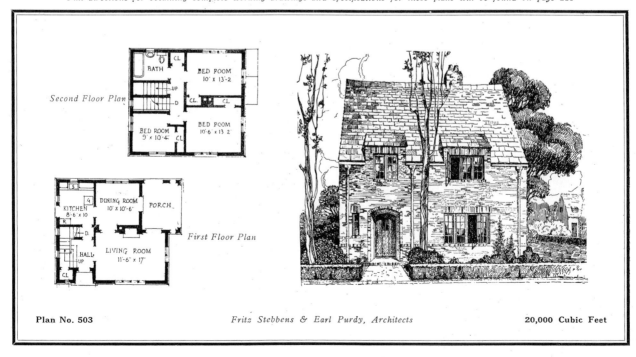

Plan No. 503   *Fritz Stebbens & Earl Purdy, Architects*   **20,000 Cubic Feet**

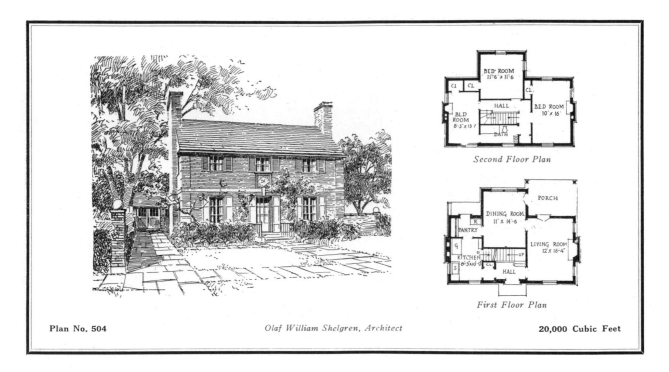

Plan No. 504   *Olaf William Shelgren, Architect*   **20,000 Cubic Feet**

(Description of house shown in above plans)

THIS simple, formal house would fit admirably on a lot with a frontage of fifty feet. It should preferably face the west, affording morning sun in the dining room and southern exposure for the living room. The kitchen has a window overlooking the street, making it a pleasant workplace. The floor plan has been carefully worked out for the maximum utility of space. Exterior of face brick.

(Description of house shown in plans below)

THIS house would be appropriate for a narrow lot on a suburban street, which would afford a pleasant outlook from the attractive living room bay. The extreme width of the house is 35 ft. and its depth 28 ft. It could occupy a 50-ft. frontage with ample space for a drive at the right side to a garage in the rear. The plans of both floors show a compact and convenient arrangement. Exterior of face brick.

Full directions for obtaining complete working drawings and specifications for these plans will be found on page 281

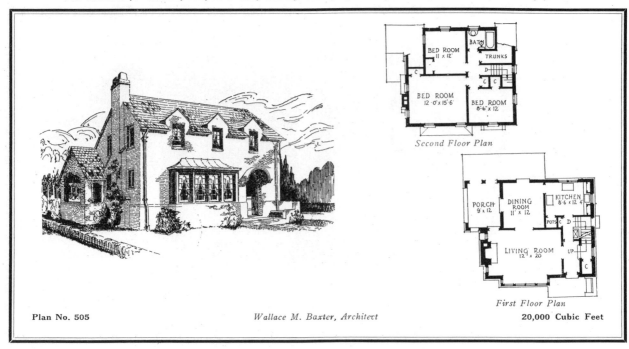

Plan No. 505   *Wallace M. Baxter, Architect*   **20,000 Cubic Feet**

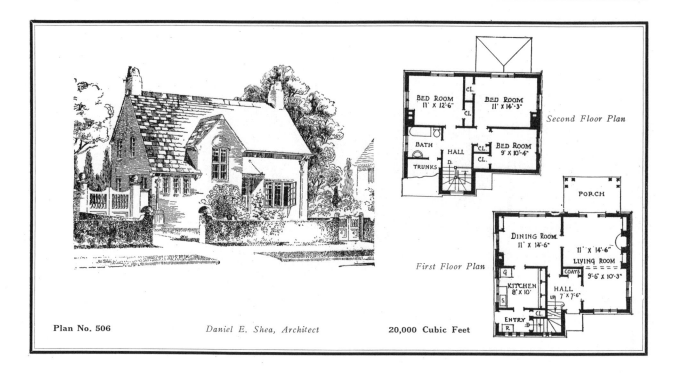

Plan No. 506   *Daniel E. Shea, Architect*   **20,000 Cubic Feet**

(Description of house shown in above plans)

ALTHOUGH the illustration shows this house on a level, it could readily be adapted to a sloping or irregular site if there were a level space at the rear to form a lawn and garden across the living and dining rooms. The first floor rooms are nicely grouped, and the stairs are especially attractive with the large window. Although the roof is low in front, the bedrooms have full height because the rear is two stories high.

(Description of house shown in plans below)

AN unusual solution of the "square" house for the very narrow lot is presented in this house, which is only 22'6" by 26'0". Wide siding, symmetrical placing of the twelve light windows with their characteristic shutters and slender porch columns are pleasing exterior details. From the spacious front porch one enters directly into the living room, extending across the front of the house.

Full directions for obtaining complete working drawings and specifications for these plans will be found on page 281

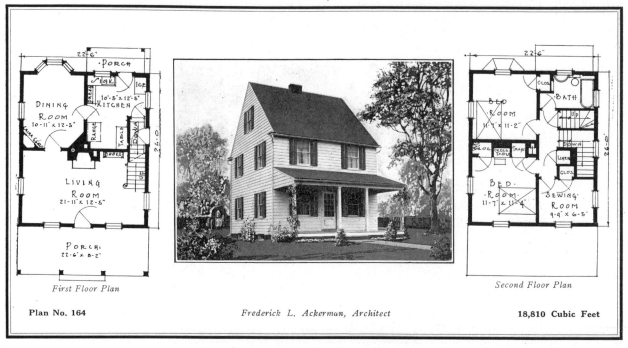

First Floor Plan   *Second Floor Plan*

Plan No. 164   *Frederick L. Ackerman, Architect*   **18,810 Cubic Feet**

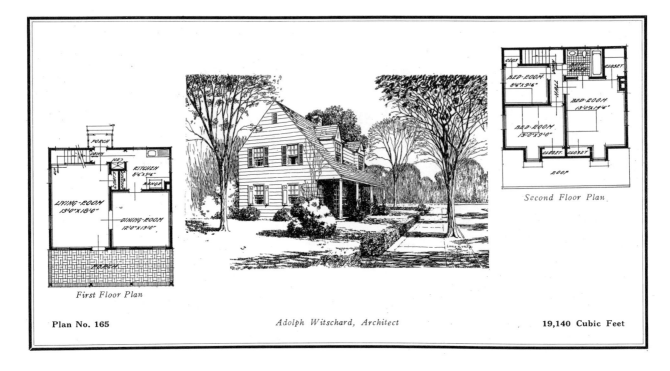

First Floor Plan

Second Floor Plan

Plan No. 165   *Adolph Witschard, Architect*   **19,140 Cubic Feet**

(Description of house shown in above plans)

IT is hardly possible to overestimate the beauty of this Colonial home. The exterior is of shingles painted white with green blinds, and the porch floor is of brick. The long roof-slope over the porch is successfully broken by the use of two well placed dormers connected by a shed dormer slightly set back, and containing closets. The plans are very economical both regarding construction costs and time taken to attend to housework.

(Description of house shown in plans below)

FOR a small country house it would be difficult to find anything more charming than the simplicity of this design. The large wall surfaces would give dignity to the brickwork and the grouping of the casement windows suggests comfortable, homelike rooms within. The living room and dining room extend across the rear, which should preferably face the south, thus providing two rooms that will be very livable and altogether charming.

Full directions for obtaining complete working drawings and specifications for these plans will be found on page 281

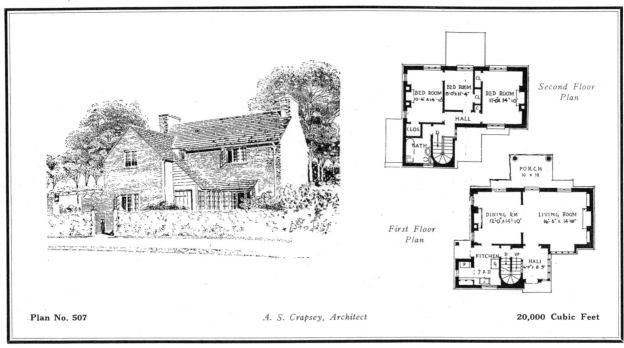

Second Floor Plan

First Floor Plan

Plan No. 507   *A. S. Crapsey, Architect*   **20,000 Cubic Feet**

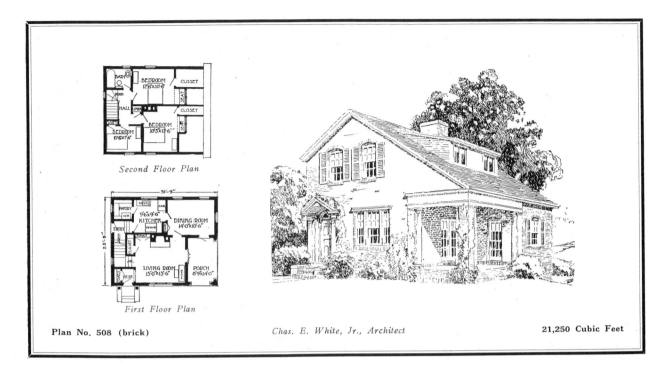

Second Floor Plan

First Floor Plan

Plan No. 508 (brick)   *Chas. E. White, Jr., Architect*   **21,250 Cubic Feet**

(Description of house shown in above plans)

HERE is another excellent example of the Colonial style. This plan has the side porch which is becoming so popular. The delightful little hooded entrance opens into a vestibule with a coat closet at one side. The living room is well planned with fireplace, double French doors leading to the porch, a long bookcase, and a large closet. The low stair landing from the living room adds charm, and the window gives light and ventilation on that side of the house.

(Description of house shown in plans below)

HERE is another Colonial design, and it leaves nothing to be desired. The illustration shows the house carried out in stucco, but it is adaptable to almost any desired construction material. The main entrance is recessed, forming an outdoor vestibule. A unique feature of the dining room is a bay window with a French door leading out to the garden. On each side of this bay is a corner china cupboard, a decorative as well as a useful feature.

Full directions for obtaining complete working drawings and specifications for these plans will be found on page 281

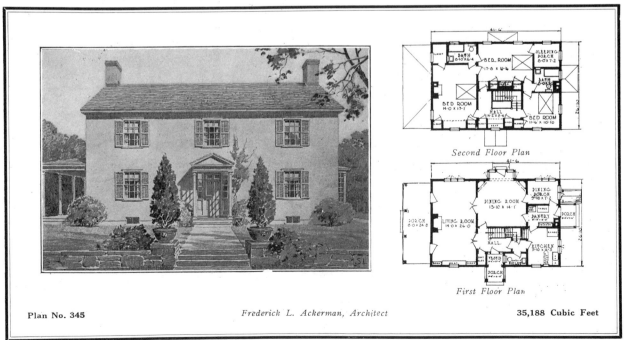

Second Floor Plan

First Floor Plan

Plan No. 345   *Frederick L. Ackerman, Architect*   **35,188 Cubic Feet**

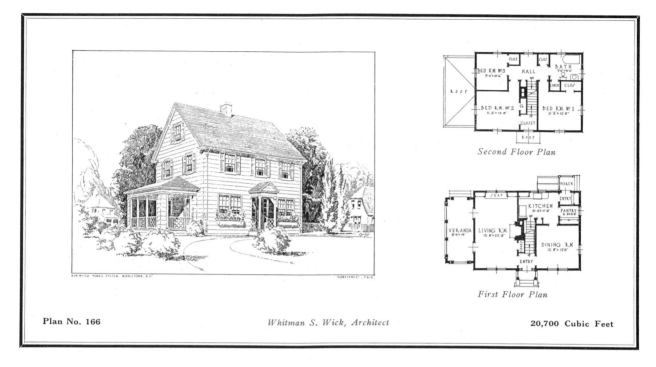

Plan No. 166   *Whitman S. Wick, Architect*   **20,700 Cubic Feet**

(Description of house shown in above plans)

THIS six-room Colonial home would look well on any lot, but for best exposure should face the east. The living room is large and light and has several built-in features such as fireplace, window seat with bookcases either side, and a closet. The entrance hall occupies the minimum of space and the stairs to the second floor are directly in front of the door. There is a large attic which could contain two additional bedrooms if desired. The exterior finish is either of shingles or wide siding painted white.

(Description of house shown in plans below)

THIS interesting little house is derived from the English cottage. It has a nice relation between the rooms on both floors; the living room is large, well lighted and has a pleasant feature in the fireplace ingle with seats on either side. The hall is simply a vestibule space with an entrance to the kitchen through a coat closet. The kitchen is conveniently arranged for efficient operation. On the second floor there are three bedrooms reached from an ample hall. Exterior is of face brick.

Full directions for obtaining complete working drawings and specifications for these plans will be found on page 281

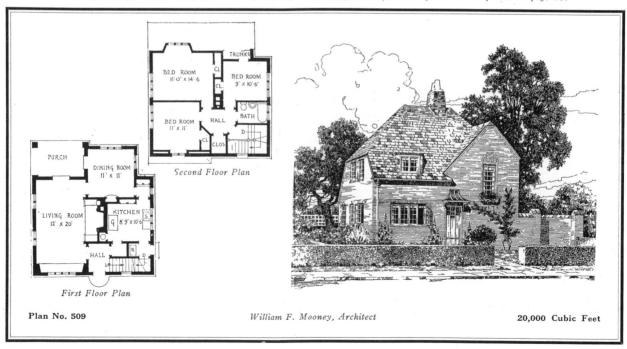

Plan No. 509   *William F. Mooney, Architect*   **20,000 Cubic Feet**

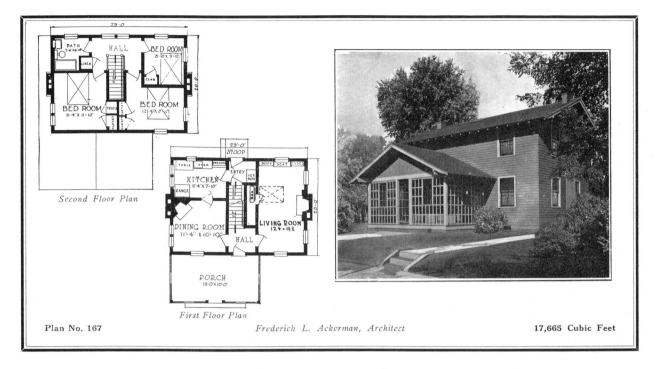

Second Floor Plan

First Floor Plan

Plan No. 167   *Frederick L. Ackerman, Architect*   **17,665 Cubic Feet**

(Description of house shown in above plans)

HERE is another bungalow of the Western type. In this plan, siding is brought down over the foundation with a desirable effect. Two fireplaces in the house mean a saving in the fuel bill. One of them is in the living room centered on the longest of the three outside walls. A built-in seat between the bookcases at the rear is an added decorative feature. There is another fireplace in the dining room, and both dining room and living room are accessible from the front vestibule, which is a convenient arrangement.

(Description of house shown in plans below)

TO add to the appearance of this house the designer very wisely changed the material from brick to stucco above the second story windows in the gables. A spacious, all-open porch spans nearly the entire front of the house. Both the living room and dining room face the street, and the kitchen is in the rear. The stairs go around the fireplace in the back of the living room. Besides three bedrooms, bath and plenty of closets there is also a sleeping porch on the second floor. Common brick with wide bond.

Full directions for obtaining complete working drawings and specifications for these plans will be found on page 281

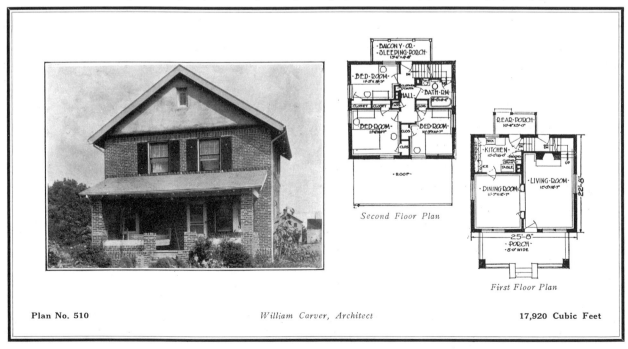

Second Floor Plan

First Floor Plan

Plan No. 510   *William Carver, Architect*   **17,920 Cubic Feet**

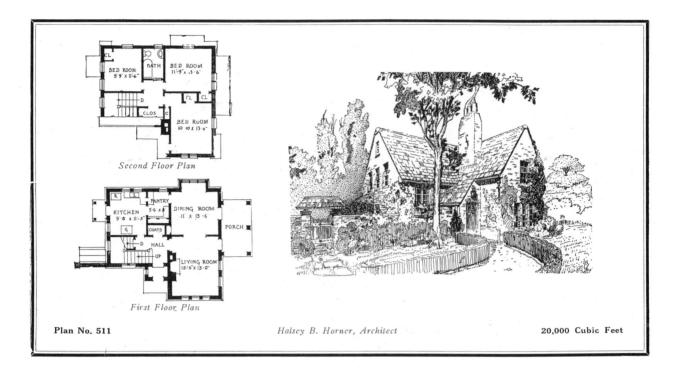

Second Floor Plan

First Floor Plan

Plan No. 511   *Halsey B. Horner, Architect*   **20,000 Cubic Feet**

(Description of house shown in above plans)

HERE is a house that shows a very compact and practical floor plan. The hall is attractive with a large window lighting the stairs. The living room and dining room are separated only by an inter-room opening so that there is a fine vista through the living room to the large bay in the dining room. The kitchen is conveniently arranged and connected with the dining room by a large pantry. The exterior is of rough-textured face brick.

(Description of house shown in plans below)

THIS house has a dignified Colonial doorway as its principal exterior feature. It is well suited to a suburban plot of 50-ft. frontage and can be placed near the street with the rear reserved for a lawn and garden treatment. The kitchen is conveniently arranged and is equipped with built-in dressers instead of having a separate pantry. The entrance is into a hall of good size from which stairs lead to the second floor where there are three bedrooms.

Full directions for obtaining complete working drawings and specifications for these plans will be found on page 281

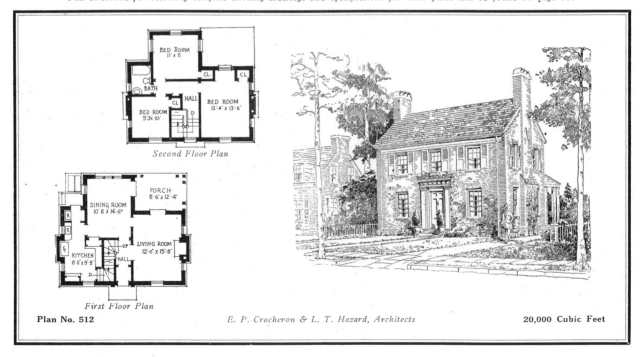

Second Floor Plan

First Floor Plan

Plan No. 512   *E. P. Crocheron & L. T. Hazard, Architects*   **20,000 Cubic Feet**

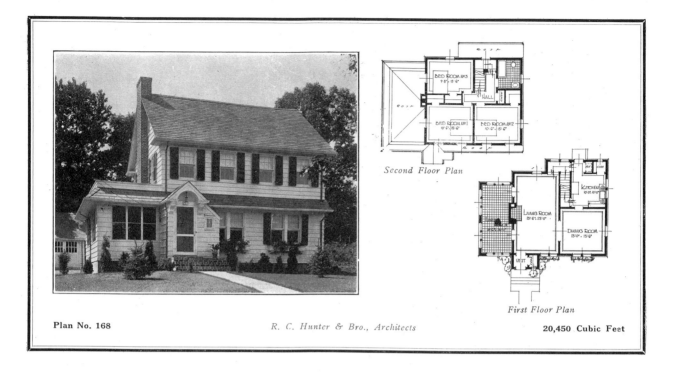

Plan No. 168   *R. C. Hunter & Bro., Architects*   **20,450 Cubic Feet**

(Description of house shown in above plans)

THIS is a modified Colonial type of home which is quite different from the usual. The treatment of the vestibule and coat closet is quite novel in exterior appearance. The house is finished in wide Colonial siding with slate roofs. One can go upstairs from either the living room or the kitchen, thereby saving steps and needless wear of rugs. The bedrooms are all large and well ventilated and there is an abundance of closet space. A large attic gives space for storage.

(Description of house shown in plans below)

AN outside living room is made by screening the large front porch of this home, as shown in the exterior view. The indoor living room extends across the entire front of the house. In one corner of the living room is the stair, and near it a mirror door. The kitchen is well-lighted and is supplemented by a large screened porch. One of its best features is its direct access to the front door and stair. Windows on two sides furnish ample light for sink and dresser.

Full directions for obtaining complete working drawings and specifications for these plans will be found on page 281

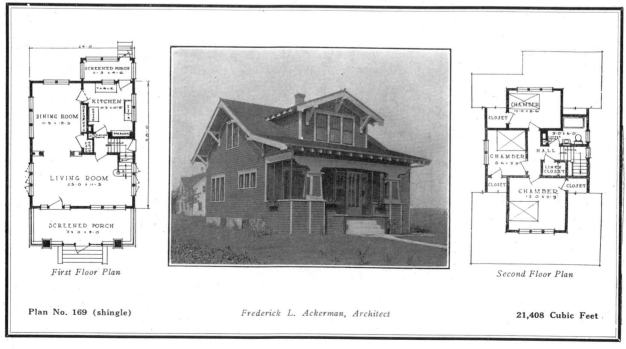

Plan No. 169 (shingle)   *Frederick L. Ackerman, Architect*   **21,408 Cubic Feet**

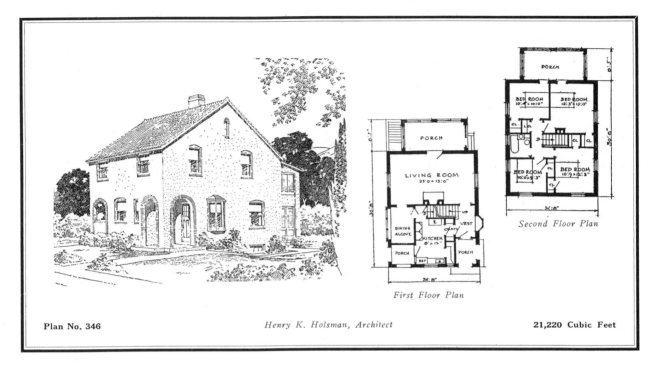

Plan No. 346   Henry K. Holsman, Architect   21,220 Cubic Feet

Second Floor Plan

First Floor Plan

(Description of house shown in above plans)   *(Description of house shown in plans below)*

HERE is a clever solution of the problem of a lot that faces north. The kitchen has been placed in the front of the house, leaving the more desirable location in the rear for the living room, which extends the entire width of the house, and beyond it is a spacious screened porch looking into the garden at the rear of the lot. The living room and porch get all the sunshine. Between living room and kitchen is the popular dining alcove. The upper floor comprises four bedrooms, sleeping porch and bathroom. Exterior of stucco on concrete blocks.

HERE is a cozy bungalow that has ample room on a city lot, yet has six livable rooms, including two bedrooms and a den which may be used as an emergency bedroom, as it contains a closet which accommodates a disappearing bed. The sleeping quarters have been well separated from the living rooms and all rooms are well ventilated and bright. The living room and dining room are separated only by an inter-room opening which provides bookcases in the pedestals. The window seat in the dining room bay is an attractive feature. The kitchen is compact.

Full directions for obtaining complete working drawings and specifications for these plans will be found on page 281

Floor Plan

Plan No. 170   *Frederick L. Ackerman, Architect*   23,543 Cubic Feet

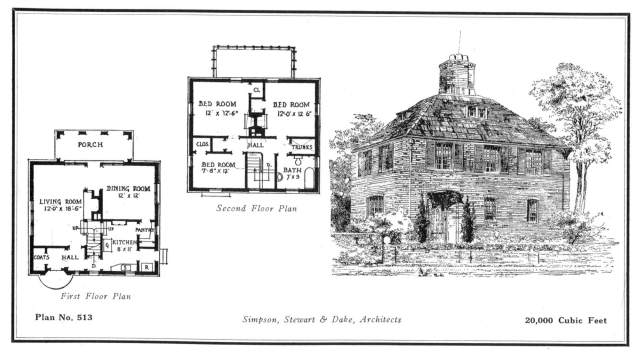

PORCH

LIVING ROOM
12'-0" x 18'-6"

DINING ROOM
12' x 12'

UP   PANTRY

KITCHEN
8' x 11'

COATS   HALL

First Floor Plan

BED ROOM
12' x 12'-6"   CL   BED ROOM
12'-0" x 12'6"

CLOS.   HALL   TRUNKS

BED ROOM
7'-6" x 12'   BATH
7' x 9'

Second Floor Plan

Plan No. 513   *Simpson, Stewart & Dake, Architects*   **20,000 Cubic Feet**

(Description of house shown in above plans)

THE massive chimney of this house suggests cheery open fires within. The interior arrangement is informal and planned with a minimum of waste space. The entrance is into a hall with convenient coat closet to the left. The stair is an architectural feature of the living room. The kitchen is placed on the front so that the rear may be treated as a garden and enjoyed from the living room and dining room. The second floor provides three bedrooms of good size, each of which has cross-ventilation and is well supplied with closets.

(Description of house shown in plans below)

THE simplicity of this house will commend it to many. It can be built inexpensively and its well arranged rooms will provide a comfortable home. It can be placed with the entrance on the side as in the illustration, or on the front if the view of the street is more interesting, when this will be had from the porch. The bedrooms have square ceilings and are well supplied with large closets. Dark-toned brick with occasional darker headers is recommended for the walls, while the roof should preferably be of slate and the exterior woodwork brown stained.

Full directions for obtaining complete working drawings and specifications for these plans will be found on page 281

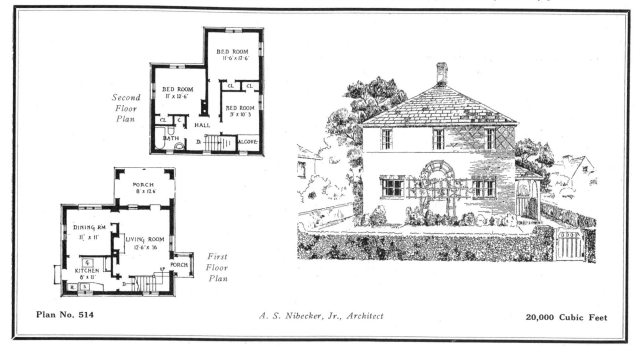

Second Floor Plan

BED ROOM
11'-6" x 12'-6"

BED ROOM
11' x 12'-6"   CL   CL

CL   C   BED ROOM
9' x 10'-3"

BATH   HALL

D.   ALCOVE

PORCH
8' x 12'6"

DINING RM
11' x 11'   LIVING ROOM
12'-6" x 16

KITCHEN
8' x 11'   UP   PORCH

First Floor Plan

Plan No. 514   *A. S. Nibecker, Jr., Architect*   **20,000 Cubic Feet**

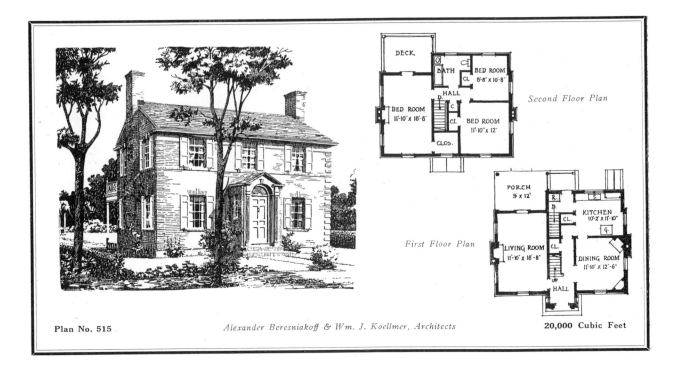

Plan No. 515   *Alexander Beresniakoff & Wm. J. Koellmer, Architects*   **20,000 Cubic Feet**

(Description of house shown in above plans)

HERE is a Colonial house that would look well set close to the street in a suburb or small town, with the left side of the space in the rear devoted to a garden. The remainder of the plot can be occupied by a garage, drying yard, and kitchen garden. The enclosed stoop, the rowlock sill course and the brick quoins add a charm consistent with the simple lines of the façade. The arrangement of the six rooms has been carefully worked out.

(Description of house shown in plans below)

A PORCH enclosed on two sides, and a widely overhanging roof gives a sheltered appearance to this economically constructed house. The porch is included within the rectangle of its floor plan. On the first floor, in addition to the living room, dining room and kitchen, there is the always desirable feature of a bedroom and bath. The chief object of interest in the living room is the handsome open stair. There is a coat closet just outside, in the hall.

Full directions for obtaining complete working drawings and specifications for these plans will be found on page 281

Plan No. 171   *Frederick L. Ackerman, Architect*   **20,400 Cubic Feet**

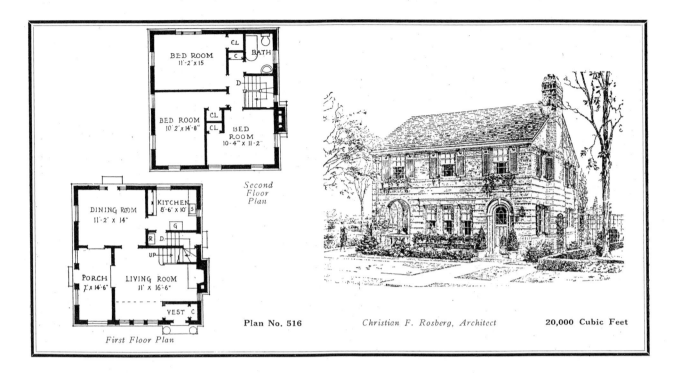

BED ROOM
11'-2" x 15

BED ROOM
10'2" x 14'-8"   BED
ROOM
10'-4" x 11'-2"

*Second
Floor
Plan*

DINING ROOM
11'-2" x 14'   KITCHEN
8'-6" x 10'

PORCH
7' x 14'-6"   LIVING ROOM
11' x 16'-6"

VEST C

First Floor Plan

Plan No. 516   *Christian F. Rosberg, Architect*   **20,000 Cubic Feet**

(Description of house shown in above plans)

THE entrance to this house is directly into the living room, but an ample vestibule with coat closet would shut off drafts in cold weather. The staircase starts from the living room and, with the vestibule, frames an ingle-nook about the fireplace which adds a decorative feature to the room. The second floor provides three bedrooms of good size, well equipped with clothes closets. The porch overlooks the street and side lawn. Face brick.

(Description of house shown in plans below)

THERE is an irregularity of outline in the rooms of this plan that is much more alluring than strictly rectangular rooms. Sunny alcoves at the front of the living room and dining room seclude the entrance porch. Casements add to their attractiveness, though double-hung windows with divided lights could be used effectively. In the living room there is an alcove opposite the fireplace, making a splendid location for a davenport or piano. Stucco on frame.

Full directions for obtaining complete working drawings and specifications for these plans will be found on page 281

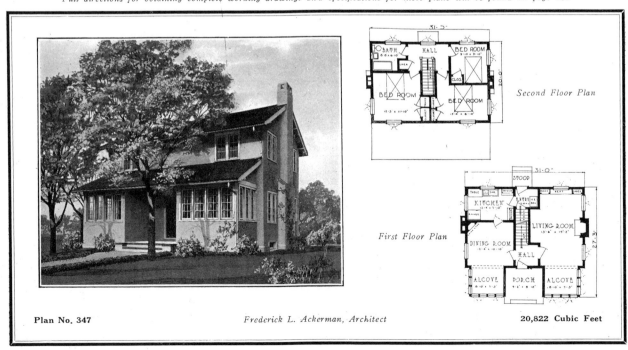

BATH   HALL   BED ROOM

BED ROOM   BED ROOM

Second Floor Plan

First Floor Plan

STOOP

KITCHEN   ENTRY   LIVING ROOM

DINING ROOM   HALL

ALCOVE   PORCH   ALCOVE

Plan No. 347   *Frederick L. Ackerman, Architect*   **20,822 Cubic Feet**

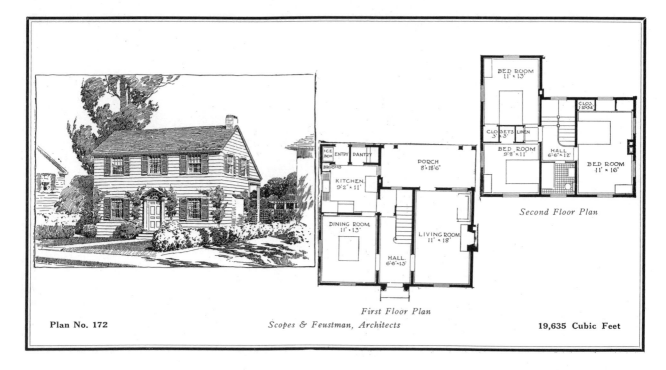

Plan No. 172   *Scopes & Feustman, Architects*   **19,635 Cubic Feet**

(Description of house shown in above plans)

IN this design the large porch is placed at the rear of the house, where the family may sit in privacy. The rooms are all large and the principal bedroom is nearly the same size as the living room. The bath is convenient to all bedrooms, each of which has an ample closet. The exterior is of wide siding in white stained shingles, and the roof also is shingled. Note the unusual arrangement of the chimney, how it is built out on the first floor and is inside the house above. This house is economical to build.

(Description of house shown in plans below)

THE first floor arrangement of this house is especially convenient. All the rooms are reached from the hall, and the dining room and living room are connected with a wide opening which increases the apparent size of the house. The living room is built almost as a separate unit, affording plenty of light and air, and there is a fireplace somewhat off-center which makes this a very pleasant room. To carry out the designer's idea, the garden development should be on the porch side and in the rear. Face brick walls.

Full directions for obtaining complete working drawings and specifications for these plans will be found on page 281

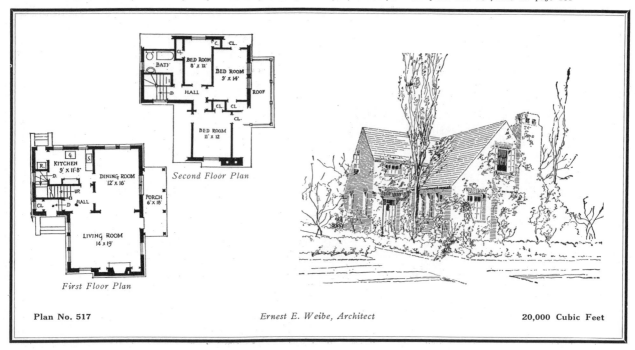

Plan No. 517   *Ernest E. Weibe, Architect*   **20,000 Cubic Feet**

First Floor Plan

Second Floor Plan

Plan No. 518   George H. Schwan, Architect   **21,152 Cubic Feet**

(Description of house shown in above plans)

ALL of us know that, size for size, the more nearly square a house is the more economical it is to build. This brick house contains six well planned rooms of ample size, all within a space of 20 ft. by 26 feet. There is no hall on the first floor; hence, that space is eliminated. The stairs are placed at one end of the living room. The cellar stairs and grade entrance are directly under them. There are four closets on the second floor, one in connection with each of the three bedrooms, and a large one out of the bathroom.

(Description of house shown in plans below)

HERE is a substantial home which would look well with a brick exterior. It has full height square rooms on the second floor and a cozy arrangement of rooms on the first floor. The staircase is at the rear and is attractively arranged in a separate projection with a large Colonial window at the landing. The living room fireplace is set in an ingle-nook, thereby increasing the size of the room, which is of generous proportions. The porch is composed of a series of brick arches, giving a cloister effect that is very quaint.

Full directions for obtaining complete working drawings and specifications for these plans will be found on page 281

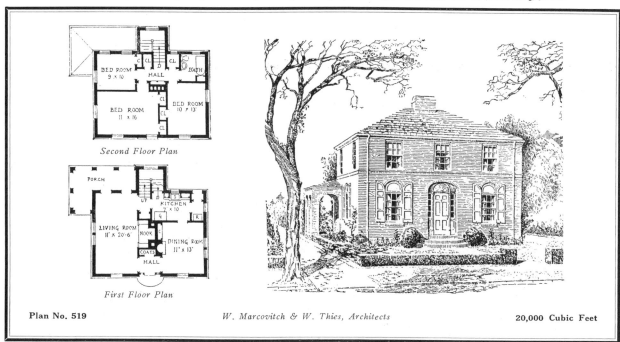

Second Floor Plan

First Floor Plan

Plan No. 519   *W. Marcovitch & W. Thies, Architects*   **20,000 Cubic Feet**

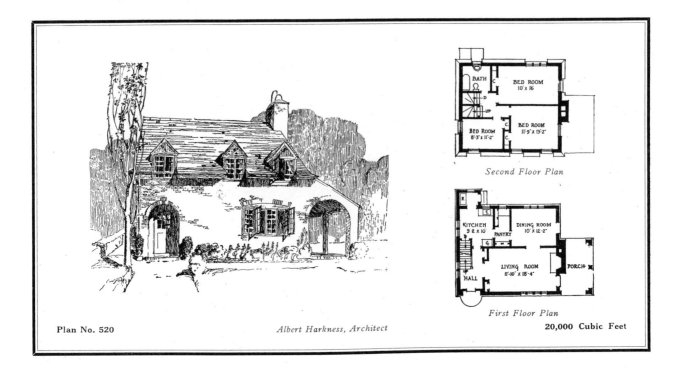

BATH   BED ROOM
10' x 16

BED ROOM
8'-3" x 11'-2"   BED ROOM
11'-9" x 13'-2"

Second Floor Plan

KITCHEN
9 x 10   DINING ROOM
10' x 12'-2"
PANTRY

LIVING ROOM
11'-10" x 18'-4"   PORCH

HALL

First Floor Plan

Plan No. 520   *Albert Harkness, Architect*   **20,000 Cubic Feet**

(Description of house shown in above plans)

THERE is a comfortable cottage-like character to this house that would make it especially desirable for a country or small town home. Its simple gable roof broken by dormers would be very attractive and it has good wall space for vines to ramble over. The plan of both floors is direct and simple; the living room is of pleasing proportions and opens directly on the porch. Weathered timber work in the dormers is suggested, filled in with brick.

(Description of house shown in plans below)

THE design of this house is quite unusual both in exterior and interior treatment. The lower portion is stucco on concrete blocks or tile and the upper portion shingles or wide siding. The living room occupies the front of the house and has a group of five windows to light it. The fireplace is directly opposite. The three bedrooms are large and each has good light and cross-ventilation. There is ample closet space. Roof of cement tile or slate.

Full directions for obtaining complete working drawings and specifications for these plans will be found on page 281

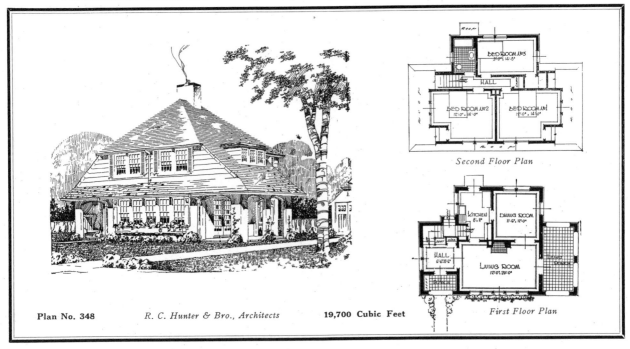

BED ROOM N°3
9'-10" x 14'-8"

HALL

BED ROOM N°2
12'-0" x 14'-0"   BED ROOM N°1
11'-0" x 14'-0"

Second Floor Plan

KITCHEN
8'-11"   DINING ROOM
11'-6" x 11'-0"

HALL
6'-6" x 6'-6"   LIVING ROOM
12'-0" x 20'-0"

First Floor Plan

Plan No. 348   *R. C. Hunter & Bro., Architects*   **19,700 Cubic Feet**

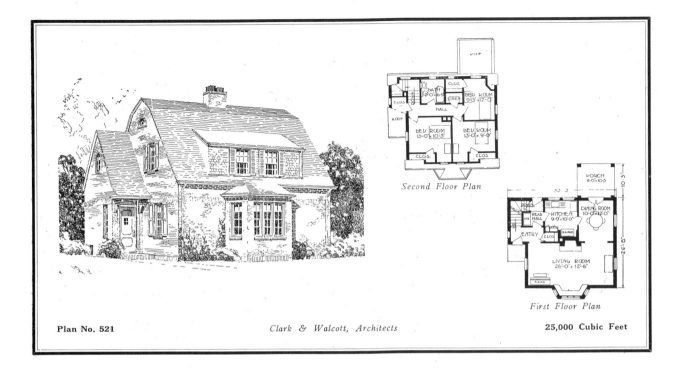

Plan No. 521   *Clark & Walcott, Architects*   **25,000 Cubic Feet**

Second Floor Plan

First Floor Plan

(Description of house shown in above plans)

IN this house of Dutch Colonial type we have long lower rafters and short upper ones, giving a large, well ventilated attic which will tend to keep the upper rooms cool in summer. The unusually large living room occupies the entire front portion of the house. The attractive bay and the fireplace opposite are features not usually found in houses of this size. The dining room opens from the living room, beyond which is a rear porch. Exterior is of face brick.

(Description of house shown in plans below)

HERE is a well planned six-room cottage. A special feature of the first floor is a den in which there is a closet accommodating a disappearing bed, thus providing an extra sleeping room on occasion. The large living room has a delightful bay at one side and just opposite are French doors that lead to the den. Notice the location of the boxed stair, and the basement steps between the living room and kitchen, and the accessibility of the rooms.

Full directions for obtaining complete working drawings and specifications for these plans will be found on page 281

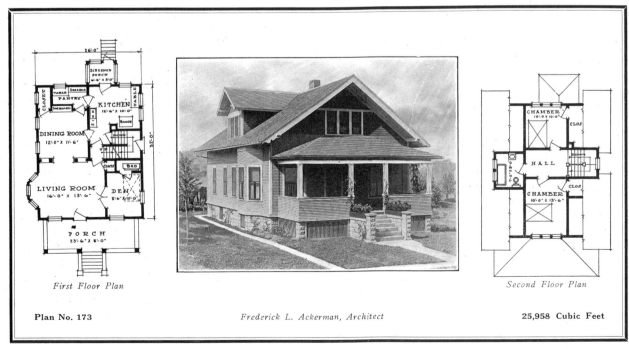

First Floor Plan

Second Floor Plan

Plan No. 173   *Frederick L. Ackerman, Architect*   **25,958 Cubic Feet**

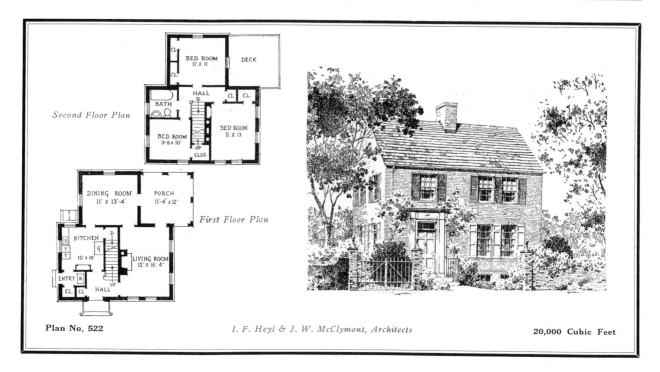

Second Floor Plan

BED ROOM
11' X 11

DECK

CL.

CL.

BATH

HALL

CL. CL.

BED ROOM
9'-6 X 10'

BED ROOM
11 X 13

UP

CLOS.

First Floor Plan

DINING ROOM
11' X 13'-4"

PORCH
11'-4" x 12'

KITCHEN
10' X 10'

LIVING ROOM
12' X 16'-4"

ENTRY   R

CL. CL.   HALL   UP

Plan No. 522   *I. F. Heyl & J. W. McClymont, Architects*   **20,000 Cubic Feet**

(Description of house shown in above plans)   *(Description of house shown in plans below)*

HERE is a design that is equally suitable for a suburban or small town location. It can be placed close to the street with the rear of the lot reserved for a lawn and garden. The rooms on the first floor are independent units without wide connecting doorways. This affords coziness without making the house appear small. The porch leading from the dining room is an attractive feature. There are three bedrooms on the second floor, and a sleeping porch could be provided over the rear porch.

THOSE who like bungalows should find this home, of the Western type, especially enticing. Its lines and proportions are good, and there is a ruggedness about its exterior that makes it picturesque. The long slope of the roof, broken by a flat-roofed dormer, includes under its protection the spacious porch. A good attic, ventilated by louvres, keeps the bedrooms cool. These three rooms are unusually practical. They are of good size and have plenty of windows and large closets.

Full directions for obtaining complete working drawings and specifications for these plans will be found on page 281

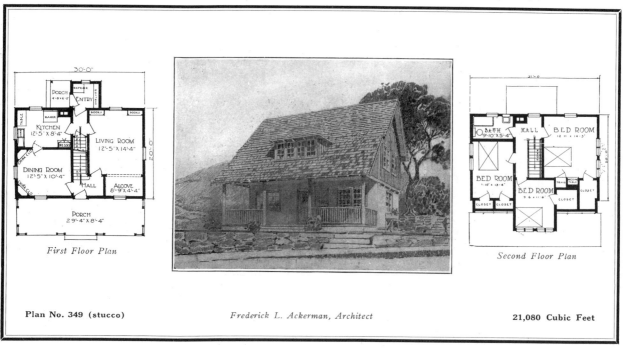

First Floor Plan   *Second Floor Plan*

Plan No. 349 (stucco)   *Frederick L. Ackerman, Architect*   **21,080 Cubic Feet**

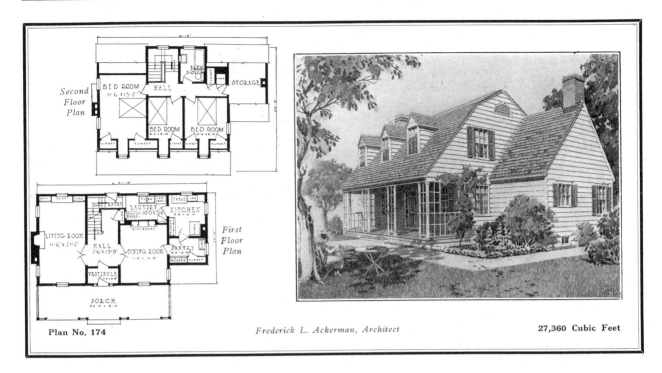

Plan No. 174   *Frederick L. Ackerman, Architect*   **27,360 Cubic Feet**

(Description of house shown in above plans)

A MODIFIED gambrel roof distinguishes this house from ordinary houses. Well-proportioned dormers lend interest to the three bedrooms upstairs, and two of these have windows on a second side also. Downstairs there is an unusually good room arrangement. At the rear of the vestibule there is a generous hall, with its typical Colonial staircase. On each side of this hall are French doors, permitting the living room, dining room and hall to be opened together on occasions. Frame construction throughout.

(Description of house shown in plans below)

HERE is a house with central hall separating the living room and dining room and containing at the rear the main stairway. In the living room is an open fireplace, on either side of which is a French door leading into the large sun porch. The kitchen is very conveniently arranged. On the second floor are three bedrooms and two baths, one of which is in connection with the owner's bedroom. The exterior finish is of white Portland cement stucco applied on structural wall of concrete blocks.

Full directions for obtaining complete working drawings and specifications for these plans will be found on page 281

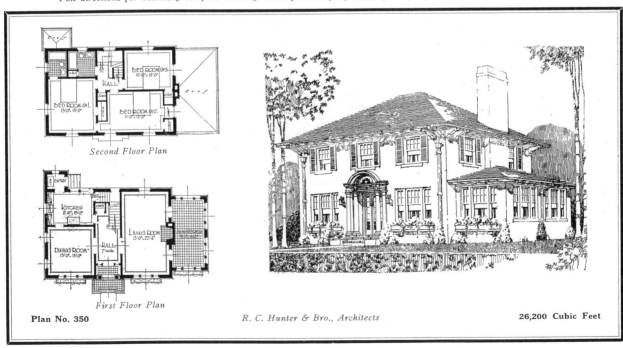

Plan No. 350   *R. C. Hunter & Bro., Architects*   **26,200 Cubic Feet**

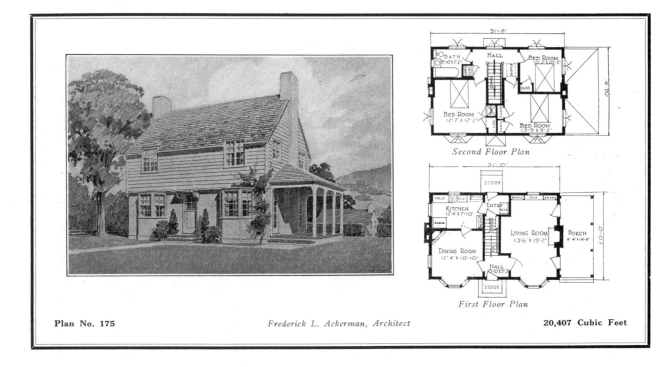

Second Floor Plan

First Floor Plan

Plan No. 175   *Frederick L. Ackerman, Architect*   **20,407 Cubic Feet**

(Description of house shown in above plans)

EVERY room in this distinctive house has windows on two sides and in addition there is an attractive bay on the front elevation. The overhang of the second story, and the use of stucco for the first floor and siding above, tend to accentuate the horizontal lines and give the house a low comfortable appearance. The living room extends across the entire right half of the first floor and glazed doors on each side of the fireplace lead to the porch.

(Description of house shown in plans below)

HERE is a bungalow of unusually attractive design and plan. It is especially suited to the country but would look well in a suburban location, though it would need a good sized plot to enable its full beauty to be seen. A garage is suggested in the illustration, tied into the house by a brick wall. In this arrangement the garden and lawn would be at the opposite end with a terrace outside the living room windows. The construction of exterior walls is face brick.

Full directions for obtaining complete working drawings and specifications for these plans will be found on page 281

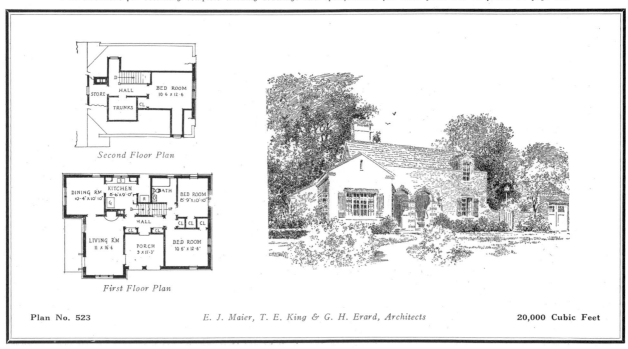

Second Floor Plan

First Floor Plan

Plan No. 523   *E. J. Maier, T. E. King & G. H. Erard, Architects*   **20,000 Cubic Feet**

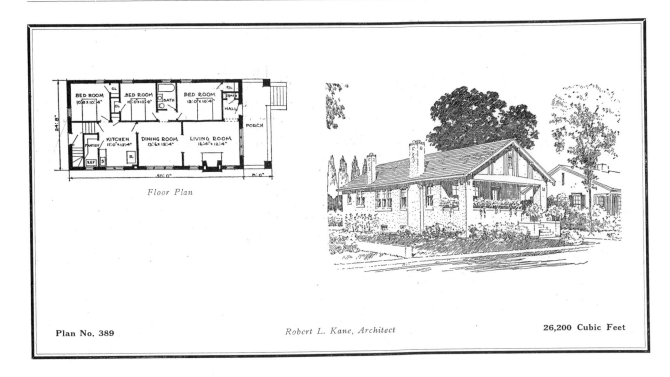

Floor Plan

Plan No. 389   *Robert L. Kane, Architect*   **26,200 Cubic Feet**

(Description of house shown in above plans)

HERE is a small bungalow that should be economical to build because of its simple design, and it is this very simplicity that makes it so attractive. The long straight lines of the roof are pleasingly broken by the chimney stacks. Their red brick capping and wrought iron staybolts will make a pleasing contrast with the white stucco walls and the red or gray of the roofing. Stucco on concrete block walls.

(Description of house shown in plans below)

THIS semi-bungalow is of the so-called California type with its wide overhanging cornices and massive construction. The roof is comparatively flat and is not recommended for shingles in the eastern states. One enters directly into the living room from the large front porch. The stairs are opposite the entrance and are a feature of the living room. Many closets and built-in features are to be found in this house.

Full directions for obtaining complete working drawings and specifications for these plans will be found on page 281

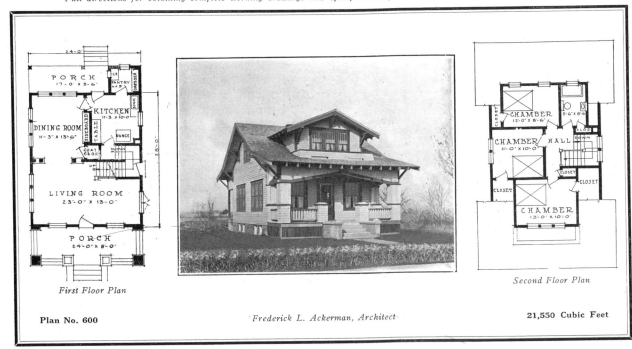

First Floor Plan

Second Floor Plan

Plan No. 600   *Frederick L. Ackerman, Architect*   **21,550 Cubic Feet**

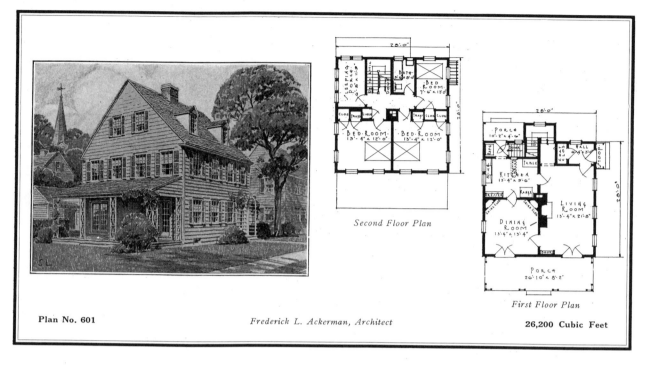

Second Floor Plan

First Floor Plan

Plan No. 601   *Frederick L. Ackerman, Architect*   **26,200 Cubic Feet**

(Description of house shown in above plans)

THIS Colonial house would best fit a corner lot facing southeast. However, if placed in the middle of the block, either the living room side or the porch side could become the front of the house. The rooms are large and well arranged, and have many built-in features. The exterior walls and roofs are of stained shingles, and a neat trellis graces the front entrance. There is a sleeping porch on the second floor. Two or more rooms can be finished in the attic if desired. The construction is frame throughout.

(Description of house shown in plans below)

THIS simple design makes an attractive, practical home. From the small entrance hall one enters a spacious living room extending across the front of the house, with a comfortable dining room at the rear. Three sets of French doors to the porch in the side wall of the dining room and living room give the effect of one large room, although the rooms are separated by the projecting fireplace. Three bedrooms are well arranged on the second floor with ample closet space and plenty of windows, insuring good light and air.

Full directions for obtaining complete working drawings and specifications for these plans will be found on page 281.

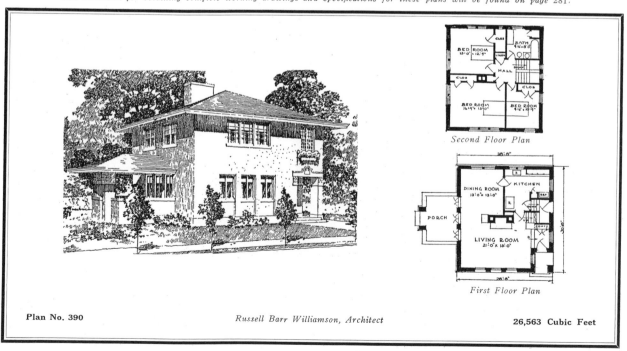

Second Floor Plan

First Floor Plan

Plan No. 390   *Russell Barr Williamson, Architect*   **26,563 Cubic Feet**

First Floor Plan

Plan No. 391   *Gordon Robb, Architect*   **21,773 Cubic Feet**

Second Floor Plan

(Description of house shown in above plans)

HERE is a slender house designed for a very narrow site. However, the plan is very commodious. The entrance through the sun porch is into the living room the full width of the house with a corner fireplace, and through a deep recess we enter the well lighted dining room with a glazed rear door that will provide cross-ventilation through the house. The kitchen has no pantry, but cupboards on the walls give plenty of shelf room. On the second floor are three good bedrooms with large clothes closets.

(Description of house shown in plans below)

THIS attractive house of English cottage type has exterior walls of timber and stucco on wide sheathing. It contains six rooms and one bath. The living room is large and lighted by three windows, including a small bay. An open fireplace is an added feature of the living room as also are the built-in book shelves. The dining room also has a bay window and two built-in china closets. The kitchen is well arranged with rear entry from which stairs lead to cellar and in which the ice box is located.

Full directions for obtaining complete working drawings and specifications for these plans will be found on page 281

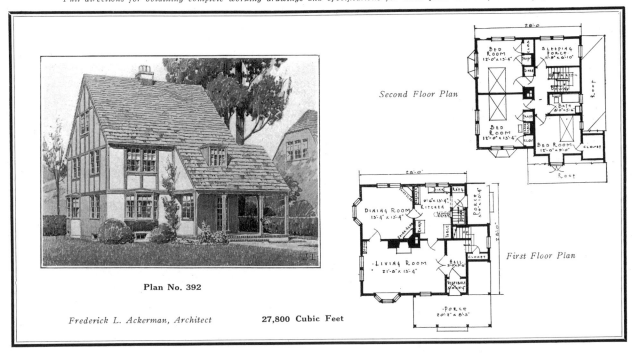

Second Floor Plan

First Floor Plan

Plan No. 392

Frederick L. Ackerman, Architect   **27,800 Cubic Feet**

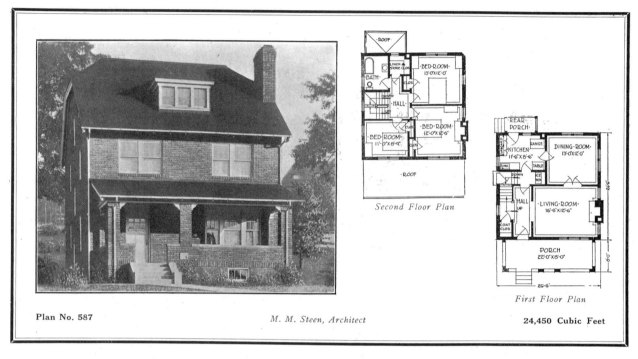

Second Floor Plan

First Floor Plan

Plan No. 587   M. M. Steen, Architect   24,450 Cubic Feet

(*Description of house shown in above plans*)

THE exterior walls of this well arranged six-room house are of common brick with roof of slate or patented shingles. Entrance is into a large hall in which a stairway is located. The living room has an open fireplace flanked by small windows. The dining room and kitchen are conveniently arranged. The square plan of the house makes possible a very convenient arrangement of bedrooms on the second floor. This type of arrangement also means economy in construction because it provides an opportunity to use standard sizes in design.

(*Description of house shown in plans below*)

THERE are six rooms in this excellently designed house, with provision for additional rooms on the third floor if needed. Three glazed doors open from the artistic front porch to the living room, but the main entrance is through the vestibule at the side. The living room occupies the front half of the first floor. The fireplace at the rear makes use of the same central chimney as the furnace and range. A pair of Colonial corner cupboards are a decorative feature of the dining room. The kitchen is a model of efficiency with ironing board, dresser and work table built in.

Full directions for obtaining complete working drawings and specifications for these plans will be found on page 281

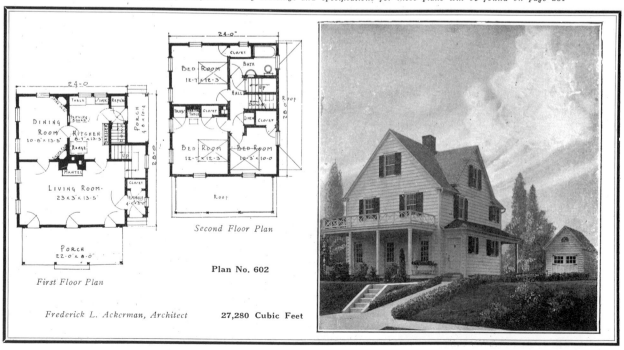

First Floor Plan

Second Floor Plan

Plan No. 602

Frederick L. Ackerman, Architect   27,280 Cubic Feet

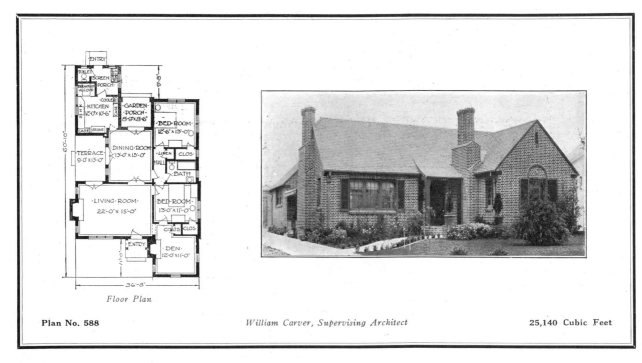

Floor Plan

Plan No. 588   *William Carver, Supervising Architect*   **25,140 Cubic Feet**

(Description of house shown in above plans)

HERE is an unusually attractive six-room brick bungalow of English character. The exterior walls are of common brick laid in a geometric design of wide white mortar joints. The entrance is directly into a large living room equipped with open fireplace. From this living room a small entry leads to coat closet, guest room and den. The den is an interesting room lighted on three sides and also provided with an open fireplace. A special feature of the living room is the brick floored terrace entered through French doors. The dining room also opens on terrace.

(Description of house shown in plans below)

THIS little cottage includes four porches—two are latticed, and there is a rear porch and sleeping porch. The porch roofs have a pergola effect, while the main roof is a combination gable and hip that permits the attic to be ventilated by louvres in the gables. The floor plan is a perfect rectangle though its interesting exterior is very unlike the usual economical rectangular house. The six rooms are well arranged and the sleeping rooms are effectively isolated from the living portion of the house. French doors make two front porches a part of living room.

Full directions for obtaining complete working drawings and specifications for these plans will be found on page 281

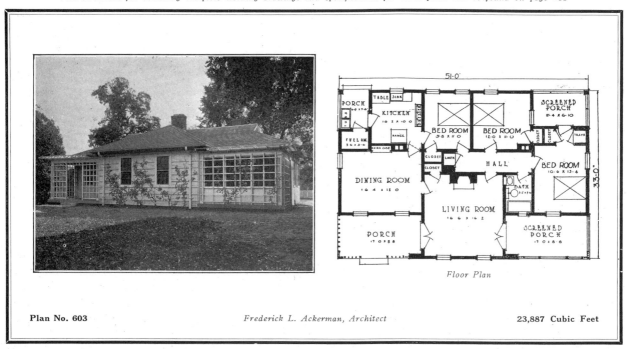

Floor Plan

Plan No. 603   *Frederick L. Ackerman, Architect*   **23,887 Cubic Feet**

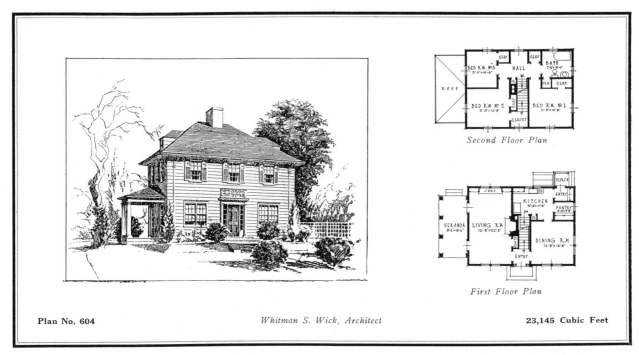

Plan No. 604   *Whitman S. Wick, Architect*   **23,145 Cubic Feet**

(Description of house shown in above plans)   *(Description of house shown in plans below)*

THIS is a simple Colonial frame six-room house with exterior of wide siding and roof of wood or patented shingles. The plan of this house is such that construction is economical and there is no waste space. There is a large veranda from which French doors open into a spacious living room. At the main entrance a small entry is provided which also opens into the living room. The living room is lighted on three sides and has the special features of built-in window seat and bookcases, large open fireplace and a large coat closet. On the second floor are three bedrooms of good size, provided with large closets.

HERE is a house of substantial appearance and the interior is a very comfortable arrangement of five rooms and bath. The living room and dining room share the front of the house and each has many windows on two sides. French doors are effectively used between these two rooms. One of the charms of the dining room is a simple, dignified sideboard, built in flush with one wall. From the living room one may pass directly into the hall which connects the two bedrooms at the rear, the bathroom between them. The kitchen projects four feet beyond the rest of the house, so that it gets light from three sides.

Full directions for obtaining complete working drawings and specifications for these plans will be found on page 281

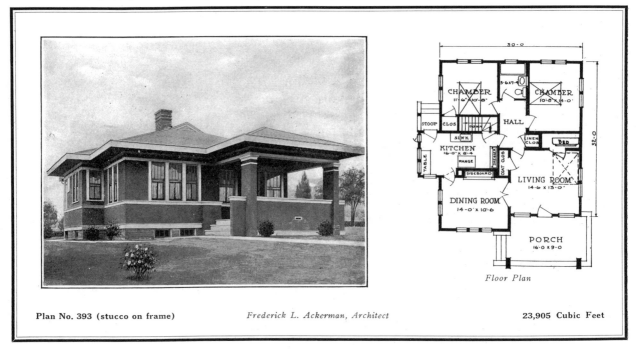

Plan No. 393 (stucco on frame)   *Frederick L. Ackerman, Architect*   **23,905 Cubic Feet**

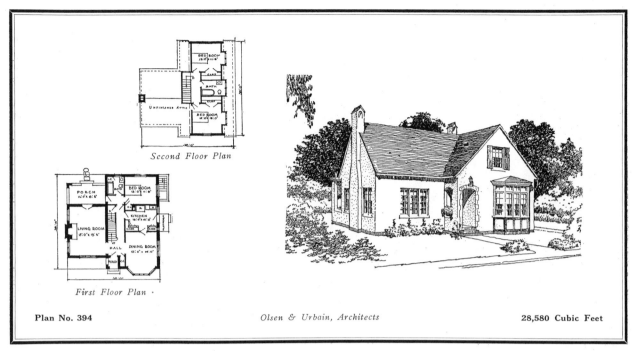

Second Floor Plan

First Floor Plan ·

Plan No. 394   *Olsen & Urbain, Architects*   **28,580 Cubic Feet**

(*Description of house shown in above plans*)   (*Description of house shown in plans below*)

THE principal feature of the first floor of this house is the fine living room, lighted on three sides and having a lofty beamed ceiling. The ground floor bedroom has a bath adjoining. The dining room and kitchen are of ample size and upstairs are two good bedrooms with an additional bath. For the man who is looking forward to a good home, but lacking the funds to complete it at the start, this house has been especially designed. The dining room, kitchen, bedroom and bath form a complete unit, so that the upstairs might be left unfinished or the building of the living room wing left till later.

CONNECTING with the living and dining rooms, the enclosed sun porch in this bungalow will radiate its cheerfulness to both. At the other side of the living room is the outdoor summer porch, over which extends the roof, thus connecting it with the house in a very harmonious manner. The breakfast room in this plan is a most attractive feature. It is located in the rear of the house, overlooking the garden, and is convenient to the kitchen and bedrooms. A fireplace in the dining room is a welcome feature. The two bedrooms are of good size and have commodious closets. Exterior walls are finished in face brick.

Full directions for obtaining complete working drawings and specifications for these plans will be found on page 281

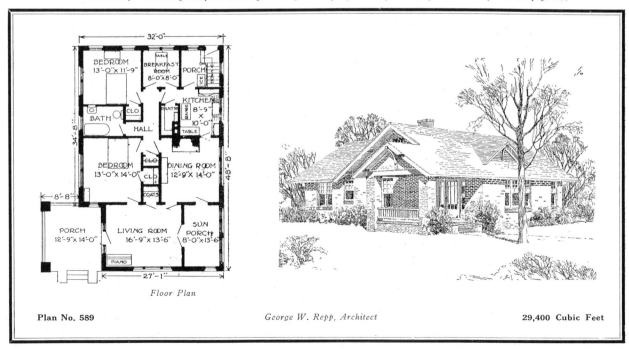

Floor Plan

Plan No. 589   *George W. Repp, Architect*   **29,400 Cubic Feet**

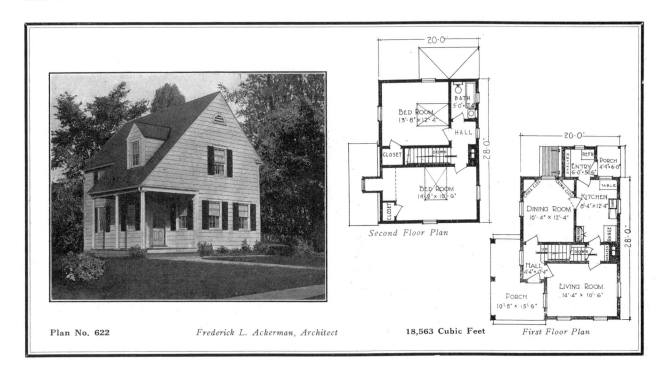

Plan No. 622   *Frederick L. Ackerman, Architect*   **18,563 Cubic Feet**   *First Floor Plan*

(Description of house shown in above plans)

HERE is another attractive five-room Colonial house. The construction is of frame with exterior walls of wide siding. The corner porch takes advantage of every breeze. The front door leads directly to a reception hall with a boxed stair, which is an economical feature, as it saves space and material. From this hall one may pass to the living room at the right or the dining room at the rear. The living room, while rather small, has openings on three sides, so that it is unusually bright.

(Description of house shown in plans below)

THIS interesting five-room dwelling is of the popular type with first story of stucco. Although the ground space is not large, every room is good sized. The square central hall with its beautiful open stair has direct access from the kitchen entry by way of the landing. The coat closet on the landing is a convenient feature. The living room is of good size and is entered from both the hall and through the entry from the kitchen. The living room has a fireplace and built-in seat with bookcases flanking.

Full directions for obtaining complete working drawings and specifications for these plans will be found on page 281

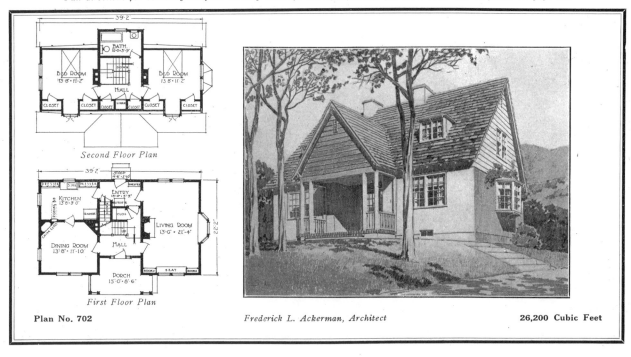

Plan No. 702   *Frederick L. Ackerman, Architect*   **26,200 Cubic Feet**

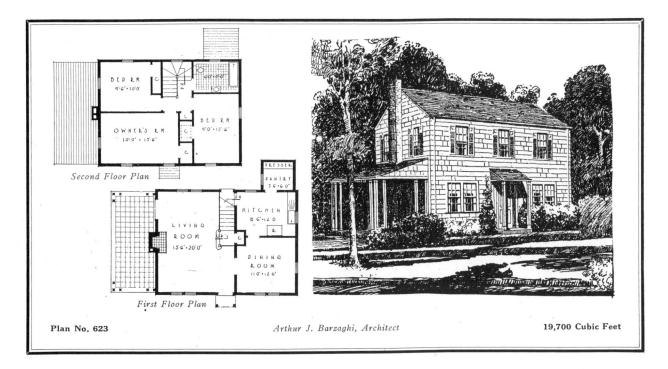

Second Floor Plan

First Floor Plan

Plan No. 623   *Arthur J. Barzaghi, Architect*   19,700 Cubic Feet

(Description of house shown in above plans)

HERE is an economical type of small six-room Colonial house, having exterior of shingles with shingle roof. The plan is subdivided in the most simple manner possible with entrance directly into the living room. There is a large porch extending across the entire width of house. The dining room and kitchen are arranged in a practical manner, and there is a large, light pantry built as an extension to the kitchen. On the second floor there are three bedrooms and large tiled bath.

(Description of house shown in plans below)

THIS type of simple, economical Colonial home is greatly favored where it is necessary to conserve the original investment. The house is of frame construction throughout with wide siding and chimneys of brick. A broad porch extends almost the entire width of the house, and entrance is into a small hall from which central staircase leads upward. An open fireplace is provided in the living room with the additional feature of a door-bed and dressing closet, thus adding a guest room.

Full directions for obtaining complete working drawings and specifications for these plans will be found on page 281

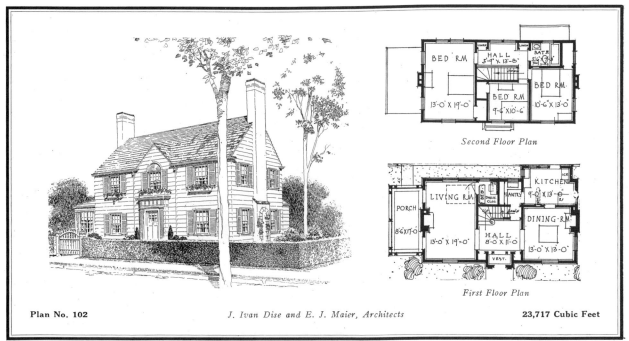

Second Floor Plan

First Floor Plan

Plan No. 102   *J. Ivan Dise and E. J. Maier, Architects*   23,717 Cubic Feet

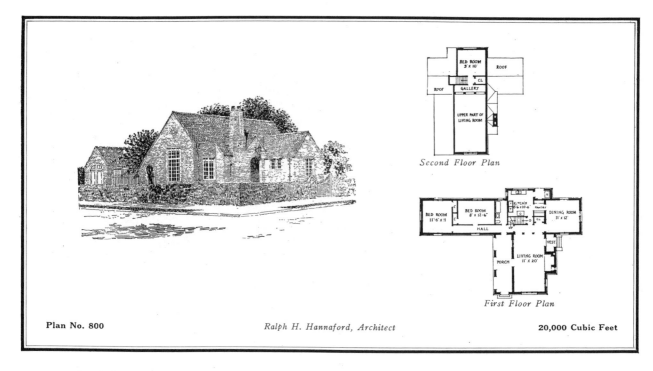

Plan No. 800   *Ralph H. Hannaford, Architect*   20,000 Cubic Feet

Second Floor Plan

First Floor Plan

(Description of house shown in above plans)

QUITE out of the ordinary is this bungalow of brick construction. Its chief feature is an opentimbered, high-ceiled living room. This room also has an attractive fireplace set in an ingle-nook. The dining room is of generous size, and as there are windows on three sides it is a cheerful, sunny room. The kitchen is well arranged and has convenient access to the dining room. The two bedrooms and bath are entirely separated from the living quarters and are well lighted.

(Description of house shown in plans below)

THIS is another of the economically-built square type of homes. The exterior has simple lines with principal walls of wide siding. The brick foundation and porch walls afford an opportunity to use color. The expense of the small roofs over the second story and attic windows might be saved without detracting from the appearance of the house. The reception hall serves as a vestibule. Here there is an impressive stairway to the second floor. There is a pretty bay in the dining room.

Full directions for obtaining complete working drawings and specifications for these plans will be found on page 281.

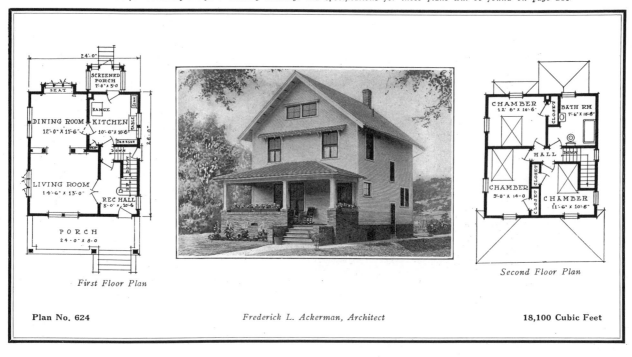

First Floor Plan

Second Floor Plan

Plan No. 624   *Frederick L. Ackerman, Architect*   18,100 Cubic Feet

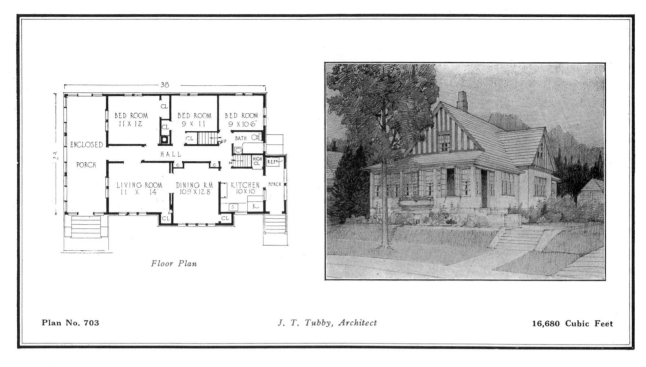

Floor Plan

Plan No. 703   *J. T. Tubby, Architect*   **16,680 Cubic Feet**

(*Description of house shown in above plans*)

AN extremely practical and attractive type of six-room bungalow with exterior of stucco and half-timbered gables and shingle roof applied with double lap at intervals to provide parallel shadow lines. At the side of the house there is an unusually large enclosed porch which may be omitted for economy when the house is first constructed. This porch constitutes the main entrance and if omitted entrance must be directly into living room. From the porch a central hall connects with all rooms in the house.

(*Description of house shown in plans below*)

THIS is an excellent type of five-room house for a narrow lot. This house is designed for exterior construction of face brick, with roof of slate or asbestos shingles. This house virtually becomes a six-room house by introduction of a door-bed into the sewing room. On the first floor there is a living room of fair size which is entered from the porch through a small hall. The dining room is well lighted and kitchen is located for convenient service and has rear entry with ice box.

Full directions for obtaining complete working drawings and specifications for these plans will be found on page 281

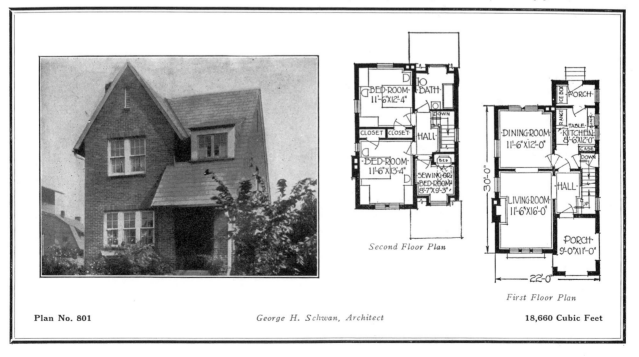

Second Floor Plan

First Floor Plan

Plan No. 801   *George H. Schwan, Architect*   **18,660 Cubic Feet**

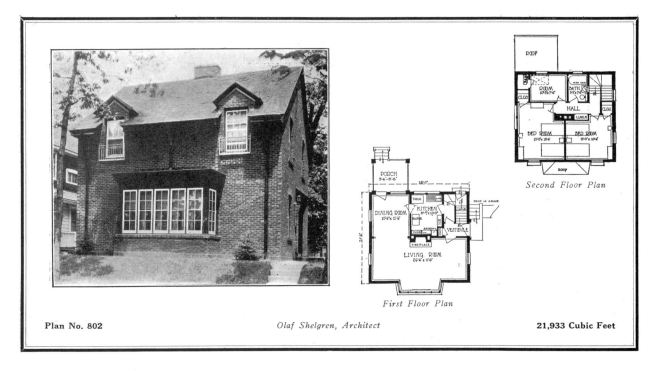

Plan No. 802   *Olaf Shelgren, Architect*   **21,933 Cubic Feet**

(Description of house shown in above plans)

THE first floor plan of this house offers an unusual arrangement. The entrance is at the side of the house into the small vestibule leading into a very large living room, extending across the entire front of the house. There is no partition between living room and dining room, which provides an unusual amount of undivided space. At the rear of the dining room is a large living porch. The feature of the second floor is the introduction of a door-bed, providing a small extra bedroom.

(Description of house shown in plans below)

THE graceful spring of the roof, the chimney pots, the plain wall surfaces of stucco, casement sash—some of which break the roof line—all characterize this as an English home. Entrance from the brick-floored porch is into a vestibule from which the main stair leads up to the second floor. The living room extends across the entire house and has casements on three sides. The dining room is well lighted and a wood ceiling, with beams, is an interesting feature of this room.

Full directions for obtaining complete working drawings and specifications for these plans will be found on page 281

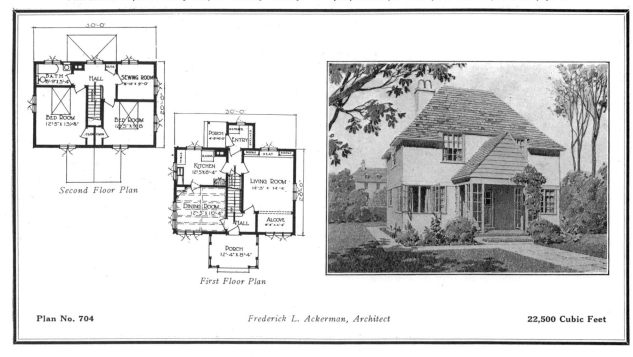

Plan No. 704   *Frederick L. Ackerman, Architect*   **22,500 Cubic Feet**

Second Floor Plan

First Floor Plan

Plan No. 302   *Amedo Leone, Architect*   **20,194 Cubic Feet**

(Description of house shown in above plans)

THIS attractive home would be exceptionally appropriate for a small suburban lot where sufficient space could be had in the rear to develop a garden. The construction is stucco on back-plastered metal lath. The arrangement of the first floor is roomy and convenient. The living room is of good size and opens from a wide hall with an attractive staircase. The dining room is entered from the end of this hall and the porch is reached from both rooms by French windows.

(Description of house shown in plans below)

HERE is another well-planned six-room Colonial house of frame construction with exterior walls of wide siding painted white. No little attractiveness is added to this design by the long roof slope broken by a dormer section, and extending over the brick porch. French doors give access to a large porch off the living room and the fireplace adds an artistic note. The staircase to the second floor is in one corner of this room. Here three sizable bedrooms and bath are well arranged.

Full directions for obtaining complete working drawings and specifications for these plans will be found on page 281.

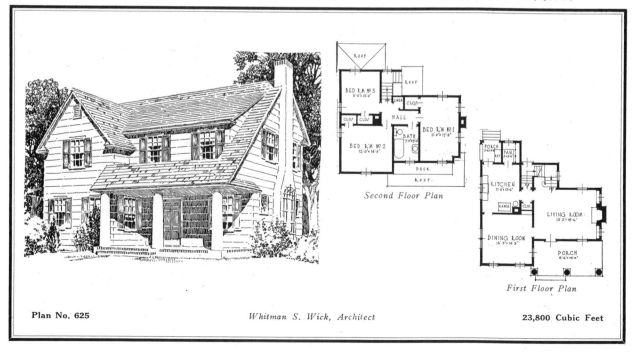

Second Floor Plan

First Floor Plan

Plan No. 625   *Whitman S. Wick, Architect*   **23,800 Cubic Feet**

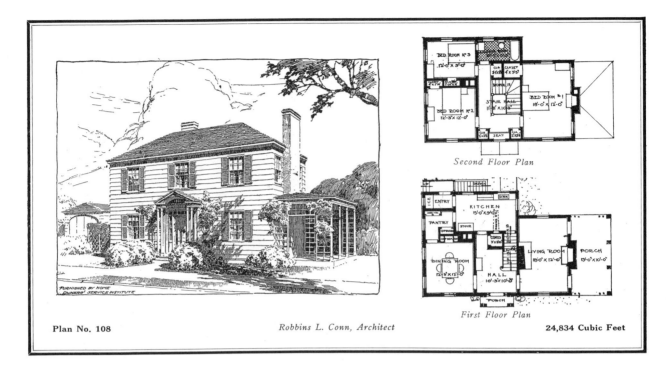

Second Floor Plan

First Floor Plan

Plan No. 108   *Robbins L. Conn, Architect*   **24,834 Cubic Feet**

(Description of house shown in above plans)

A SIMPLE type of Colonial frame six-room house showing efficiency of space as developed through the architect's design. This plan was submitted in a recent architectural competition. The architect suggests that shingles on the side walls be white-washed; all millwork to be painted white and the shutters painted green; the roof to be left to weather. One enters into a good-sized hall, having convenient coat closet, and stairs to the second floor. On each side of the fireplace is a door to the latticed porch.

(Description of house shown in plans below)

HERE is an attractive six-room cottage of the popular Dutch Colonial type. The architects suggest that side walls be of shingles, whitewashed; trim painted white and shutters dark green, the roof to be of silver gray shingles. Entrance is into a hall from which stairs lead to the second floor. Thence one may pass into the living room or to the kitchen through a passage where coats may be hung. The living room has an open fireplace and there is a door opening on to the porch.

Full directions for obtaining complete working drawings and specifications for these plans will be found on page 281

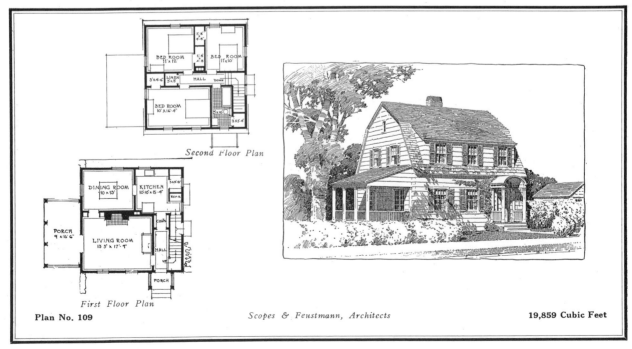

Second Floor Plan

First Floor Plan

Plan No. 109   *Scopes & Feustmann, Architects*   **19,859 Cubic Feet**

First Floor Plan

Second Floor Plan

Plan No. 314   *A. B. Hoffmeyer, Architect*   **19,818 Cubic Feet**

(Description of house shown in above plans)

THIS attractive six-room home has been designed for construction of stucco on back-plastered metal lath. The architect suggests that the stucco be light buff or cream tone; exterior trim to be stained early English brown; roof to be sea green variegated slate; roof of bay and entrance to be copper, to weather green; chimney of buff brick. The living room is of excellent size and the bay window adds much to this room, as does the fireplace. Three bedrooms are well arranged on the second floor.

(Description of house shown in plans below)

HERE is an attractive six-room home of face brick construction. The architect suggests that exterior walls be velvet texture of variegated colors, and laid up in English diamond bond with half-inch thick joints in white mortar; roof to be of wood shingles laid with thatched effect. The living room is well lighted by a bay and windows on two sides. The porch may be entered from the dining room and living room. An attractive feature is the breakfast nook, conveniently located in an alcove off the kitchen.

Full directions for obtaining complete working drawings and specifications for these plans will be found on page 281

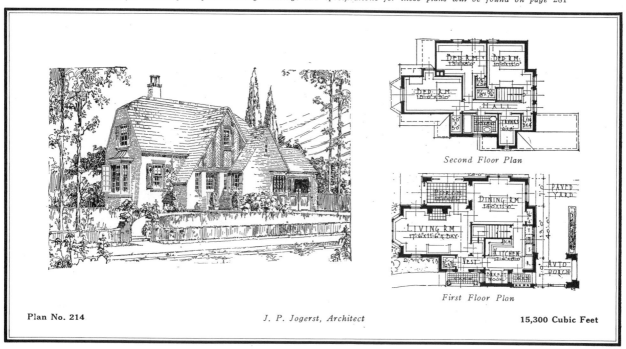

Second Floor Plan

First Floor Plan

Plan No. 214   *J. P. Jogerst, Architect*   **15,300 Cubic Feet**

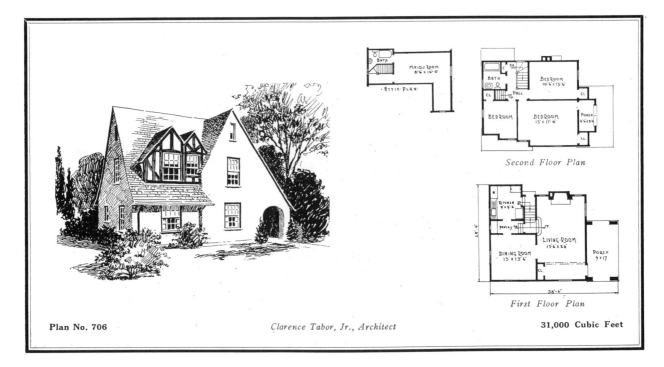

Plan No. 706   *Clarence Tabor, Jr., Architect*   **31,000 Cubic Feet**

(Description of house shown in above plans)

THIS attractive six-room house of English type is constructed of stucco on hollow tile or metal lath with half-timbered work in the dormers adding an interesting touch. From the porch one enters a living room of generous size with an open fireplace at one end. Between the dining room and kitchen is a butler's pantry. The kitchen is well arranged for efficient operation and the service entry is an added convenience. The attic would permit of the addition of a maid's room and bath if desired.

(Description of house shown in plans below)

THIS little house would be charming in its simplicity set well back from the street with an ample lawn. The plan is very compact, and the principal rooms of the first floor are arranged to give as great a sense of space as possible. The living room has an open fireplace with doors on each side; open onto porch. The kitchen is convenient and supplied with closets and built-in dresser instead of a separate pantry. Three bedrooms and bath are well arranged on the second floor.

Full directions for obtaining complete working drawings and specifications for these plans will be found on page 281

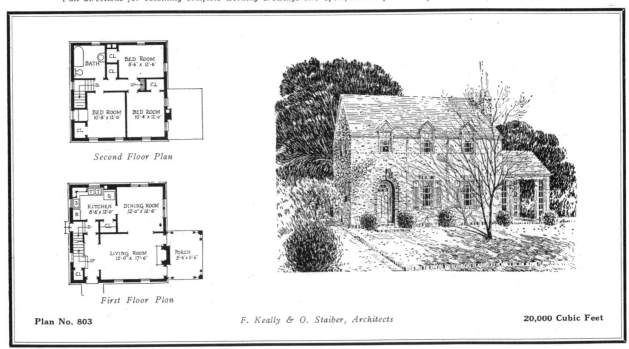

Plan No. 803   *F. Keally & O. Staiber, Architects*   **20,000 Cubic Feet**

First Floor Plan

Second Floor Plan

Plan No. 804   Paul R. Smith, Architect   17,850 Cubic Feet

(Description of house shown in above plans)

A N attractive effect has been obtained in this six-room home by the use of common brick for the first story, with gables and trim of stucco on metal lath. The entry is directly into the living room, and there is also a door from this room to the porch. The den off the living room is an attractive feature, and the introduction of a closet in this room which accommodates a disappearing bed provides an extra bedroom on occasion. The service entry is a convenient feature of the kitchen.

(Description of house shown in plans below)

H ERE is an interesting six-room house of frame construction with stone chimney. Exterior walls are of wide siding and roof of shingles. Entrance is into a small vestibule in which there is a convenient coat closet. The staircase to the second floor is in the living room, and this adds an attractive note as does the open fireplace with brick hearth. The porch may be entered either from the living room or dining room. There is a service entry, and from this the refrigerator may be iced.

Full directions for obtaining complete working drawings and specifications for these plans will be found on page 281

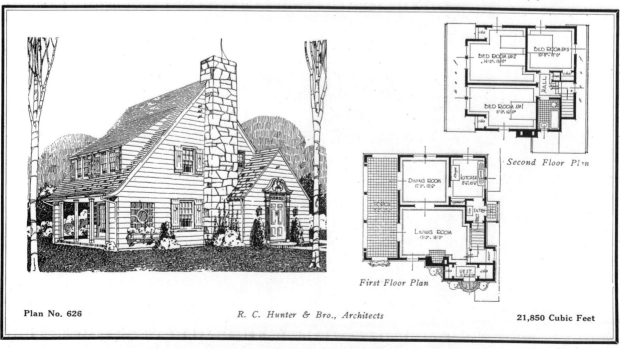

Second Floor Plan

First Floor Plan

Plan No. 626   R. C. Hunter & Bro., Architects   21,850 Cubic Feet

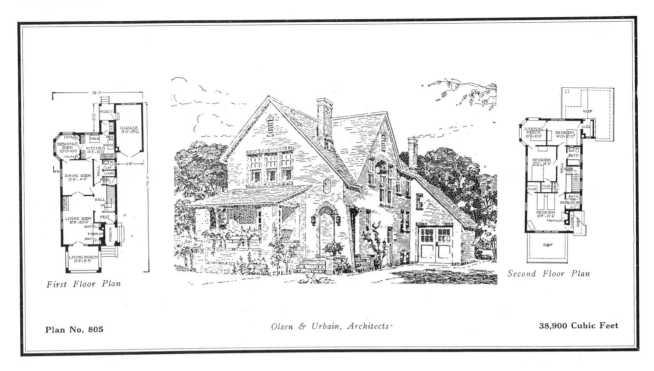

First Floor Plan

Second Floor Plan

Plan No. 805   *Olsen & Urbain, Architects·*   **38,900 Cubic Feet**

(Description of house shown in above plans)

THE quaint gabled effect in this six-room house is characteristic of the English cottage, which always has a cozy, homelike atmosphere about it. If the brickwork is laid in English Cross Bond, the resulting diagonal lines throughout the wall will harmonize with the roof lines. Flemish, English, or Garden Wall Bond would also be effective. Placed on a fifty-foot lot there will be plenty of room for a driveway to the garage, which is attached to the building, a feature many will appreciate.

(Description of house shown in plans below)

THIS attractive six-room home is designed for exterior walls of common brick. The floor plan has been carefully worked out, and the garage, which is connected by a small hall to the house, is an interesting feature. The living room is of good size, and French doors open onto the sun porch. At one end is a fireplace flanked by bookcases, and in the opposite corner a stairway leads to the second floor. The balcony outside the main bedrooms is unusual and attractive.

Full directions for obtaining complete working drawings and specifications for these plans will be found on page 281

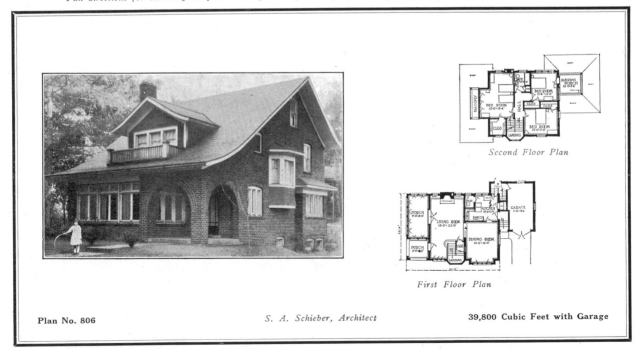

Second Floor Plan

First Floor Plan

Plan No. 806   *S. A. Schieber, Architect*   **39,800 Cubic Feet with Garage**

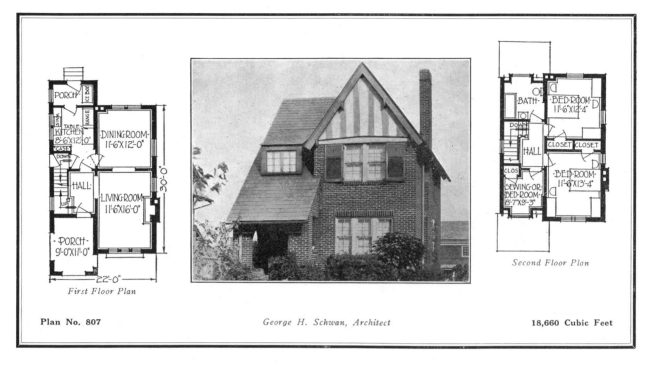

First Floor Plan

Second Floor Plan

Plan No. 807   *George H. Schwan, Architect*   18,660 Cubic Feet

(Description of house shown in above plans)

ON this page there are shown two homes which are particularly attractive for suburban areas. The house shown above has exterior walls of common brick with gables of half-timbered stucco and roof of slate. The entrance is from a large corner porch into a hall in which the stairs are located. Dining room and living room are of conventional type. The kitchen is well arranged and provided with large service entry. On the second floor there are three bedrooms and a large bath.

(Description of house shown in plans below)

THIS is a particularly attractive dwelling, which is excellently suited for a small country home. It is English in its architectural characteristics, and designed for exterior walls of stucco. Here the front entry consists of a small vestibule with coat closet, from which one passes directly into a large living room with wide inter-room opening to dining room, making a cross sweep of approximately 38 feet. At one end of the living room is located a large fireplace with tiled or brick hearth.

Full directions for obtaining complete working drawings and specifications for these plans will be found on page 281

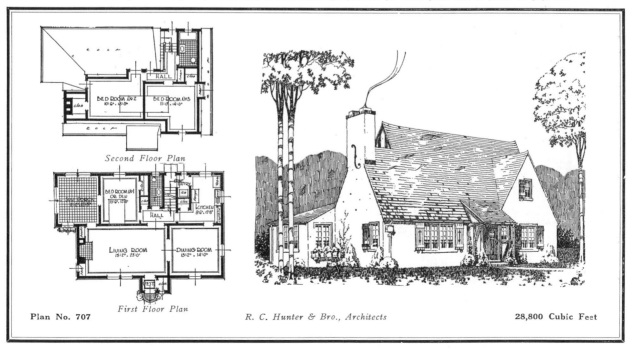

Second Floor Plan

First Floor Plan

Plan No. 707   *R. C. Hunter & Bro., Architects*   28,800 Cubic Feet

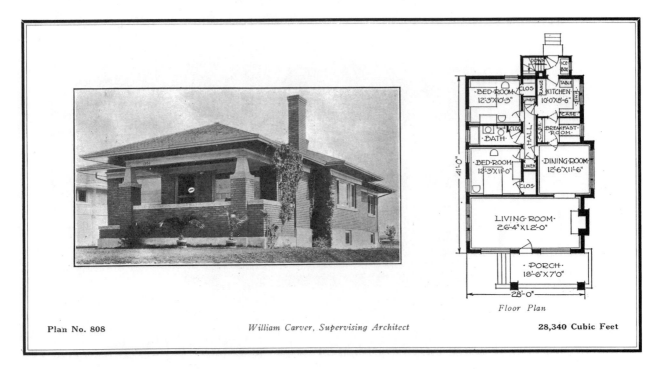

Plan No. 808   William Carver, *Supervising Architect*   28,340 Cubic Feet

(Description of house shown in above plans)

A WELL-PLANNED bungalow, having exterior walls constructed of common brick. From the large entrance porch one enters directly into a living room which extends across the entire front of the house. The open fireplace is located at the end of this room with small flanking windows. The sleeping quarters, consisting of two bedrooms and bath, are entirely separated from living quarters, connected by a small hall. An attractive breakfast room is arranged in an alcove between dining room and kitchen.

(Description of house shown in plans below)

THE most striking feature of this six-room brick dwelling is the exceptionally broad porch, which, with the porte-cochère, occupies the entire front of the house. The living room entered from this porch is ample, lighted by casement windows on two sides. There is a fine fireplace with built-in bookshelves on one side and the entrance to dining room on the other. The kitchen is of good size and well arranged. Cabinets on both sides of the sink, as well as over the refrigerator, take the place of a pantry.

Full directions for obtaining complete working drawings and specifications for these plans will be found on page 281

Plan No. 809   George W. Repp, *Architect*   31,500 Cubic Feet

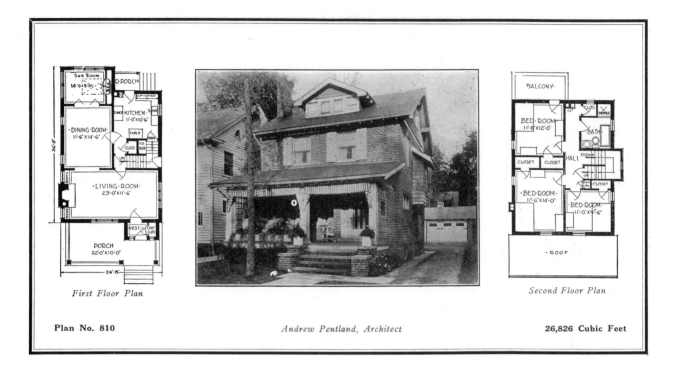

First Floor Plan

Second Floor Plan

Plan No. 810   *Andrew Pentland, Architect*   **26,826 Cubic Feet**

(Description of house shown in above plans)

FOR the exterior of this six-room home common brick has been used with wide white mortar joints. This is a type of house which can be used to good advantage in closely built sections. A vestibule is provided as part of the large front porch, and opens directly into the living room, which extends across the house. The dining room is connected with a large sun room by French doors. This sun room can well be used as a breakfast room if desired.

(Description of house shown in plans below)

HERE is a plan that would be economical to build. There are no expensive breaks, either in the wall surfaces or the roof. Stucco is a material that is economical to apply and to maintain. The floor plan is the typical one for a square six-room house, but there are many little conveniences in the plan that show careful study. The passage from the kitchen to the receiving hall eliminates the necessity of passing through the main rooms to reach the front door.

Full directions for obtaining complete working drawings and specifications for these plans will be found on page 281

First Floor Plan

Second Floor Plan

Plan No. 708   *Frederick L. Ackerman, Architect*   **21,336 Cubic Feet**

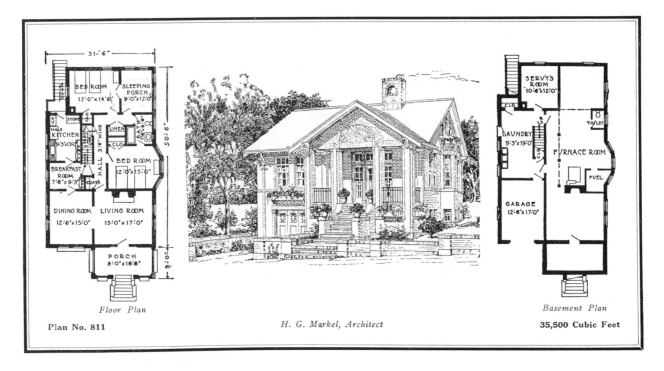

Floor Plan

Plan No. 811

H. G. Markel, Architect

35,500 Cubic Feet

Basement Plan

(Description of house shown in above plans)

HERE is a five-room brick bungalow which would be very attractive on a hillside location, but could be built successfully on a level plot. The living room, entered directly from the porch, together with the dining room, occupy the entire front of the house, and the dining room and kitchen are connected by a breakfast room. The kitchen is well lighted with double window over the sink and has a cabinet which replaces a pantry. The basement contains a garage, laundry, servant's room, furnace room and toilet.

(Description of house shown in plans below)

THIS is an interesting six-room dwelling which was designed for construction of white Portland cement on concrete blocks. This plan is developed as a replica of an old Colonial house which served as Washington's headquarters at Valley Forge. The large living room extends entirely across the house and has a brick fireplace flanked by French doors opening to an extensive porch which may be open or enclosed, as desired. The stairway is located directly off the living room at the rear of the house.

Full directions for obtaining complete working drawings and specifications for these plans will be found on page 281

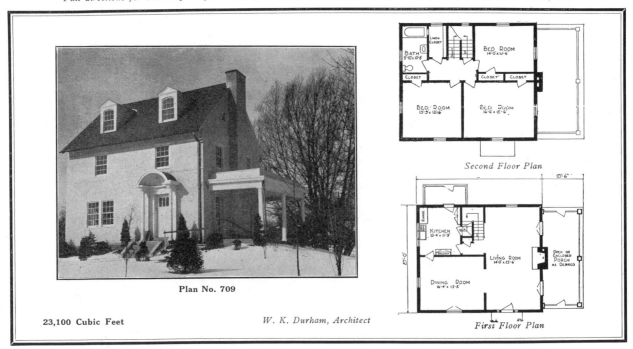

Second Floor Plan

Plan No. 709

23,100 Cubic Feet

W. K. Durham, Architect

First Floor Plan

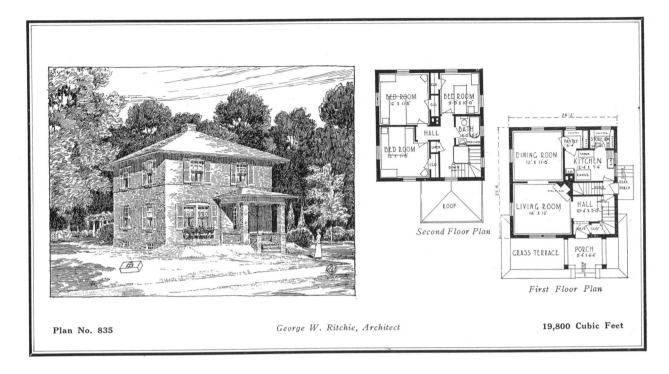

Second Floor Plan

First Floor Plan

Plan No. 835   *George W. Ritchie, Architect*   19,800 Cubic Feet

(Description of house shown in above plans)

THIS attractive six-room home would look equally well on a city or suburban lot, or out in the country. Exterior walls are of brick and with white window sash and outside blinds painted olive green, this is a home which anyone might be proud to own. Entrance is into a vestibule containing a convenient coat closet, and this leads to a hall where there is a wide opening into the living room. The pantry between the kitchen and dining room is an added feature.

(Description of house shown in plans below)

HERE is a home that is designed to provide ample accommodations for an average family in a small and economical house—only twenty feet wide by twenty-four deep. The living room extends across the front of the house with stair on one side. There is a wide opening into the dining room, which has windows on two sides. The kitchen is conveniently arranged and has a service entry. There are three bedrooms and bath on the second floor.

Full directions for obtaining complete working drawings and specifications for these plans will be found on page 281

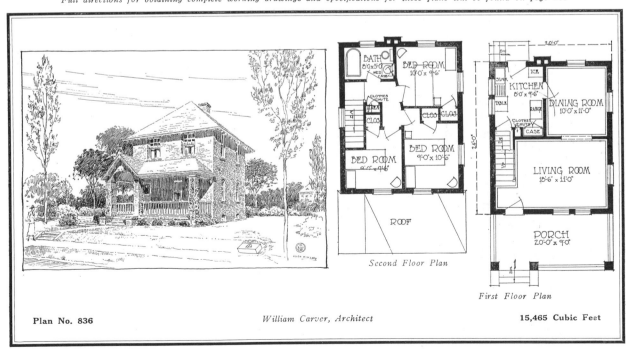

Second Floor Plan

First Floor Plan

Plan No. 836   *William Carver, Architect*   15,465 Cubic Feet

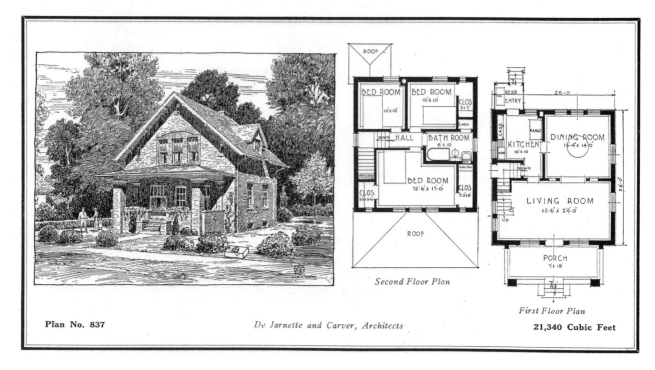

Plan No. 837   *De Jarnette and Carver, Architects*   **21,340 Cubic Feet**

Second Floor Plan

First Floor Plan

(Description of house shown in above plans)

(Description of house shown in plans below)

ALTHOUGH the total area of this home is comparatively small, the plan has been carefully worked out to provide the maximum accommodations. The living room extends across the front of the house and is augmented in size by the open porch. There is a wide opening into the dining room which is well lighted. The kitchen is laid out to save steps and to give ample space for china, dishes and food, and there is a small entry containing the icebox. Construction is of brick.

HERE is another house of brick construction with an excellent floor plan. The entrance is into a vestibule with large closets on each side. The living room is of generous size and has two doors to the large porch and an open fireplace on the opposite side of the room. The main stair leads directly from the living room and is detailed to present a most artistic appearance. The sleeping porch could easily be converted into a bedroom by the introduction of a door bed in the large closet.

Full directions for obtaining complete working drawings and specifications for these plans will be found on page 281

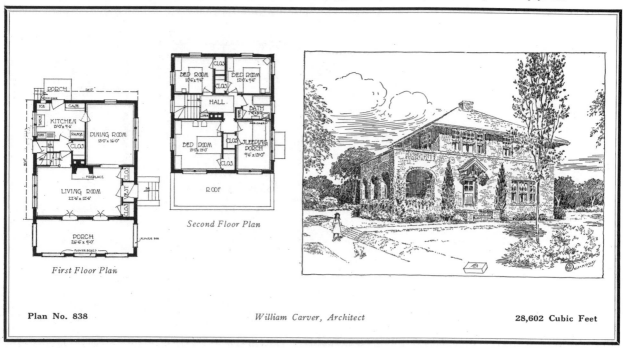

First Floor Plan

Second Floor Plan

Plan No. 838   *William Carver, Architect*   **28,602 Cubic Feet**

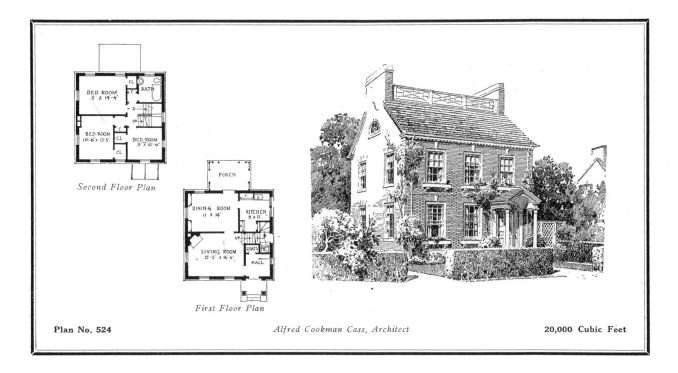

Second Floor Plan

First Floor Plan

Plan No. 524   *Alfred Cookman Cass, Architect*   **20,000 Cubic Feet**

(Description of house shown in above plans)

THE plan of this six-room house is very compact and the simplicity of construction would enable it to be built inexpensively. The porch is on the rear, reached from the dining room. A pleasant garden could be arranged on this part of the lot. The living room has splendid proportions and the fireplace in the corner adds an interesting decorative feature. The exterior walls are constructed of face brick with deeply raked joints; roof is of slate shingles.

(Description of house shown in plans below)

ALTHOUGH only twenty-six feet square this house has four pleasant rooms downstairs, and two bedrooms upstairs. It is built of stucco and shingles, with overhanging eaves and a screened-in porch. The living room and dining room together extend across the front of the house. The plans may be reversed to give the living room the pleasantest exposure. Between the dining room and kitchen is a pantry with built-in dresser. The basement steps lead from here.

Full directions for obtaining complete working drawings and specifications for these plans will be found on page 281

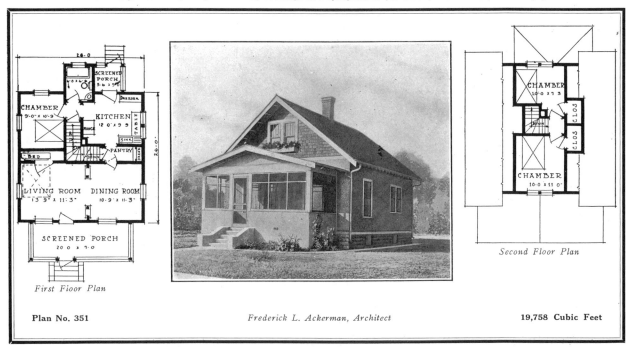

First Floor Plan   *Second Floor Plan*

Plan No. 351   *Frederick L. Ackerman, Architect*   **19,758 Cubic Feet**

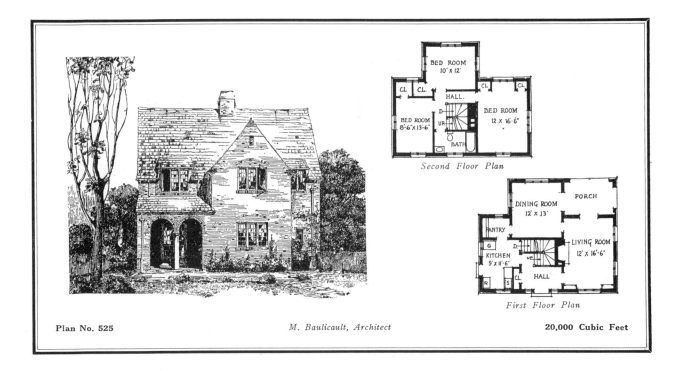

Plan No. 525   *M. Baulicault, Architect*   **20,000 Cubic Feet**

(Description of house shown in above plans)

THIS house is planned to be placed near the street, and facing the northwest. The living rooms will have southern exposure and the rear of the lot could be developed with a lawn and garden to afford a pleasant outlook. The illustration shows a view of the rear. The first floor is well arranged, the porch being reached from both dining room and living room. The three bedrooms are provided with ample closets.

(Description of house shown in plans below)

HALF-TIMBERS in an overhanging second story, and clipped gable ends are picturesque features of this English house. Equally fascinating are its grouped casements, tall chimney, and the severely simple formal entrance. The living porch is at the rear, an excellent plan where the front or side of the house is exposed to the afternoon sun. There is another good porch at the side.

Full directions for obtaining complete working drawings and specifications for these plans will be found on page 281

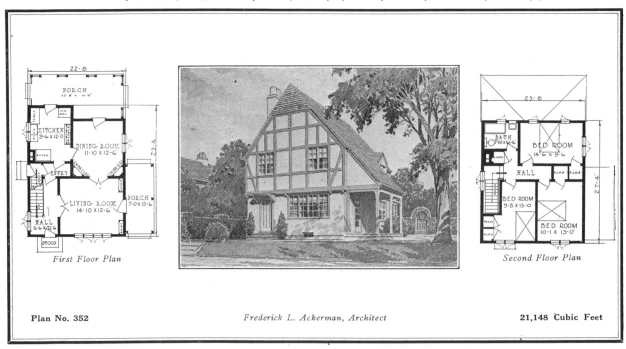

Plan No. 352   *Frederick L. Ackerman, Architect*   **21,148 Cubic Feet**

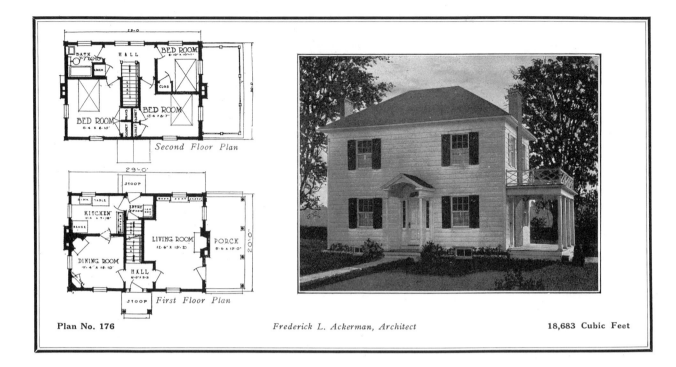

Plan No. 176   *Frederick L. Ackerman, Architect*   **18,683 Cubic Feet**

(Description of house shown in above plans)

IT would be hard to plan a house with a more comfortable and convenient layout, and a more attractive exterior, that could be built as economically as this pretty six-room home. The over all dimensions are twenty-nine feet by twenty feet. This will fit an ordinary lot and still leave space for lawn and garden. The charming Colonial entrance is inviting. The main stair is a straight boxed run.

(Description of house shown in plans below)

THIS type of brick Colonial house would adapt itself well to any suburban location. It would probably look its best placed near the street, with the rear reserved for a garden and lawn. The kitchen has a window overlooking the street and is well placed with respect to the dining room and entrance hall. The bedrooms are of good size and well equipped with closet space. Roof of slate or asbestos shingles.

Full directions for obtaining complete working drawings and specifications for these plans will be found on page 281

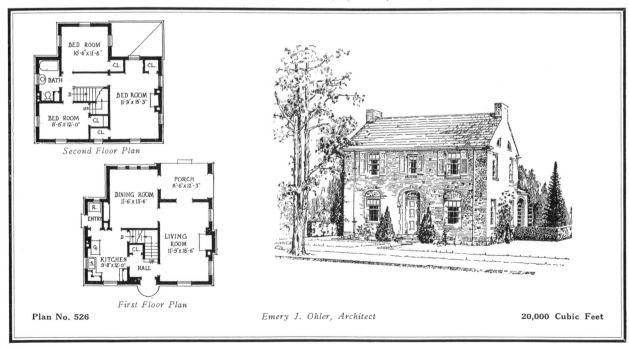

Plan No. 526   *Emery J. Ohler, Architect*   **20,000 Cubic Feet**

LEFT: *This is a detailed view of the attractive entrance door of the Washington model house. All woodwork and trim in this house was furnished from stock designs originally developed under careful architectural supervision.*

CENTER: *A view of the interior, indicating the interesting possibilities of attractively designed built-in features when carefully selected from good stock designs.*

RIGHT: *A view in the living room of the model house showing attractive brick fireplace with mantel selected from stock design.*

The breakfast nook in the model house is one of the particularly attractive features. Table, seats and dressers from stock designs.

A general view of the kitchen showing an unusually attractive arrangement of well selected utility features and flooring of cork tile.

For photographs and revised plans of this house see pages 4, 25 and 41

Note attractive background provided by well selected wallpaper in living room and dining room above.

Interesting Interiors of Model House at Washington, D. C.

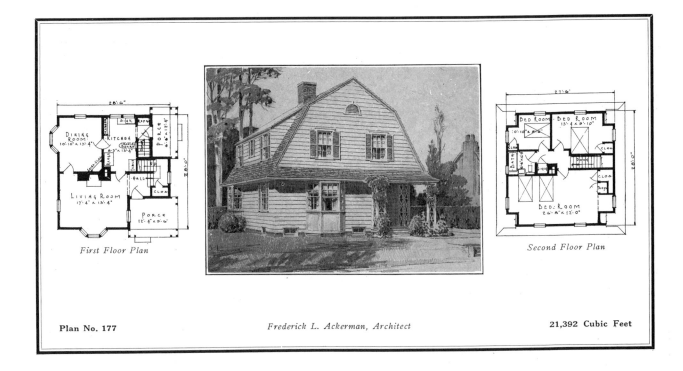

First Floor Plan

Second Floor Plan

Plan No. 177   Frederick L. Ackerman, Architect   21,392 Cubic Feet

(Description of house shown in above plans)

HERE is another excellent example of the Dutch Colonial with the popular gambrel roof. Two bays, in the living room and dining room respectively, are attractive features of the exterior. The front door leads to an alcove off the living room, containing the stair and coat closet, and just opposite the bay at the front of the living room is the fireplace. Every bit of wall space is utilized in the kitchen for equipment.

(Description of house shown in plans below)

THIS house is modern in character but possesses many Colonial features. It could be placed on a corner lot with the front on the narrow side as shown in the illustration, or it could equally well occupy an inside lot. The living room is especially attractive with the broad bay window, and is built almost as a separate unit. There is also a fine fireplace at the side of the room, an added decorative feature.

Full directions for obtaining complete working drawings and specifications for these plans will be found on page 281

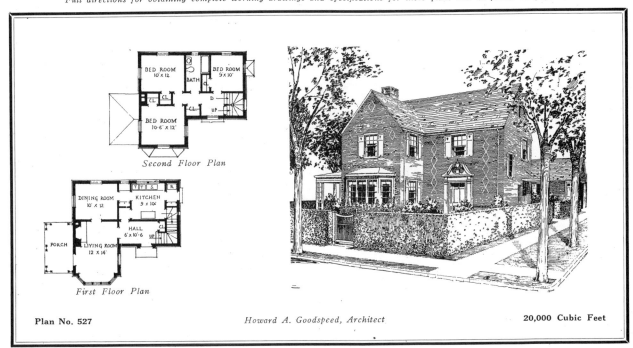

Second Floor Plan

First Floor Plan

Plan No. 527   Howard A. Goodspeed, Architect   20,000 Cubic Feet

Second Floor Plan

First Floor Plan

Plan No. 178   *R. C. Hunter & Bro., Architects*   16,200 Cubic Feet

(Description of house shown in above plans)

THIS house would look well facing as it does in the illustration or with the living room in front and the porch on the left. The original position would be required for a narrow lot. The plan is very compact and complete. The hall space on the second floor is reduced to the minimum, yet all rooms are convenient to it. There are six closets, all of good size, and three large bedrooms. It is of frame construction.

(Description of house shown in plans below)

IN a small house it is often desirable to have a larger space than the usual room provides, and this is recognized in this plan in making the dining and living rooms practically one. If desired, this could be furnished as a living room, the dining table at other than meal times serving as a library table. With the porch opening from the room and groups of windows at each end it would give the appearance of a large house, all actually in a very small space.

Full directions for obtaining complete working drawings and specifications for these plans will be found on page 281

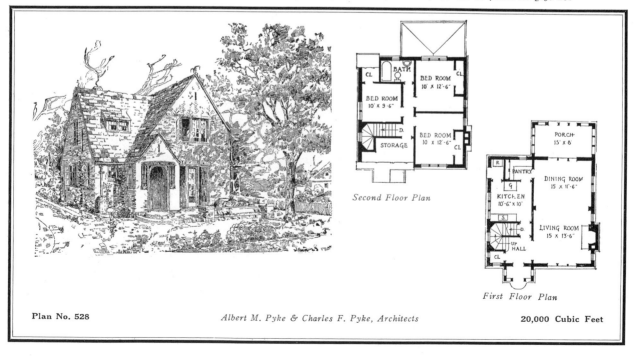

Second Floor Plan

First Floor Plan

Plan No. 528   *Albert M. Pyke & Charles F. Pyke, Architects*   20,000 Cubic Feet

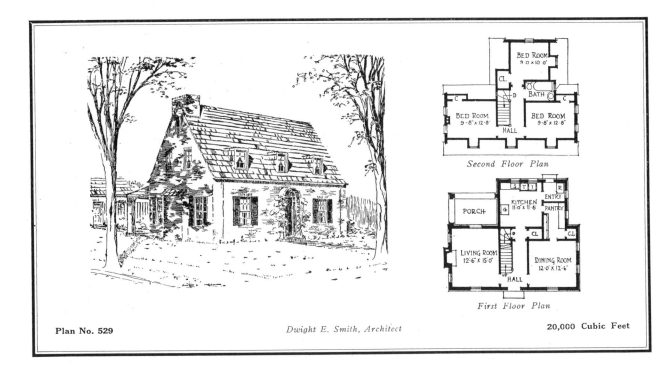

Plan No. 529   *Dwight E. Smith, Architect*   20,000 Cubic Feet

(Description of house shown in above plans)

HERE is another small cottage of Colonial design with all the character of the simple village type so much admired. It can be placed near the street, and would look equally well on a corner or an inside lot of 50-foot frontage. The front should preferably face the southeast to have morning sun in the dining room. Windows on three sides of the living room will give sun all day. Exterior walls of face brick.

(Description of house shown in plans below)

EXCELLENT floor plans, an attractive, sensible exterior and economical construction, make this a house among thousands. Both double hung windows and casement sash are used with good effect. The entrance opens upon a vestibule with a straight boxed stair. Both vestibule and rear entry are included within the rectangle of the floor plan, forming an alcove in the living room. Exterior of stucco.

Full directions for obtaining complete working drawings and specifications for these plans will be found on page 281

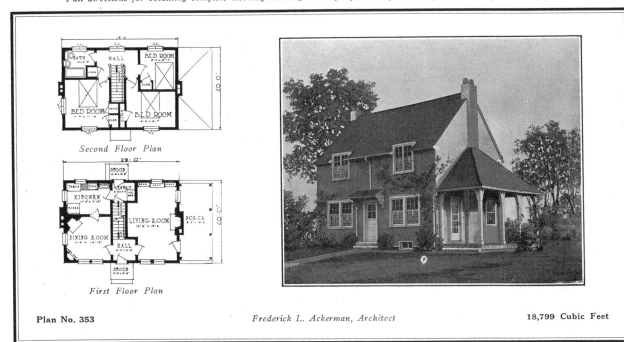

Plan No. 353   *Frederick L. Ackerman, Architect*   18,799 Cubic Feet

Plan No. 530   *Herman Brookman & Karl Bradley, Architects*   20,000 Cubic Feet

(Description of house shown in above plans)   *(Description of house shown in plans below)*

HERE is a house that is modeled after the small Georgian houses of England. It would look well placed close to the road, and if on a corner lot with the front parallel to the long side, the garage could be placed at the extreme right, opposite the porch, with the garden between. A hedge along the street will give a setting to the house and afford privacy for the garden. A good exposure would be northwest for the front. This will give morning sun in the dining room.

THERE is a special compactness about the plan of this house and a simplicity in its exterior design that would make it inexpensive to build. The living room is of good size and is separated from the dining room only by an inter-room opening affording a long vista to the porch in the rear. The three bedrooms are of ample size and provided with good closet space and plenty of windows, insuring good light and ventilation. Exterior of face brick and stucco.

Full directions for obtaining complete working drawings and specifications for these plans will be found on page 281

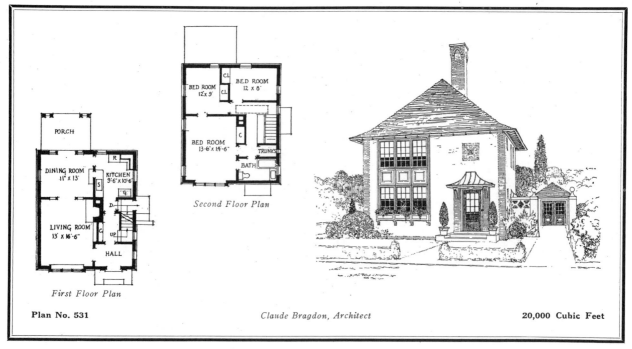

Plan No. 531   *Claude Bragdon, Architect*   20,000 Cubic Feet

Plans for 3-, 4- and 5-Room Houses

On the following pages there will be found a wide selection of plans for three-, four- and five-room houses. The majority of these plans are for five-room houses, as it has been determined that there is a greater demand for this size than those of smaller type. The plans include, in all room sizes, both bungalows and two-story houses, with many unusual arrangements which will appeal to those who desire unique and artistic layouts. It should, of course, be realized that from the viewpoint of conserving the original investment, it is possible to build a three- or four-room house, having in mind future extensions which will provide the required additional rooms. If such extensions are planned it is important that the builder should know it in advance, so that he may make proper preparations in order to keep down costs when remodeling is carried out.

See page 281 for full information on the practical use of this plan book

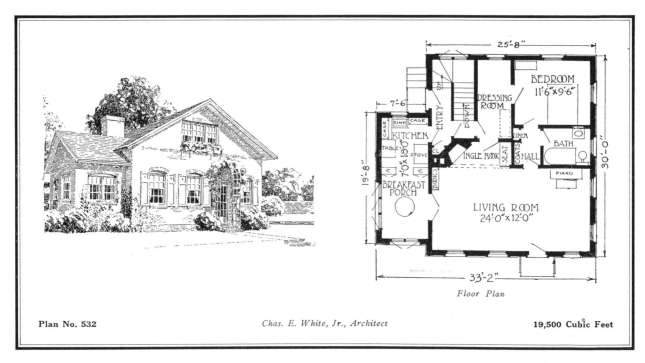

25'-8"

7'-6"

19'-8"

BEDROOM
11'6"x9'6"

DRESSING
ROOM

ENTRY

DOWN

30'-0"

CASE SINK CASE

KITCHEN
7'0"x18'0"

TABLE

STOVE

CL

LINEN

SEAT

COATS

BATH

HALL

INGLE NOOK

PIANO

BREAKFAST
PORCH

BOOKS

LIVING ROOM
24'-0"x12'-0"

33'-2"

Floor Plan

Plan No. 532   *Chas. E. White, Jr., Architect*   **19,500 Cubic Feet**

(Description of house shown in above plans)

THIS attractive Colonial bungalow is designed along apartment lines for those who wish the convenience of the apartment combined with the pleasures of their own home. It is not large or expensive to build and is suitable for a small lot, which would reduce the total investment. The bungalow feeling predominates in the exterior, but the roof is high enough to allow the finishing of two more bedrooms and a bath, or a den, upstairs, if desired. Any shade or texture of brick would be adaptable to this design, for which shrubbery and vines are especially suitable.

(Description of house shown in plans below)

THIS is a charming and livable home, necessitating the minimum amount of care, and should make an ideal home for two people. The living room is large enough for entertaining and has a real fireplace. A valuable feature is a disappearing bed in an adjoining closet which makes a second bedroom when required for an occasional guest. There is no dining room, as the dining room alcove in the kitchen will serve all family requirements, while upon more formal occasions, a gate-leg table in the living room will accommodate a large dinner party.

Full directions for obtaining complete working drawings and specifications for these plans will be found on page 281

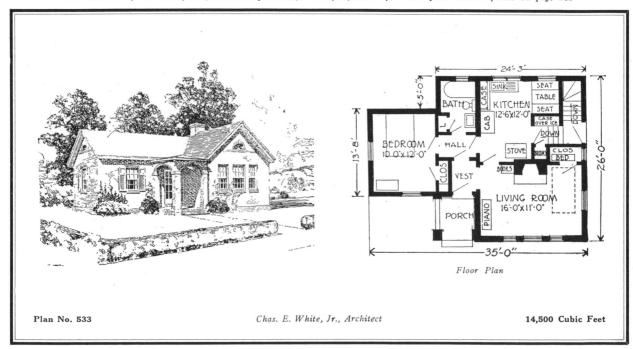

24'-3'

5'-0"

13'-8"

BATH

CASE

SINK

KITCHEN
12'-6"x12'-0"

SEAT

TABLE

SEAT

DOWN

CAB

CASE
OVER ICE

DOWN

26'-0"

BEDROOM
10'-0"x12'-0"

HALL

STOVE

CLOS
BED

CLOS

VEST

BOOKS

PORCH

PIANO

LIVING ROOM
16'-0"x11'-0"

35'-0"

Floor Plan

Plan No. 533   *Chas. E. White, Jr., Architect*   **14,500 Cubic Feet**

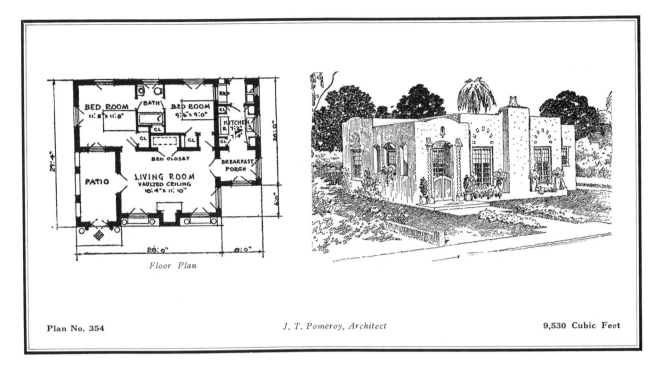

Plan No. 354   *J. T. Pomeroy, Architect*   9,530 Cubic Feet

Floor Plan

(Description of house shown in above plans)

HERE is a bungalow of the popular Spanish Mission style of design. Entering the open patio through a wooden gate, we find ourselves in a walled exclusure open to the sky; from this we enter a well-proportioned living room with vaulted ceiling and a fireplace. There is a wall bed concealed in the closet in this room, a very convenient feature to accommodate the occasional guest. The kitchen is separated from the living room by a breakfast porch that is large enough for three or four people.

(Description of house shown in plans below)

THIS four-room bungalow has many attractive features. The fireplace adds much to the cheerfulness of the living room, being placed in an ingle-nook at one side of the room. French doors at the end of this room open to the porch which, placed at the side of the house, obtains more privacy than if it were on the front as an entrance porch. The bedroom with a large closet having a window, and the bath are connected with the living room by a short hall, which serves at the same time to isolate them completely.

Full directions for obtaining complete working drawings and specifications for these plans will be found on page 281

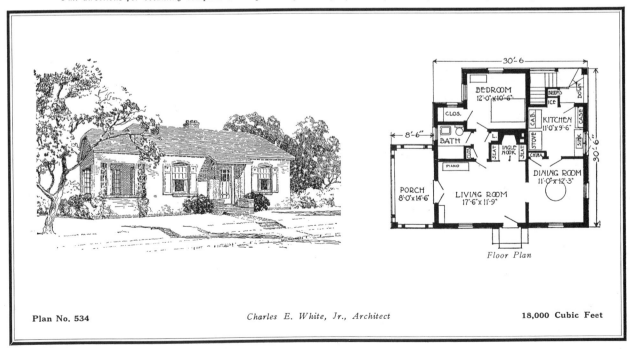

Floor Plan

Plan No. 534   *Charles E. White, Jr., Architect*   18,000 Cubic Feet

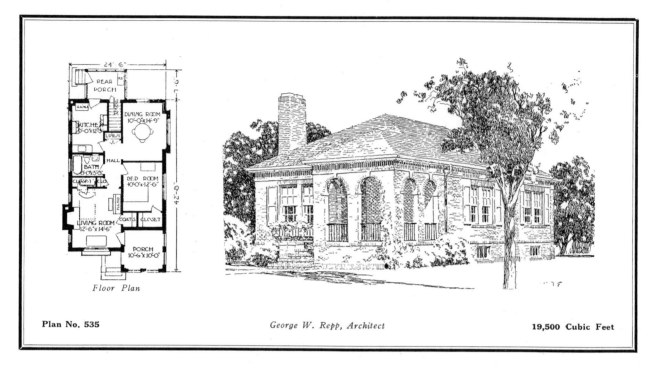

Floor Plan

Plan No. 535   George W. Repp, Architect   **19,500 Cubic Feet**

(Description of house shown in above plans)   *(Description of house shown in plans below)*

THE arcaded porch of this four-room bungalow gives a suggestion of the Italian Renaissance. This design offers a rare chance for the artistry of brickwork. While the field could be treated with a simple running bond, much could be made of the frieze under the eaves, the base and band courses, window lintels and sills, and the arches of the porch columns, by the handling of analogous color tones. Striking contrasts should not be used. A brick walk, of the same color as the house, would intimately link the landscape and house together. Exterior of face brick.

SO compactly and efficiently has this four-room bungalow been arranged that all the conveniences of the up-to-date apartment are to be found in it. The dining alcove is so close to the kitchen as to become almost a part of it, and yet is entirely shut off from both kitchen and living room. This is a spacious room and has a delightful open fireplace and two convenient closets. A large bedroom and a smaller guest room are found at the rear. A splendid porch runs across the front of the house and can be screened in or glazed if desired. Stucco on concrete block.

Full directions for obtaining complete working drawings and specifications for these plans will be found on page 281

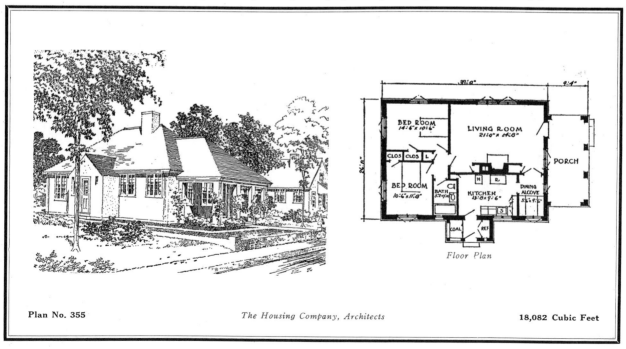

Floor Plan

Plan No. 355   *The Housing Company, Architects*   **18,082 Cubic Feet**

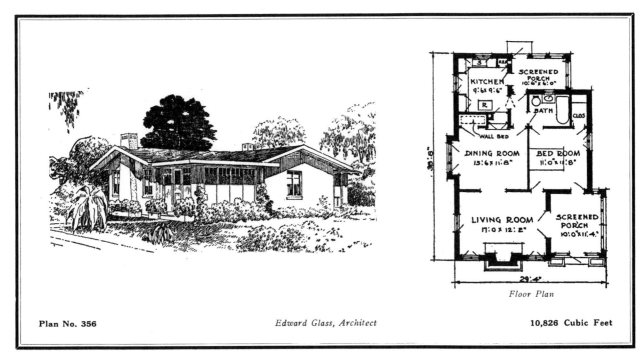

Plan No. 356   *Edward Glass, Architect*   **10,826 Cubic Feet**

(Description of house shown in above plans)

(Description of house shown in plans below)

HERE is a bungalow of the popular California type. The low-pitched roof, wide shady eaves, and the fireplace chimney in the center of the front wall are typical of the western bungalow type of design. The house is entered from the large screened porch in front, and with the large enclosed porch there is no need of a vestibule. The porch opens through French doors into the living room, which has a cheerful fireplace. The dining room is equipped with a modern wall bed, concealed in the closet, giving extra sleeping accommodation for guests. Stucco on concrete block.

HERE is an attractive, cozy and convenient four-room bungalow of the Colonial type. The inviting fireplace directly opposite the entrance offers a cheering hospitality. The living and dining rooms, while separated by the coat closet and seat, form practically one big room across the front of the house. A large closet at the end of the living room holds a disappearing bed, which will prove to be very convenient for an occasional guest. The small hall, which communicates with bedroom, bath and kitchen, is conveniently located and contains a linen closet.

Full directions for obtaining complete working drawings and specifications for these plans will be found on page 281

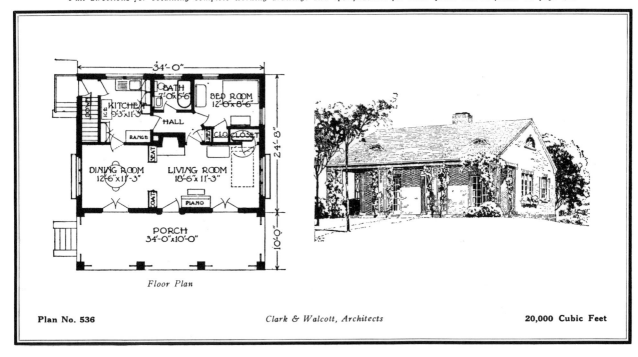

Floor Plan

Plan No. 536   *Clark & Walcott, Architects*   **20,000 Cubic Feet**

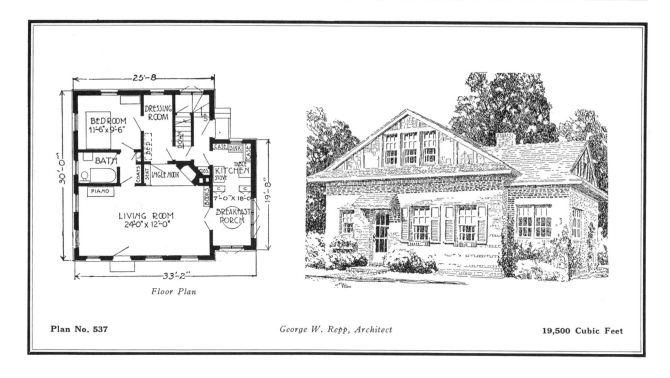

Floor Plan

Plan No. 537   *George W. Repp, Architect*   19,500 Cubic Feet

(Description of house shown in above plans)

THIS interesting plan for a studio type four-room brick bungalow is well worth careful study. The upper part of the house is of brick and exposed timbers with roof of slate or metal patented shingles. The arrangement of the floor plan is quite unique. The kitchen and breakfast porch are practically thrown into one room, while the feature of the plan is a very large living room with fireplace arranged at an angle providing an extremely attractive ingle-nook and seat.

(Description of house shown in plans below)

THIS four-room house is designed for an exterior of red brick with cornice, entrance, blinds, porch and bay painted white, or blinds can be light green. The roof is recommended to be slate or other type of heavy shingle. No dining room is provided, but there is a complete kitchen and pantry for service at one end of the large living room. Two bedrooms of fair size are located on the second floor. This is a simple, inexpensive type of house.

Full directions for obtaining complete working drawings and specifications for these plans will be found on page 281

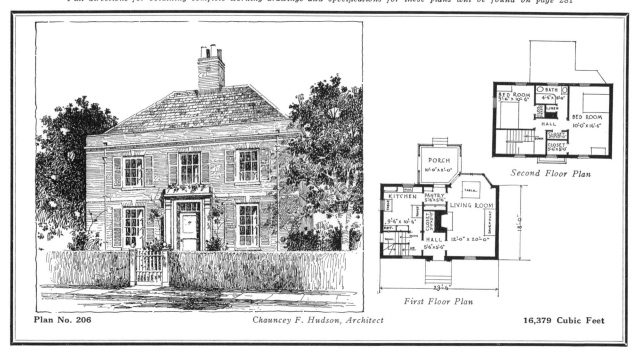

Second Floor Plan

First Floor Plan

Plan No. 206   *Chauncey F. Hudson, Architect*   16,379 Cubic Feet

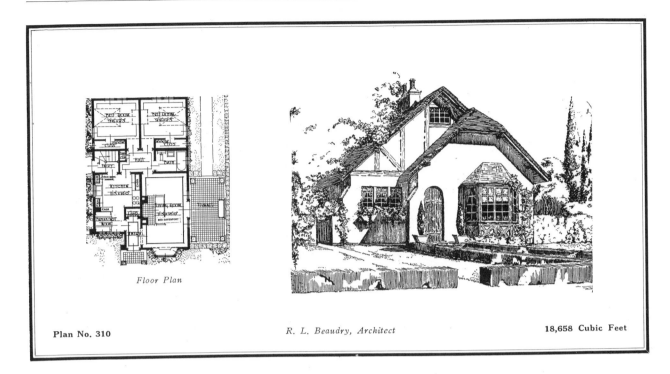

Floor Plan

Plan No. 310   *R. L. Beaudry, Architect*   **18,658 Cubic Feet**

(Description of house shown in above plans)

IN this four-room bungalow are combined compactness of plan and beauty of exterior design. Of stucco and timber construction, and roof of thatched effect, the outward appearance would surely appeal to any lover of the English cottage. It should be noted in particular that the bedrooms, though on the same floor, are quite apart from the living quarters. Each has a large closet and is close to the bathroom. The kitchen is well arranged.

(Description of house shown in plans below)

HERE is a well planned four-room bungalow. The wide siding and vertical batten strips, with overhanging eaves and exposed rafter ends, create a rustic impression for the exterior that is novel and artistic. One may enter the living room from the stoop or from the porch. This room extends across the entire end of the house. Instead of an ordinary dining room there is a sunny little breakfast room, separated from the kitchen by a broad opening.

Full directions for obtaining complete working drawings and specifications for these plans will be found on page 281

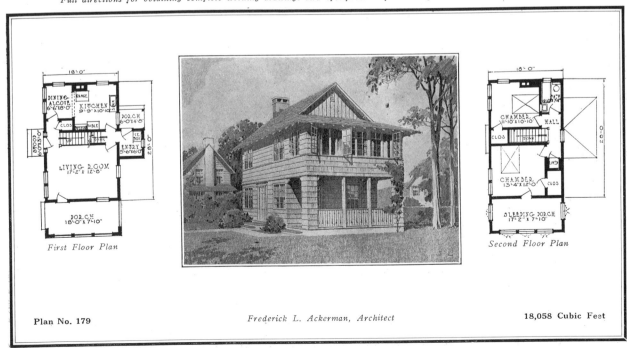

First Floor Plan   *Second Floor Plan*

Plan No. 179   *Frederick L. Ackerman, Architect*   **18,058 Cubic Feet**

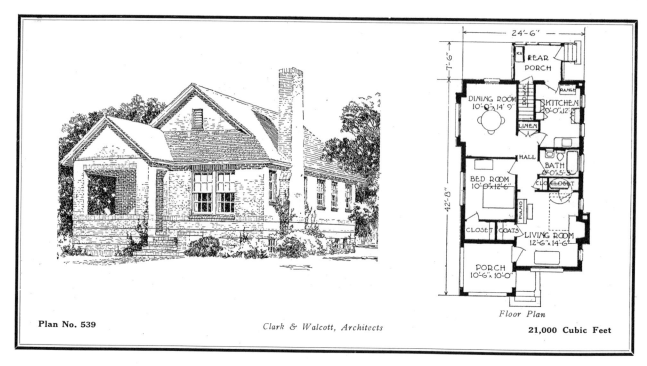

Plan No. 539   *Clark & Walcott, Architects*   **21,000 Cubic Feet**

(Description of house shown in above plans)

Here is a small house which has real architectural merit. The fine chimney, the roof, the gabled porch, the proportion of height to length and breadth, and the fenestration combine into a very pleasing whole. The large square porch forms a complete protection for the entrance, which is directly into the ample living room. A closet for a disappearing bed practically makes of the living room another bedroom when occasion demands. A short hall leads to the dining room and kitchen, and connects the bedroom with the bath. Exterior is of face brick.

(Description of house shown in plans below)

This charming Colonial home could be built on a narrow city lot to good advantage. Preferably it should set back from the street, as the sketch indicates. The exterior treatment is stucco on back-plastered metal lath; roof of stained wood shingles or slate. The combined living and dining room is large and well lighted. There are also plenty of blank wall spaces for the placing of furniture. Two large bedrooms, bathroom and many closets occupy the second story. The space taken up by stairs and hall is reduced to the minimum.

Full directions for obtaining complete working drawings and specifications for these plans will be found on page 281

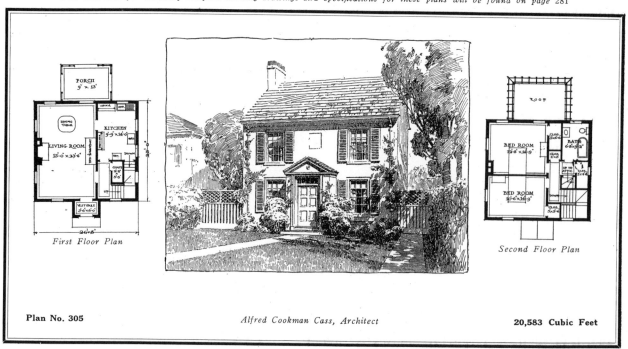

Plan No. 305   *Alfred Cookman Cass, Architect*   **20,583 Cubic Feet**

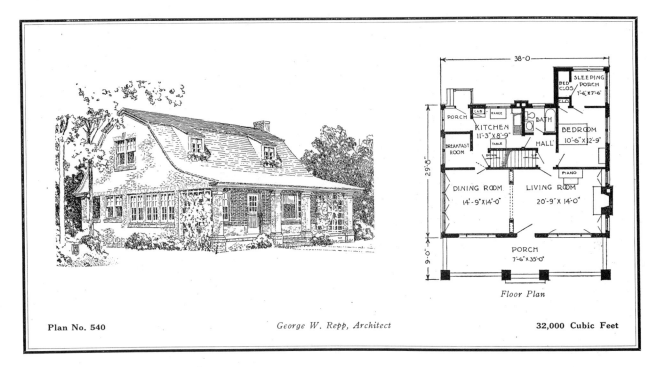

Plan No. 540   *George W. Repp, Architect*   **32,000 Cubic Feet**

Floor Plan

(Description of house shown in above plans)

THIS five-room bungalow is a fine example of the Colonial type. The gambrel roof, always charming, gives additional space in the attic that may be utilized for a billiard room, a playroom for the children, or divided into two bedrooms and a bath, thereby gaining more space at a slight additional cost. Careful consideration of color and texture of both brick and mortar joint is all that is further required to make it a marked success. There is a fine basement under the rear half, reached by a stairway from the breakfast room above.

(Description of house shown in plans below)

HERE is a five-room bungalow with an interior arrangement as distinctive as its exterior. The uneven texture of cobblestones, combined with siding, shingles, brick and stucco, and the low-lying effect of broad frontage and sweeping roof contribute to the charm of this house. A reception hall not only provides shelter and privacy, but also makes it possible to reach any room in the house with a minimum of intrusion into other rooms. At the left, through an inter-room opening, is the living room, and at the right, through French doors, the dining room.

Full directions for obtaining complete working drawings and specifications for these plans will be found on page 281

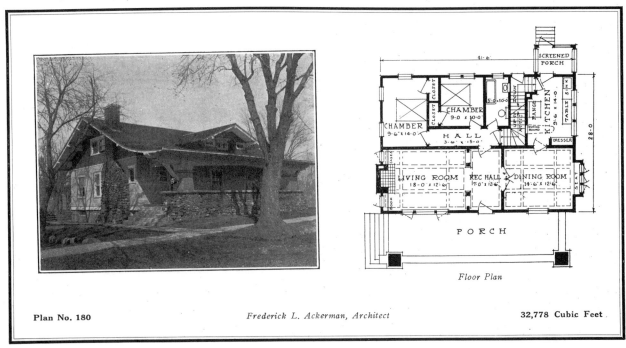

Floor Plan

Plan No. 180   *Frederick L. Ackerman, Architect*   **32,778 Cubic Feet**

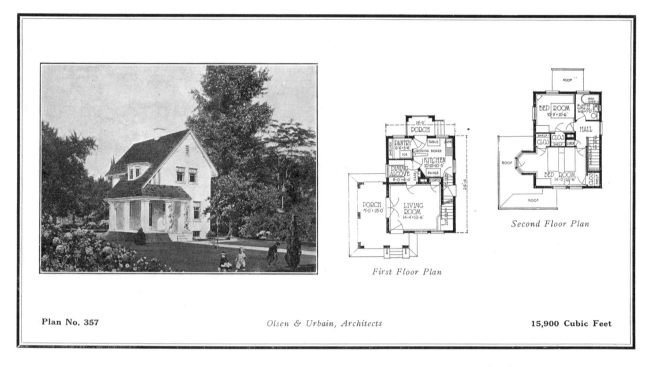

Plan No. 357   *Olsen & Urbain, Architects*   **15,900 Cubic Feet**

First Floor Plan

Second Floor Plan

(Description of house shown in above plans)

THE plans of this two-story residence have been well worked out to provide a spacious living room with two entrances off the porch. Well-finished seats with high curved backs and a refectory type table are built in the dining cove and together with a wall case for chinaware constitute practically all the furniture needed. The kitchen is delightfully planned to permit plenty of ventilation. The front bedroom runs across the front of the house and contains two clothes closets. The second bedroom has a closet and two windows.

(Description of house shown in plans below)

A FOUR-ROOM house with exterior walls of stucco on metal lath and roof of slate. This is an English design in which it is recommended that exterior woodwork be stained dark brown with gutters and leaders to match or in copper. Exterior sash painted cream color; living room and halls in sand-finished plaster. Structural ceiling beams recommended for the living room, together with fireplace and hearth of brick. A large window seat is an attractive feature of the well-arranged living room.

Full directions for obtaining complete working drawings and specifications for these plans will be found on page 281

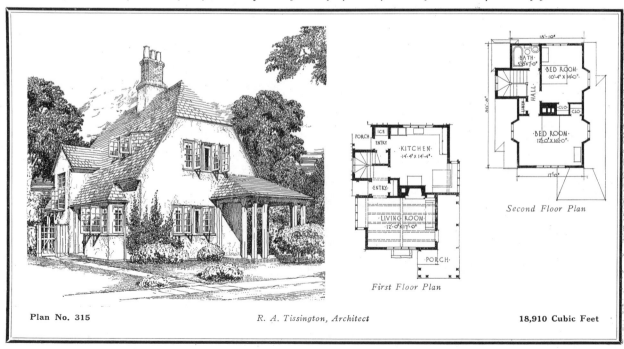

First Floor Plan

Second Floor Plan

Plan No. 315   *R. A. Tissington, Architect*   **18,910 Cubic Feet**

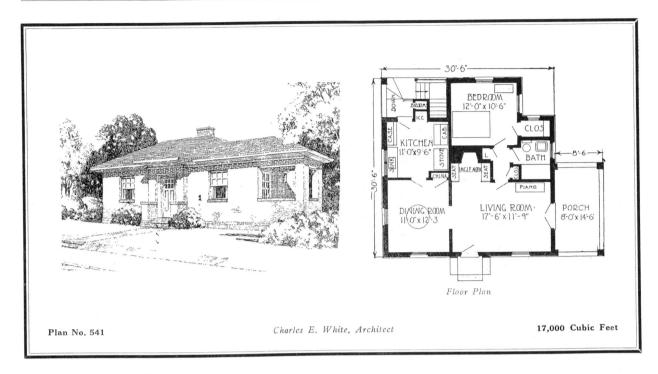

Floor Plan

Plan No. 541   *Charles E. White, Architect*   **17,000 Cubic Feet**

(Description of house shown in above plans)

HERE is a plan which should appeal to a small family, as it is unusually complete for a small house. The living room and dining room, together with the porch, extend across the entire front and give splendid space for entertaining. All the rooms in the house are corner rooms, securing fine light and air. There is a basement under the entire house well lighted by windows on the rear and end, while access from both the outside and inside is had by means of the stairs on the enclosed rear porch. Face brick.

(Description of house shown in plans below)

THIS four-room two-story house has two bedrooms, living room, kitchen and dining alcove. Casement windows, the secluded latticed porch, and 10″ siding in the gable are unusual features which add greatly to the attractiveness of the exterior. There is a side as well as a front door from the porch to the living room at the front of the house, and across one side of the room is a handsome open stair with a landing platform. The kitchen is unusually well arranged with built-in dresser and sink placed under casements.

Full directions for obtaining complete working drawings and specifications for these plans will be found on page 281

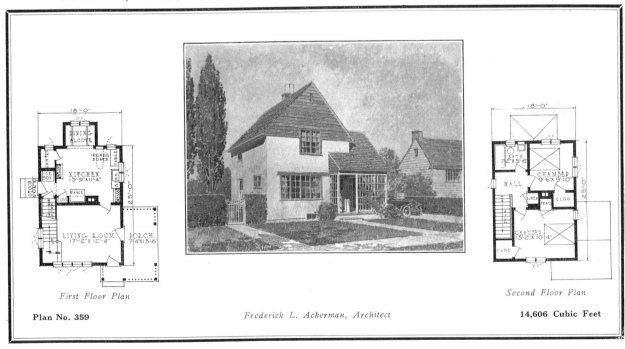

First Floor Plan   *Second Floor Plan*

Plan No. 359   *Frederick L. Ackerman, Architect*   **14,606 Cubic Feet**

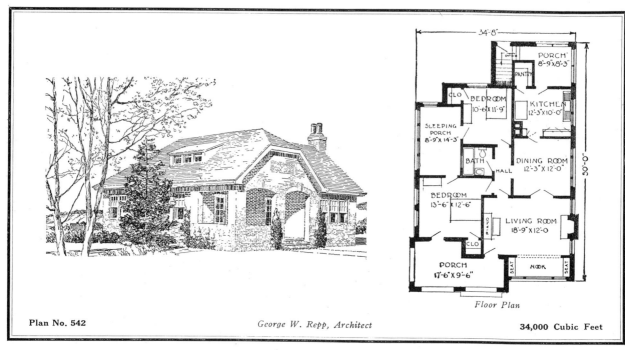

Plan No. 542　　　　　*George W. Repp, Architect*　　　　　**34,000 Cubic Feet**

Floor Plan

(Description of house shown in above plans)　　　　*(Description of house shown in plans below)*

THE exterior of this house is distinctive and un-usual, following English example, and affords an excellent opportunity for the display of charming brickwork. The fine sleeping porch, with its wide expanse of windows is well sheltered within the main body of the house, and may be closed and heated during the day, if so desired. The snug brick fireplace and wide window nook make the living room cozy and comfortable with a pleasant outlook. French doors, a decorative feature in themselves, give privacy to the dining room while still allowing it to be made practically a part of the living room.

ALTHOUGH at first glance this house appears to be built entirely of stucco, the main part of the house is covered with four-inch siding, and the stucco and panel strips are used for decorative purposes, as are the brackets. There are five large rooms in this design, but they do not have the arrangement common to most bungalows. The long living room occupies the entire front of the house, so that it has openings on three sides. The fireplace is desirably located at the narrow end, with bookcases and seat on the sides. Through an inter-room opening one gets a glimpse of a built-in sideboard in the dining room.

Full directions for obtaining complete working drawings and specifications for these plans will be found on page 281

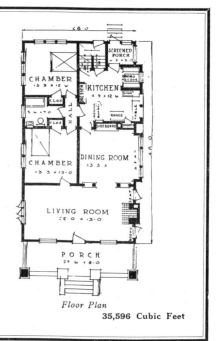

Floor Plan

Plan No. 360　　　　　*Frederick L. Ackerman, Architect*　　　　　**35,596 Cubic Feet**

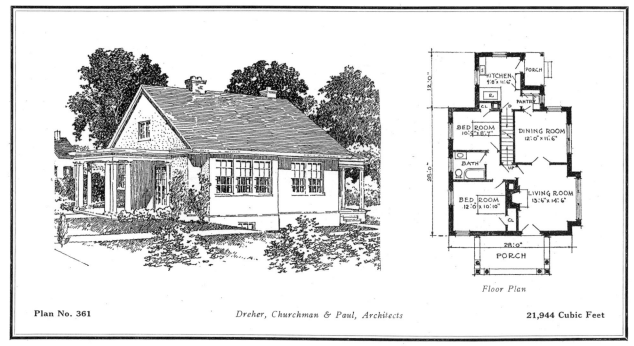

Plan No. 361   *Dreher, Churchman & Paul, Architects*   **21,944 Cubic Feet**

Floor Plan

(Description of house shown in above plans)   *(Description of house shown in plans below)*

THIS little cottage is compact and well planned, and will make a comfortable home. It will be economical to build; for the square, simple character of the plan means efficiency in labor and no waste of material. The living room is entered direct from the porch through French doors, and has a fireplace and triple window set into a square bay, large enough to place a davenport in. The fireplace is on an inside wall to insure maximum conservation of heat and the cellar flue is in the same stack. By combining the dining and living rooms the result would be a fine room over twenty-six feet long. Stucco on concrete blocks.

PRIVACY is suggested by this porch, walled across the front and entered from the side. The house is built of stucco, with brick chimneys and buttresses, and shingle roof. It is only twenty-four feet wide, so will require only a narrow lot, and since it is strictly rectangular in layout, it should be economical to build. Two essentials of a real living room are prominent features here—the fireplace and bookcases. The latter are the pedestals of the inter-room opening between living room and dining room. In the dining room their paneled backs suggest wainscoting, which would be an attractive and inexpensive stock finish.

Full directions for obtaining complete working drawings and specifications for these plans will be found on page 281

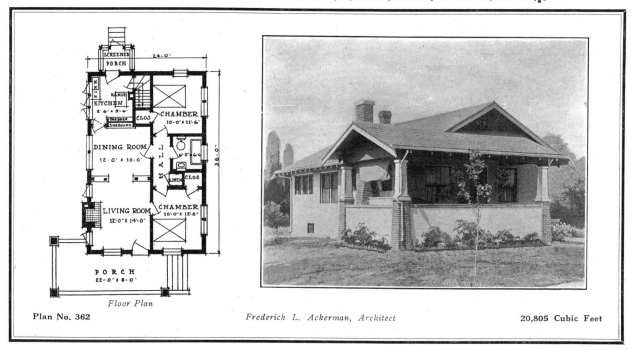

Floor Plan

Plan No. 362   *Frederick L. Ackerman, Architect*   **20,805 Cubic Feet**

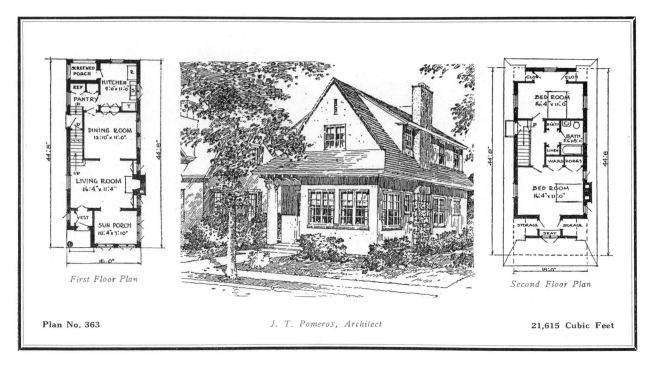

First Floor Plan

Second Floor Plan

Plan No. 363　　　　　　　　*J. T. Pomeroy, Architect*　　　　　　　　**21,615 Cubic Feet**

(Description of house shown in above plans)　　　　　　*(Description of house shown in plans below)*

THIS Dutch Colonial house can be placed very comfortably on a thirty-foot lot, and can be used on a twenty-five-foot lot without crowding. Three features save this house from having a pinched look: First, it is built close to the ground; second, it has lawn on both sides, and third, the skilful handling of the red cement shingle roof, particularly the broad expanse over the front entrance and sun parlor. It is remarkable what spacious rooms have been contrived in this small house. The living room is the full width of the house with fireplace and bookshelves at the end.

HERE is a plan which would solve the narrow-lot problem for many. Although it occupies small ground space this house has all the comforts of a home, even including a reception hall, coat closet, dining alcove and towel closet. The fireplace is the center of interest in the living room and the casements at each side are high enough that permanent bookcases may be built in beneath them. The dining room has double windows on two sides, so that it is light and cheerful. There is a built-in sideboard which may also be utilized as a dresser from the kitchen.

Full directions for obtaining complete working drawings and specifications for these plans will be found on page 281

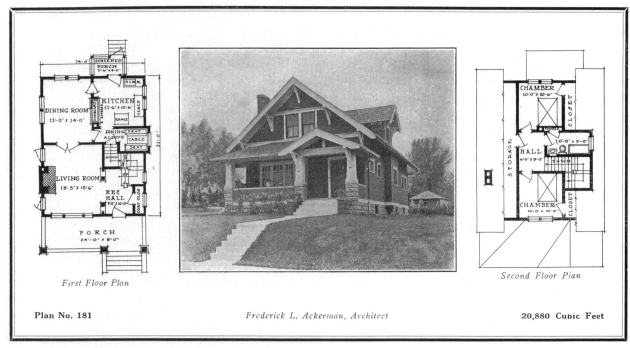

First Floor Plan

Second Floor Plan

Plan No. 181　　　　　　　　*Frederick L. Ackerman, Architect*　　　　　　　　**20,880 Cubic Feet**

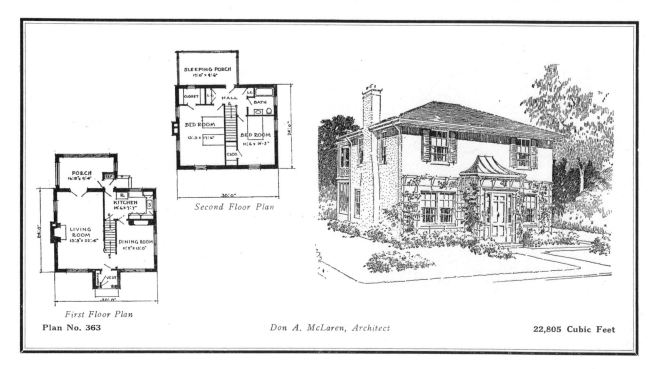

Second Floor Plan

First Floor Plan

Plan No. 363   *Don A. McLaren, Architect*   **22,805 Cubic Feet**

(Description of house shown in above plans)

THE plan of this house is of the popular Colonial type, containing living room the full depth of the house with fireplace on one side and dining room and kitchen on the other. The porch leading from the living room augments the size of this room and if screened in or glazed would be a delightful spot at all times. The larger of the bedrooms has a fine sleeping porch leading from it and both rooms have ample clothes closets. The front entrance, with curved hood and trellis around, gives a striking and individual appearance to the house. Stucco on concrete blocks.

(Description of house shown in plans below)

THE floor plan of this interesting little house includes a small room convenient to the front entrance, which may be used as an office or den. It might also be utilized as an extra bedroom, as it contains a closet which accommodates a disappearing bed. The partition between the living room and dining room is an inter-room opening with bookcases on each side. Directly opposite the opening, in the dining room, is a sideboard which is combined with the kitchen dresser that is set back-to-back with it. A window at the side, above the work-table, affords ample light.

Full directions for obtaining complete working drawings and specifications for these plans will be found on page 281

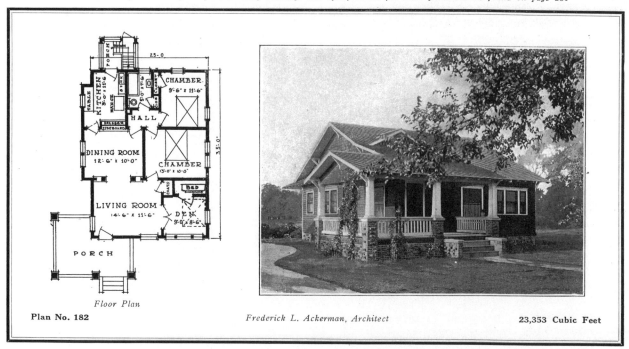

Floor Plan

Plan No. 182   *Frederick L. Ackerman, Architect*   **23,353 Cubic Feet**

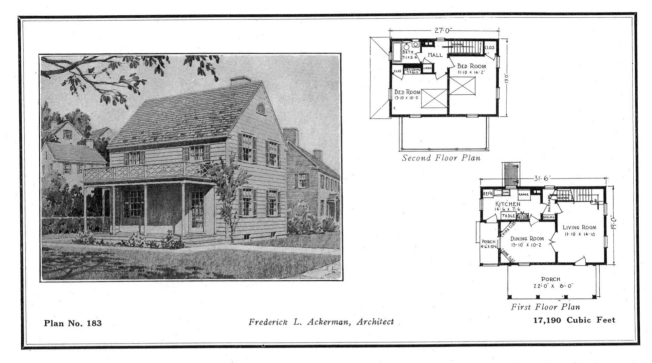

Second Floor Plan

First Floor Plan

Plan No. 183   Frederick L. Ackerman, Architect   17,190 Cubic Feet

(Description of house shown in above plans)

HERE is a small house of the Colonial type which could be placed to advantage on a small lot. Although the dimensions are only nineteen by thirty-one it has been well designed and skillfully planned. The balustrade above the big open porch is characteristic and pretty. The entrance door faces the open stair on the opposite side of the living room, and French doors invite one into the dining room, or one may go directly to the kitchen through a small passage. The most notable feature in the dining room is a pair of Colonial corner china closets.

(Description of house shown in plans below)

HOW charming is this little Dutch Colonial home, and how simple, too! The entrance is well protected from the weather by the wide overhang of the low cornice. A seat and wrought iron lamp adorn the entrance and are balanced by a window on the opposite side. The fireplace and stairway occupy the far end of the living room and a large open porch extends the whole depth of the house, reached from the living room through a French door. There are two large bedrooms together, with bath and closets, on the second floor. Frame construction throughout.

Full directions for obtaining complete working drawings and specifications for these plans will be found on page 281

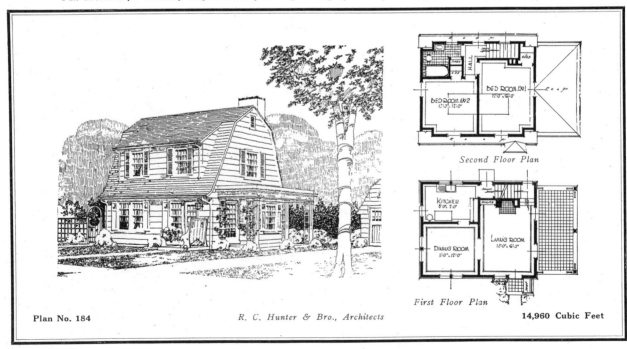

Second Floor Plan

First Floor Plan

Plan No. 184   R. C. Hunter & Bro., Architects   14,960 Cubic Feet

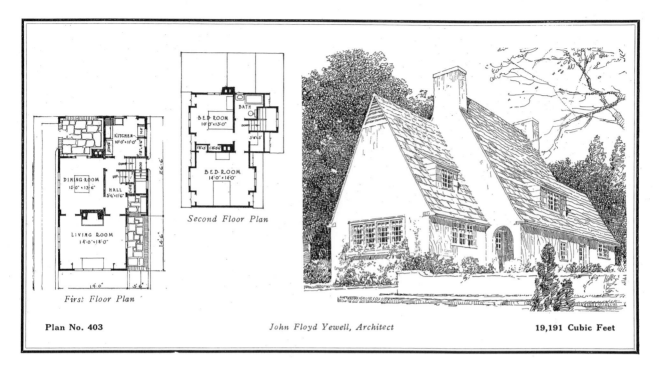

Second Floor Plan

First Floor Plan

Plan No. 403   *John Floyd Yewell, Architect*   **19,191 Cubic Feet**

(Description of house shown in above plans)

THIS five-room house of English cottage type has been designed by the architect in a manner which provides maximum architectural effect. The exterior walls are constructed of back plastered metal lath and stucco. For the exterior color scheme the architect recommends that the roof be of green and purple, the stucco a warm gray and the woodwork painted cream color. Entering across a stone and brick flagged terrace and passing through a small covered porch one finds a fairly large entrance hall with stairs leading up and entrances to dining room and living room.

(Description of house shown in plans below)

IN this type of bungalow, suitable for the narrow city lot, the porch extends the full width of the house but the roof does not, thereby affording plenty of light for the living room. The spacious living room with its wide fireplace at one end has plenty of wall space for furniture and a good coat closet convenient to the entrance. The bedrooms, with good closets, and the bath are well isolated from the principal rooms and have plenty of light and ventilation. As there is no pantry in this plan, the kitchen is provided with a large cupboard and kitchen cabinet.

Full directions for obtaining complete working drawings and specifications for these plans will be found on page 281

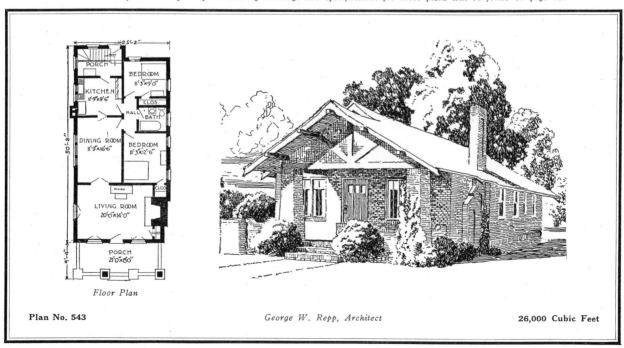

Floor Plan

Plan No. 543   *George W. Repp, Architect*   **26,000 Cubic Feet**

Floor Plan

Plan No. 544   *William Carver, Architect*   **25,642 Cubic Feet**

(*Description of house shown in above plans*)   (*Description of house shown in plans below*)

ADDITIONAL rooms can be provided in this five-room brick bungalow by finishing the attic and introducing dormers for additional windows and head room. The plan shown herewith provides rooms only on the first floor, which is well arranged. A small vestibule with clothes closet is entered from the front porch and leads directly into a combination living room and sun parlor. A central hallway is provided for entrance to the two bedrooms and bath, while kitchen, dining room and living porch are arranged at the rear. Exterior is of common brick.

THE simple roof lines and window arrangement of this bungalow at once attract attention. The entrance leads directly into the living room. This room is L-shaped, with the fireplace so situated as to be enjoyed from both living and dining rooms. In the dining room is a fine, built-in sideboard. The kitchen, at one side of the dining room, is a model of convenience, with good light over the sink, well equipped cupboards, and a built-in garbage incinerator. The bedrooms and bath are well isolated from the rest of the house. Exterior is of face brick.

Full directions for obtaining complete working drawings and specifications for these plans will be found on page 281

Floor Plan

Plan No. 545   *George W. Repp, Architect*   **26,000 Cubic Feet**

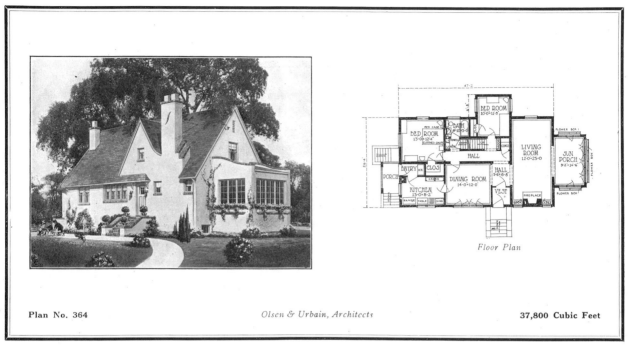

Plan No. 364   *Olsen & Urbain, Architects*   **37,800 Cubic Feet**

Floor Plan

(Description of house shown in above plans)   *(Description of house shown in plans below)*

ESPECIALLY well suited for a suburban district, or for a residential section is this charming, individual English home. The main entrance is at the left side, permitting the full frontage to be used for the living room. A fireplace at the right end of the living room has bookcases on either side of it, with windows overhead, and the sun parlor, leading from this room through a cased opening, adds to the size of the room. Both bedrooms have windows on two sides, giving plenty of light and ventilation, and both have clothes closets. Exterior of stucco on hollow tile.

HERE is a bungalow which is comfortable and homelike in appearance and so planned that it would be possible to obtain three rooms and a bath on the second floor. The arrangement of the first floor is unusual. Note the extent of space from dining room to sun porch, which may be thrown together if desired, or closed off by French doors. The kitchen is well arranged and has three windows. Cabinets in the breakfast room and kitchen take the place of the pantry. There is a garbage incinerator in connection with the kitchen chimney. Exterior is of face brick.

Full directions for obtaining complete working drawings and specifications for these plans will be found on page 281

Plan No. 546   *Geo. W. Repp, Architect*   **37,000 Cubic Feet**
Garage, 3,000 Cubic Feet

Floor Plan

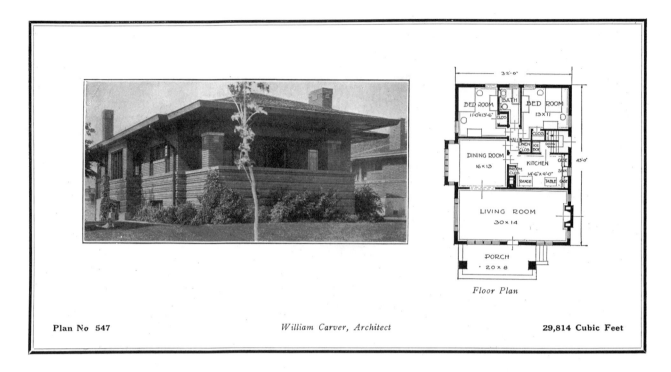

Floor Plan

Plan No 547   *William Carver, Architect*   **29,814 Cubic Feet**

(Description of house shown in above plans)

A TYPE of five-room bungalow which is particularly popular in the West. The exterior walls are constructed of common brick laid in a series of extending courses to provide an unusually interesting pattern. The large front porch with wide overhanging eaves adds considerably to the visual size. An unusually large living room is provided. The kitchen and service section is well arranged. The dining room has an interesting window seat with casement windows.

(Description of house shown in plans below)

HERE is an attractive bungalow of the southern type. This house could be built on a sixty-foot lot with room for a driveway. Corner posts and gate posts of the same brickwork as in the house would serve to tie the house into the landscape. The living room is well situated to command the view toward the front. It opens to a fine porch. The kitchen is compact, well lighted, and conveniently arranged. There are two comfortable bedrooms.

Full directions for obtaining complete working drawings and specifications for these plans will be found on page 281

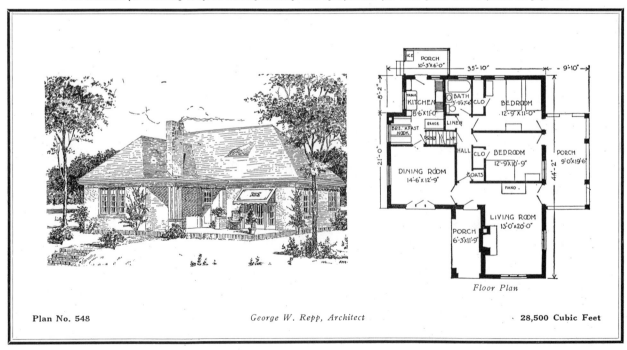

Floor Plan

Plan No. 548   *George W. Repp, Architect*   **28,500 Cubic Feet**

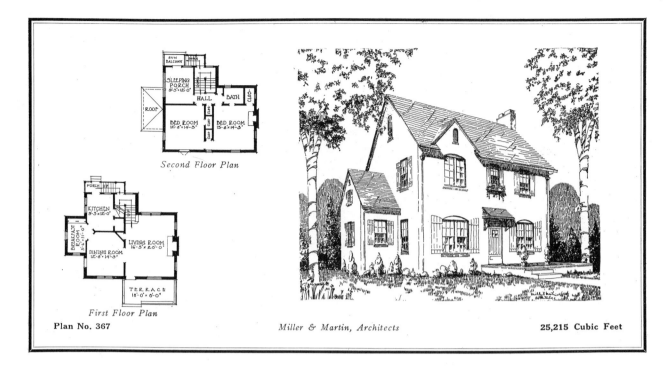

Second Floor Plan

First Floor Plan

Plan No. 367   *Miller & Martin, Architects*   **25,215 Cubic Feet**

(Description of house shown in above plans)

THIS design is an American expression of the English cottage. As pictured it is built of hollow tile or concrete blocks and stuccoed, but would be equally as attractive if built of brick or stone. The house is comparatively small in plan yet gives rooms of excellent size and shape on both floors. There are two added features in this house that ought not be overlooked. They are the convenient breakfast room on the first floor and the airy sleeping porch on the second, conveniently reached from all the bedrooms.

(Description of house shown in plans below)

THERE is a suggestion of the Swiss chalet in the vertical clapboards and stucco, and the second-story overhang of this home. Brackets and rafter ends embellish its simple exterior. The large dormer makes it possible to have three bedrooms upstairs. The formal dining room is replaced in this design by a practical dining alcove with permanent table and benches. It opens directly off the front hall, which is just wide enough for the coat closet. A hanging china closet decorates one wall of the living room.

Full directions for obtaining complete working drawings and specifications for these plans will be found on page 281

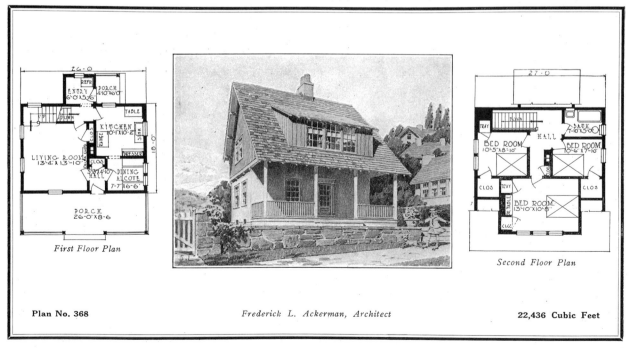

First Floor Plan

Second Floor Plan

Plan No. 368   *Frederick L. Ackerman, Architect*   **22,436 Cubic Feet**

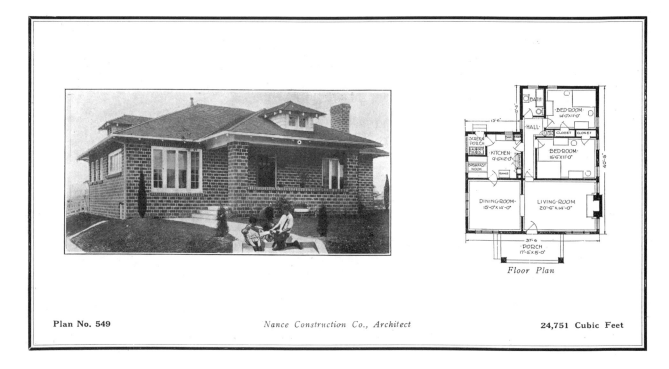

Plan No. 549   *Nance Construction Co., Architect*   **24,751 Cubic Feet**

(Description of house shown in above plans)

HERE is a carefully planned bungalow, having exterior walls (hollow) of common brick. The construction is simplified and cost consequently reduced by compact arrangement and unbroken wall and partition lines. The house contains five rooms and bath. Living room is entered directly from porch and has open brick fireplace flanked by windows. Bedrooms and bath are arranged in a well-separated unit. Kitchen is well arranged with attractive breakfast nook.

(Description of house shown in plans below)

IT is hard to find an ideal plan for the narrow lot, as the problems to be solved are many. However, this plan will be found as near ideal as can be hoped for. The entrance and kitchen have been placed about the middle of the house, thus leaving both ends free for light and air. The treatment of the exterior is very simple. Note the pleasing effect of the soldier courses running about the house. The low-pitched roof has ventilating dormers on the four sides.

Full directions for obtaining complete working drawings and specifications for these plans will be found on page 281

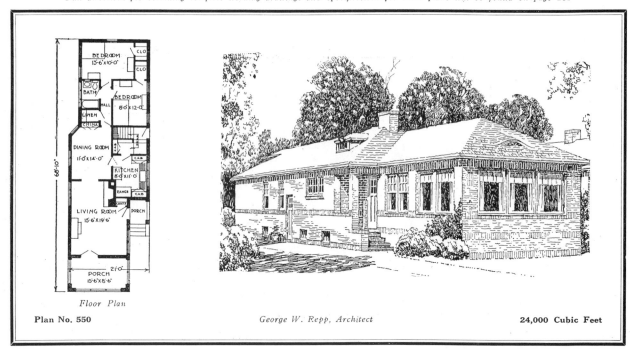

Floor Plan

Plan No. 550   *George W. Repp, Architect*   **24,000 Cubic Feet**

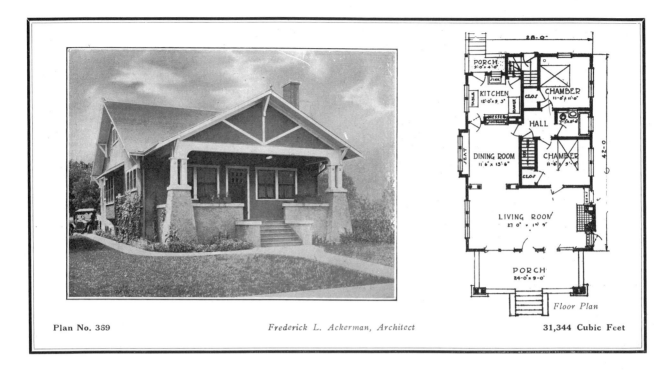

Plan No. 389   *Frederick L. Ackerman, Architect*   31,344 Cubic Feet

Floor Plan

(Description of house shown in above plans)

HERE is another design in which the living room extends across the entire front of the house. In this case there are openings on three sides and to make it even more livable, there is a fireplace, flanked by a bookcase and window seat. At the narrow end of the room these simplify the furnishings of the room and leave much space for the other furniture. The two bedrooms are comfortable but not overly large. The construction is of stucco on wood sheathing.

(Description of house shown in plans below)

THIS typical Western five-room bungalow seems to nestle snugly down to the ground and should appeal to those wishing a low, restful feeling in their home. The low horizontal effect is not only attractive but is economical in that it reduces the height of the exterior wall. Although the illustration shows this bungalow on a level site it would be as suitable for a lot that slopes toward the rear, as simple plan changes can be made at the rear entrance to permit this.

Full directions for obtaining complete working drawings and specifications for these plans will be found on page 281

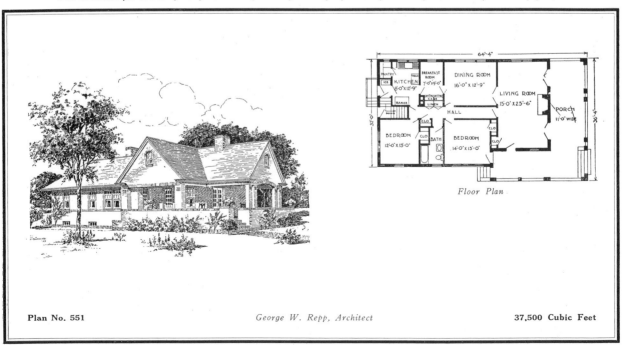

Floor Plan

Plan No. 551   *George W. Repp, Architect*   37,500 Cubic Feet

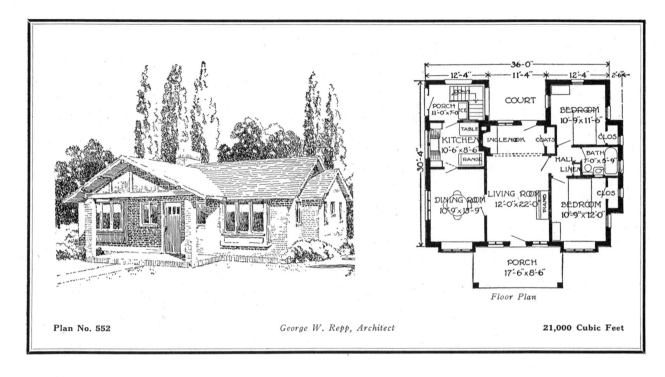

Plan No. 552   *George W. Repp, Architect*   **21,000 Cubic Feet**

Floor Plan

(Description of house shown in above plans)

AN attractive face brick bungalow containing five rooms and bath. The roof of this house should be of masonry or slate surfaced shingles. Interesting features of this plan include a fireplace with large ingle-nook arranged as an extension of the living room. The living quarters of the house are well separated from sleeping rooms. An enclosed entry porch adds to the convenience of the kitchen. Bedrooms have ample closet space with a window in each closet.

(Description of house shown in plans below)

THIS is a simple, easily constructed five-room frame cottage. Exterior walls call for wood shingles with 10″ to the weather. Shingles and trim to be painted white; shutters dark green and roof shingles grayish green. The living room is arranged with open fireplace flanked by French doors opening on to a large living porch. Small entry porch is provided and stairs lead up from a narrow central hall to the second floor containing two large, light bedrooms and bath.

Full directions for obtaining complete working drawings and specifications for these plans will be found on page 281

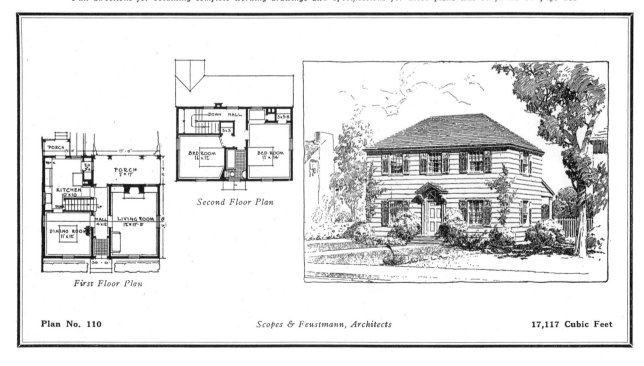

Second Floor Plan

First Floor Plan

Plan No. 110   *Scopes & Feustmann, Architects*   **17,117 Cubic Feet**

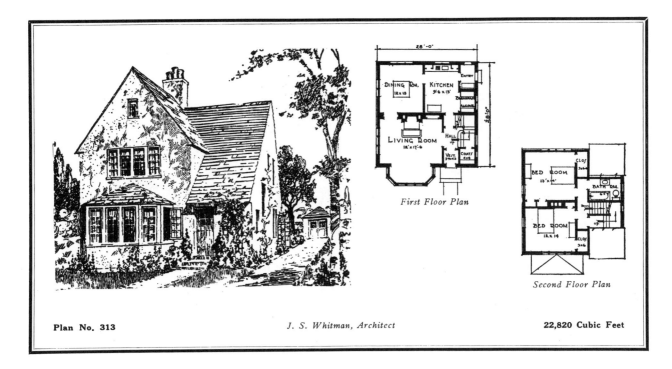

First Floor Plan

Second Floor Plan

Plan No. 313   *J. S. Whitman, Architect*   **22,820 Cubic Feet**

(Description of house shown in above plans)

A FIVE-ROOM house of English cottage type. Exterior walls of stucco on back plastered metal lath. It is recommended that the stucco be applied rough, leaving trowel marks for pattern. Roof to be of weathered green slate or stained shingles and laid rough. Entrance door of weathered oak with iron strap hinges; entrance and curbing of brick. The living room is designed in an interesting manner with large bay containing seven windows.

(Description of house shown in plans below)

THIS is a popular design for a brick house, offering unusual architectural charm. It is recommended that roof be of green and purple slate; brickwork to be of dull red and exterior woodwork painted in French gray. Entrance door of oak. The living room and dining room are separated by a wide arch, allowing a clear vista through to the rear garden. The stairs lead up from a small entry hall to the second floor, containing two large bedrooms and tiled bath.

Full directions for obtaining complete working drawings and specifications for these plans will be found on page 281

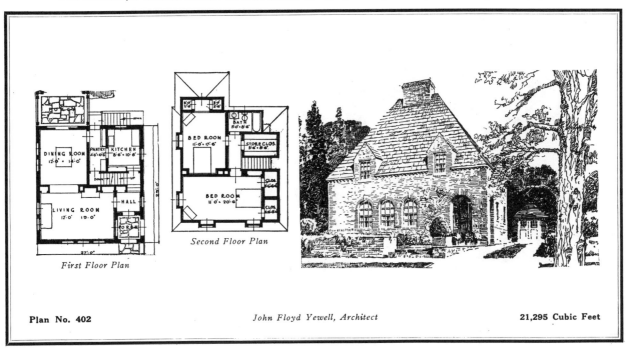

First Floor Plan

Second Floor Plan

Plan No. 402   *John Floyd Yewell, Architect*   **21,295 Cubic Feet**

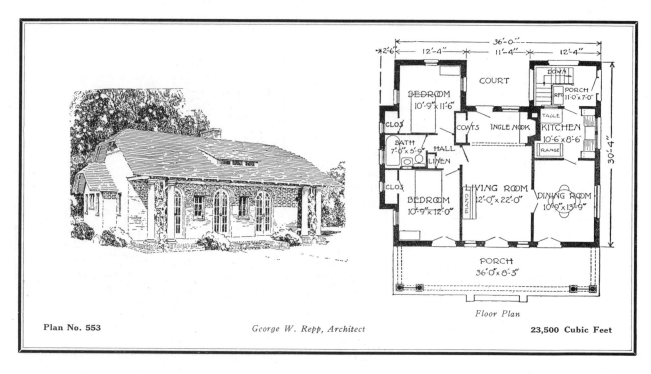

Plan No. 553   *George W. Repp, Architect*   **23,500 Cubic Feet**

(*Description of house shown in above plans*)

IN this attractive Colonial design the living room has both front and rear exposure, thereby permitting the house to face north without losing the cheerful sunlight in the living room. The floor plan is conveniently arranged, the living centrally located, separating the bedrooms from the kitchen and dining room. This room opens from the living room with a pair of French doors. The kitchen is compact and convenient with cupboards built in at both sides of the well-lighted sink. Exterior walls of face brick.

(*Description of house shown in plans below*)

HERE is a handsome little bungalow in which an individual touch is given by the quaintly gabled roof and the paneling in the upper half of all the windows, even those of the attic. The floor plan is well arranged with the sleeping quarters segregated in the rear of the house. Each bedroom has a clothes closet, and the attic, which reaches from one end of the house to the other, will afford ample storage accommodation. The basement also has plenty of storage space. Exterior walls of stucco on hollow tile.

Full directions for obtaining complete working drawings and specifications for these plans will be found on page 281

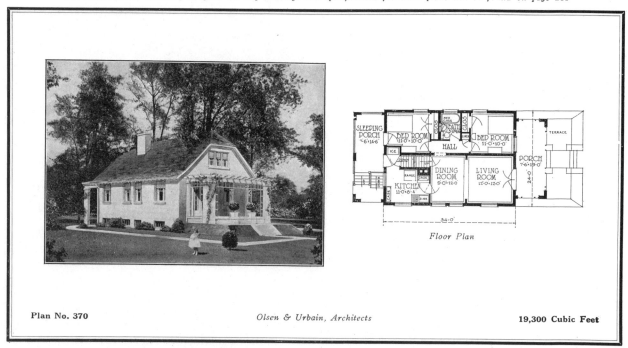

Plan No. 370   *Olsen & Urbain, Architects*   **19,300 Cubic Feet**

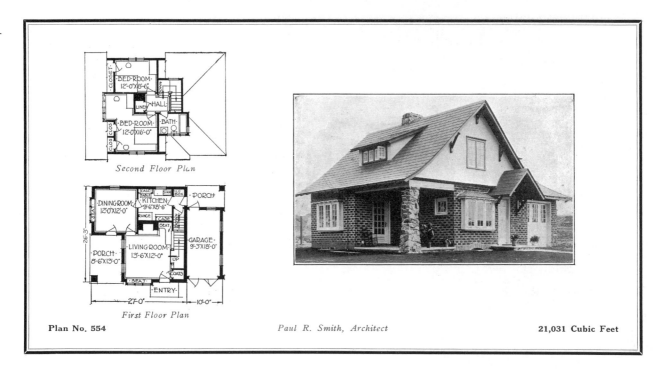

Second Floor Plan

First Floor Plan

Plan No. 554   *Paul R. Smith, Architect*   **21,031 Cubic Feet**

(Description of house shown in above plans)

A N interesting combination of materials for exterior purposes is shown in this attractive five-room house. The walls of the first floor are of common brick laid with wide white mortar joints. The gables are of white stucco on brick, while stone is introduced in the heavy corner column. Roof may be of slate, asbestos cement or patented shingles. This use of various materials provides an excellent opportunity to introduce an interesting combination of texture, pattern and color, providing a pleasing exterior.

(Description of house shown in plans below)

B ROAD and low, imparting its coolness to the balance of the house, the porch is here the dominant feature. Extending across the front of the house, the living and dining rooms, separated only by a colonnade, make one spacious room. At the end of the living room and flanked by bookcases, is the open fireplace. The bedroom and bath are isolated from the main rooms yet connected with the kitchen. The sleeping porch has a closet that will accommodate a disappearing bed. Exterior is of face brick.

Full directions for obtaining complete working drawings and specifications for these plans will be found on page 281

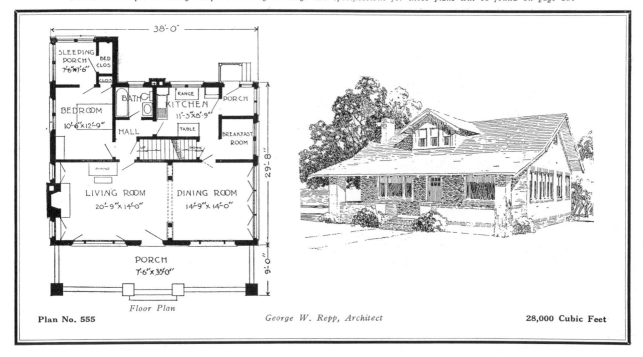

Floor Plan

Plan No. 555   *George W. Repp, Architect*   **28,000 Cubic Feet**

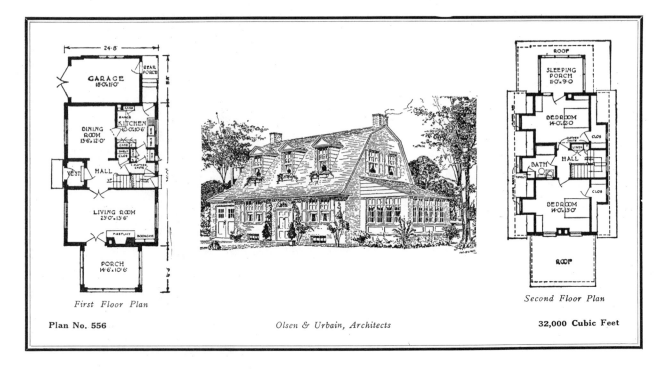

First Floor Plan

Second Floor Plan

Plan No. 556   *Olsen & Urbain, Architects*   32,000 **Cubic Feet**

(Description of house shown in above plans)

HERE is an example of a Dutch Colonial five-room house which is quaint and charming. The sheltering eaves give a low one-story effect, while the graceful gambrel roof makes good second-story rooms possible. Flemish or English cross bond treatment of the brickwork with a flush cut mortar joint that contrasts in color with the brick, would be most appropriate and effective. The garage is built in connection with and heated from the house. One may enter it from the outside by way of the back porch under cover.

(Description of house shown in plans below)

THIS plan combines many popular features. The living room occupies one end of the house and obtains good light and excellent outlook on three sides. The cheerful fireplace, with the adjacent built-in book shelves, will become the heart of the home. Double French doors open from the living room to the porch, and a wide opening leads to the hall. On the second floor there are two good bedrooms, each occupying an end of the house, and a sleeping porch at one end is an added feature. Exterior is of face brick.

Full directions for obtaining complete working drawings and specifications for these plans will be found on page 281

First Floor Plan

Second Floor Plan

Plan No. 557   *Olsen & Urbain, Architects*   32,000 **Cubic Feet**

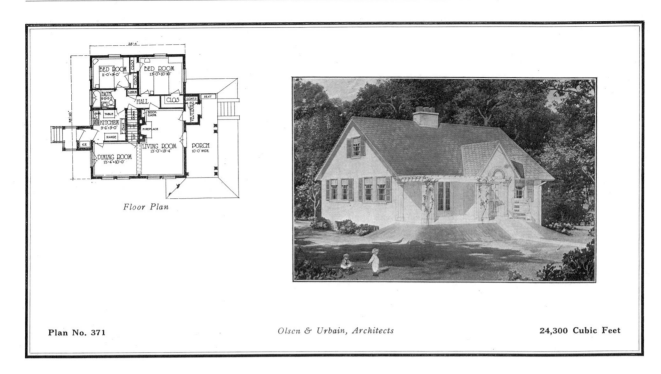

Floor Plan

Plan No. 371   *Olsen & Urbain, Architects*   **24,300 Cubic Feet**

(Description of house shown in above plans)

HERE is a five-room cottage of the Colonial type, which is very popular. The deep gabled roof continues across the front of the house over the open porch, its breadth most effectively broken by the gabled hood over the entrance vestibule. The floor plan has been splendidly arranged. The rooms are all light and well ventilated, with plenty of closet space. An attractive feature of the living room is the handsome brick-trimmed open fireplace with a bookcase to the right of it, opposite the entrance vestibule.

(Description of house shown in plans below)

THE twin-gabled porch of this attractive Colonial bungalow adds a distinctive touch to the pleasing proportions and roof lines. No other ornamentation is necessary than that obtained by a good brick bond and a well-considered color scheme of brickwork and mortar joint. A large closet at the end of the living room holds a disappearing bed, which will prove to be very convenient for an occasional guest. The small hall which communicates with bedroom, bath, and kitchen is conveniently located and has a linen closet.

Full directions for obtaining complete working drawings and specifications for these plans will be found on page 281

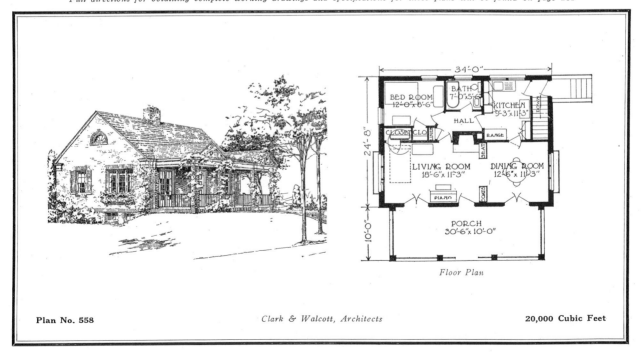

Floor Plan

Plan No. 558   *Clark & Walcott, Architects*   **20,000 Cubic Feet**

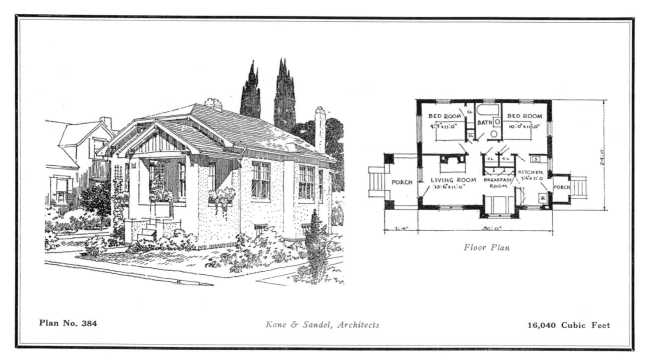

Plan No. 384   *Kane & Sandel, Architects*   **16,040 Cubic Feet**

Floor Plan

(Description of house shown in above plans)

ALTHOUGH this house is small and compact, it contains all the comforts and conveniences of the modern home, and can be built at a minimum of cost. It is so planned that it can easily be added to, making a larger home as the family grows. From the well shaded front porch with its massive piers and half timbered gable one enters a comfortable living room with a good fireplace. Instead of a dining room the architects have planned one of the popular breakfast nooks, just large enough for four, with china closets and cupboards facing. Stucco on concrete blocks.

(Description of house shown in plans below)

ALL the essentials for comfortable living have been incorporated within the walls of this attractive little English bungalow. There is a fine fireplace in the corner of the living room as well as built-in bookcases on the sides of the entrance from the porch, which add considerably to the decoration of the room. A large closet off the living room accommodates a disappearing bed, which really adds another bedroom. Two good corner bedrooms with closets and a connecting hall are arranged on one side of the house and from this hall open the stairs to the basement.

Full directions for obtaining complete working drawings and specifications for these plans will be found on page 281

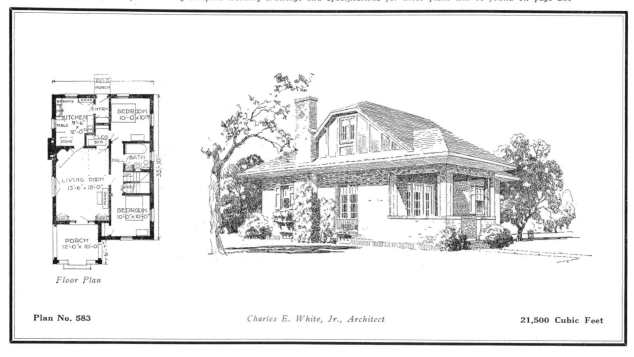

Floor Plan

Plan No. 583   *Charles E. White, Jr., Architect*   **21,500 Cubic Feet**

First Floor Plan

Second Floor Plan

Plan No. 385   *Dean & Dean, Architects*   **21,044 Cubic Feet**

(Description of house shown in above plans)   *(Description of house shown in plans below)*

IN this house the heavy overhang of the roof, so typical of western design, gives an air of warmth, security and comfort. The entrance hall is entered direct from both kitchen and living room, and there is a coat closet on the first floor landing. An attractive feature of the living room is the corner fireplace with handsome brick mantel. Archways separate the dining room and living room, but if desired these two rooms could be combined at a slight saving in construction cost. The kitchen is well supplied with closets, and has a pantry and rear entry under a lean-to at the back.

ALL the advantages of the regular bungalow plan are incorporated in this cottage. It may be built of brick or siding, although it is illustrated in stucco. The wide side of the house is toward the street, so that a very shallow lot may be used. This allows the placing of the kitchen at the front of the house, together with the living room and dining room, so that the sleeping quarters are well isolated on the opposite side of the house. The living room and dining room are practically one long room, with the inter-room opening between them.

Full directions for obtaining complete working drawings and specifications for these plans will be found on page 281

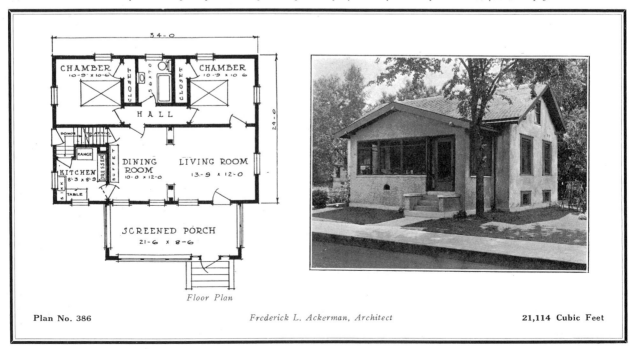

Floor Plan

Plan No. 386   *Frederick L. Ackerman, Architect*   **21,114 Cubic Feet**

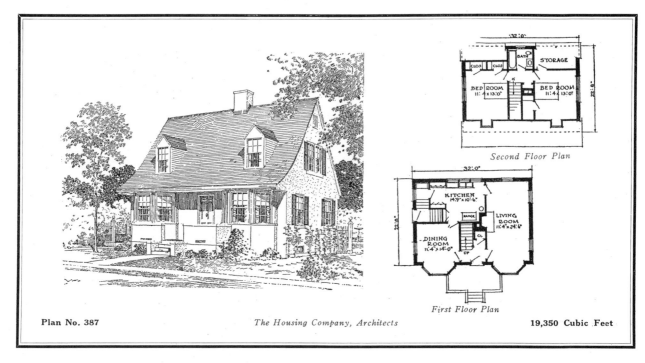

Plan No. 387   *The Housing Company, Architects*   **19,350 Cubic Feet**

(Description of house shown in above plans)

THIS five-room house, of English type, represents a maximum in comfort, space and beauty for a minimum cost. Entering the hall we pass into a long living room with a fine fireplace and windows on three sides. On the other side of the hall is a dining room with a kitchen of good size leading from it. The rear entrance and cellar steps lead from the kitchen. Upstairs are two good bedrooms lighted on both sides, and both have large closets. This house would look equally well on a wide suburban lot, a narrow city street or in the country. Stucco and frame.

(Description of house shown in plans below)

THIS house could be placed on a forty-foot lot, yet it has five large rooms, and is as well arranged and planned as many houses that occupy a great deal more ground space. The living room occupies the entire front half of the first floor, thus it has light from the three sides. Opposite the bay at the front, with its built-in seat, is the open stair. The dining room door is just at the foot of the stair and the kitchen is reached from the other end of the room, so that the stair is easily accessible to all of them. Built-in corner china closets contribute charm to the dining room.

Full directions for obtaining complete working drawings and specifications for these plans will be found on page 281

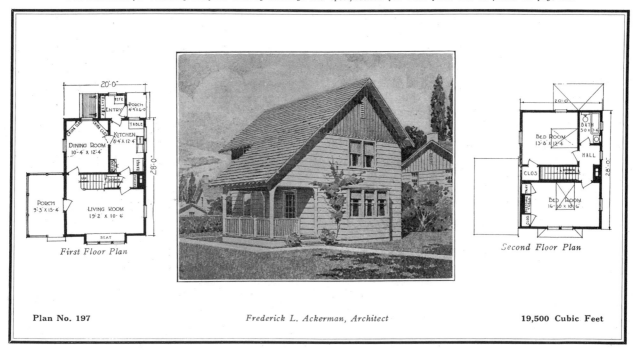

Plan No. 197   *Frederick L. Ackerman, Architect*   **19,500 Cubic Feet**

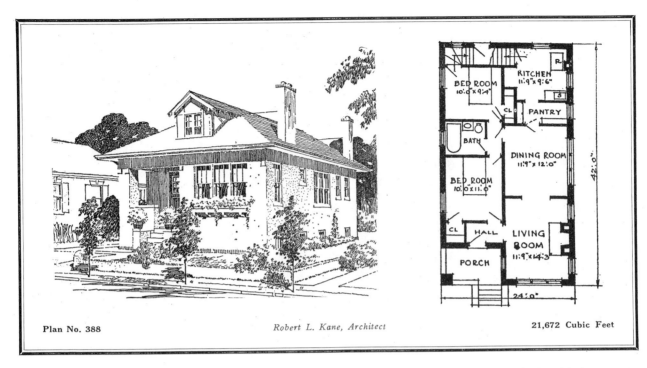

Plan No. 388   *Robert L. Kane, Architect*   21,672 Cubic Feet

(Description of house shown in above plans)

(Description of house shown in plans below)

HERE is a plan that is very popular. The roof extends over the porch and makes it part of the main structure. It has a concrete floor and steps and although it is shown open, can be enclosed and glazed if desired, making a permanent sun parlor. From the porch one enters a small reception hall into the living room. This has a front bay with windows on three sides, insuring plenty of light, and an inviting brick fireplace adds a decorative feature. The dining and living rooms could be used as one long room in which case the pantry could be used as a breakfast nook.

A DECORATIVE effect is obtained in this five-room home by color-contrast in the painting. Because of the plain lines and simple roof this should be an economical house to build. The front porch is a pleasant outdoor living room; from it a door with sidelights forms the entrance to the reception hall. This hall has a door to the front bedroom, and a cased opening connects it with the living room. A double-acting door permits easy passage between the bright dining room and the kitchen, a room so small and compact that it saves many steps.

Full directions for obtaining complete working drawings and specifications for these plans will be found on page 281

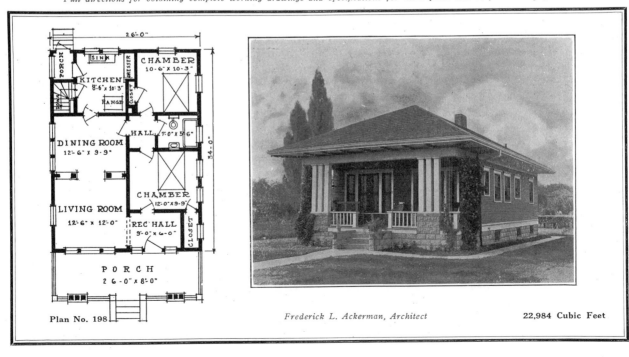

Plan No. 198   *Frederick L. Ackerman, Architect*   22,984 Cubic Feet

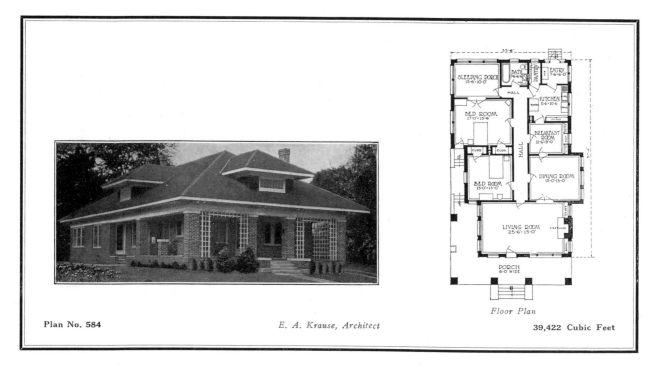

Plan No. 584   *E. A. Krause, Architect*   **39,422 Cubic Feet**

Floor Plan

(Description of house shown in above plans)

THIS brick bungalow has five main rooms and in addition a sleeping porch and breakfast room which, on account of their size, might be considered as rooms. The living room is very large and light, and is entered from the large porch which extends on two of its sides. A central hall through the house gives access to all the rooms. Although as shown no provision has been made for a cellar, the plan could easily be altered to include this portion in climates where it is necessary. Exterior walls of common brick.

(Description of house shown in plans below)

HERE is an interesting exterior in which there are two open terraces. One of the gabled porches could be glazed and turned into a sun parlor if desired. From the side porch the main entrance door leads into the large living room with a coat closet close at hand. This room is splendidly lighted on three sides, and has a fine brick fireplace on the broad side. Opposite the fireplace French doors lead to the dining room. Between the dining room and kitchen is a breakfast room with a china cabinet. Face brick.

Full directions for obtaining complete working drawings and specifications for these plans will be found on page 281

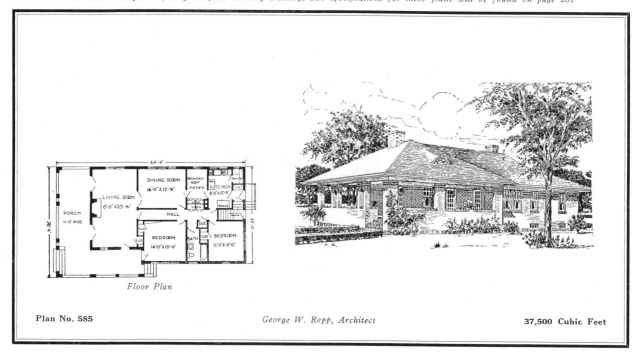

Floor Plan

Plan No. 585   *George W. Repp, Architect*   **37,500 Cubic Feet**

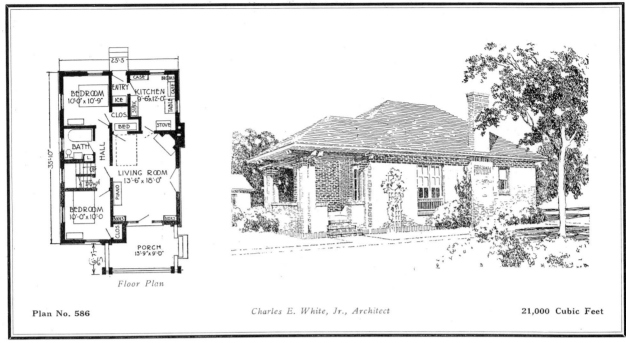

Floor Plan

Plan No. 586   *Charles E. White, Jr., Architect*   **21,000 Cubic Feet**

(Description of house shown in above plans)   *(Description of house shown in plans below)*

THE fine chimney, the simple and attractive roof lines, the fenestration and the brick steps leading to the outside vestibule, combine here in a very pleasing whole. The floor plan has been carefully worked out. The living room, well lighted and ventilated, has a cheery fireplace in the corner, while a large closet off the living room accommodates a disappearing bed, which really adds another bedroom. The kitchen is equipped with two large cabinets, extending to the ceiling, taking the place of the pantry. The entrance from the porch to the living room is flanked by bookcases and with the fireplace in the opposite corner.

A LOW, homey appearance is produced in this house by having the wide side to the front. The exterior shows the use of stucco to the sill-line, siding above, and shingles in the gables and roof. Windows with sash divided to match the front door, form sidelights for the entrance. The long living room to which the entrance admits receives light indirectly from a third side, through the inter-room opening which separates it from the dining room. The wide window stool below triple windows in the dining room bay is a charming place for a row of potted plants. The kitchen is small, compact and well-equipped.

Full directions for obtaining complete working drawings and specifications for these plans will be found on page 281

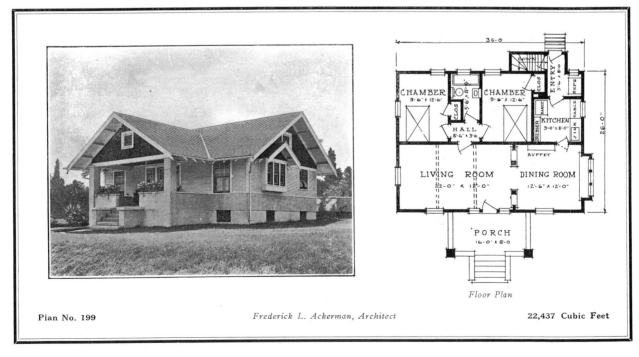

Floor Plan

Plan No. 199   *Frederick L. Ackerman, Architect*   **22,437 Cubic Feet**

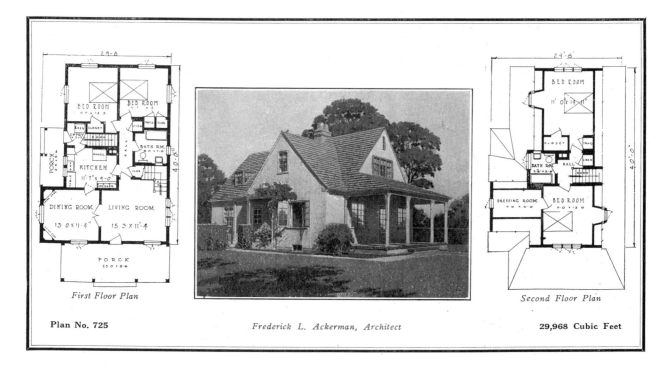

First Floor Plan

Second Floor Plan

Plan No. 725   *Frederick L. Ackerman, Architect*   **29,968 Cubic Feet**

(Description of house shown in above plans)

VERY often a downstairs bedroom and bathroom are a great convenience, especially where there are children or elderly people in the family. Being at the back of the house in this plan, they are undisturbed by the noise of the street and enjoy privacy from the day portion of the house. Two upstairs bedrooms, a second bathroom and a large dressing room supplement the downstairs sleeping rooms. The open stairs is located in the living room.

(Description of house shown in plans below)

THIS type of bungalow is very popular in California and some southern states, and is rapidly spreading east. The contrasting color tones of a red or a green tile roof against the cream tinted stucco walls and piers, set off by the painted woodwork of the pergola and the red brick window sills, base course and chimney cap, will give a pleasant appearance to this house. The interior arrangement is very attractive and includes many unusual features.

Full directions for obtaining complete working drawings and specifications for these plans will be found on page 281

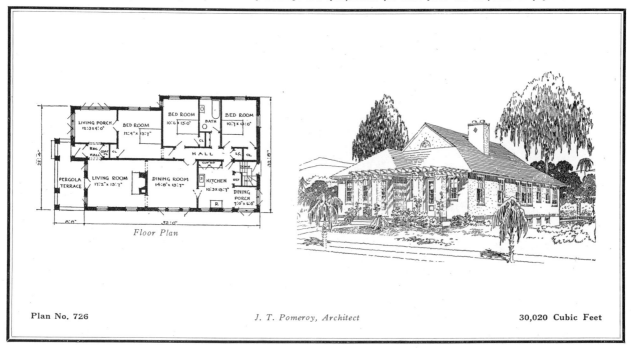

Floor Plan

Plan No. 726   *J. T. Pomeroy, Architect*   **30,020 Cubic Feet**

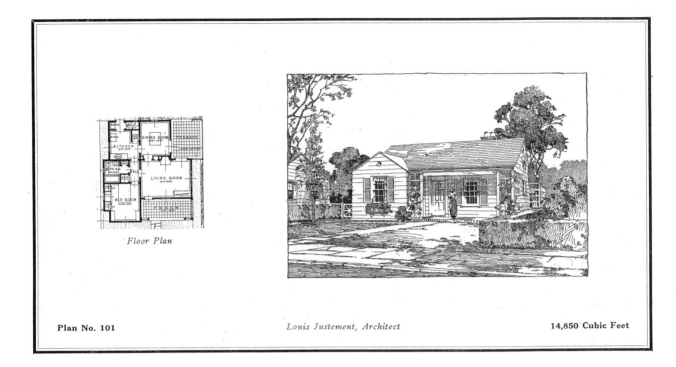

Floor Plan

Plan No. 101   *Louis Justement, Architect*   **14,850 Cubic Feet**

(Description of house shown in above plans)

THIS frame house with exterior walls of wide siding is planned along bungalow lines and is attractively designed in simple Colonial style. Entrance is directly into the living room which is generous in size. Beside the fireplace in the living room is a French window opening onto a terrace which overlooks the rear of the lot where a simple garden treatment could be carried out. The dining room also faces the garden and has a French window opening on terrace.

(Description of house shown in plans below)

HERE is another of the popular English type of houses with exterior walls of stucco. A porch entirely glazed in, and included under the sweep of the main roof, becomes really a sixth room and is usable the year round. The layout is almost square and the simple treatment of the exterior, and sound construction, make it an economical home. The five rooms are of good average size and in addition there is a large storage space in the attic.

Full directions for obtaining complete working drawings and specifications for these plans will be found on page 281

First Floor Plan   *Second Floor Plan*

Plan No. 396   *Frederick L. Ackerman, Architect*   **20,558 Cubic Feet**

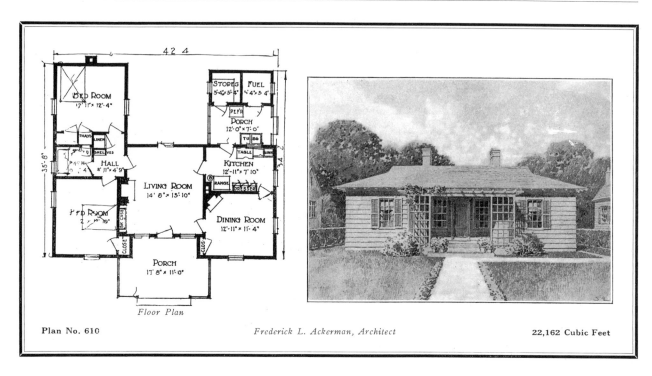

Plan No. 610   *Frederick L. Ackerman, Architect*   **22,162 Cubic Feet**

Floor Plan

(*Description of house shown in above plans*)

HERE is a frame bungalow which has been economically designed but which gives a maximum
amount of privacy and convenience in a one-story arrangement. Each room has outside openings on two
sides to make it airy and light, while shutters and wide
eaves protect the interior from the direct rays of the
sun, and there are long wall spaces for furniture.
There are plenty of closets and cupboards, which are
a necessity when there is neither attic nor basement.
Bedrooms are large and supplied with ample closets.

(*Description of house shown in plans below*)

ALTHOUGH this is only a four-room cottage it has
real architectural merit. Its exterior type of
wide siding painted white is Colonial. The simple
rectangular layout, plain hip roof and the omission
of any unnecessary ornamentation, make it economical
to build. The front entrance admits directly to the
living room, at the right of the house. Beyond is the
dining room, a pleasant corner room with a pair of
corner china closets. At the left are the bedroom and
kitchen with bathroom between.

Full directions for obtaining complete working drawings and specifications for these plans will be found on page 281

Floor Plan

Plan No. 611   *Frederick L. Ackerman, Architect*   **21,437 Cubic Feet**

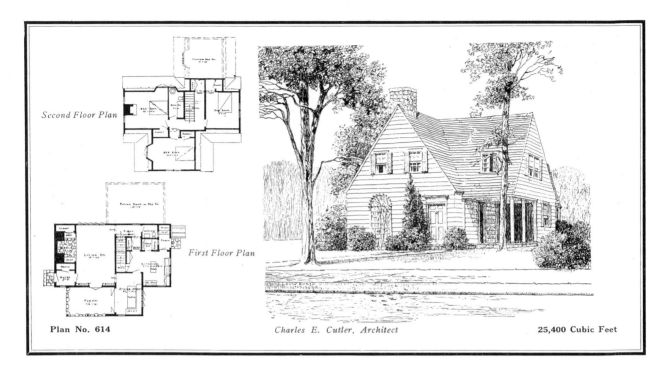

Second Floor Plan

First Floor Plan

Plan No. 614   *Charles E. Cutler, Architect*   **25,400 Cubic Feet**

(Description of house shown in above plans)   *(Description of house shown in plans below)*

THE exterior of this five-room frame house is very attractive. It could occupy any site, fitting a sloping lot equally as well as a level one, and it has the further advantage of affording a choice of positions with reference to street frontage. The exterior walls are of wide siding with roof of shingles. The living room has an open fireplace with stone hearth set in an ingle-nook, and on each side of the door leading to the porch there is a built-in bookcase. The lavatory on first floor is a convenient feature.

THIS house shows the inspiration of the English cottage in its architecture and is both unique and pleasing. The construction is of stucco on back-plastered metal lath. Entrance is through a vestibule with large closet, the stairs starting opposite the doorway to the living room. The plan shows one large room to serve both living and dining purposes. The bay window near fireplace affords a pleasant feature for the living room end, and the three windows an attractive note for the dining room end.

Full directions for obtaining complete working drawings and specifications for these plans will be found on page 281

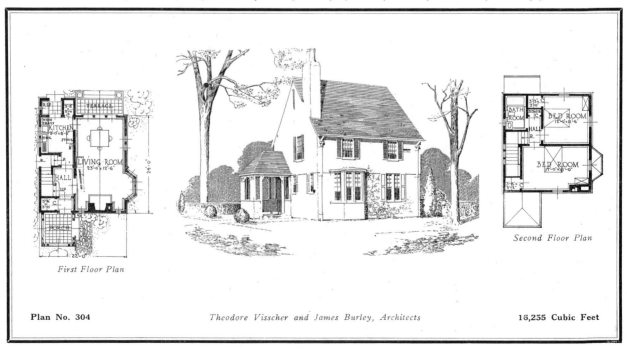

First Floor Plan

Second Floor Plan

Plan No. 304   *Theodore Visscher and James Burley, Architects*   **16,255 Cubic Feet**

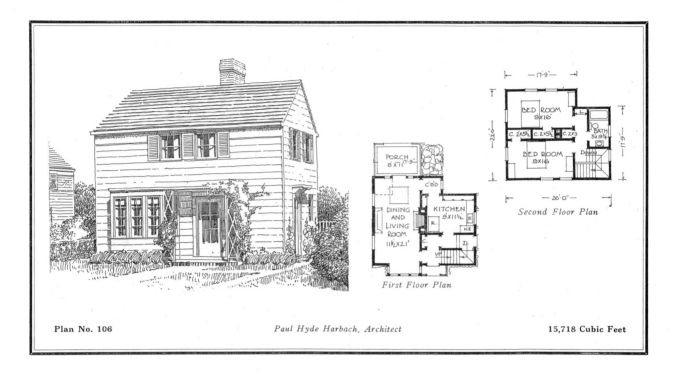

Plan No. 106   *Paul Hyde Harbach, Architect*   15,718 Cubic Feet

(Description of house shown in above plans)

THIS is a simple, economical type of Colonial design, using frame construction throughout, and with exterior of wide siding. The architect suggests that this siding be of 10-inch, rabbetted type, to give a thin exposed edge. The siding, trim and sash to be painted white, and blinds light blue-green. Selected common brick with half-inch flush struck joints to be used for the base, entrance platform and chimney. First floor contains a large combination living and dining room and has an open brick fireplace.

(Description of house shown in plans below)

THIS is an unusually attractive bungalow with exterior of common brick and roof of slate. There is a high living room of studio type lighted by one unusually large window at the end and small casing in the side. The dining room and sun room are planned together to provide an attractive vista; or the sun room can be used as a breakfast room. There are two bedrooms and bath connected by a small hall and well separated from living quarters. Careful but inexpensive planting adds considerable value.

Full directions for obtaining complete working drawings and specifications for these plans will be found on page 281

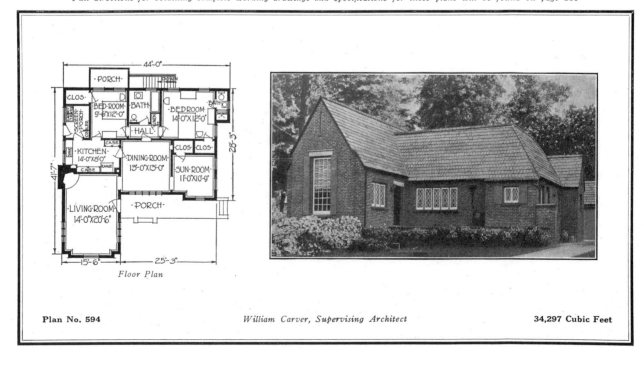

Plan No. 594   *William Carver, Supervising Architect*   34,297 Cubic Feet

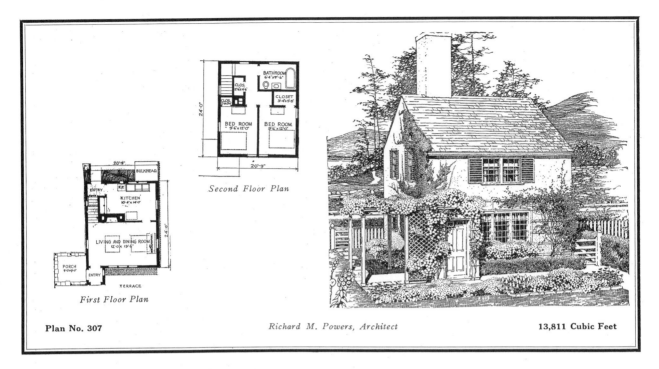

Second Floor Plan

First Floor Plan

Plan No. 307   *Richard M. Powers, Architect*   **13,811 Cubic Feet**

(Description of house shown in above plans)

THIS attractive four-room home has exterior walls of stucco on back-plastered metal lath. The architect suggests that roof be covered with shingle tile, fire-flashed. Exterior walls to be of white Portland cement with uneven surface, hand-floated with a steel trowel. Sash, doors, all exterior finish and lattice to be painted cream white. Blinds to be painted pea green. The combination living and dining room extends across the front of the house. It is well lighted on three sides, and has an attractive fireplace.

(Description of house shown in plans below)

HERE is a five-room house which may be built on a forty-foot lot, facing in any direction. The illustration shows four-inch siding as the main exterior material, with shingled gables and roof; foundation of concrete blocks and piers of brick. Besides the three windows with the flower box beneath them, there are two other windows in the living room. The inter-room opening makes the dining room and living room one large room, while also serving as bookcase. The combination sideboard and dresser is convenient.

Full directions for obtaining complete working drawings and specifications for these plans will be found on page 281

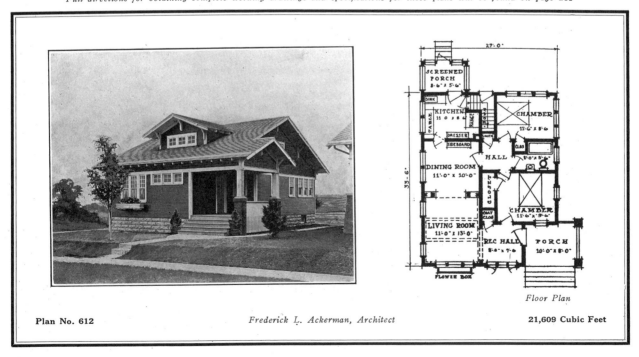

Floor Plan

Plan No. 612   *Frederick L. Ackerman, Architect*   **21,609 Cubic Feet**

First Floor Plan

Second Floor Plan

Plan No. 104   *Walter F. Bogner & Carl A. Rehse, Architects*   **15,553 Cubic Feet**

(Description of house shown in above plans)

THIS simple little house of four rooms is designed for wide siding or shingle exterior. The plan shows a most compact arrangement in small space, the whole area of the house being only 18x30 feet. The living room is entered through a vestibule. The stairs to the second floor lead out of this room, forming an attractive feature. Opposite the stairs are a group of windows and French door giving access to the porch. At the rear of the living room is a conveniently planned kitchen.

(Description of house shown in plans below)

HERE is a bungalow that is very compact in its arrangement and provides many labor-saving features. It is unpretentious and economically built and has the typical bungalow floor plan. In the living room there is a long inside wall space for the piano, and on the opposite side there are triple casements high above the floor, so that another large piece of furniture may be set beneath them. The glass-enclosed cases of the inter-room opening face the dining room and serve as china cases.

Full directions for obtaining complete working drawings and specifications for these plans will be found on page 281

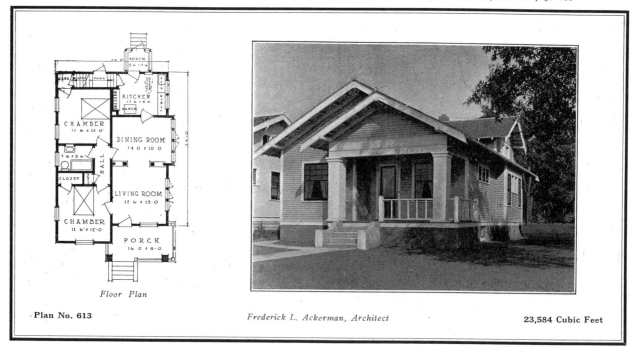

Floor Plan

Plan No. 613   *Frederick L. Ackerman, Architect*   **23,584 Cubic Feet**

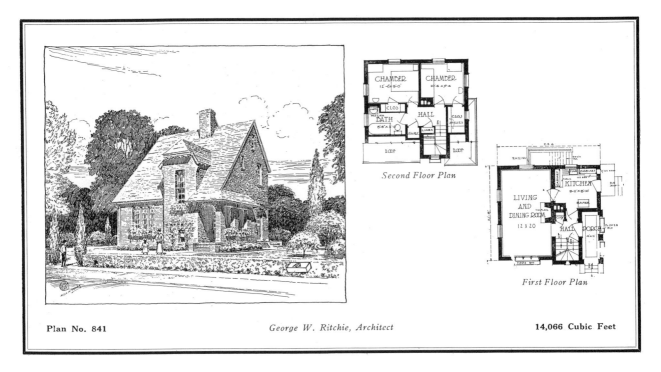

Plan No. 841   *George W. Ritchie, Architect*   14,066 Cubic Feet

(Description of house shown in above plans)

HERE is an attractive home of English type with a picturesque grouping of gables and long sweeping roof. The plan, which calls for brick construction, is thoroughly modern, and the principal room conforms to the new idea of combining the living and dining room. This room is light and cheery, with casement windows in front and a large brick fireplace. The kitchen is compact, with the cupboards, sink and icebox close together. The icebox is placed under one of the cabinets and has an outside icing door.

(Description of house shown in plans below)

THIS bungalow of brick construction will suit almost any part of this country. Because of the open plan this bungalow is remarkably cool. Every room is a corner room except the combined living and dining room, and that room has windows on two opposite sides so the breeze can sweep through it. The sleeping porch could easily be converted into an additional bedroom by the introduction of a door bed in the closet. The bedrooms have spacious closets, and the additional linen closet is an excellent feature.

Full directions for obtaining complete working drawings and specifications for these plans will be found on page 281

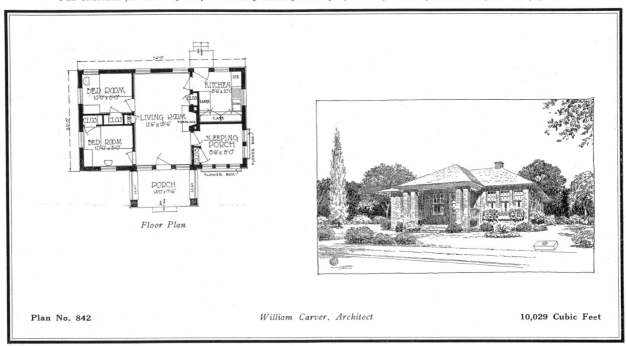

Floor Plan

Plan No. 842   *William Carver, Architect*   10,029 Cubic Feet

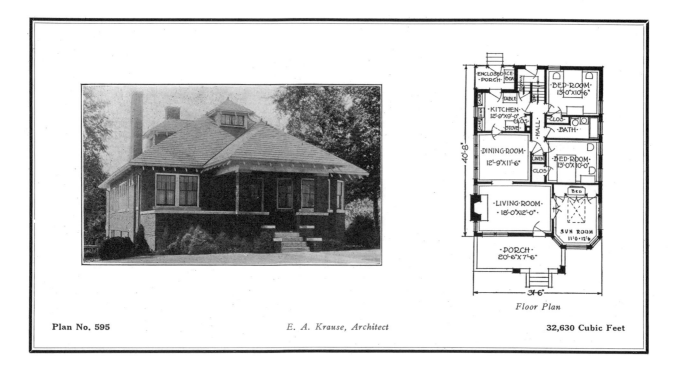

Plan No. 595   *E. A. Krause, Architect*   32,630 Cubic Feet

(Description of house shown in above plans)

THE floor plan of this five-room brick house has been very carefully worked out. From the porch one enters the living room, which has an open fireplace with a window on each side. French doors open into the sun room and the provision of a closet which accommodates a disappearing bed makes of this an extra bedroom. The bedrooms have been entirely separated from the living quarters, and they are connected by a small hall in which there is a linen closet.

(Description of house shown in plans below)

THIS attractive plan for a face brick bungalow has an interior arrangement that is at once out of the ordinary and at the same time most practical and convenient. The large central room which extends from the front to the back of the house is intended to serve both as living and dining room. The kitchen with pantry arrangements, cellar stairs and outside entrance are at the left of living room, and the wing at the right contains two good-sized chambers.

Full directions for obtaining complete working drawings and specifications for these plans will be found on page 281

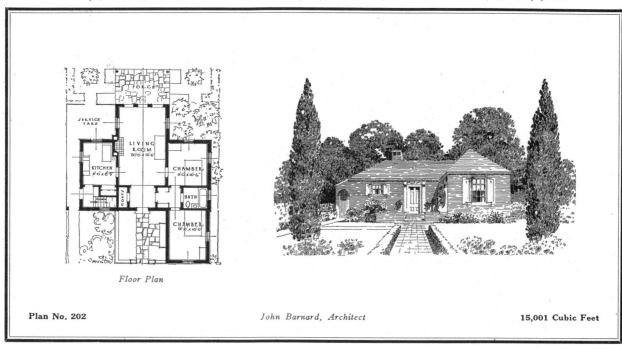

Floor Plan

Plan No. 202   *John Barnard, Architect*   15,001 Cubic Feet

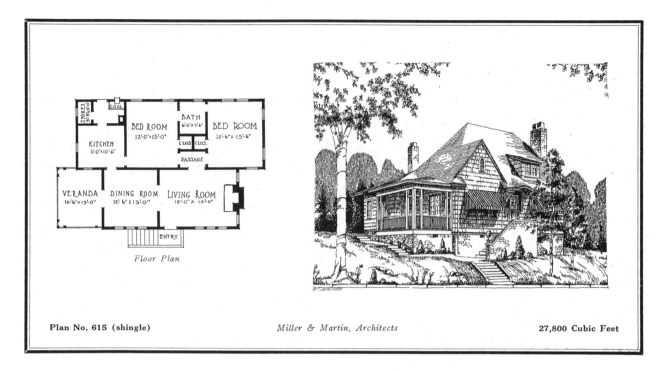

Plan No. 615 (shingle)   *Miller & Martin, Architects*   **27,800 Cubic Feet**

(Description of house shown in above plans)

THIS design is particularly adapted to a lot which slopes away from the street, although it could nearly as well be erected on a level lot. The treatment of roof lines in this case is very interesting and quite out of the ordinary. The arrangement of rooms is very good, and the plan in general quite compact. The bedrooms are separated from the living room by a passage, thus making them more private, and the bath is placed between them and directly connected with each of them. Frame with shingle exterior.

(Description of house shown in plans below)

HERE is a house which has been well planned from the basement to the light attic. The laundry room in the basement is located just below the kitchen, so that plumbing is conserved. Other rooms are partitioned off for drying, storage and coal. The main floor includes five rooms—two bedrooms and bath being arranged on one side, well separated from the living rooms. In the living room and dining room bay there are triple casements high off the floor, so that pieces of furniture may stand beneath them.

Full directions for obtaining complete working drawings and specifications for these plans will be found on page 281

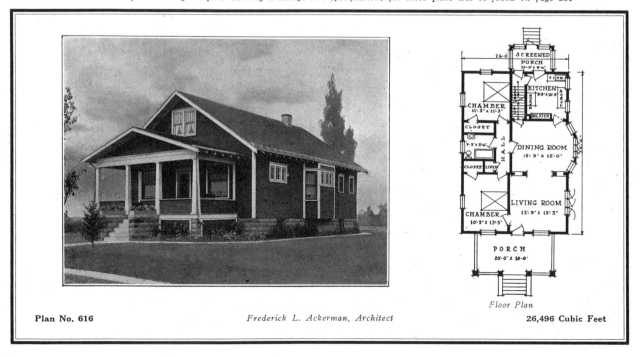

Plan No. 616   *Frederick L. Ackerman, Architect*   **26,496 Cubic Feet**

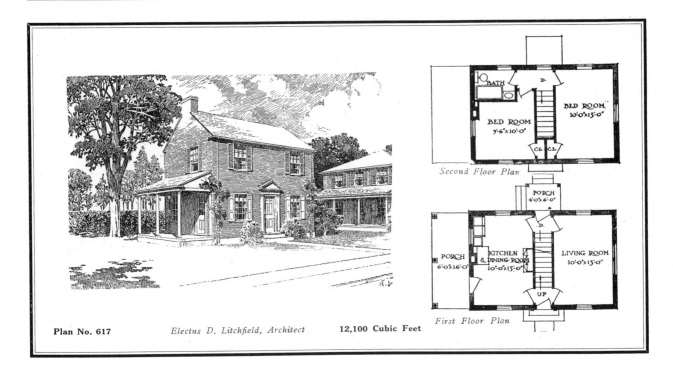

Plan No. 617   *Electus D. Litchfield, Architect*   **12,100 Cubic Feet**

(Description of house shown in above plans)

THIS is a four-room house of unusual interior arrangement. The construction is of brick. The first floor is divided into two rooms of equal size, the one a living room and the other being intended to serve the purpose of a kitchen and dining room. The utility features are all at one end of the room, leaving the other end for dining, and here there is a door opening onto the porch. The second floor contains two bedrooms of good size and a bath room.

(Description of house shown in plans below)

HERE is a well-designed stucco house of the modern English cottage type. This design calls for a five-room house with dining alcove, and special arrangement for a future two-room, two-story addition. The plan as illustrated, however, is complete in itself without the extension. Entrance is through a vestibule with coat closet, directly off the living room. The living room is roomy, attractive and homelike, with f... ., open stairway and adjoining dining alcove.

Full dire   for these plans will be found on *page* 281

Second Floor Plan

First Floor Plan

Plan No. 397   *Harry C. Starr, Architect*   **19,750 Cubic Feet**

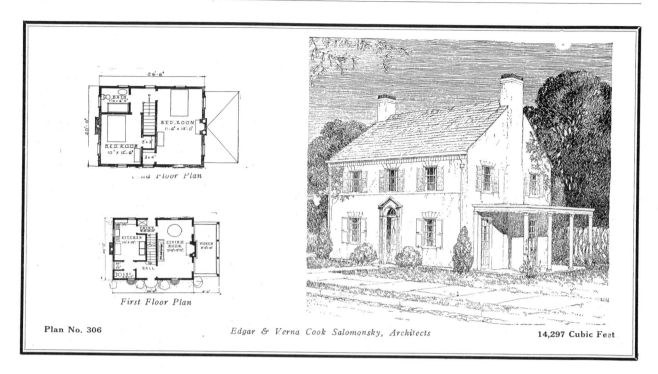

Second Floor Plan

First Floor Plan

Plan No. 306   *Edgar & Verna Cook Salomonsky, Architects*   **14,297 Cubic Feet**

(Description of house shown in above plans)

THIS attractive five-room house is one of the designs submitted in a recent architectural competition. The architects suggest that exterior walls be of light gray stucco; entrance door and cornice to be of wood painted white; roof of weathered shingles. Living room extends the width of the house and one end may be used as a dining room. The fireplace is flanked by doors which open onto the porch. The kitchen has a convenient entry to the living room as well as to the hall.

(Description of house shown in plans below)

THERE is more than the usual convenience of the five-room bungalow in this little house. The illustration shows the exterior of stucco, a material which owes its popularity to its appearance, its durability, its low upkeep cost and its adaptability in color and texture. The porch is small with boxed rail, and can be screened or glazed at low cost. The small lights at the top of entrance door, and even the doors in the pedestal bookcases and the sideboard, harmonize in design with the windows.

Full directions for obtaining complete working drawings and specifications for these plans will be found on page 281

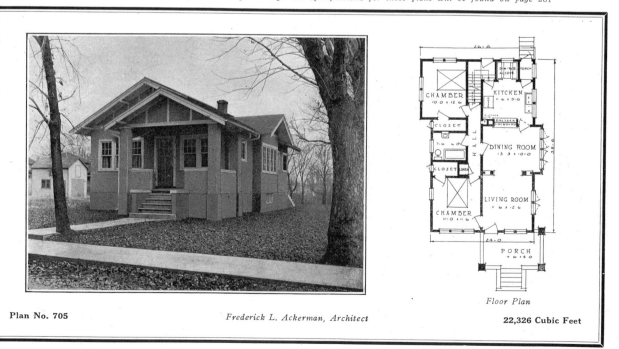

Floor Plan

Plan No. 705   *Frederick L. Ackerman, Architect*   **22,326 Cubic Feet**

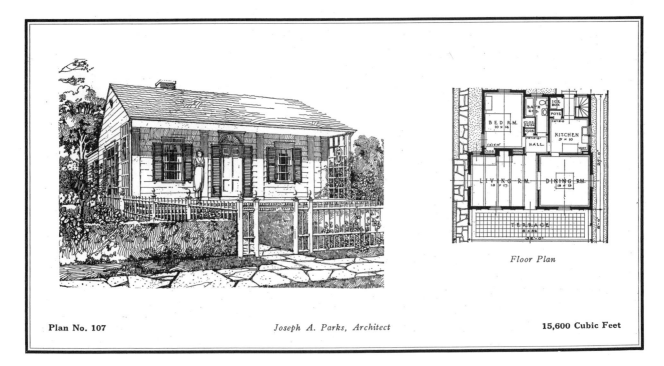

Plan No. 107   *Joseph A. Parks, Architect*   **15,600 Cubic Feet**

Floor Plan

(Description of house shown in above plans)

ALTHOUGH this house contains only four rooms the floor plan has been carefully worked out to secure the maximum of efficiency in a small area. The architect suggests that the exterior walls of wide siding be painted three coats Old Virginia white; shutters bottle green; roof to be shingles unstained, terrace to be cement with brick edge and steps; beams in living room to be 4x6-inch band sawed, stained brown. From the terrace one may enter the living room or the dining room.

(Description of house shown in plans below)

THIS five-room house is designed for an exterior of red brick with roof of slate or other type of heavy shingle. From the porch one enters the living room, which is separated from the dining room only by an inter-room opening. Opposite this opening is a fireplace with windows on each side. This is virtually a six-room house because of the introduction of a closet containing a disappearing bed in the sleeping porch. The sleeping quarters are separated from the living rooms by a narrow hall.

Full directions for obtaining complete working drawings and specifications for these plans will be found on page 281

Floor Plan

Plan No. 596   *William Carver, Supervising Architect*   **29,894 Cubic Feet**

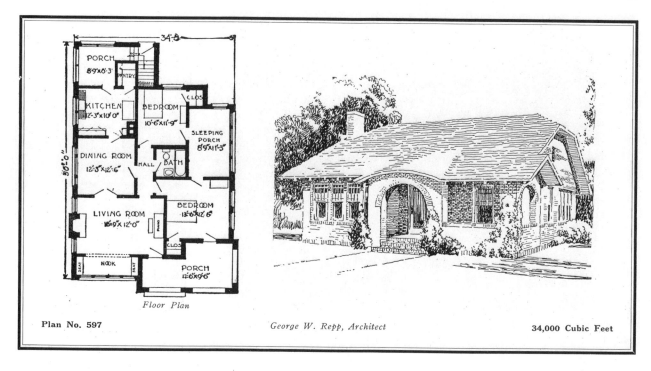

Plan No. 597   George W. Repp, Architect   34,000 Cubic Feet

Floor Plan

(Description of house shown in above plans)

THIS is a simple, compact little brick bungalow with airy porches, plenty of windows, and eaves to shade the walls. It has a pleasing exterior and the plan is of unusual merit. The snug brick fireplace and wide window-nook make the living room cozy and comfortable. French doors give privacy to the dining room while still allowing it to be made practically a part of the living room. The bedrooms are well isolated and the sleeping porch may be divided to give a private porch for each room.

(Description of house shown in plans below)

THIS little home has many features which distinguish it from the average, including gable ends that are cut off; exposed timbers; a belt course that forms the head casing of the windows. There is a coat closet with a mirror door in the vestibule, and a cased opening to the living room, which occupies the rest of the front of the house. French doors could be used here if preferred. An inter-room opening utilizes the partition space between the living room and dining room for bookcases. Frame with stucco exterior.

Full directions for obtaining complete working drawings and specifications for these plans will be found on page 281

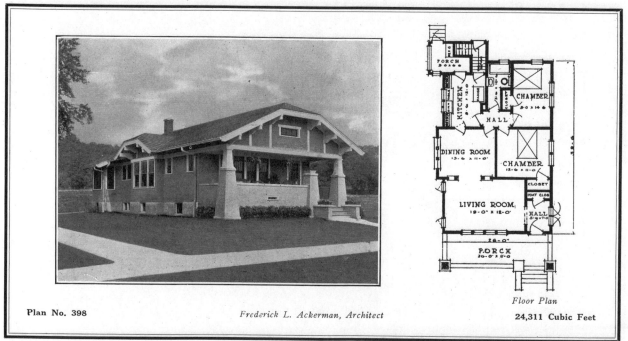

Plan No. 398   Frederick L. Ackerman, Architect

Floor Plan

24,311 Cubic Feet

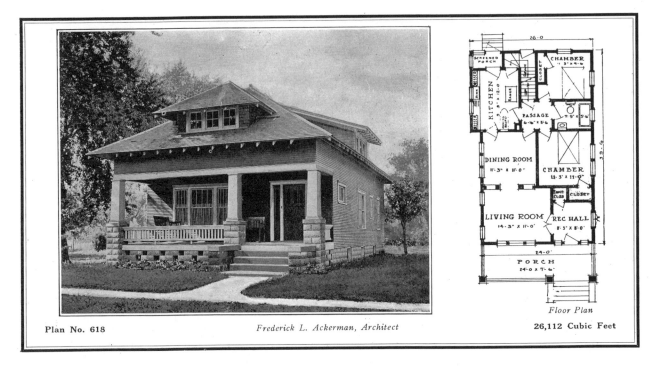

Plan No. 618   *Frederick L. Ackerman, Architect*   **26,112 Cubic Feet**

Floor Plan

(Description of house shown in above plans)

THIS plan provides for additional rooms to be finished later if desired. A stair is already incorporated in the plan, leading to the attic, which can be finished into two good rooms. Four dormers with triple windows provide ample light and air. The plan includes a light reception hall with a coat closet. French doors lead to the living room, and an inter-room with bookcases separates living room and dining room. The walls are of siding, and concrete columns support the porch.

(Description of house shown in plans below)

HERE is an attractive bungalow of the New Orleans type that meets conditions where it is desirable, on account of a high water line, to have the basement built entirely above the ground. Although this feature often results in a very stilted, ill-proportioned exterior, the designer here has very cleverly utilized a terrace in front of the house to reduce its height, while the stairs set attractively in the corner tend toward the same effect. The color and texture of the brick affords pleasing possibilities in design.

Full directions for obtaining complete working drawings and specifications for these plans will be found on page 281

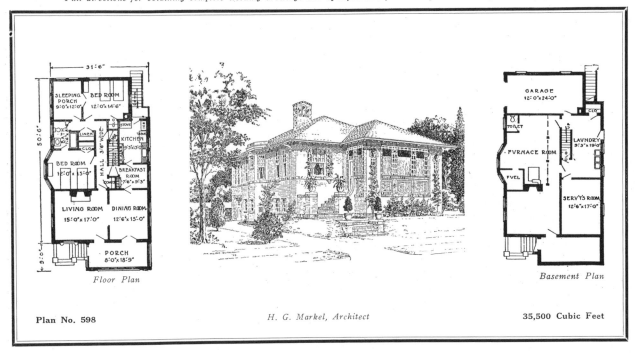

Floor Plan

Basement Plan

Plan No. 598   *H. G. Markel, Architect*   **35,500 Cubic Feet**

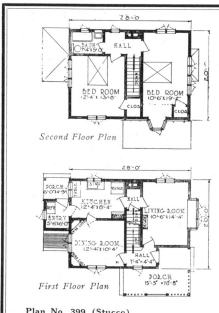

Second Floor Plan

First Floor Plan

Plan No. 399 (Stucco)   *Frederick L. Ackerman, Architect*   **19,088 Cubic Feet**

(Description of house shown in above plans)

IN this five-room house stucco of various tints and textures, brick, limestone or other material of fire-resisting nature could be used to good advantage. A small hall with a straight boxed stair preserves the privacy of every room in the house, and is a convenience in cold weather. Each of the rooms has windows on at least two sides, to make it light and airy. The two bedrooms have roomy closets and the larger of the rooms has a small dormer forming an alcove.

(Description of house shown in plans below)

HERE is a design that is particularly adapted to the long, narrow lot, but the gable roof, presenting its wide side to the street, gives a desirable appearance of width. The porch is included under the main roof. There is no vestibule so the front entrance admits directly to the living room, which has windows on two sides. There is a long inside wall space for the piano, and the inter-room opening affords place for books. This house is of frame construction with brick columns.

Full directions for obtaining complete working drawings and specifications for these plans will be found on page 281

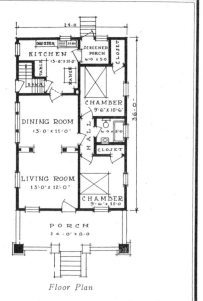

Floor Plan

Plan No. 619   *Frederick L. Ackerman, Architect*   **22,176 Cubic Feet**

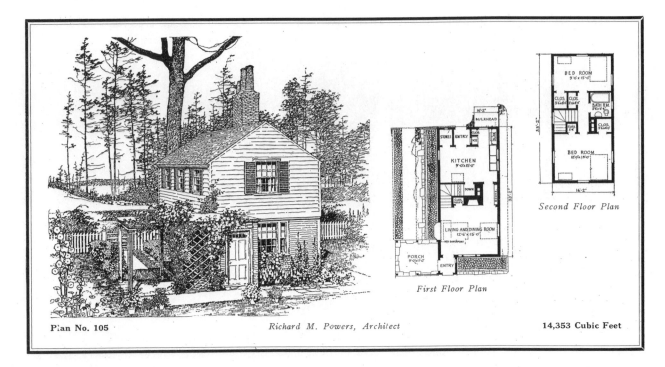

Plan No. 105

Richard M. Powers, Architect

14,353 Cubic Feet

Second Floor Plan

First Floor Plan

(Description of house shown in above plans)

THIS attractive little four-room house was one of the prize-winning designs in a recent competition. The architect suggests the roof covering to be unfading green slate; front wall in lower story and walls of entry to be covered with narrow clapboards, remainder of walls to be covered with wide clapboards, all painted pearl gray. Exterior of sash and doors, exterior finish, and lattice painted cream white. Blinds to be painted olive green. Entrance to the combination living and dining room is through the entry.

(Description of house shown in plans below)

THREE bedrooms in a five-room house is an unusual feature of this attractive home. This greater housing capacity is possible because a dining alcove is substituted for the regular dining room. This house is of frame construction with exterior walls of broad siding. The living room extends across the front of the house and has the attractive features of a fireplace and built-in seat with bookcases flanking. In the dining alcove there is a hanging china closet which is both decorative and useful.

Full directions for obtaining complete working drawings and specifications for these plans will be found on page 281

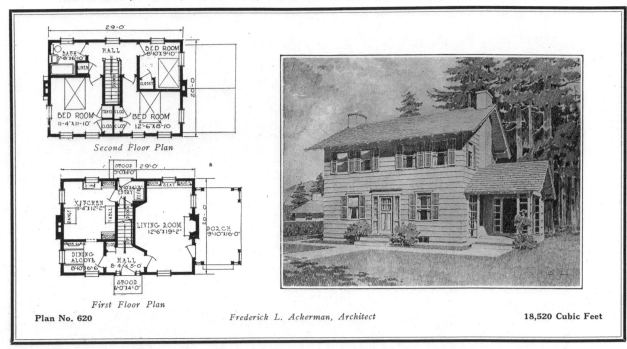

Second Floor Plan

First Floor Plan

Plan No. 620

Frederick L. Ackerman, Architect

18,520 Cubic Feet

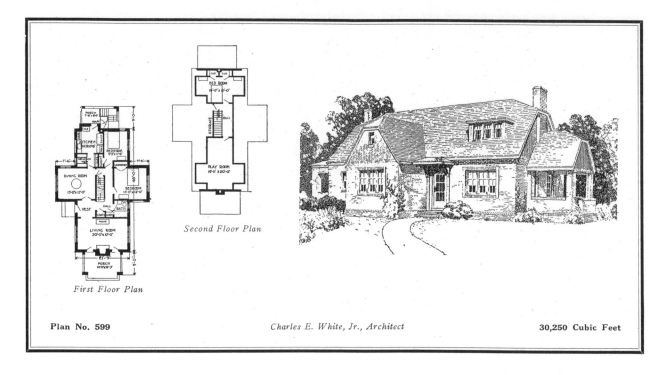

Second Floor Plan

First Floor Plan

Plan No. 599   *Charles E. White, Jr., Architect*   **30,250 Cubic Feet**

(*Description of house shown in above plans*)

THIS charming English bungalow would be especially attractive with its broad side to the road, but it is also very well suited to a narrow lot. If the porch were turned toward the street, a fifty-foot lot would leave ample room for a driveway at the side. It would also be very attractive placed on a knoll with side entrance at grade, and the two end porches well above the ground. A garage could then be placed beneath one of the porches. Exterior walls of face brick.

(*Description of house shown in plans below*)

THIS cottage demonstrates the statement that good design is not a matter of size, nor of great cost. This five-room cottage of stucco is carefully planned from the well-ventilated attic to the basement, divided into clean, light rooms. From the pleasant living porch one enters a hall in which a coat closet is provided. A most inviting room-end in the living room is composed of bookcases and window seat, while in the dining room are a pair of corner china closets.

Full directions for obtaining complete working drawings and specifications for these plans will be found on page 281

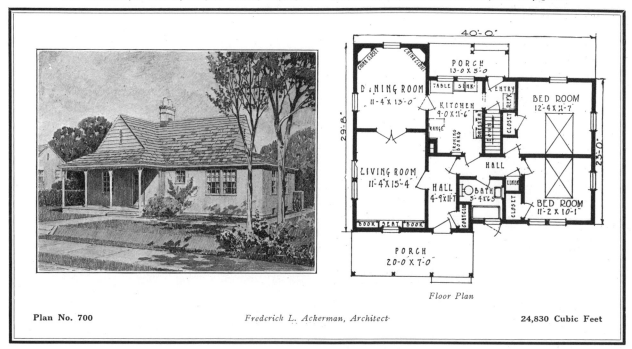

Floor Plan

Plan No. 700   *Fredrick L. Ackerman, Architect*   **24,830 Cubic Feet**

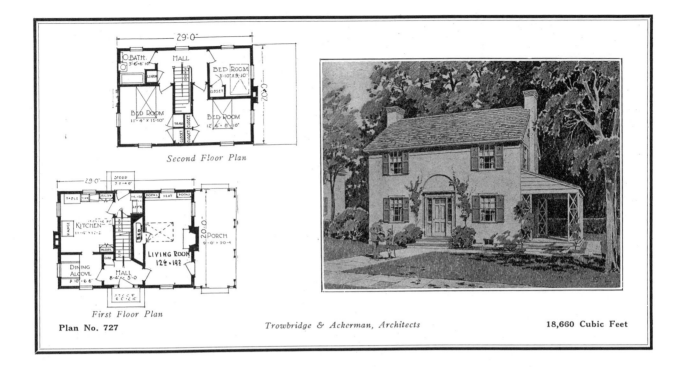

Second Floor Plan

First Floor Plan

Plan No. 727   *Trowbridge & Ackerman, Architects*   **18,660 Cubic Feet**

(Description of house shown in above plans)   *(Description of house shown in plans below)*

THIS attractive little home has exterior walls of stucco. The floor plans have been carefully worked out and include three bedrooms on the second floor. The dining room has been dispensed with, but an attractive alcove is provided, opening from the vestibule and kitchen. The living room is attractively arranged with fireplace on one side and a built-in seat flanked by bookcases. Work-table, dresser and sink occupy one end of the kitchen.

HERE is a house that is specially designed for a narrow lot. The dimensions of the main part of the house are only eighteen feet wide by thirty-four feet, six inches deep. The living room is placed across the front of the house. The entrance to the house is at the side, thus leaving a large room in front, well lighted by windows on three sides. There is a wide cased opening to the dining room. A built-in sideboard is an attractive feature of this room.

Full directions for obtaining complete working drawings and specifications for these plans will be found on page 281

Second Floor Plan

First Floor Plan

Plan No. 843   *Olsen & Urbain, Architects*   **19,862 Cubic Feet**

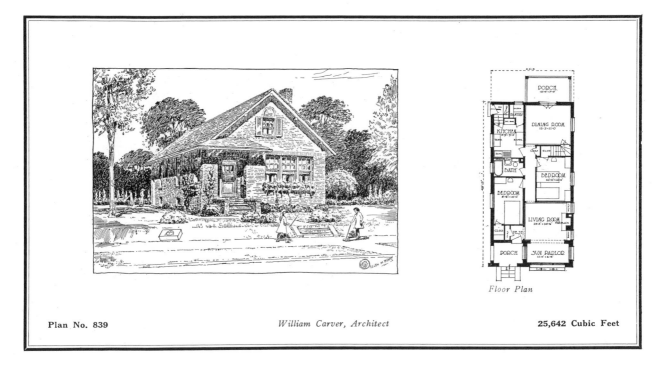

Plan No. 839   *William Carver, Architect*   **25,642 Cubic Feet**

Floor Plan

(Description of house shown in above plans)

A FIVE-ROOM house of simple design with exterior walls of common brick. Entrance from the porch is into a small vestibule, with a convenient coat closet. The living room is augmented in size by the sun parlor, into which there is a wide opening. The living room has also an attractive fireplace with bookcases on each side. The dining room is of generous size and French doors open onto a porch. Stair from the dining room leads to a useful storage room in the attic.

(Description of house shown in plans below)

WITH wide spreading porches, very large rooms, and good ventilation, this is an exceptionally cool house for the hottest climate. Entrance is directly into the living room which has an attractive fireplace flanked by bookcases with small windows above. The dining room is cheerfully lighted and there is a door to the large pergola. The dining porch is glassed in and forms a comfortable feature. The bedrooms are well arranged on one side of the house with bathroom between. Construction is of brick.

Full directions for obtaining complete working drawings and specifications for these plans will be found on page 281

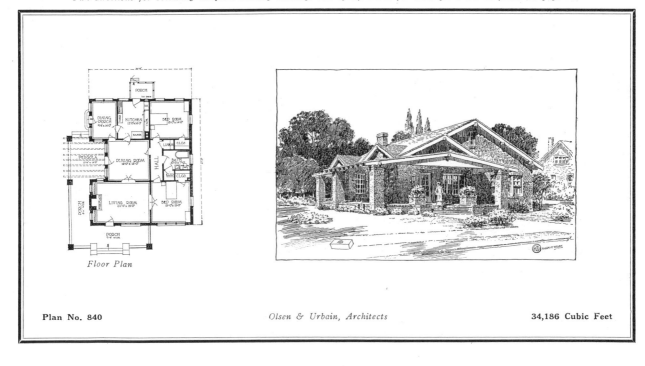

Floor Plan

Plan No. 840   *Olsen & Urbain, Architects*   **34,186 Cubic Feet**

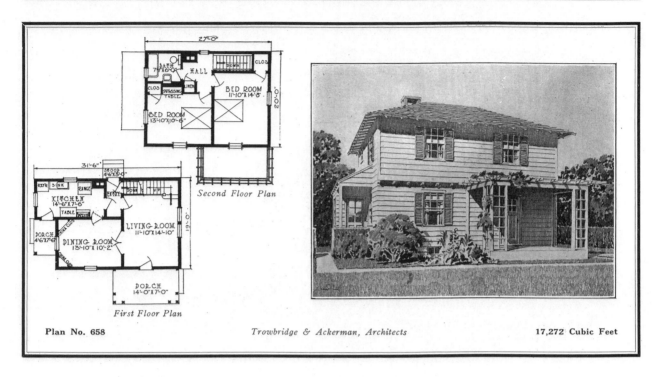

Second Floor Plan

First Floor Plan

Plan No. 658   *Trowbridge & Ackerman, Architects*   **17,272 Cubic Feet**

(Description of house shown in above plans)

EACH of the five rooms of this pretty home has a front facing. The construction is of frame with exterior walls of wide siding. The pergola-like front porch shelters the front entrance, saving the space of a vestibule. Opposite the entrance is an open stair, turning with a platform at the corner. Windows on two sides make the dining room cheerful and it has the added attractiveness of French doors and corner china closets. The bedrooms are both good-sized, and have windows on two sides.

(Description of house shown in plans below)

THERE is a homey appeal about this house with its low eaves toward the street. Furthermore it is a design well adapted to brick construction and would be economical to build because of its rectangular plan. The first floor plan shows comfortably-sized living and dining rooms together with a convenient kitchen supplied with rear entry. The living porch is reached from the dining room by French windows and overlooks the rear of the lot. On the second floor there are two good-sized bedrooms and ample closet space.

Full directions for obtaining complete working drawings and specifications for these plans will be found on page 281

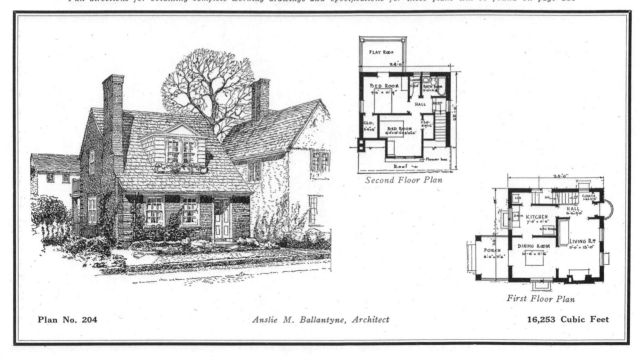

Second Floor Plan

First Floor Plan

Plan No. 204   *Anslie M. Ballantyne, Architect*   **16,253 Cubic Feet**

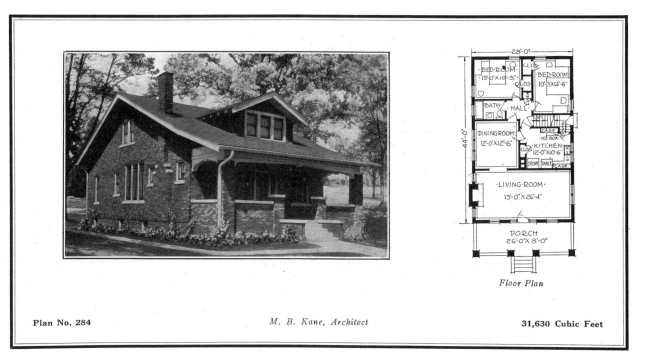

Floor Plan

Plan No. 284   M. B. Kane, Architect   31,630 Cubic Feet

(Description of house shown in above plans)

THIS is a very popular type of brick bungalow, designed for economy and comfort. The exterior is of common brick laid with wide joints to give an attractive texture. The roof could well be of slate-surfaced asphalt shingles or asbestos-cement shingles. Leaders and gutters of copper add to attractiveness of design. The exterior woodwork could be painted white. In this five-room bungalow a large living room occupies the entire front of the floor plan.

(Description of house shown in plans below)

THE unusual shape in the plan of this five-room bungalow gives all rooms a corner, which means fine ventilation. Another excellent feature is the easy communication made possible by the central hall. The living room and dining room are connected by the entrance hall. A breakfast nook, with cabinets, connects the dining room and kitchen. The kitchen is compact and well lighted by windows above the sink. The bedrooms are of a good size and arrangement.

Full directions for obtaining complete working drawings and specifications for these plans will be found on page 281

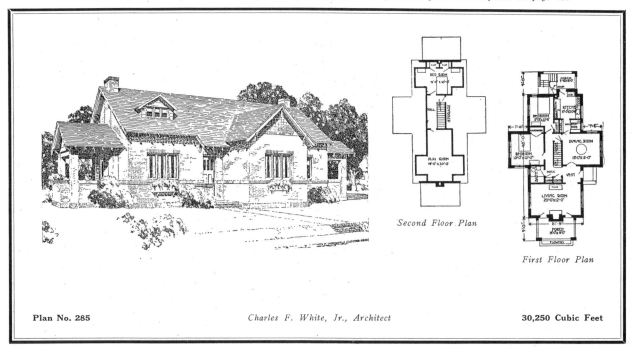

Second Floor Plan

First Floor Plan

Plan No. 285   Charles F. White, Jr., Architect   30,250 Cubic Feet

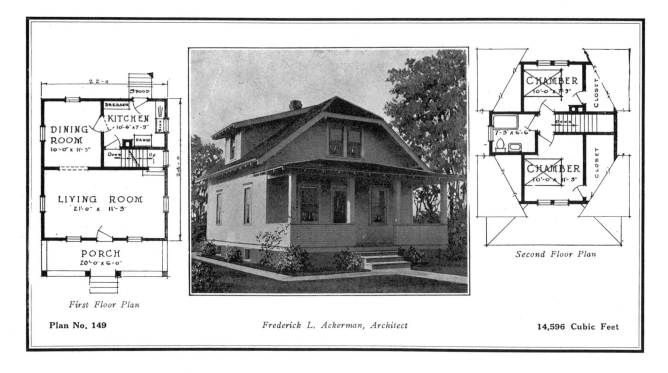

DINING ROOM
10'-0" x 11'-5"

KITCHEN
10'-6" x 7'-9"

DRESSER

RANGE

STOOP

22-0

24-0

LIVING ROOM
21'-0" x 11'-3"

PORCH
20'-0" x 6'-0"

First Floor Plan

CHAMBER
10'-0" x 7'-9"

CLOSET

7'-3" x 6'-6"

CHAMBER
10'-0" x 11'-3"

CLOSET

Second Floor Plan

Plan No. 149   *Frederick L. Ackerman, Architect*   **14,596 Cubic Feet**

(Description of house shown in above plans)

PLAIN square construction, ordinary materials, and an absence of unnecessary ornamentation make the construction of this house economical. It occupies a space only 22 feet by 24 feet, yet its accommodations are ample. The living room extends across the house and receives light from three sides. In one corner is the boxed stair, with a plaster arch above. At the rear a cased opening admits to the dining room, which has windows on two sides.

(Description of house shown in plans below)

HERE is a house in which the Dutch and English characteristics are combined in a pleasing manner. The result is a purely American home. There is a spacious porch on the right side, but only a small entry-way in front. The living room is equipped with a fireplace and the stairs are found at the far end beyond. The kitchen and service quarters are unusually well worked out and guarantee few steps for the housewife. Exterior is of common brick.

Full directions for obtaining complete working drawings and specifications for these plans will be found on page 281

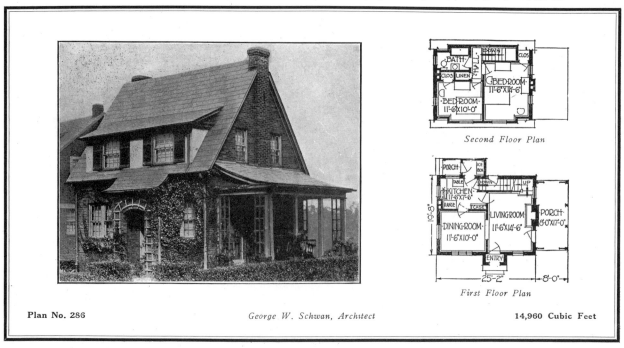

BATH

CLOS   LINEN

CLOS

BEDROOM
11'-6" x 10'-0"

BEDROOM
11'-6" x 14'-6"

CLOS

Second Floor Plan

PORCH

ICE BOX

KITCHEN
11'-6" x 7'-6"

RANGE

CASE

DINING ROOM
11'-6" x 10'-0"

LIVING ROOM
11'-6" x 14'-6"

PORCH
15'-0" x 17'-0"

ENTRY

UP

DOWN

TABLE

19'-8"

25'-2"   8'-0"

First Floor Plan

Plan No. 286   *George W. Schwan, Architect*   **14,960 Cubic Feet**

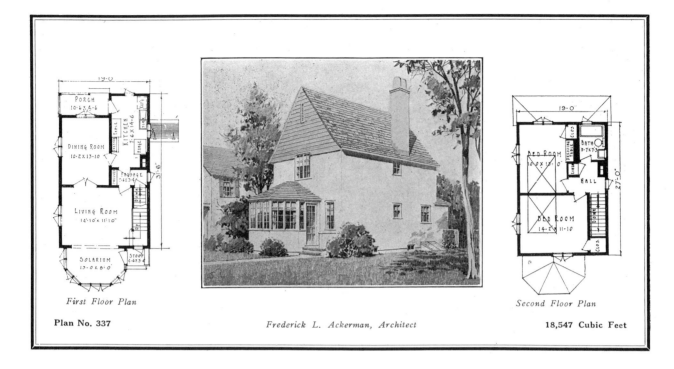

First Floor Plan

Second Floor Plan

Plan No. 337   *Frederick L. Ackerman, Architect*   **18,547 Cubic Feet**

(Description of house shown in above plans)   *(Description of house shown in plans below)*

IN addition to its five rooms, this plan includes a splendid solarium separated from the main living room only by a plaster opening. It greatly increases the size of the living room and, because of its semi-octagonal shape and its many casements, every passing breeze will find its way in. It is this room which one enters from the little brick-bordered cement stoop. Perhaps the chief architectural feature of the living room proper is the handsome stair.

HERE again the influence of the old Dutch settlers is found in this modern five-room brick cottage. The small dormers are more in accordance with old Dutch design than the usual modern long "shed" dormer, but give less room in the bedrooms. One enters the living room directly from the porch, there being no hall. The stairs to the second floor wind around the fireplace in the far end of the room. The entire arrangement is very compact and simple.

Full directions for obtaining complete working drawings and specifications for these plans will be found on page 281

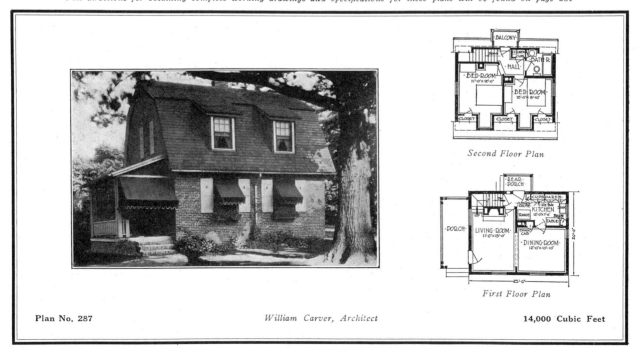

Second Floor Plan

First Floor Plan

Plan No. 287   *William Carver, Architect*   **14,000 Cubic Feet**

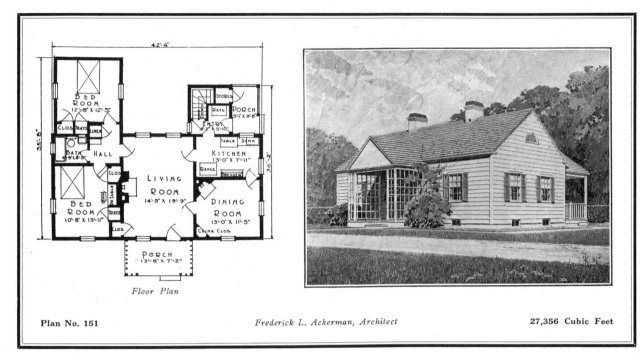

Floor Plan

Plan No. 151   *Frederick L. Ackerman, Architect*   **27,356 Cubic Feet**

(Description of house shown in above plans)

(Description of house shown in plans below)

THERE is a fine simplicity about this little cottage that wins the heart at once. Long horizontal lines, symmetrical openings, a plain roof with a delicately molded cornice, all produce a restful design. The semicircular louver ventilates the attic space. The living room is a splendidly large room with a fireplace in the center of one long wall, and opposite that an inside wall space for the piano. On one side are the dining room and kitchen, each having openings on two sides. Two corners of the dining room are occupied by fireplace and corner china cupboard.

SIMPLE roof lines and window arrangements give a cozy effect to this design. Horizontal bands in the brickwork have been used very effectively. Common bond with the joints raked out would be quite appropriate. This house may be placed on a narrow lot with the driveway and entrance at the side. The garage is separate from the house but connected by the back porch over which the main roof extends. It is readily accessible and heated from the house. French doors flanked by bookcases connect the sun porch and living room.

Full directions for obtaining complete working drawings and specifications for these plans will be found on page 281

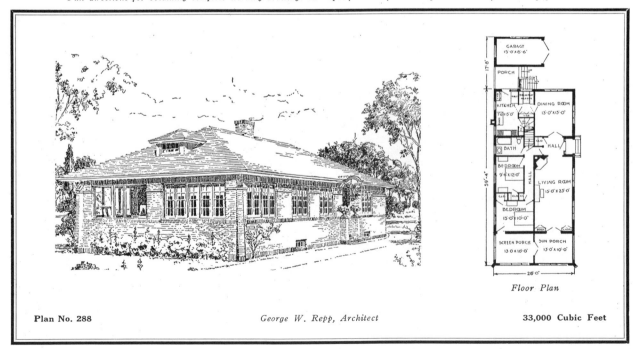

Floor Plan

Plan No. 288   *George W. Repp, Architect*   **33,000 Cubic Feet**

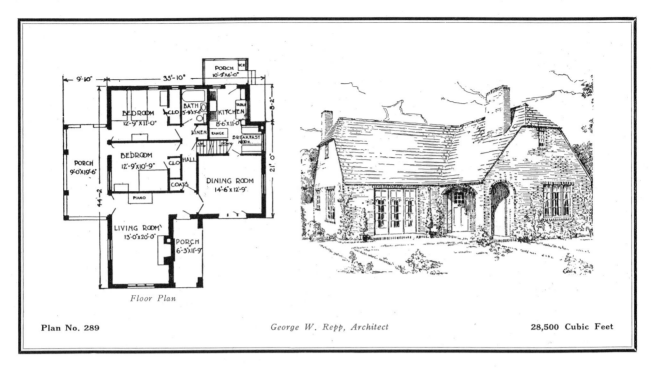

Floor Plan

Plan No. 289   *George W. Repp, Architect*   **28,500 Cubic Feet**

(Description of house shown in above plans)

HERE is a bungalow that is reminiscent of the English cottage and perfectly preserves the tradition of simple charm, dignity and comfort which we associate with that type. The living room is especially well situated to command the view toward the front, and opens to a fine porch not seen in the picture. The dining room is of generous proportions, with three French doors opening on the terrace and a double casement window on the adjoining side. One of the most charming features is the breakfast nook between the dining room and kitchen. Face brick.

(Description of house shown in plans below)

ALTHOUGH this house is shown with the exterior of stucco it would be equally attractive of brick or hollow tile. The latticed porch, with brick-bordered cement floor, is recessed and could be used early in spring and late in fall. The living room extends clear through the house, with casements toward front and back, and contains a fireplace. The sleeping quarters are isolated in a separate wing, a splendid arrangement, and are provided with convenient closets and chiffonier-like tray cases. The kitchen and service entry are well arranged.

Full directions for obtaining complete working drawings and specifications for these plans will be found on page 281

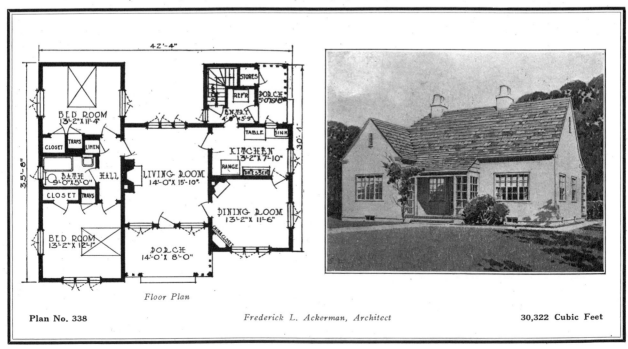

Floor Plan

Plan No. 338   *Frederick L. Ackerman, Architect*   **30,322 Cubic Feet**

Floor Plan

Plan No. 152   *Frederick L. Ackerman, Architect*   **25,524 Cubic Feet**

(Description of house shown in above plans)

THE floor plan of this five-room bungalow has been well arranged, with the living portion of the house on one side and the sleeping rooms and bath on the other. The glazed entrance door furnishes light for the vestibule and coat closet. The living room at the left has groups of windows on two sides, with top sash divided into small panes. Between the living room and the dining room is an inter-room opening, a type of treatment for wide openings which is rapidly gaining favor over the old-style colonnade.

(Description of house shown in plans below)

SIMPLE and effective, this five-room bungalow of the Western type should be a very economical one to build. The use of an attractive face brick laid in some distinctive bond and mortar joint greatly enhances the value and attractiveness of this design. It would look exceedingly well with wide, deeply raked horizontal joints and very thin vertical joints. The effect would be a series of horizontal shadow lines banding the entire building. The interior arrangement has been carefully planned for convenient living.

Full directions for obtaining complete working drawings and specifications for these plans will be found on page 281

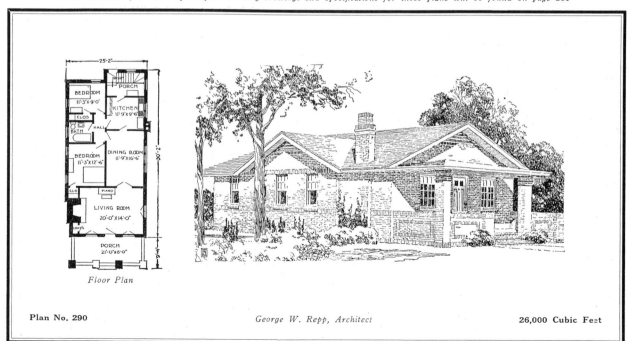

Floor Plan

Plan No. 290   *George W. Repp, Architect*   **26,000 Cubic Feet**

First Floor Plan

Second Floor Plan

Plan No. 291 *George H. Schwan, Architect* 16,337 Cubic Feet

(Description of house shown in above plans)

THE English type house with its steep roof lines, small dormers, casement windows and extending bays presents a charm seldom surpassed by other common types. This one of brick is especially well proportioned and the masses well balanced. The rooms are all large and light, and placed so as to eliminate all possible unusable space. The whole house, including the porch, occupies a space but twenty-five feet square. The roof and sides of the dormer are slate covered and the porch is of cement.

(Description of house shown in plans below)

HERE is an excellent design especially intended for narrow lots. This could be built as a double house, for no essential openings would be sacrificed and each half would have entire privacy. The simple, almost rustic entrance is at the foot of the stairway, so that the living room is not made a passageway. The stair, with its open balustrade, ascending along one wall, is one of the decorative features of the living room. French doors transmit light between this room and the dining room.

Full directions for obtaining complete working drawings and specifications for these plans will be found on page 281

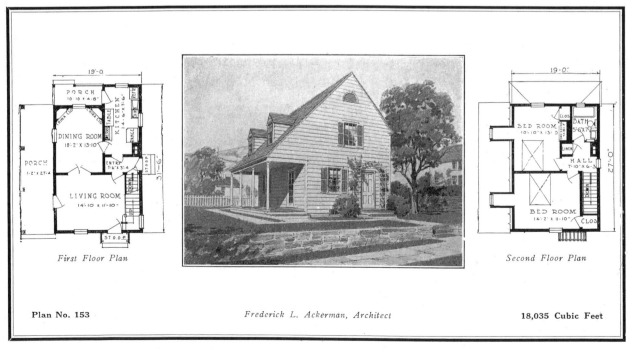

First Floor Plan

Second Floor Plan

Plan No. 153 *Frederick L. Ackerman, Architect* 18,035 Cubic Feet

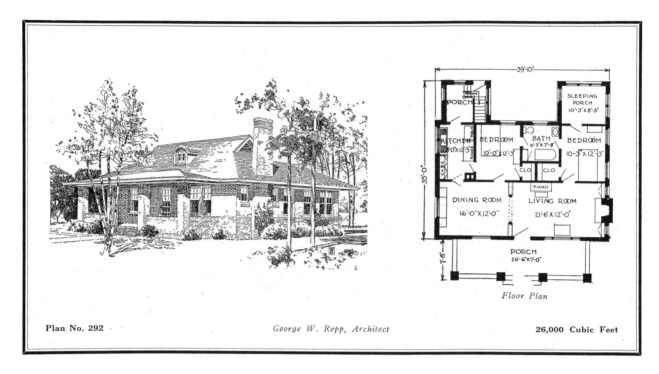

Plan No. 292   *George W. Repp, Architect*   **26,000 Cubic Feet**

(Description of house shown in above plans)

HERE is a five-room bungalow which combines symmetry, simplicity, dignity and comfort. The roof lines are low and sweeping, yet the attic is well ventilated with louvers at the ends so that the house will be cool in summer. The living room and dining room extend across the entire front of the house, in a sweep of thirty-eight feet, broken only by a light colonnade into which bookcases are built. At one end is the brick fireplace, flanked by a second pair of bookcases. Exterior is of face brick.

(Description of house shown in plans below)

HERE is a cottage which has the unusual feature of a solarium. It is separated from the living room by attractive French doors and, since the dining room is divided from them only by an inter-room opening, the three rooms may be thrown together into one large room. The central hall makes it possible for one in the living room to reach the basement, bathroom, kitchen or bedrooms without passing through any other room. The living room contains a closet which accommodates a door-bed.

Full directions for obtaining complete working drawings and specifications for these plans will be found on page 281

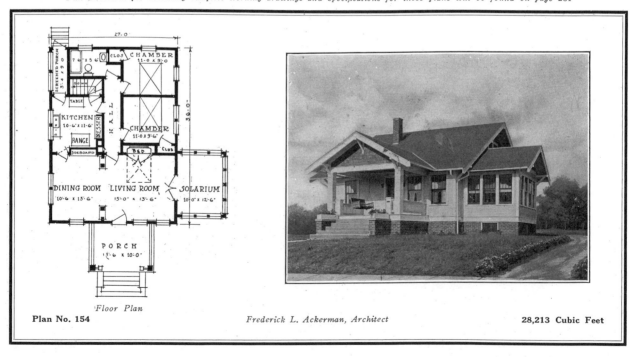

Plan No. 154   *Frederick L. Ackerman, Architect*   **28,213 Cubic Feet**

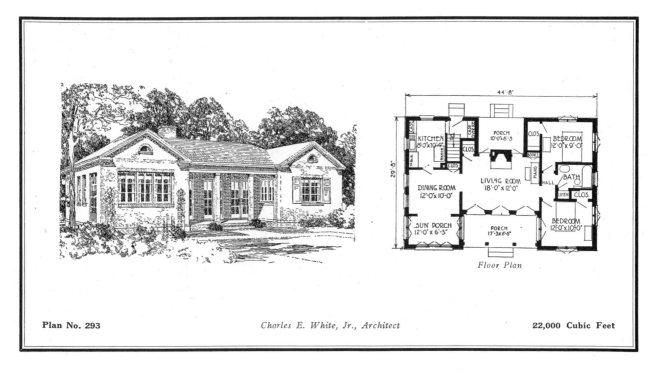

Plan No. 293   *Charles E. White, Jr., Architect*   22,000 Cubic Feet

Floor Plan

(Description of house shown in above plans)

THERE is a feeling of comfort and hominess about this five-room Colonial bungalow. The dignity of the Colonial style is retained and accentuated by the symmetrical gables. The living room is centrally located with the bedrooms and bath isolated on one side, while the kitchen and dining room occupy the other wing. Directly opposite the entrance is the fireplace and beyond is the brick-paved porch overlooking the garden. The dining room is augmented in size by the glazed sun porch. Face brick exterior.

(Description of house shown in plans below)

WIDE siding makes this little house appear larger and white paint would further increase the impression. Perhaps the most distinctive feature of the exterior is the pergola-like terrace. The rooms are so arranged that living room, dining room and kitchen may share the pleasantest exposure, and the plans could be reversed to take advantage of your particular location. The living room is almost square and the beamed ceiling adds a homey touch. The fireplace is in an ingle-nook with built-in seats.

Full directions for obtaining complete working drawings and specifications for these plans will be found on page 281

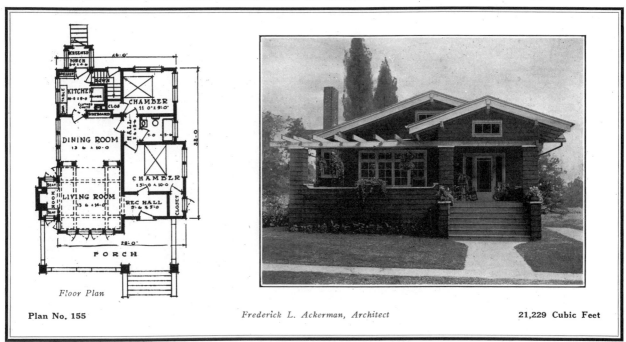

Floor Plan

Plan No. 155   *Frederick L. Ackerman, Architect*   21,229 Cubic Feet

First Floor Plan

Plan No. 294   *George W. Schwan, Architect*   14,750 Cubic Feet

Second Floor Plan

(Description of house shown in above plans)

FOR a small family this design should be very appealing. Much usable space is contained within a very small area. The rooms are all sufficiently large to answer their respective requirements and absolutely no space is wasted. The exterior walls, except dormers, are of brick, and the roofs of slate. The dormers are shingled, and all trim is painted white. A bit of trellis work here and there and a window flower box add to the attractiveness of this house. Common brick exterior.

(Description of house shown in plans below)

HERE is a small house which has been planned very carefully and contains five uncrowded rooms, a splendid solarium, bathroom, rear entry, and many closets. The solarium has a pretty semi-octagonal shape and opens off both living room and dining room. The living room occupies the right half of the house, while dining room and kitchen share the left. An open stair occupies the rear side of the room, and direct access is arranged to the kitchen, basement and rear entry. Stucco on frame.

Full directions for obtaining complete working drawings and specifications for these plans will be found on page 281

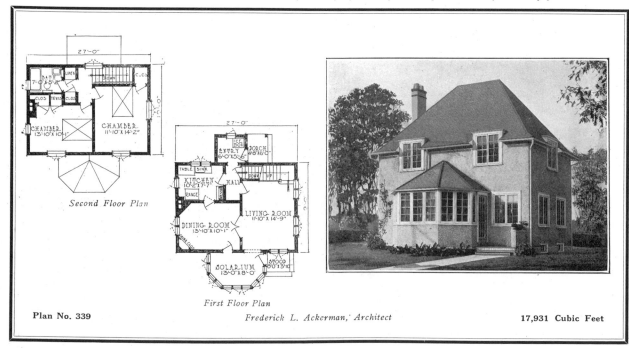

Second Floor Plan

First Floor Plan

Plan No. 339   *Frederick L. Ackerman, Architect*   17,931 Cubic Feet

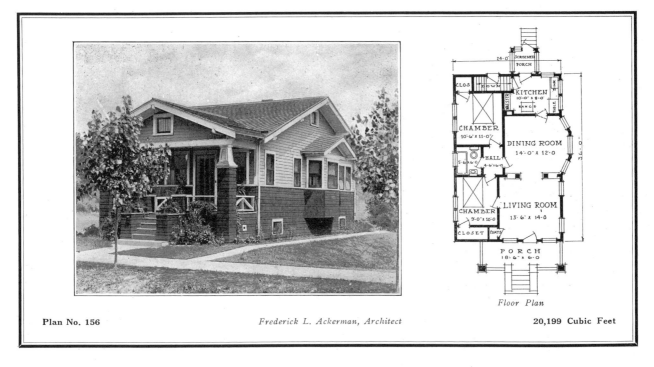

Plan No. 156   *Frederick L. Ackerman, Architect*   **20,199 Cubic Feet**

Floor Plan

(Description of house shown in above plans)

THE illustration shows the use of alternate wide and narrow courses of shingles below the sill-line, and six-inch siding above. However, practically any desired building material may be used. There are four windows, on two sides, in the living room, and it is lighted indirectly, also, through the opening which divides it from the dining room. The sunny bay is a delightful feature of the dining room. There are two long wall spaces which permit of the artistic arrangement of furniture. The kitchen is efficiently arranged.

(Description of house shown in plans below)

NO matter how small a house may be, it is always possible to work out a satisfactory plan if enough thought is put into it. There are five exceptionally fine rooms contained in this house and it has but 440 square feet of area. The open stairs are a feature of one end of the living room, and this room opens nicely into the dining room through a wide cased opening. Plenty of closets and storage space are to be found on the second floor. Exterior is of common brick with roof of slate or other shingle type.

Full directions for obtaining complete working drawings and specifications for these plans will be found on page 281

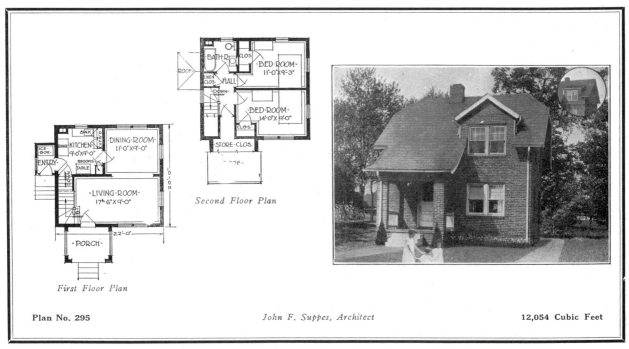

Second Floor Plan

First Floor Plan

Plan No. 295   *John F. Suppes, Architect*   **12,054 Cubic Feet**

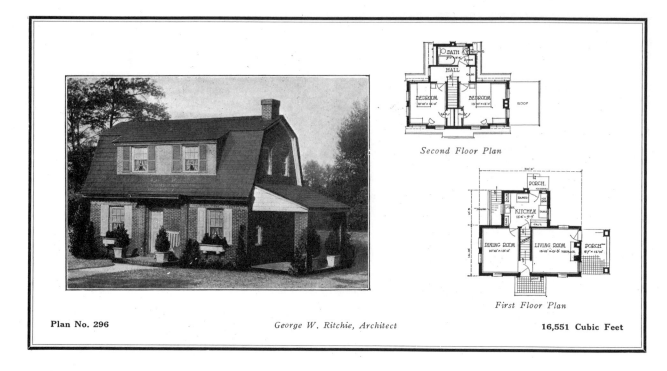

Second Floor Plan

First Floor Plan

Plan No. 296   *George W. Ritchie, Architect*   **16,551 Cubic Feet**

(Description of house shown in above plans)

HERE are shown plans and photograph of a five-room brick home designed along Dutch Colonial lines. As shown here, the house of this character should be built close to the ground to produce the most desired effect. Little space is used in the entrance hall and the living and dining rooms are on opposite sides of the house and both face the street. Two large bedrooms, bath and several closets make up the second floor.

(Description of house shown in plans below)

HERE is a small house of the Colonial type which embodies simplicity, symmetry and unassuming dignity. Its simple details make for economy of construction as does the rectangular shape of the house itself. Wide siding has a tendency to make a house look larger and would be suitable for this plan. The central hall has been omitted in this plan but the advantages of this idea are retained by modifying it to a small reception hall.

Full directions for obtaining complete working drawings and specifications for these plans will be found on page 281

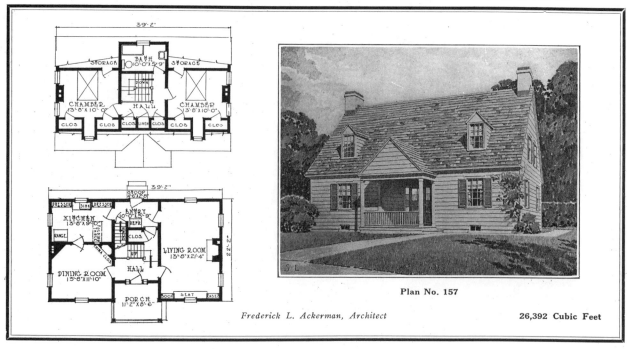

Plan No. 157

Frederick L. Ackerman, Architect   **26,392 Cubic Feet**

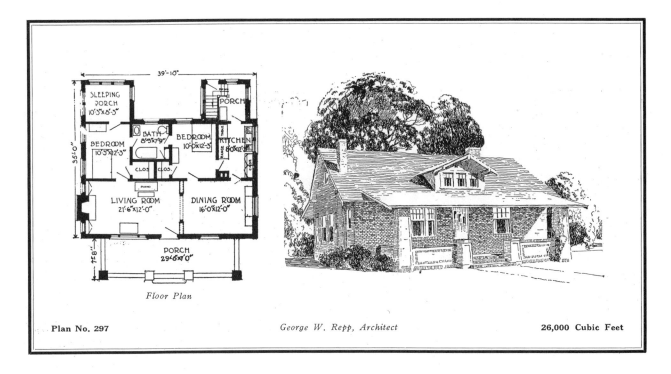

Floor Plan

Plan No. 297   *George W. Repp, Architect*   26,000 Cubic Feet

(*Description of house shown in above plans*)

PORCHES are an American institution. This Western bungalow has three. Note especially the wide, low and inviting front porch which preserves a touch of privacy by reason of the low brick parapet which surrounds it. The living and dining rooms occupy the entire front of the house and a very interesting feature is the fireplace at one end flanked by bookcases. At the other end of the long vista in the dining room is an attractive built-in buffet of simple design.

(*Description of house shown in plans below*)

BRICK veneer construction is used for this house which contains five rooms. The architect suggests the use of cement porch coping and lintels and sills. This five-room bungalow has the typical bungalow layout of rooms, being divided by a straight partition wall. The entrance from the porch is into the living room. This room is almost square, with windows on two sides, and beamed ceiling. An interroom opening has bookcases on each side.

Full directions for obtaining complete working drawings and specifications for these plans will be found on page 281

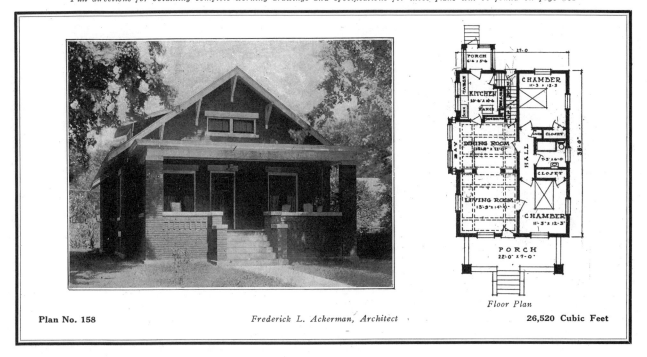

Floor Plan

Plan No. 158   *Frederick L. Ackerman, Architect*   26,520 Cubic Feet

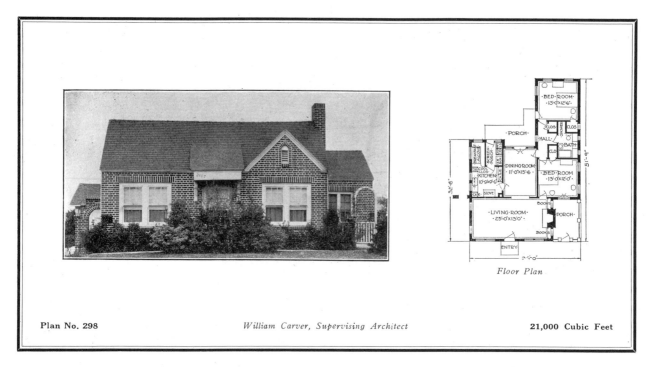

Plan No. 298   *William Carver, Supervising Architect*   **21,000 Cubic Feet**

(Description of house shown in above plans)

THERE is only one reason why a bungalow can't be made as attractive with brick as with any other material and that is the lack of feeling on the part of the designer. This five-room home was well thought out and though simple is beautiful on account of rather than in spite of its simplicity. The bedrooms with bath and closets are well removed from the living room, which insures privacy for those who care to retire earlier. The living and dining rooms are large and on account of their position may be used to good advantage to entertain.

(Description of house shown in plans below)

HERE is a house with a strictly Colonial exterior treatment in which the space usually allotted to a central hall is thrown into the living room. The open stairway to the second floor occupies a corner opposite the front entrance. This room has outside openings on three sides which affords splendid light and ventilation. On each side of the door leading to the living porch is a built-in bookcase, a splendid decorative feature. French doors lead to the dining room provided with a handsome corner china closet. The kitchen is conveniently arranged.

Full directions for obtaining complete working drawings and specifications for these plans will be found on page 281

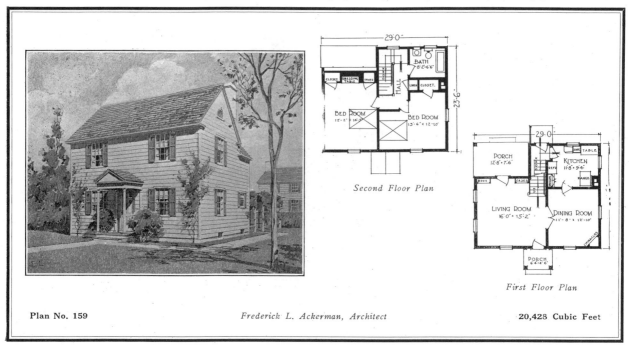

Plan No. 159   *Frederick L. Ackerman, Architect*   **20,428 Cubic Feet**

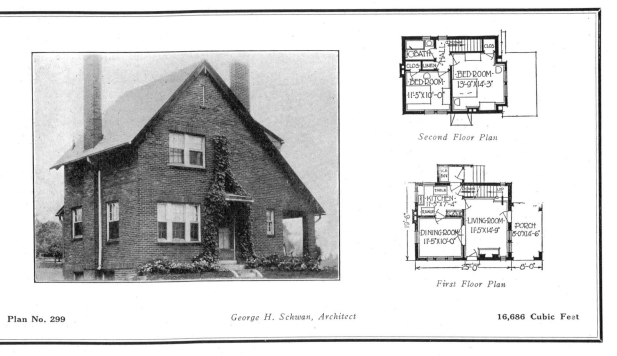

Second Floor Plan

First Floor Plan

Plan No. 299   *George H. Schwan, Architect*   16,686 Cubic Feet

(Description of house shown in above plans)

THE most interesting point about this house is the manner in which the main roof slope is continued down over the porch. The effect gained thereby is quite pleasing and gives an opportunity for a larger room on the second floor. The living room has two features; the fireplace in the front end and the open stairway in the rear. The two bedrooms on the second floor are large and well arranged. Although the illustration shows the use of brick this house might be built of stucco over hollow tile, or other construction materials.

(Description of house shown in plans below)

THIS five-room house would be suitable for a short lot, for it has no rear porch, and the front porch is practically included within the rectangle of the floor plan. The entrance to the living room is from the left of the porch. The broad opening into the dining room, which increases the apparent size of both rooms, is attractively finished with French doors, and triple windows form a sunny bay in the dining room. The center of interest in this room is the built-in sideboard of beautiful design. There are plenty of bins and drawers in the kitchen dresser.

Full directions for obtaining complete working drawings and specifications for these plans will be found on page 281

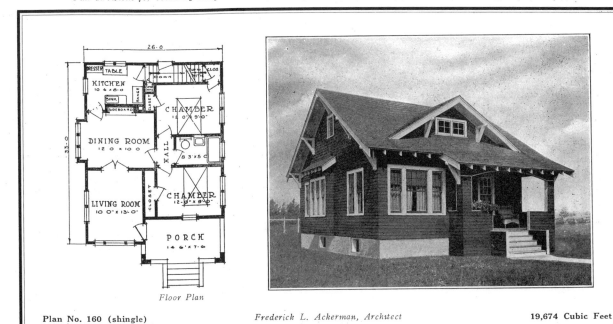

Floor Plan

Plan No. 160 (shingle)   *Frederick L. Ackerman, Architect*   19,674 Cubic Feet

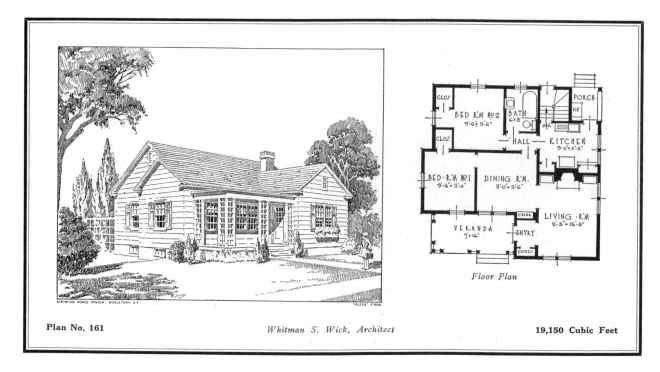

Plan No. 161   *Whitman S. Wick, Architect*   **19,150 Cubic Feet**

Floor Plan

(Description of house shown in above plans)

HERE is a dainty little Colonial bungalow containing five rooms. The exterior finish is of stained white shingles with wide exposure, and the roofs, except of the porch, are shingled also. The porch details are light and simple but in correct relation to all other details of the house. The plan is compact and windows are well placed to give proper light and air to all rooms. The fireplace with a bookcase on either side is a feature of the living room. The bathroom is conveniently located.

(Description of house shown in plans below)

THIS charmingly simple bungalow would fit the summer waterside as naturally as do the low hills and sandy beach. But its versatile lines make it suitable for a village or suburban street. The living room, with its splendid fireplace, is well lighted, and with the adjacent dining room gives ample space for entertaining. The bedrooms on the other side of the house have cross light and ventilation and are equally convenient to the bathroom through a short connecting hall. Exterior is of face brick.

Full directions for obtaining complete working drawings and specifications for these plans will be found on page 281

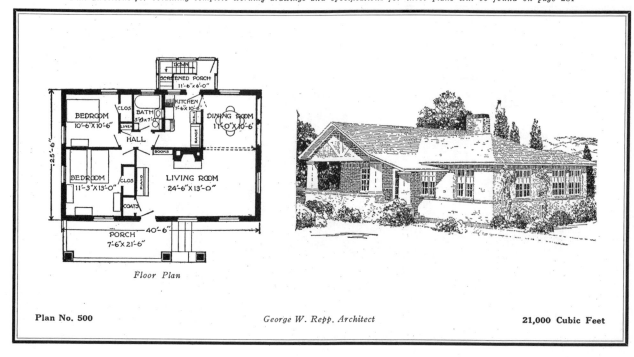

Floor Plan

Plan No. 500   *George W. Repp, Architect*   **21,000 Cubic Feet**

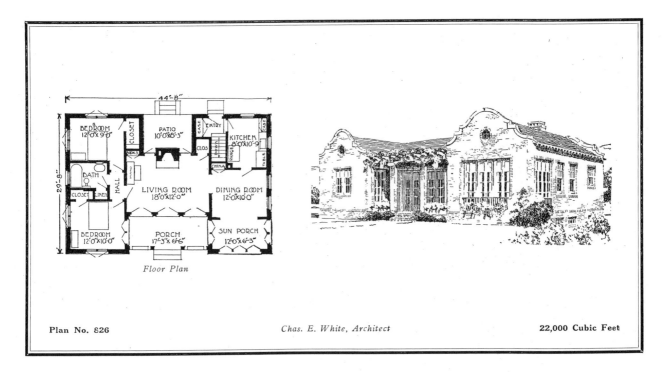

Floor Plan

Plan No. 826   *Chas. E. White, Architect*   22,000 Cubic Feet

(Description of house shown in above plans)

THE Spanish type of bungalow, so well liked in some Western states, is fast gaining popularity throughout the country. This one may be fitted to any frontage desired, but retains the outlook on the garden, through the patio. The color and texture of the brickwork will be determined greatly by the location. A tile, slate, or other substantial roof is recommended. All rooms have exposure on two sides, giving the maximum of light, air and outlook. Some special features are built-in bookcase and china cabinets.

(Description of house shown in plans below)

THIS distinctive type of five-room bungalow is constructed with brick walls and slate roof. The architect recommends the use of mingled shades of blue to red rough textured brick with 5/8″ rough-cut flush mortar joints. For the roof he recommends unfading mottled green and purple slate in graduated effect with 10″ exposure at the eaves and 4″ at ridge; the porch to be of red quarrytile with 1/2″ black joints. Garden wall and garage are designed in harmony with the house, providing an attractive unit.

Full directions for obtaining complete working drawings and specifications for these plans will be found on page 281

Floor Plan

Plan No. 210   *L. W. Rummell, Jr., Architect*   19,884 Cubic Feet

From Plans to Finished Homes

*O*N this page there are presented illustrations of typical homes constructed from the plans shown in this book. Here are three distinctly differing types indicating the wide range of this plan service.

The simple Colonial house shown above was constructed at Teaneck, N. J., from working drawings and specifications provided through the Home Owners Service Institute. Exterior is of wide siding; roof is of patented shingles and chimney of common brick.

This attractive small country home has exterior walls of stucco and roof of slate. Plans for this house are shown on page 161. Note the artistic design of the garage which harmonizes with the house exterior.

At the left is shown a six-room dwelling recently built in Brooklyn, N. Y., from plans furnished by the Home Owners Service Institute. The construction of the exterior walls of this house is stucco on concrete blocks. Roofing is of copper shingles, and face brick has been used for decorative effect on sills and porch trim.

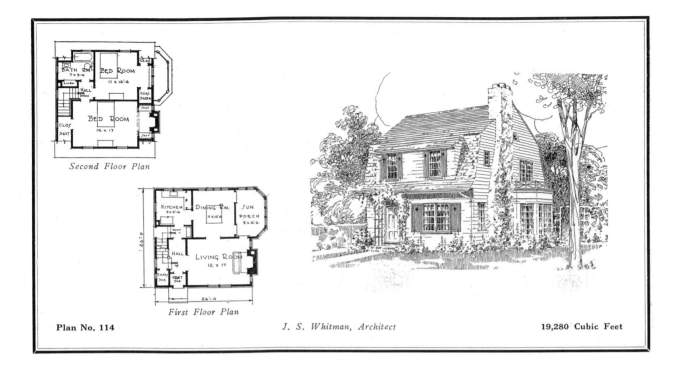

Second Floor Plan

First Floor Plan

Plan No. 114   *J. S. Whitman, Architect*   **19,280 Cubic Feet**

(Description of house shown in above plans)

THIS Dutch Colonial five-room home is particularly attractive both outside and in. The arrangement of rooms on each floor is ideal and shows thought in planning. The sun porch is reached both from the living room and the dining room. The two bedrooms are large and light and have ample closet space. The front one has a fireplace with a seat on each side. Frame construction, brick chimney.

(Description of house shown in plans below)

QUITE out of the ordinary is this brick bungalow, yet how attractive. The almost flat roofs bring the height down so that it almost seems to be part of the landscape. The living room is large and opens into the dining room through a very wide opening. What an excellent place to entertain one's friends! The bedrooms are entirely separated from the rest of the house and have large closets and good ventilation.

Full directions for obtaining complete working drawings and specifications for these plans will be found on page 281

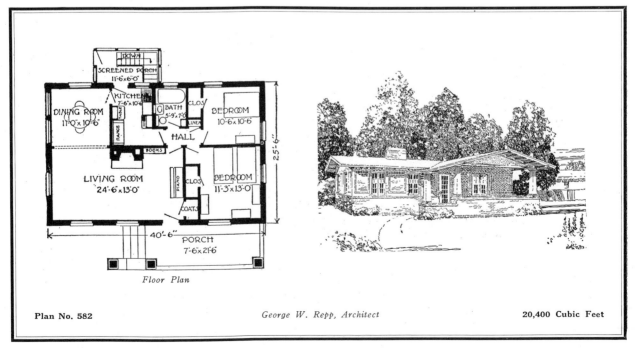

Floor Plan

Plan No. 582   *George W. Repp, Architect*   **20,400 Cubic Feet**

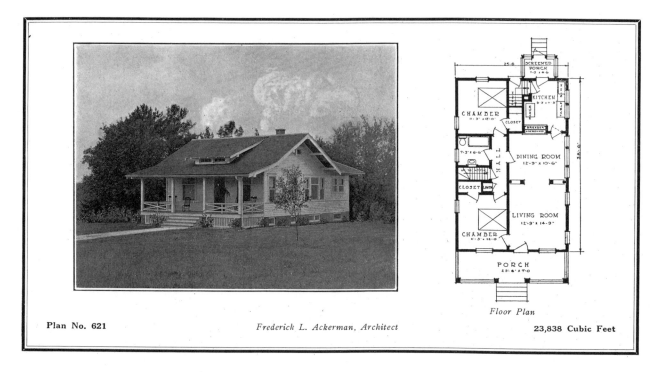

Plan No. 621   *Frederick L. Ackerman, Architect*   23,838 Cubic Feet

Floor Plan

(Description of house shown in above plans)

THE exterior of this little frame house suggests a summer home, because of its wide, sheltering eaves, ventilated attic and open porch, yet its convenient floor plan makes it a very livable home the year round. The shape of the house is rectangular, which makes for economy of construction. The basement is divided into furnace room, laundry room, coal room with chutes, a storage room and a separate fruit room, all well lighted.

(Description of house shown in plans below)

THE problem of isolating the various parts of the house is well worked out in this five-room house. In the right wing of the house are grouped two corner bedrooms with ample closets, an excellent bathroom and a linen closet with trays and drawers. Opening back of entrance hall is the dining room provided with a built-in sideboard having a central section of shelves to give it a charming antique effect. The exterior walls are of stucco with roof of patented shingles.

Full directions for obtaining complete working drawings and specifications for these plans will be found on page 281

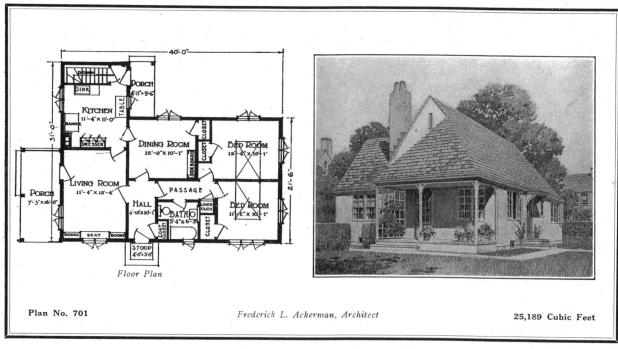

Floor Plan

Plan No. 701   *Frederick L. Ackerman, Architect*   25,189 Cubic Feet

Plans for 7- and 8-Room Houses

On the following sixty pages there are presented a large number of plans for seven- and eight-room houses. These plans have been selected with great care in order to provide houses which represent economy of first investment and maintenance. Among these plans will be found large bungalows and two-story houses constructed of practically every known material and standard method of building. Many of these plans are adaptable for the purpose of building a first unit of four or five rooms and adding additional rooms at some future time. This can easily be arranged in conference with the building contractor. While many of these houses are presented with one bath only, it will be found that plans can easily be changed to allow for another bath or for an additional lavatory if desired.

See page 281 for full information on the practical use of this plan book

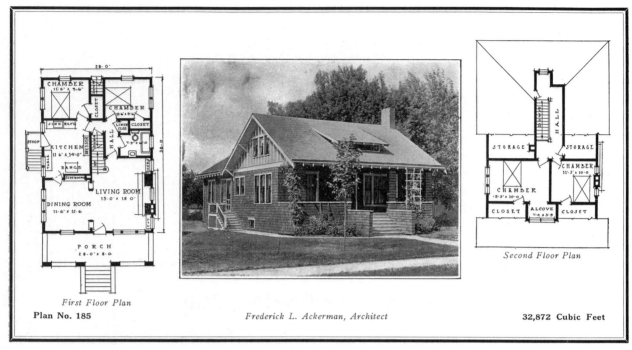

First Floor Plan

Plan No. 185   *Frederick L. Ackerman, Architect*   **32,872 Cubic Feet**

Second Floor Plan

(Description of house shown in above plans)   *(Description of house shown in plans below)*

HERE is a shingle house, with beamed stucco in the gables, that has a very interesting floor plan on two floors. The spacious front porch is designed so that it may be easily screened or glazed. The living room has an unusual number of attractive features. There is the tiled hearth, with its simple wood mantel shelf, flanked by a bookcase and a window seat that is also a receptacle for firewood. In the corner opposite the front door is a handsome open stair. The built-in sideboard is a pleasing and useful feature in the dining room. Room for second bath upstairs.

HERE is another excellent plan for a seven-room house with a downstairs bedroom. The reception hall provides easy communication between the kitchen and the front door, as well as the second floor. An inter-room opening and a built-in sideboard add to the attractiveness of the roomy, light living room and dining room. The kitchen is very compact and is conveniently arranged. It has a room-end of dressers, with sink between them under double windows. There is also a wall-cabinet ironing board, a broom closet, and inside basement steps. Stucco and frame construction.

Full directions for obtaining complete working drawings and specifications for these plans will be found on page 281

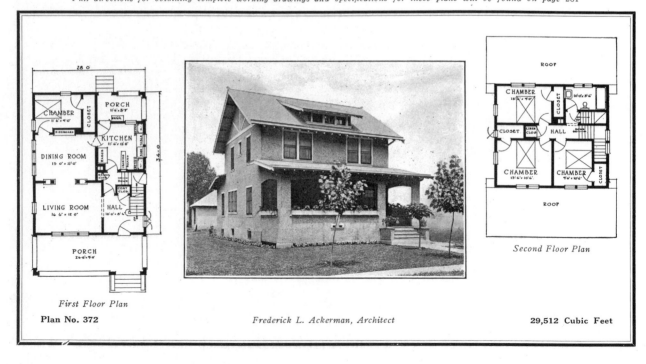

First Floor Plan

Plan No. 372   *Frederick L. Ackerman, Architect*   **29,512 Cubic Feet**

Second Floor Plan

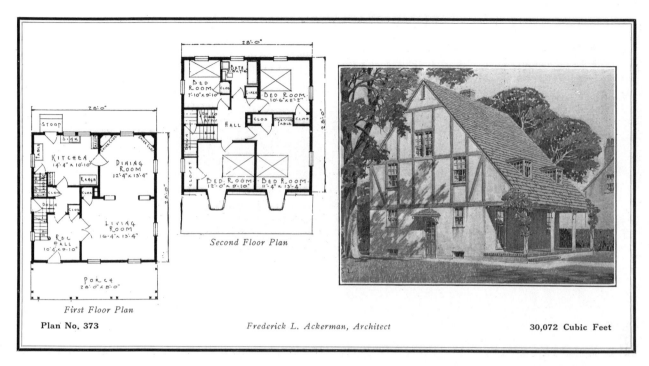

Second Floor Plan

First Floor Plan

Plan No. 373   *Frederick L. Ackerman, Architect*   **30,072 Cubic Feet**

(Description of house shown in above plans)

THIS house is an unusual and unconventional example of the half-timbered house that is increasing in popularity. Dormers break the long slope of the steep gable roof, affording ventilation in the two front bedrooms, and they are also attractive from inside the house. The floor plan has been carefully worked out. The living room and dining room are separated only by an inter-room opening so that there is a long vista from the porch through these two rooms. There are two artistic china closets in the dining room and many other built-in features throughout the house.

(Description of house shown in plans below)

THE Mansard roof, admired by many, has here been adapted to the small house. This plan requires a wide frontage if built with the living room to the front, but if turned with the entrance to the front and porch to the rear, it may be built on a fifty-foot lot. If one wishes to omit the present covered entrance, the house could be turned with the porch to the street, entering the house by way of the porch. An extremely large living room extends across the entire front. The fireplace and bookcases make this a very attractive room. Exterior walls of face brick.

Full directions for obtaining complete working drawings and specifications for these plans will be found on page 281

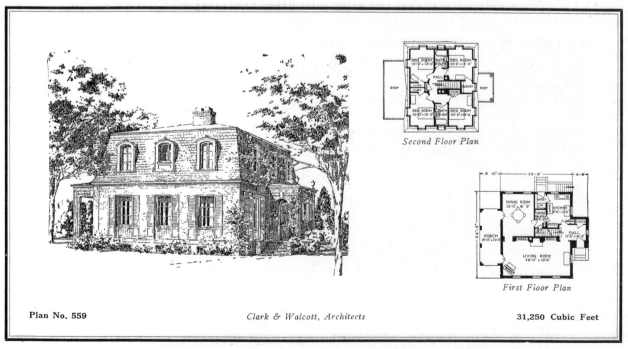

Second Floor Plan

First Floor Plan

Plan No. 559   *Clark & Walcott, Architects*   **31,250 Cubic Feet**

First Floor Plan

Second Floor Plan

Plan No. 560   *George W. Repp, Architect*   40,000 Cubic Feet

(Description of house shown in above plans)   *(Description of house shown in plans below)*

THIS house turned endwise or broadside to the street, to fit your particular lot, will be equally attractive. Following the usual Colonial plan, the hall has been centered, with the stairway ascending to landing. The living room on the left is unusually large, with a fine fireplace on the opposite wall and French doors opening to the sun porch. The dining room on the right opens on a breakfast porch beyond, directly connecting with the kitchen, pantry and rear porch. A lavatory and coat closet are conveniently placed off the hall. Note the connected garage.

ALTHOUGH the illustration shows the use of tapestry brick for the first story, with stucco above, this house could be built of almost any construction material. It would appear to best advantage on a wide lot, or a corner, using the length for the front. The inviting formal entrance admits one into a central hall with a straight flight of open stairs, and French doors at right and left leading to the dining room and living room. The latter occupies one entire end of the first floor with openings on three sides, a fireplace, bookcase, built-in seat and a long inside wall space.

Full directions for obtaining complete working drawings and specifications for these plans will be found on page 281

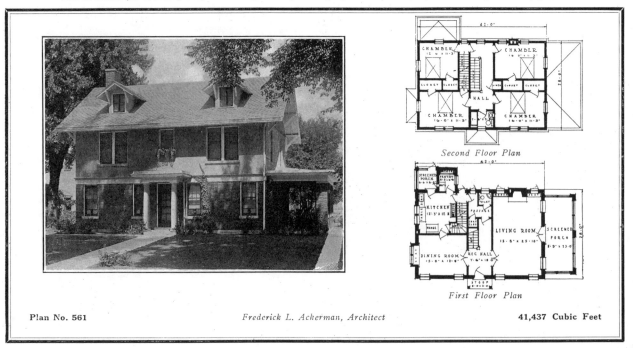

Second Floor Plan

First Floor Plan

Plan No. 561   *Frederick L. Ackerman, Architect*   41,437 Cubic Feet

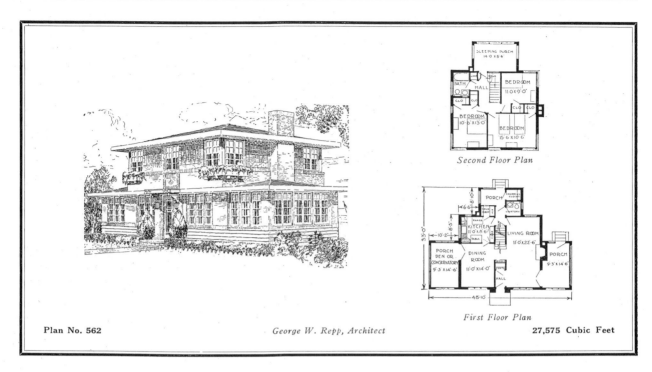

Plan No. 562   *George W. Repp, Architect*   **27,575 Cubic Feet**

Second Floor Plan

First Floor Plan

(Description of house shown in above plans)

THIS is a type of architecture developed in the middle and western states that has much to commend it. Designed along horizontal lines, it fits into the landscape of the flat or rolling prairies, and yet houses of this type have been placed in rugged, hilly countries with good effect. The broad eaves provide excellent shelter for the windows during storms. This plan is suitable for a lot facing north, as the living room and porch receive the south sun from the rear. It is a very flexible plan and should appeal to many, as it may be built as shown or with one side porch.

(Description of house shown in plans below)

HERE is a house of the economical square type, but which is nevertheless a thing of beauty, because of its good architecture. It is small enough for practically any city lot, but has every excellence of design and interior planning that a seven-room house could incorporate. The location of the living porch at the side rather than across the front has many advantages. The air of privacy expressed by the formal entrance is appropriate for a home. This is carried out by the vestibule and hall through which one passes before reaching the living room.

Full directions for obtaining complete working drawings and specifications for these plans will be found on page 281

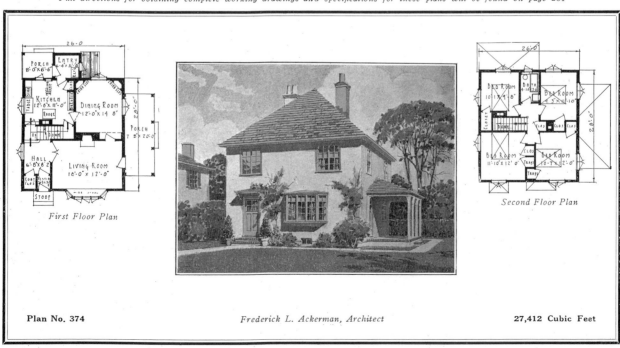

First Floor Plan

Second Floor Plan

Plan No. 374   *Frederick L. Ackerman, Architect*   **27,412 Cubic Feet**

Plan No. 375   *Frederick L. Ackerman, Architect*   33,207 Cubic Feet

Second Floor Plan

First Floor Plan

(Description of house shown in above plans)

HALF-TIMBER construction, typical of many English homes, is exemplified by this design. Twin gables are a distinctive touch, while the steep-sloping roof and the chimneys are characteristic. Stucco is indicated, but this house may be appropriately built of a combination of stucco with any locally-obtainable building material. The porch floor is cement, brick-bordered. This design includes many convenient built-in features, including bookcases on both sides of the passage into the living room.

(Description of house shown in plans below)

WHATEVER direction this house faces, some portion of the porches will always be in the shade. The front porch has direct connection with the living room by a pair of French doors, and there is a large entrance hall with an ample coat closet. The dining porch may be screened for summer use, or by glazing will make an excellent conservatory or flower room. The living room and dining room are large and together with the hall make a splendid arrangement for entertaining. Exterior walls are of rough face brick.

Full directions for obtaining complete working drawings and specifications for these plans will be found on page 281

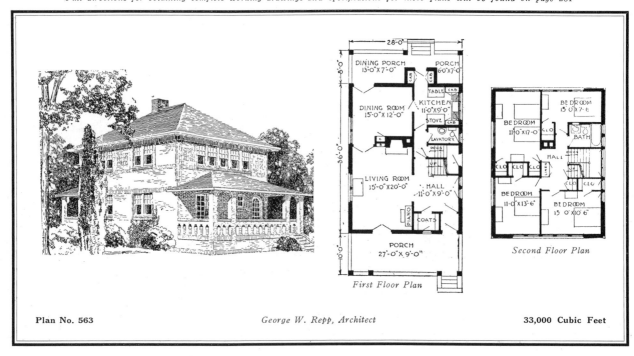

First Floor Plan

Second Floor Plan

Plan No. 563   *George W. Repp, Architect*   33,000 Cubic Feet

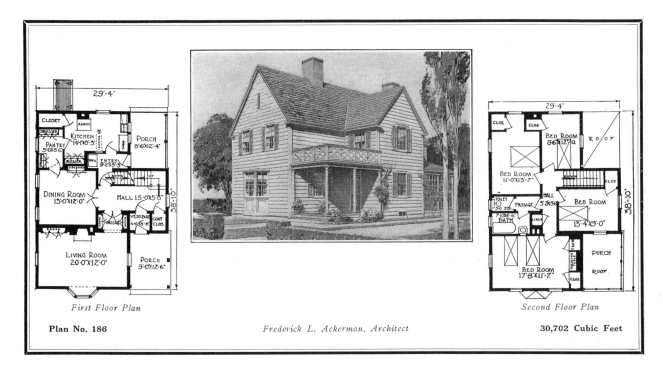

First Floor Plan   *Second Floor Plan*

Plan No. 186   *Frederick L. Ackerman, Architect*   **30,702 Cubic Feet**

(Description of house shown in above plans)

THE irregular shape of this Colonial house makes it very interesting. It is a small house, with home-like appearance, yet has seven excellent rooms, hall, pantry, vestibule, rear entry, bathroom, and many closets and built-in cabinets. The vestibule leads to a hall of good size from which the main stair rises to the second floor. This stair with its graceful, slender details, adds a valuable architectural note. The kitchen is conveniently arranged and contains several built-in features which make for efficient operation.

(Description of house shown in plans below)

HERE is a house that offers all the possibilities of fine brickwork that the old homes of England had. The general proportions and fenestration require nothing more of the wall surfaces than an appropriate bond pattern, such as Flemish, English, or Garden Wall. A brick either in mingled or uniform shades could be used. The formal Georgian entrance is very inviting and should be approached by a walk of brick the same shade as used in the house. Roof of slate or asbestos-cement shingles.

Full directions for obtaining complete working drawings and specifications for these plans will be found on page 281

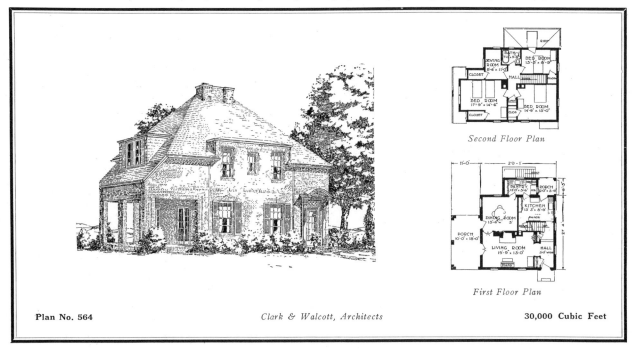

Second Floor Plan

First Floor Plan

Plan No. 564   *Clark & Walcott, Architects*   **30,000 Cubic Feet**

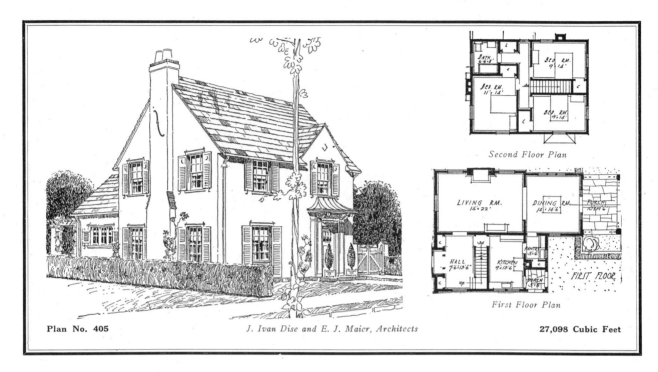

Plan No. 405   *J. Ivan Dise and E. J. Maier, Architects*   27,098 Cubic Feet

(Description of house shown in above plans)

A SIX-ROOM house with exterior walls of stucco on back plastered metal lath. The architect recommends exterior walls to be a warm white sand-finished stucco; frame sash and entrance to be painted white; blinds and entrance door blue-green. Roof to be variegated slate or weathered shingles. Cap of chimney to be painted black, with orange terra cotta pots, The first floor provides large entrance hall, large living room with open fireplace flanked by windows and a square dining room opening on to a large porch.

(Description of house shown in plans below)

THIS seven-room Colonial home would be equally attractive in stucco, in exposed tile, or with a brick veneer over hollow tile. The living room is of generous proportions, and leading from this room through French doors is the living porch. The arrangement of the service portion of the house is ideal. The ice box is located just outside the kitchen in the rear hall, and from the kitchen sink the dishes can be placed on the pantry shelf. The second floor is arranged for four bedrooms with a sleeping porch off bedrooms.

Full directions for obtaining complete working drawings and specifications for these plans will be found on page 281

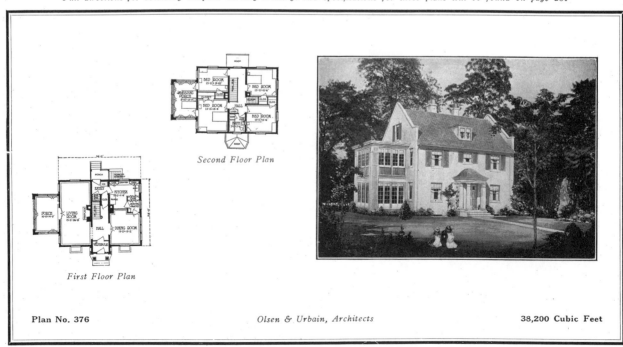

Plan No. 376   *Olsen & Urbain, Architects*   38,200 Cubic Feet

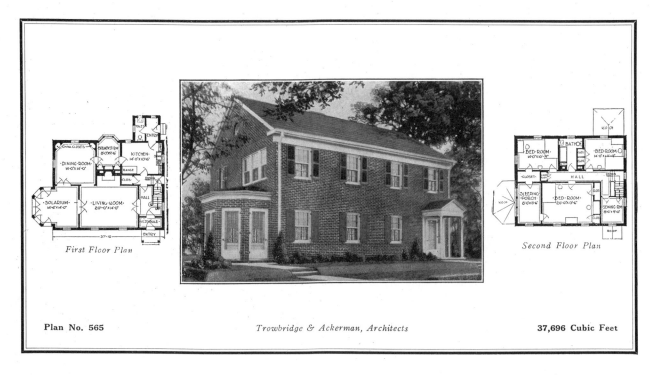

First Floor Plan

Second Floor Plan

Plan No. 565   *Trowbridge & Ackerman, Architects*   **37,696 Cubic Feet**

(Description of house shown in above plans)

THIS is an interesting example of the use of common brick in an excellent Colonial design for a large eight-room house. An attractive feature of the first floor plan is a large solarium having entrances to both living room and dining room. The dining room has the special feature of built-in china closets in the corners. A breakfast room with well-lighted bay is also provided. An attractive Colonial staircase leads up from the entrance hall. The second floor has a built-in sleeping porch and a sewing room.

(Description of house shown in plans below)

THE entrance to this charming bungalow is beneath an open pergola which extends half-way across the front of the building, thus permitting plenty of sunshine and light to come directly into the living room. The illustration shows this bungalow finished in stucco. This design would also be especially attractive with walls of hollow tile finished with a brick veneer. Extending through the center of the house and dividing the living and sleeping quarters is the hall. Stucco on hollow tile specified.

Full directions for obtaining complete working drawings and specifications for these plans will be found on page 281

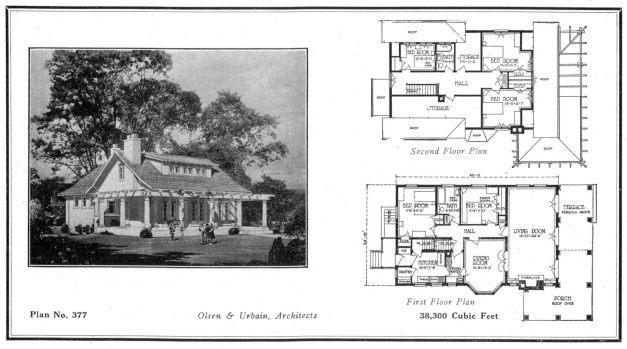

Second Floor Plan

First Floor Plan

Plan No. 377   *Olsen & Urbain, Architects*   **38,300 Cubic Feet**

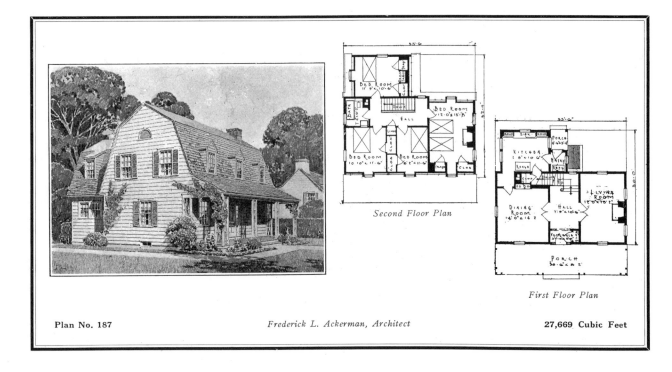

Second Floor Plan

First Floor Plan

Plan No. 187   *Frederick L. Ackerman, Architect*   **27,669 Cubic Feet**

(Description of house shown in above plans)

HERE is another house of the popular Dutch Colonial type with gambrel roof. Trellised posts add to the attractiveness of the spacious front veranda, included under the graceful sweep of the roof. A six-panel Colonial door with sidelights admits one to the house. The interior plan is of the central hall type with the kitchen in an ell at the rear. At the right as one enters is the coat closet, and straight ahead is a handsome Colonial stair.

(Description of house shown in plans below)

THE principal charm of this seven-room bungalow is its graceful roof lines and treatment of gable walls. The beauty of the wall surface will be enhanced by laying the brick in a Flemish or Garden Wall bond. If built on a corner lot the house could be set across the rear end of the lot facing the long side of the property, allowing space for a driveway at one side with ample room for a garden on the other side toward the corner. Roof of clay tile.

Full directions for obtaining complete working drawings and specifications for these plans will be found on page 281

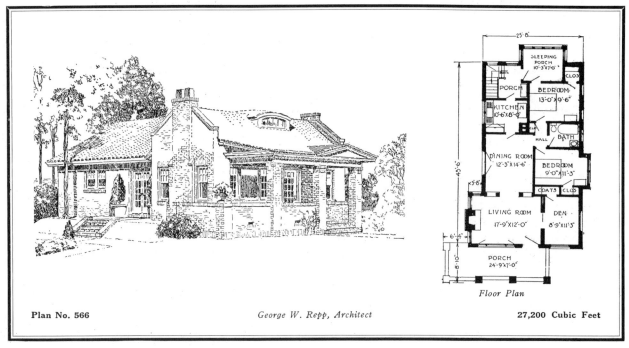

Floor Plan

Plan No. 566   *George W. Repp, Architect*   **27,200 Cubic Feet**

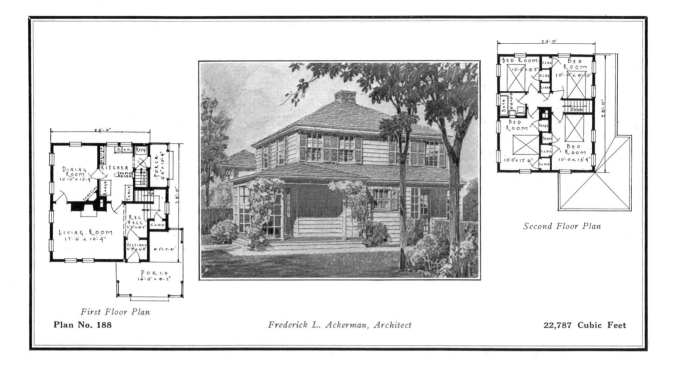

First Floor Plan

Plan No. 188   *Frederick L. Ackerman, Architect*   **22,787 Cubic Feet**

Second Floor Plan

(Description of house shown in above plans)

THIS square house demonstrates the suitability of the Colonial type for the ordinary city lot. There is an abundance of windows, and when divided into small panes they become a part of the design. The paneled shutters on the first floor and blinds upstairs are good and should blend with the roof in color. The floor plan is well arranged and provides many special features, including china closet, built-in dresser in kitchen, plenty of closets and tray cases.

(Description of house shown in plans below)

HERE is another excellent example of the Dutch Colonial type having a gambrel roof that folds down in a comfortable, protecting way over the house, leaving the dormers flush with the brick wall of the first story. Treating the gabled ends with a different colored brick from those used on the sides would form a pleasing effect. By extending the entry porch a few feet a sleeping porch could be installed directly off one of the back bedrooms. Face brick exterior.

Full directions for obtaining complete working drawings and specifications for these plans will be found on page 281

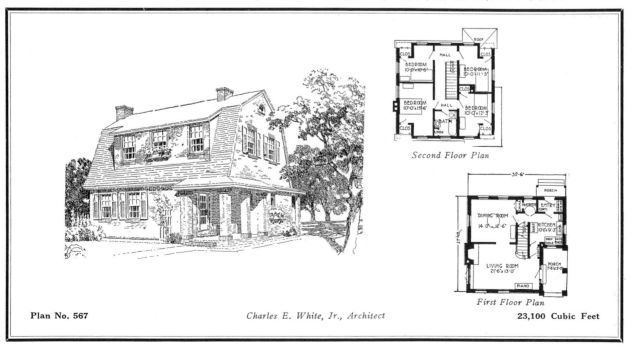

Second Floor Plan

First Floor Plan

Plan No. 567   *Charles E. White, Jr., Architect*   **23,100 Cubic Feet**

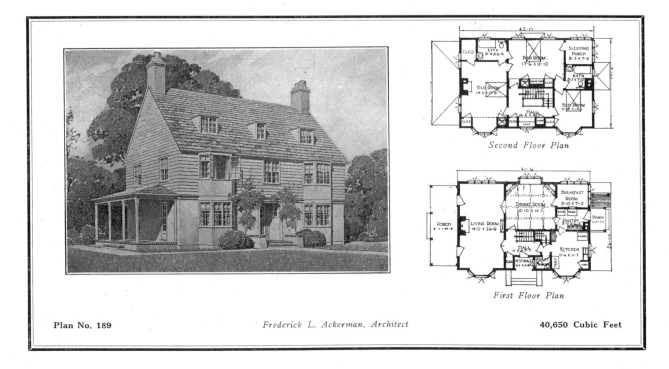

Plan No. 189   *Frederick L. Ackerman, Architect*   **40,650 Cubic Feet**

(Description of house shown in above plans)

PERFECT symmetry is observed in the composition of this handsome house in the bays, dormers, chimneys, and openings on each elevation. The illustration shows the use of wide siding for the overhanging upper story and stucco for the first story. The steep roof is shingled and the flat roofs of dormers and bays are of tin. The hall is the master-key to this home. From it one may reach directly any room and by means of it isolate any room from the rest.

(Description of house shown in plans below)

HERE is a good example of the popular rectangular house with a low, hipped roof. The plan is compact and convenient. The porch has steps to the driveway, besides those to the main walk, which make it convenient for the motorist. From the hall one may enter the living and dining rooms or go directly to the kitchen. The living room is of ample size and contains a fireplace which is attractively set in an alcove with seats at either side.

Full directions for obtaining complete working drawings and specifications for these plans will be found on page 281

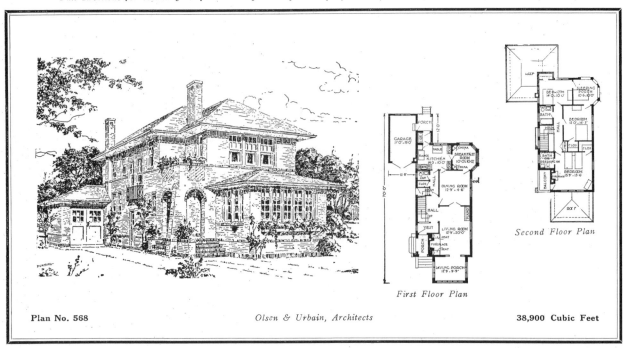

Plan No. 568   *Olsen & Urbain, Architects*   **38,900 Cubic Feet**

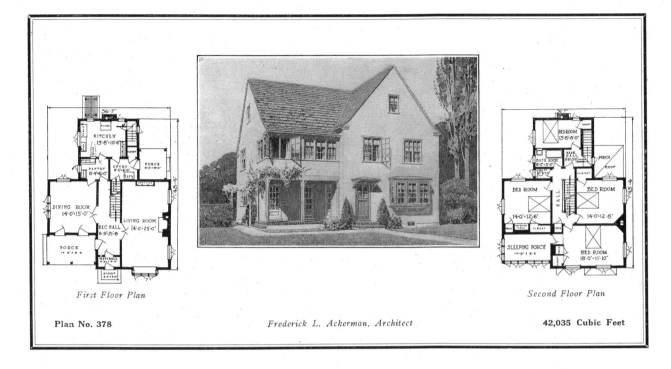

First Floor Plan

Second Floor Plan

Plan No. 378   Frederick L. Ackerman, Architect   42,035 Cubic Feet

(Description of house shown in above plans)

HERE is another English type of house designed for economical construction, and the interior has the added enticement of being a real home even before a piece of furniture is moved in because so many of the needs are taken care of by built-in features. The living room contains a fine bay and it extends through to the back porch. On the long outside wall is a fireplace, flanked by pairs of casements, and there is a built-in bookcase at the far end of the room.

(Description of house shown in plans below)

SIMPLICITY is the keynote of this design, which adapts itself to all colors and textures of brick. Two shades of brick might be used, one for the field and the other for the trim. Thus the band course at the second story window sill, the quoins, arches, and the like, might be either slightly darker or lighter than the body of the wall. The porch adjacent to the dining room and kitchen may, if desired, be converted into a maid's bedroom by omitting French doors.

Full directions for obtaining complete working drawings and specifications for these plans will be found on page 281

First Floor Plan

Second Floor Plan

Plan No. 569   George W. Repp, Architect   40,000 Cubic Feet

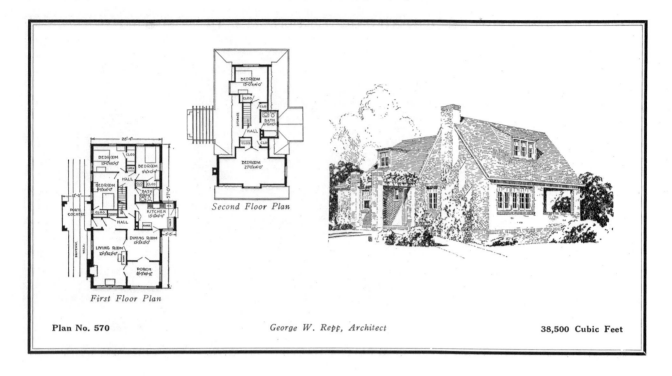

Second Floor Plan

First Floor Plan

Plan No. 570   *George W. Repp, Architect*   **38,500 Cubic Feet**

(Description of house shown in above plans)

THE exterior design here is a good example of the English cottage. The driveway and kitchen walk, at either side, leave a good expanse of unbroken lawn to be enjoyed from the living room and porch windows. The porch is under the main roof of the house and could be easily transformed into the popular sun parlor; in fact, with this style of exterior, the porch could be extended across the entire front of the house if a large open porch is desired. Face brick walls.

(Description of house shown in plans below)

HERE is a house that has many unusual features. There is a washroom adjoining the rear porch; also a bedroom on the first floor, so necessary when there is sickness; or it may be used as a bedroom for hired help. The living room owes its homelikeness to its fireplace with bookcases at each side, and two interroom openings with handy cabinets. There is a built-in sideboard in the dining room as well as a handy closet. The construction is of frame and stucco.

Full directions for obtaining complete working drawings and specifications for these plans will be found on page 281

First Floor Plan

Second Floor Plan

Plan No. 379   *Frederick L. Ackerman, Architect*   **34,450 Cubic Feet**

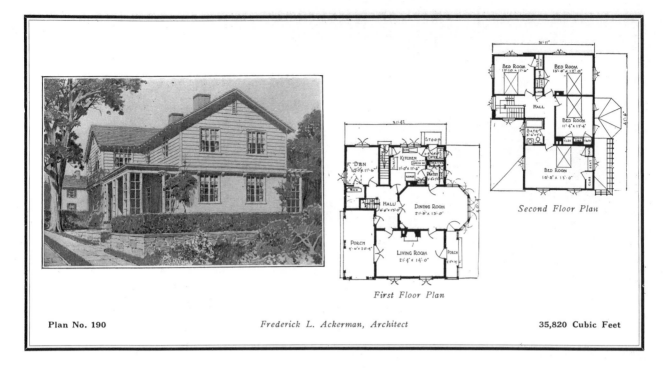

Plan No. 190   *Frederick L. Ackerman, Architect*   **35,820 Cubic Feet**

First Floor Plan

Second Floor Plan

(Description of house shown in above plans)

HERE is a house of the Western type with stucco first story, an overhanging second story with 10″ siding and brackets, louvres and latticed porch posts. There are several features about this plan that make it just as desirable for a farm or suburban home as for the city. One of these is the downstairs den which may be used as the office, or as a bedroom. Another point is the fact that the entrance hall gives direct access to every room in the house.

(Description of house shown in plans below)

THIS simple Western type has been planned for the average suburban lot. The living and dining rooms overlook the street, while the living room has a splendid view through the porch to the garden beyond. A special feature of the first floor is the splendid library with lavatory adjoining. Or, if desired, it could be changed into a bedroom by converting the present closet in the kitchen into one for the new bedroom. Exterior is of face brick.

Full directions for obtaining complete working drawings and specifications for these plans will be found on page 281

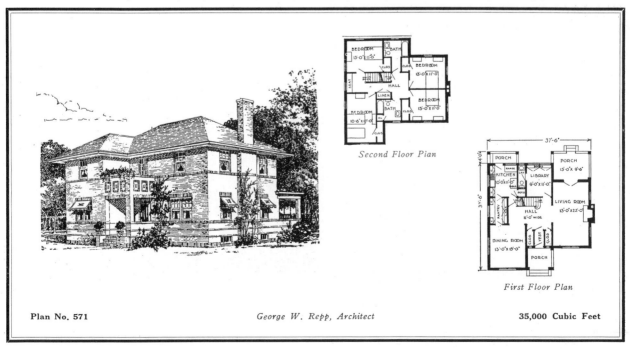

Second Floor Plan

First Floor Plan

Plan No. 571   *George W. Repp, Architect*   **35,000 Cubic Feet**

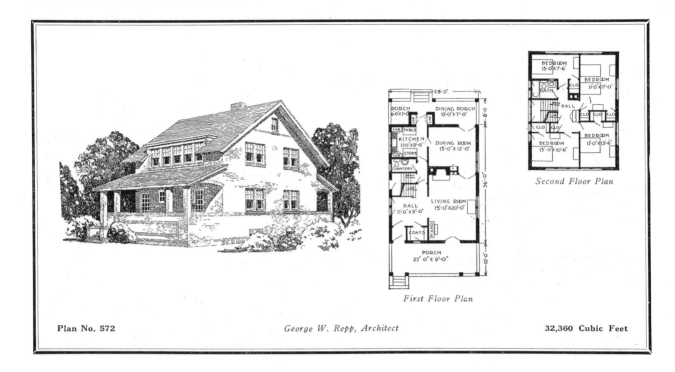

Plan No. 572   *George W. Repp, Architect*   **32,360 Cubic Feet**

(Description of house shown in above plans)

HERE we have another type of Western exterior in which the seven rooms have been well arranged. This plan, being rectangular in shape with one bearing partition through the middle, is very simple in construction, so that the house can be built for less than a smaller one that has a number of angles and breaks in its outline. This house need not be built on a level lot, as it is adaptable to a site which slopes either from front to rear or from one side to the other.

(Description of house shown in plans below)

THE illustration shows an interesting treatment of the shingled roof in which every eighth course is doubled. Siding is put on in alternate courses 4½″ and 2″ to the weather. The vestibule and central hall go straight through the house. From the hall one passes to the dining room and living room through cased openings, or may go directly to the kitchen. The living room extends across one end of the house and the fireplace is the center of attraction.

Full directions for obtaining complete working drawings and specifications for these plans will be found on page 281

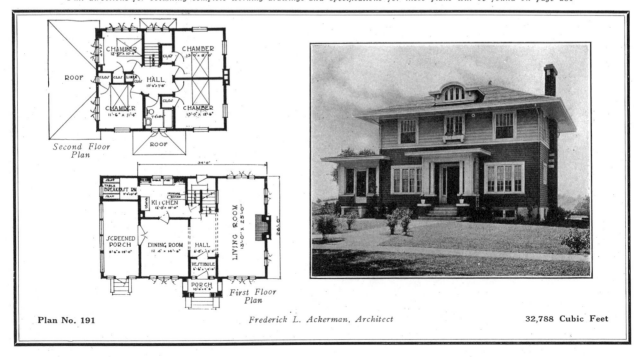

Plan No. 191   *Frederick L. Ackerman, Architect*   **32,788 Cubic Feet**

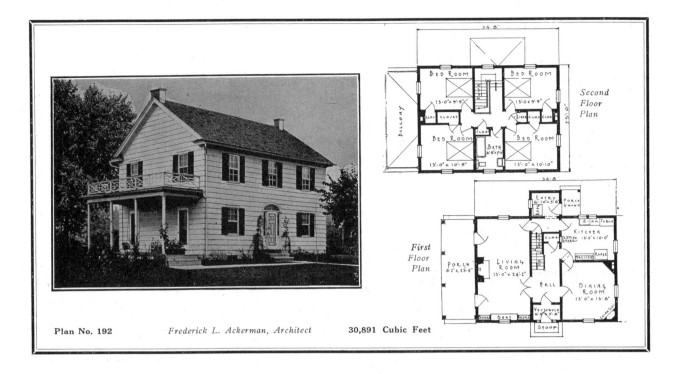

Plan No. 192   *Frederick L. Ackerman, Architect*   **30,891 Cubic Feet**

(Description of house shown in above plans)

HERE is a fine example of the Colonial tendency in architecture. The simplicity of the exterior enhances the beautiful entrance with its six-paneled molded door, sidelights and elliptical transom. The completeness of the plans is worthy of note. Beyond the vestibule is the hall, with its typical stair of mahogany and white. A coat closet is nearby. Another excellent feature is the direct entrance from the kitchen to this front hall, which saves rear stair.

(Description of house shown in plans below)

HERE is another fine example suggesting the Dutch Colonial style which is so popular. The interior arrangement is exceptionally attractive and the sleeping quarters on the first floor have been well isolated from the living rooms. The kitchen could not be better placed and is equipped with cabinets in place of a pantry. The basement includes laundry and drying room, heating plant, fuel bins, storage space and vegetable cellar. Exterior walls of face brick.

Full directions for obtaining complete working drawings and specifications for these plans will be found on page 281

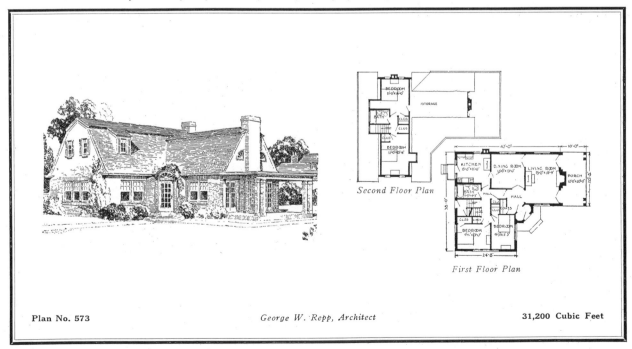

Plan No. 573   *George W. Repp, Architect*   **31,200 Cubic Feet**

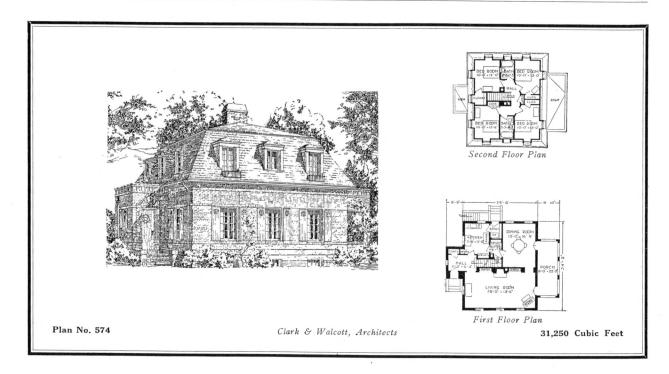

Second Floor Plan

First Floor Plan

Plan No. 574   *Clark & Walcott, Architects*   31,250 Cubic Feet

(Description of house shown in above plans)

HERE is a house of simple composition that has a graceful roof, will fit well into almost any surrounding, and affords an excellent opportunity for a display of fine brickwork in bond pattern and mortar joint. An extremely large living room extends across the entire front. The fireplace and bookcases, together with the openings to the dining room and hall, make the side of this room very attractive.

(Description of house shown in plans below)

A NORTH or east front is particularly desirable for this seven-room house. The big living room extends across the house and is lighted from three sides. At one end a handsome open stair shares honors with the homelike fireplace. There are two built-in seats near the fireplace, one beside it and one at right angles. Between the living room and dining room there is an inter-room opening with bookcases.

Full directions for obtaining complete working drawings and specifications for these plans will be found on page 281

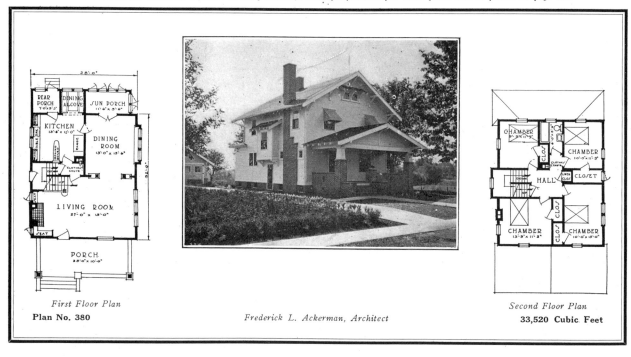

First Floor Plan

Plan No. 380   *Frederick L. Ackerman, Architect*

Second Floor Plan

33,520 Cubic Feet

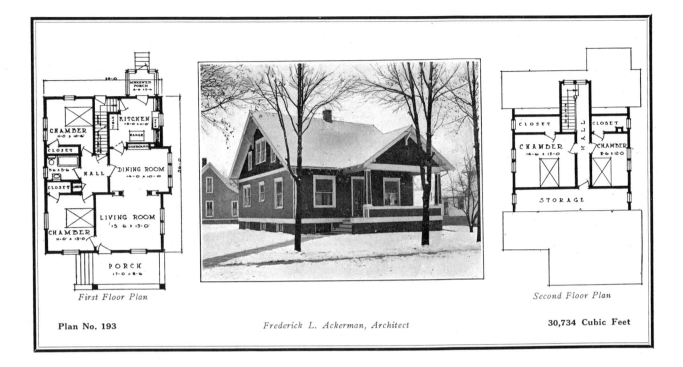

First Floor Plan

Second Floor Plan

Plan No. 193   *Frederick L. Ackerman, Architect*   **30,734 Cubic Feet**

(Description of house shown in above plans)

ONE would hardly guess, from the exterior, that this house has seven good-sized rooms. The first floor is a complete five-room bungalow in itself, while upstairs are two good bedrooms with large closets and well-lighted storage space. In this house the use of six-inch siding and shingles, with the belt courses and window frames, affords an opportunity for skilful use of color contrast accentuated by white trim.

(Description of house shown in plans below)

IT would not be hard to imagine this house covered with green vines and the red of the bricks peeping through here and there. The porch with its segmental arches is quite in keeping with the materials of construction used. The plans contain seven rooms and ample closet space, besides bath, pantry and rear porch. The second story bedrooms all have square ceilings. Roofing of slate or asbestos shingles.

Full directions for obtaining complete working drawings and specifications for these plans will be found on page 281

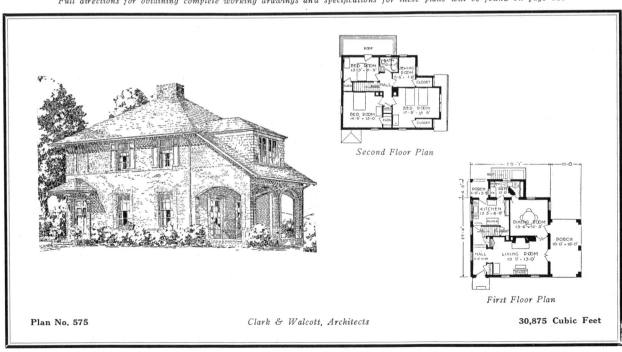

Second Floor Plan

First Floor Plan

Plan No. 575   *Clark & Walcott, Architects*   **30,875 Cubic Feet**

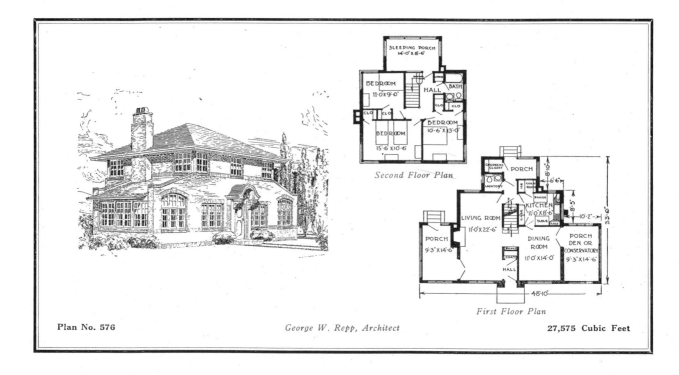

Plan No. 576   *George W. Repp, Architect*   27,575 Cubic Feet

(Description of house shown in above plans)

HERE is a house that has been carefully designed for convenience and comfort. The large living room has a fine fireplace on one side, opposite which is a broad opening connecting with the dining room. The stairway leads up from this central point and the bookshelves facing it form an attractive feature, seen from both living room and dining room. The lavatory in the back hall is a convenient feature.

(Description of house shown in plans below)

THIS plan would fit a very narrow lot, as this seven-room house is only twenty-two feet wide. Notice the good effect of having the cellar sash set down in areaways so that the house does not stand high up above the ground. The treatment of the solarium and sleeping porch makes each a real part of the house. The rooms are well planned as to size, light and ventilation, and built-in features.

Full directions for obtaining complete working drawings and specifications for these plans will be found on page 281

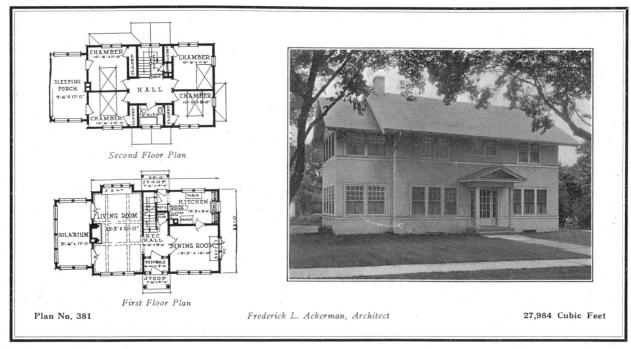

Plan No. 381   *Frederick L. Ackerman, Architect*   27,984 Cubic Feet

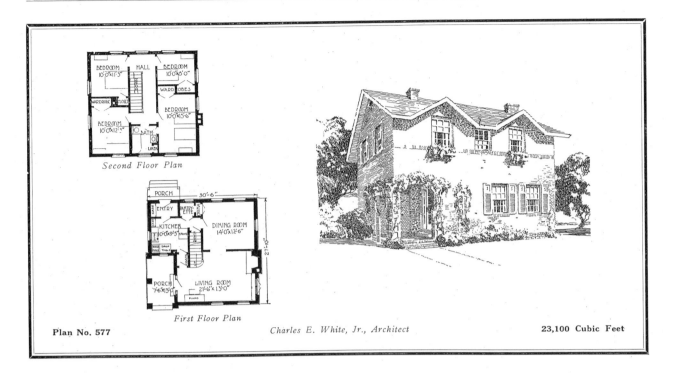

Second Floor Plan

First Floor Plan

Plan No. 577   *Charles E. White, Jr., Architect*   **23,100 Cubic Feet**

(Description of house shown in above plans)

HERE is a fine Western type of house which is suiable for a comparatively small lot. The porch, included in the floor plan, forms an outdoor vestibule for the entrance to the large living room, in which there is a cheerful fireplace. The opening into the dining room might be widened, if desired, to turn almost the entire first floor into one room. A Colonial stairway leads to the second floor. Face brick walls.

(Description of house shown in plans below)

THIS is a well designed house of the Western type and though not a large house contains seven rooms of ample size. The living room has direct light from two sides and indirect light from the French doors that lead to the dining room. The beamed ceiling is an attractive feature. A glazed door leads to the generous living porch at the side, which augments the size of the living room. Built of frame and stucco.

Full directions for obtaining complete working drawings and specifications for these plans will be found on page 281

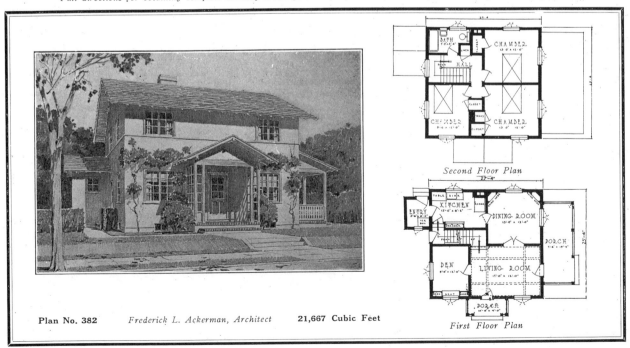

Second Floor Plan

First Floor Plan

Plan No. 382   *Frederick L. Ackerman, Architect*   **21,667 Cubic Feet**

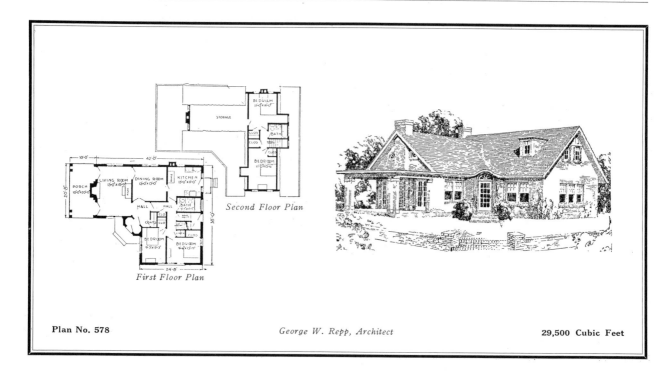

Plan No. 578   *George W. Repp, Architect*   **29,500 Cubic Feet**

(Description of house shown in above plans)

THE entrance in the angle of the house is unusually charming in its effect. The door at grade on the side of the house may serve also as a driveway entrance. The grouping of the living room, dining room, porch, and hall is the attractive feature of this house. The two bedrooms on the first floor are very convenient, especially if there are children or elderly people in the family. Exterior is of face brick.

(Description of house shown in plans below)

ALTERNATE courses of wide and narrow siding and brick porchwork are striking exterior features of this rambling little cottage. The porch and terrace extend around to the side of the house. The first floor is a complete five-room home, so that if desired the two upstairs bedrooms need not be finished up until later. The living room has a room end of fireplace, bookcase, window seat and casements.

Full directions for obtaining complete working drawings and specifications for these plans will be found on page 281

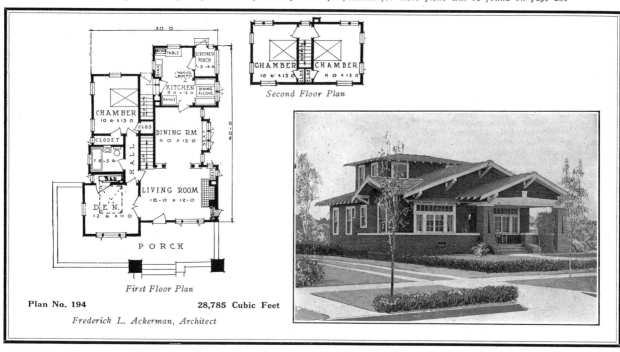

Plan No. 194   **28,785 Cubic Feet**

Frederick L. Ackerman, Architect

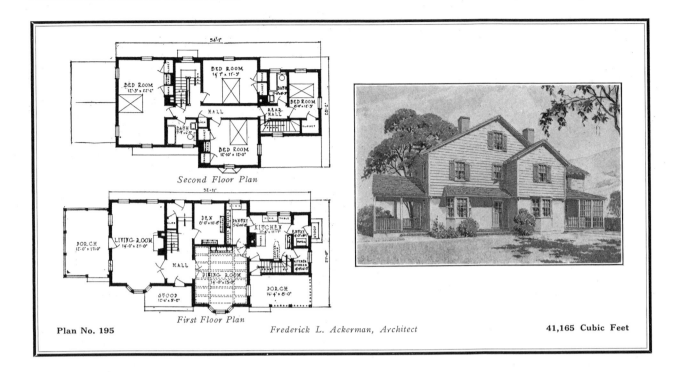

Second Floor Plan

First Floor Plan

Plan No. 195   *Frederick L. Ackerman, Architect*   **41,165 Cubic Feet**

(Description of house shown in above plans)

SOMETIMES it is more convenient to have the drive at the rear of the house, leaving the front lawn unbroken. In that case, it is a decided advantage if guests can enter the main hall directly from the rear as well as the front. For a site where space is not at a premium the illustration shows a design that is an excellent plan of this sort. The porch elevation makes an equally good front for a narrow lot.

(Description of house shown in plans below)

SIMPLE and economical in construction, this Western bungalow has a fine arrangement and disposition of rooms. The living rooms are grouped at one end, while the bedrooms and bath are isolated at the other. The living room, dining room and porch may be thrown together, or each one shut off with French doors. The entrance on the side of the house is covered with a porte-cochere, a very desirable feature.

Full directions for obtaining complete working drawings and specifications for these plans will be found on page 281

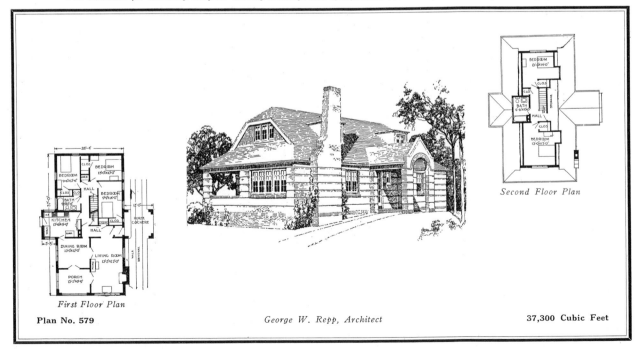

Second Floor Plan

First Floor Plan

Plan No. 579   *George W. Repp, Architect*   **37,300 Cubic Feet**

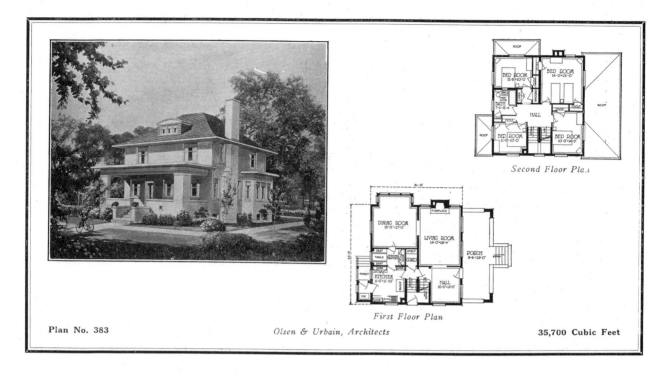

Plan No. 383   Olsen & Urbain, Architects   35,700 Cubic Feet

Second Floor Plan

First Floor Plan

(Description of house shown in above plans)

THIS seven-room residence would be equally attractive in stucco, brick veneer or with matt-faced exposed tile. From the reception room one may pass upstairs to the sleeping rooms, into the passageway leading to the rear of the house or into the commodious living room. On the first floor, in addition to the living room, dining room and kitchen, there is a breakfast alcove which can be used for serving breakfast and luncheon and is a big labor saver.

(Description of house shown in plans below)

THIS house has a dignity in its design that makes it particularly suited to brick construction. It would look well in a suburban location and would fit a corner or inside lot of 50-ft. frontage. A terrace along the front with the large living room windows opening on to it would be an attractive feature. The first floor rooms are nicely grouped and the glazed porch is attractive viewed from either living room or dining room. The dimensions are 27 ft. by 31 ft.

Full directions for obtaining complete working drawings and specifications for these plans will be found on page 281

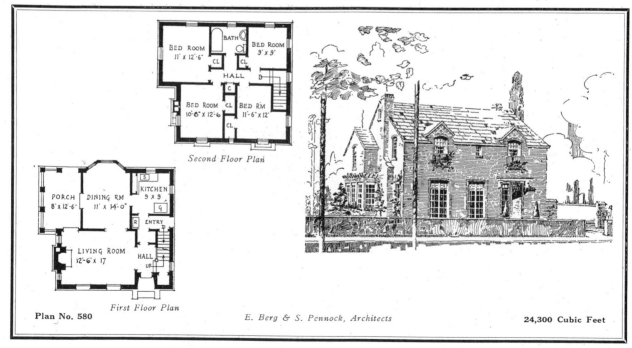

Second Floor Plan

First Floor Plan

Plan No. 580   E. Berg & S. Pennock, Architects   24,300 Cubic Feet

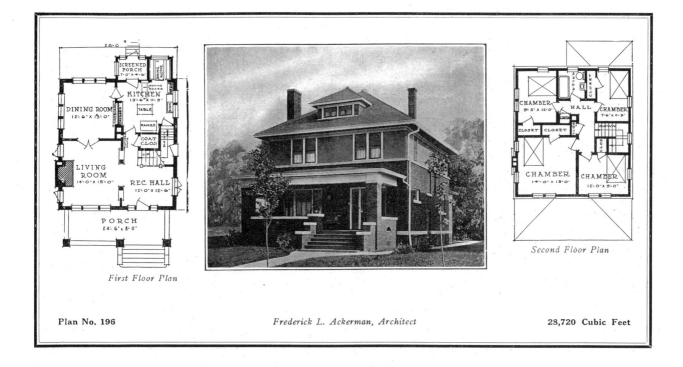

First Floor Plan

Second Floor Plan

Plan No. 196   Frederick L. Ackerman, Architect   28,720 Cubic Feet

(*Description of house shown in above plans*)

HERE is a design which combines economical, substantial construction with convenient arrangement and excellent planning of details. The reception hall and the living room, separated from it only by an inter-room opening, occupy the front of the house. The fireplace on the outside wall has a casement window on each side, and French doors lead to the dining room. Exterior of shingles and stucco.

(*Description of house shown in plans below*)

THE simple Western lines of this house are enriched by a pleasing brick pattern in the porch gable and by the pergola which forms a delightful feature when covered with rambling vines. Six rooms and a sleeping porch, which is virtually an extra bedroom, with a den that could serve as another bedroom, make this a small house for a large family, and the floor plan has been carefully worked out.

Full directions for obtaining complete working drawings and specifications for these plans will be found on page 281

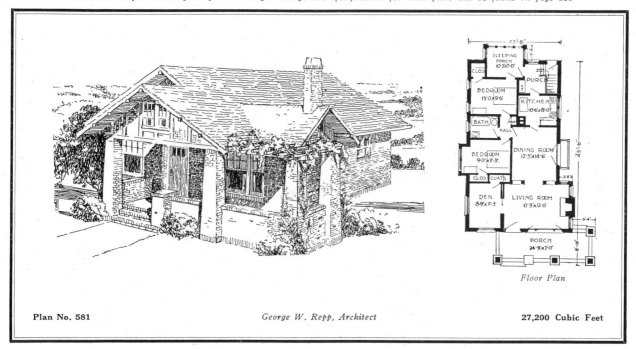

Floor Plan

Plan No. 581   George W. Repp, Architect   27,200 Cubic Feet

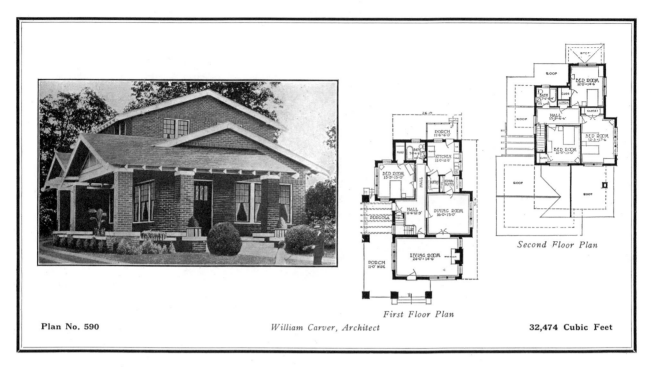

Plan No. 590   *William Carver, Architect*   32,474 Cubic Feet

(Description of house shown in above plans)   *(Description of house shown in plans below)*

HERE is an attractive dwelling of Western type with exterior of selected common brick. The roof is of shingle type with slate specified. There is a large porch which extends around the side of the house and terminates in a pergola. The living room is lighted from three sides and has an open fireplace flanked by small casement windows. The dining room is lighted by casement windows and connects with the kitchen through a large butler's pantry. On the first floor a servant's bedroom and bath is provided. On the second floor there are three large bedrooms.

IN this design a pleasing exterior is coupled with a floor plan that is nearly ideal. It has the long living room and dining room that is really a part of it. There is the sideboard and kitchen dresser back-to-back, with sliding mirrors between. There is the built-in ironing board, dining alcove with windows on two sides that occupies one corner, the broom closet, and the refrigerator entry that is within the house. Then there is the centrally located hall, separated from the living room by a cased opening, with its impressive stair, its coat closet, and lavatory opening off it.

Full directions for obtaining complete working drawings and specifications for these plans will be found on page 281

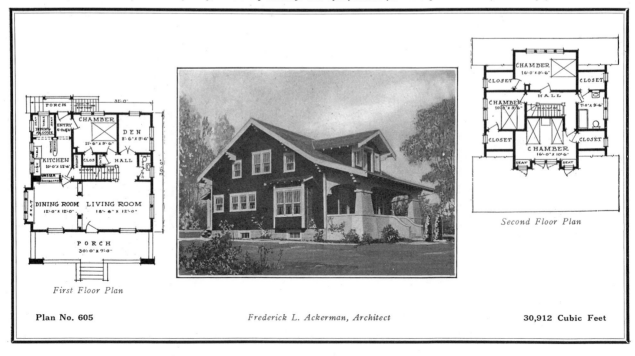

Plan No. 605   *Frederick L. Ackerman, Architect*   30,912 Cubic Feet

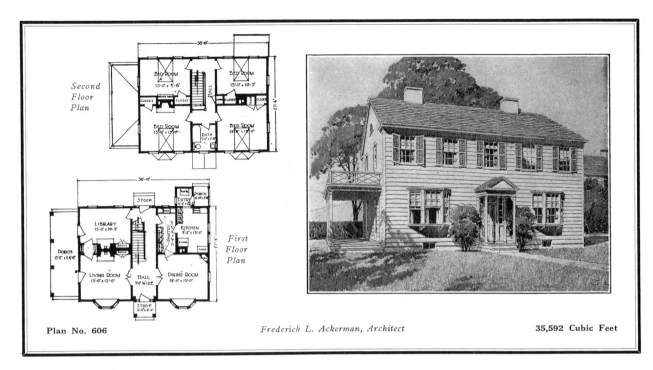

Plan No. 606   *Frederick L. Ackerman, Architect*   35,592 Cubic Feet

(Description of house shown in above plans)   *(Description of house shown in plans below)*

MANY builders regard the Colonial as the most economical type of house to build. It is so plain and simple in form and construction that there is no waste. This house is recommended for its economy and for its excellent plan. The central hall divides the house. On one side are the living room and library, both of which have fireplaces and built-in bookcases. The bedrooms are especially desirable, with excellent ventilation and plenty of closet space. An interesting feature here is the open fireplace in one of the bedrooms. This could be omitted if desired.

THIS large Colonial house has exterior walls of common brick and roof of slate shingles. The living room occupies one entire end of the house and opens directly into a large sun room. Entry is directly into a central hall from which stairs lead up. In this hall is located a large coat closet, and arched doors provide entry into the living room and into a well arranged dining room. From the dining room there is an entrance to a large living porch. The kitchen is conveniently arranged with a small service porch. Four bedrooms are provided upstairs.

Full directions for obtaining complete working drawings and specifications for these plans will be found on page 281

Plan No. 591   *William Carver, Supervising Architect*   33,608 Cubic Feet

First Floor Plan

Second Floor Plan

Plan No. 592   *Albert Sturr, Architect*   20,000 Cubic Feet

(Description of house shown in above plans)

HERE is a bungalow that would be especially attractive in brick, with the trim around openings
laid in brick of a different color tone from those in
the walls. The front of the house is given over to the
living room and dining room, and opening from the
common hall is an independent group of three bedrooms and the kitchen. A fourth bedroom can be had
in the roof of the main part, as well as a small sewing
room. Wide arch between living and dining rooms.

(Description of house shown in plans below)

IT would be very difficult to find a more compact
plan than this. Every nook and corner is put to
some good use. Likewise the stairs are placed between
the living room and kitchen, eliminating the first floor
hall entirely. On the second floor are three fine bedrooms, each having cross-ventilation and a good-sized
closet. The bathroom is larger than usual, as it also
has windows on two sides. The construction is brick,
with stucco and half timber gables, and a slate roof.

Full directions for obtaining complete working drawings and specifications for these plans will be found on page 281

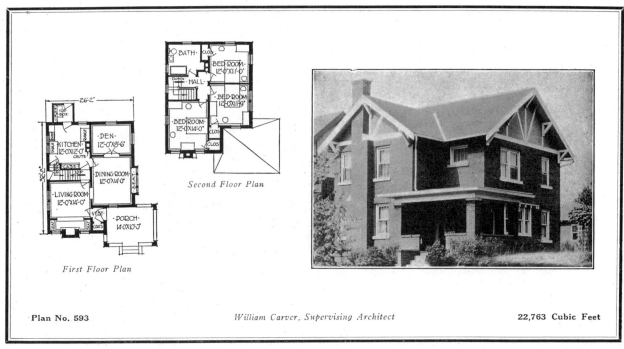

Second Floor Plan

First Floor Plan

Plan No. 593   *William Carver, Supervising Architect*   22,763 Cubic Feet

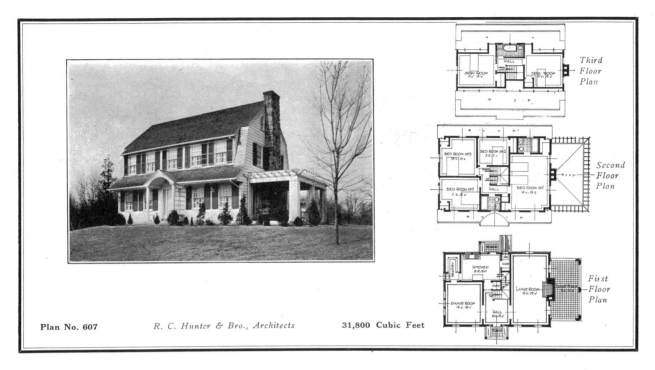

Plan No. 607   *R. C. Hunter & Bro., Architects*   31,800 Cubic Feet

(Description of house shown in above plans)   *(Description of house shown in plans below)*

THIS Dutch Colonial home has nine main rooms, and three bathrooms, counting the servants' quarters in the attic. The living room end of the house is particularly well arranged for entertaining in that the large living room opens onto a spacious open porch. This porch is built to represent a pergola but in reality has a roof over it. The owner's bedroom has a private bath as well as two closets. The other three main bedrooms are all equipped with ample closet space. The exterior walls and roof are of shingles.

FOR a narrow city lot this English cottage would be particularly adaptable. Yet it would look as well in the suburbs, especially on a wooded lot. The exterior is of shingles, stained preferably a dark color, with stucco and half timber in the front gable. The living room is large and has an open fireplace in one end. Another built-in feature is the china cabinet in the dining room. The kitchen is well arranged and step-saving, and very convenient to all the other rooms and cellar. Attractive house for closely built section.

Full directions for obtaining complete working drawings and specifications for these plans will be found on page 281

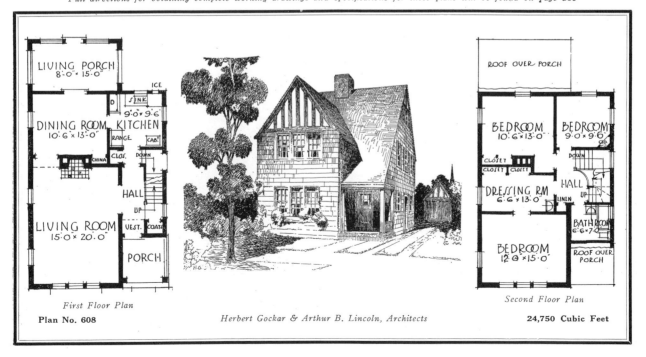

First Floor Plan

Plan No. 608   *Herbert Gockar & Arthur B. Lincoln, Architects*   24,750 Cubic Feet

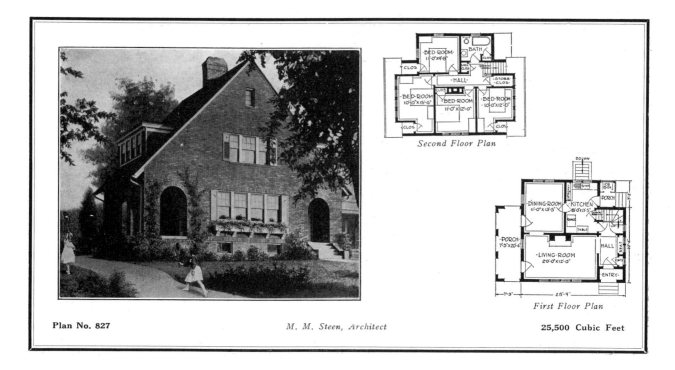

Plan No. 827   *M. M. Steen, Architect*   **25,500 Cubic Feet**

Second Floor Plan

First Floor Plan

(Description of house shown in above plans)

THIS house has quite an unusual exterior treatment, yet remarkably well designed. The circular arched openings on either side of the group of four windows are very interesting indeed. The exterior construction is of brick and the roof of slate. The living room has a large fireplace directly opposite the group of four windows. There are four bedrooms on the second floor and seven closets, which ought to be plenty for the average family.

(Description of house shown in plans below)

HERE is a house which has been planned for the larger family. It has plenty of room, yet its square shape and the absence of unnecessary ornamentation on the exterior make it economical to build. At the right of the reception hall one enters the living room through French doors. Bookcases in the pedestals of the inter-room opening between the living and dining rooms present paneled backs in the dining room.

Full directions for obtaining complete working drawings and specifications for these plans will be found on page 281

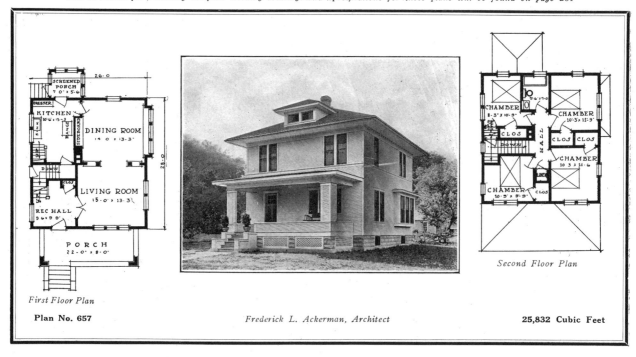

First Floor Plan

Second Floor Plan

Plan No. 657   *Frederick L. Ackerman, Architect*   **25,832 Cubic Feet**

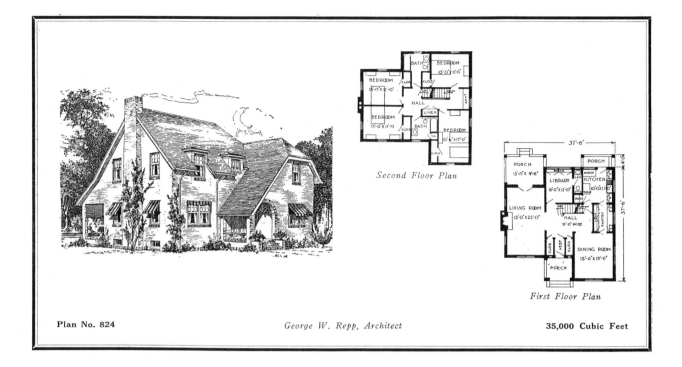

Second Floor Plan

First Floor Plan

Plan No. 824   *George W. Repp, Architect*   **35,000 Cubic Feet**

(Description of house shown in above plans)

IN this design the first floor plan has been very well
arranged so that the living room, hall, library,
and porch can be thrown into one for entertaining.
While the dining room is conveniently near, it is cut
off from the view of the rest of the house, and a well-
equipped pantry isolates the kitchen. In the kitchen
there are cabinets extending to the ceiling on both
sides of the sink, the space under the one near the
porch being reserved for the refrigerator.

(Description of house shown in plans below)

ALTHOUGH of simple rectangular type, the two
porch wings on opposite sides of this house
greatly enhance its distinctive appearance, and add
to the substantial effect produced by a broad frontage. A low hip roof with wide eaves, wide siding,
and planting about the low foundation accent the
horizontal lines. Shutters are used at the windows
to give the proper proportions to the openings. The
hooded entrance is the feature of the facade.

Full directions for obtaining complete working drawings and specifications for these plans will be found on page 281

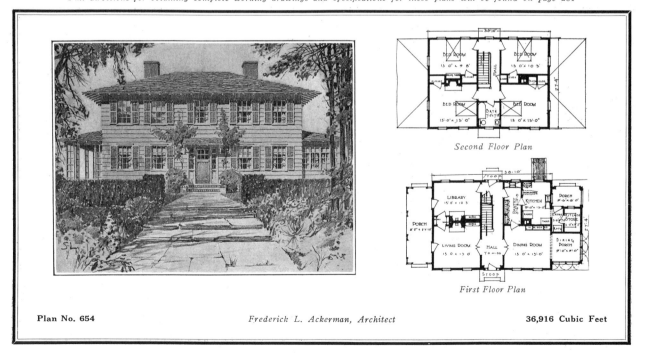

Second Floor Plan

First Floor Plan

Plan No. 654   *Frederick L. Ackerman, Architect*   **36,916 Cubic Feet**

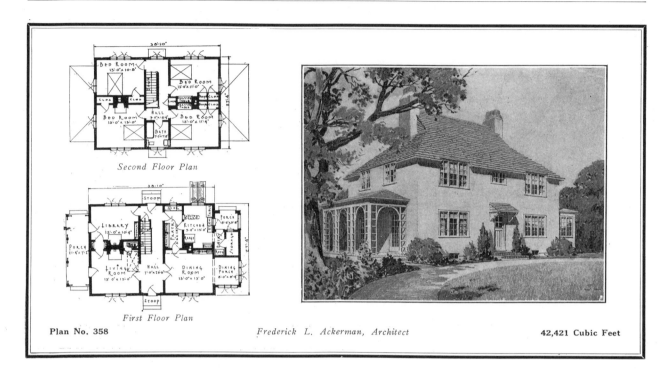

Second Floor Plan

First Floor Plan

Plan No. 358   *Frederick L. Ackerman, Architect*   **42,421 Cubic Feet**

(Description of house shown in above plans)

A STRIKING feature of this house is the hip roof with a superimposed gable, the gables being filled in with siding. Tiled chimneys at the sides of the gable give a substantial air to the building. Another unusual and pleasing touch is the dormers cutting through the eaves. The illustration shows this house built of stucco, but it may be effectively developed in other materials. The casement and the hooded entrance are typical English touches.

(Description of house shown in plans below)

ADMIRERS of pure Colonial architecture will find this a splendid example of its use in a modern home. The beautifully proportioned dormers do not mar the simple roof. The entrance is an unusually fine example of modern reproduction of old Colonial work. The main part of the plan is 36' 8" wide by 25' 10" deep, with the kitchen in an ell at the rear. Above the kitchen are a maid's room and bath. The construction is of frame with shingle roof.

Full directions for obtaining complete working drawings and specifications for these plans will be found on page 281

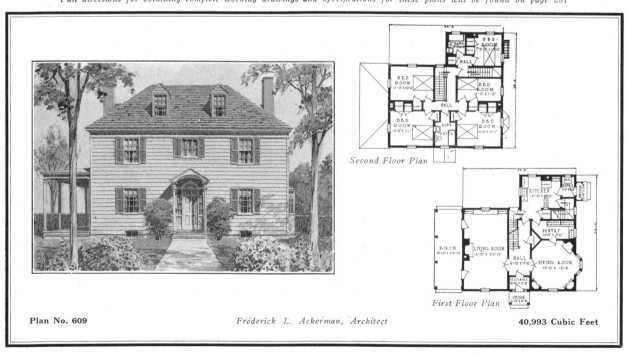

Second Floor Plan

First Floor Plan

Plan No. 609   *Frederick L. Ackerman, Architect*   **40,993 Cubic Feet**

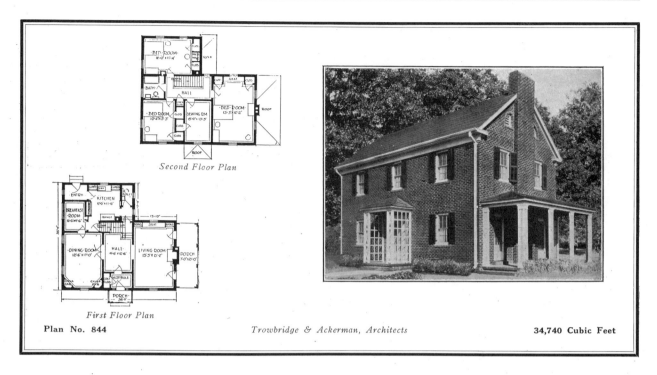

Second Floor Plan

First Floor Plan

Plan No. 844   *Trowbridge & Ackerman, Architects*   34,740 Cubic Feet

(Description of house shown in above plans)

AN eight-room dwelling of simple Colonial type with exterior walls built of common brick. A vestibule with coat closet is provided at the front entry and this leads into a large central hall from which the stairs lead upward. This hall opens directly into the dining room at the left and living room at the right. Dining room has special feature of built-in china closet. The living room has large open fireplace flanked by French doors to an open porch which might easily be glassed if desired.

(Description of house shown in plans below)

THIS attractive eight-room Colonial house is of frame construction throughout. In addition to the main body of the house a wing provides a den on the first floor equipped with a doorbed so that this room can be transformed into a bedroom when required. On the second floor an additional bedroom and the stairway is located in this wing. The living room runs across the entire front of the house and has an open fireplace with doors flanking, one leading to the central hall and the other into the dining room.

Full directions for obtaining complete working drawings and specifications for these plans will be found on page 281

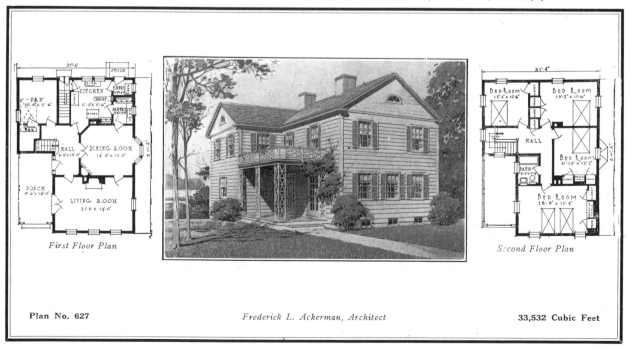

First Floor Plan

Second Floor Plan

Plan No. 627   *Frederick L. Ackerman, Architect*   33,532 Cubic Feet

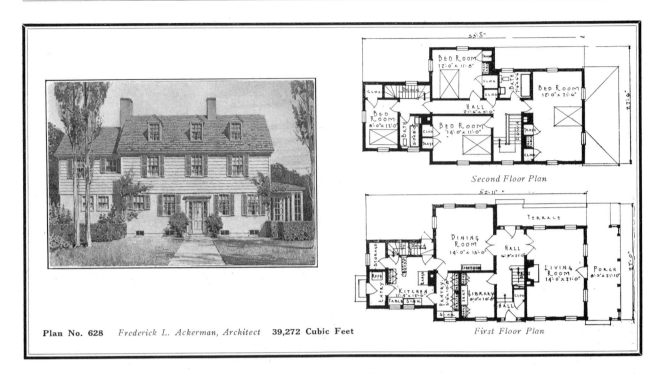

Plan No. 628   *Frederick L. Ackerman, Architect*   **39,272 Cubic Feet**

Second Floor Plan

First Floor Plan

(Description of house shown in above plans)

THE illustration shows an exterior view of this house. A broad veranda extends across one end of the house, and a terrace half way across the front, both with floors of brick-bordered cement. It is interesting to note the combination of stucco and wide siding used in the development of this Colonial house. There is a central hall straight through the house and facing the front entrance is a lovely Colonial stair and French doors at each side. The floor plan is carefully worked out with stock built-in features.

(Description of house shown in plans below)

HERE is a type of house that lends itself to development in various materials, or combinations of materials. The simple hip roof, plain walls and latticed front porch are economical of construction. The stair hall and vestibule effectually isolate the living room, which occupies half of the first floor, from the dining room and kitchen on the other side. This hall also provides convenient access between all the rooms in the house. The fireplace and built-in seat with flanking bookcases make the living room attractive.

Full directions for obtaining complete working drawings and specifications for these plans will be found on page 281

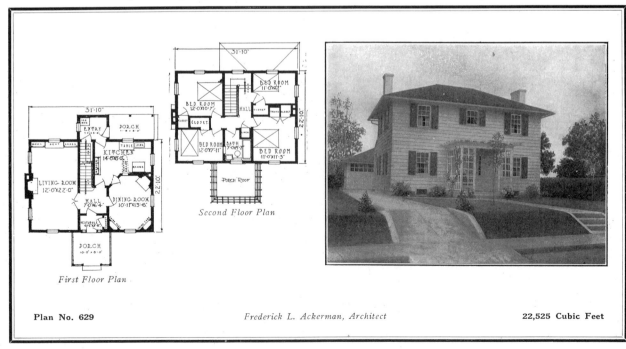

First Floor Plan

Second Floor Plan

Plan No. 629   *Frederick L. Ackerman, Architect*   **22,525 Cubic Feet**

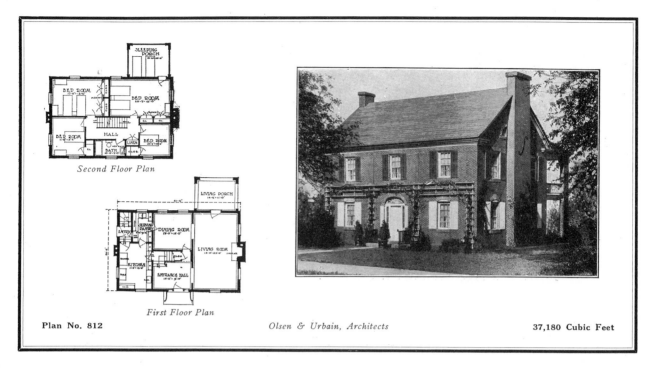

Second Floor Plan

First Floor Plan

Plan No. 812   *Olsen & Urbain, Architects*   37,180 Cubic Feet

(Description of house shown in above plans)

THIS is a large seven-room house of Colonial type, having exterior and chimneys of common brick construction. An unusually large living room with large living porch occupies one entire end of the house. There is a large central entrance hall, from which stairs lead upward. The kitchen is well arranged with service entry and serving pantry. The living porch has been extended upward to provide a sleeping porch on the second floor. This sleeping porch could be equipped with door beds if required.

(Description of house shown in plans below)

THIS is a charming example of the half-timbered stucco house. Two very attractive features are the solarium and sleeping porch. Neither is conspicuous and ugly from the outside, but each is a real part of the design, and is kept so by the use of properly divided lights in the casements. The solarium is really an alcove off the living room, separated only by cased opening, and at each side of it a glazed door leads to the lawn. The floor plan has been carefully worked out and affords many special features.

Full directions for obtaining complete working drawings and specifications for these plans will be found on page 281

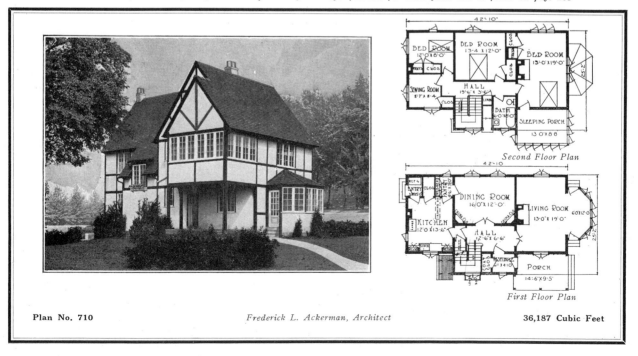

Second Floor Plan

First Floor Plan

Plan No. 710   *Frederick L. Ackerman, Architect*   36,187 Cubic Feet

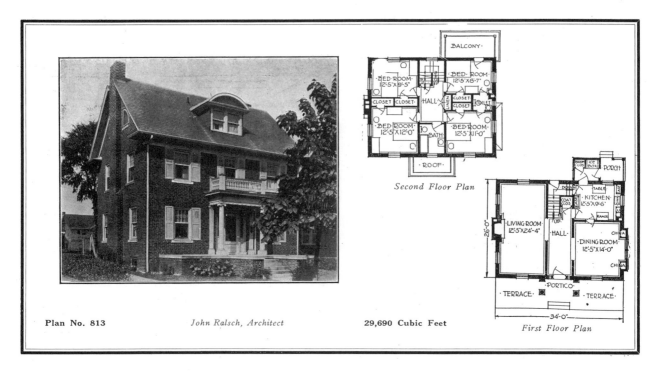

Plan No. 813   *John Ralsch, Architect*   29,690 Cubic Feet

Second Floor Plan

First Floor Plan

(Description of house shown in above plans)

THIS seven-room house is of modified Colonial type, having exterior walls of common brick. Entering a long central hall, one finds a wide opening into the dining room at the left. The kitchen is arranged with a number of practical features, including rear entry and porch. On the second floor there are four large bedrooms and one bath. The exterior is recommended as dark red with white trim; roof to be of black or mixed slate. The brick terrace is an interesting feature. Common brick used for the exterior.

(Description of house shown in plans below)

THE half-timber house combines the practical considerations of stucco construction with the decorative effect and distinctiveness of the stained wood beams. Plaster walls are warm in winter and cool in summer, and may have various textures and tints to harmonize with the surroundings. The casement windows and the chimney pots are characteristic touches. The front porch is a feature you might not find in a real English cottage, but which is desirable in many American houses because of the popular demand.

Full directions for obtaining complete working drawings and specifications for these plans will be found on page 281

First Floor Plan

Second Floor Plan

Plan No. 630   *Frederick L. Ackerman, Architect*   29,484 Cubic Feet

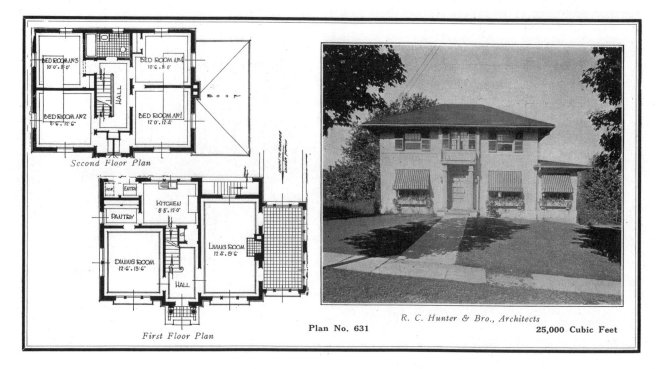

Second Floor Plan

First Floor Plan

Plan No. 631

R. C. Hunter & Bro., Architects

25,000 Cubic Feet

(Description of house shown in above plans)

THE design of this house is based somewhat on the Italian style of architecture. It is formal in character and with proper landscaping creates a very impressive effect for a small dwelling. The square shape of the house lends itself admirably to plan, layout and to construction. The exterior walls are of stucco on hollow tile. The living room is of large size with open fireplace flanked by two doors which lead to an enclosed porch. There is a large kitchen and pantry with a practical service entry.

(Description of house shown in plans below)

THIS seven-room house has exterior walls of common brick with gables of half-timbered stucco. A large porch extends across the entire front of the house with entrance into a hall from which stairs lead upward. In the plan shown, the living room is comparatively small in order to provide a den. If desired, however, the dining room can be located where the den is shown and in this manner a very large living room can be provided. The kitchen has the added features of pantry and service entry.

Full directions for obtaining complete working drawings and specifications for these plans will be found on page 281

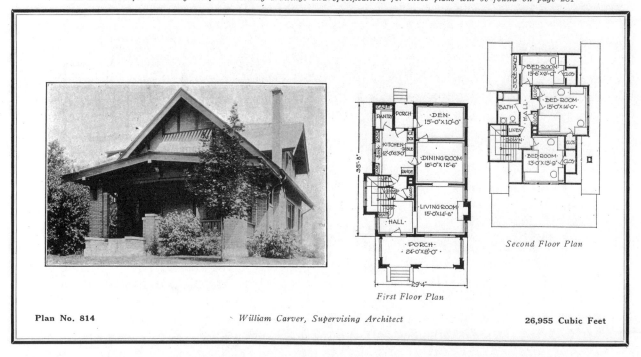

First Floor Plan

Second Floor Plan

Plan No. 814

William Carver, Supervising Architect

26,955 Cubic Feet

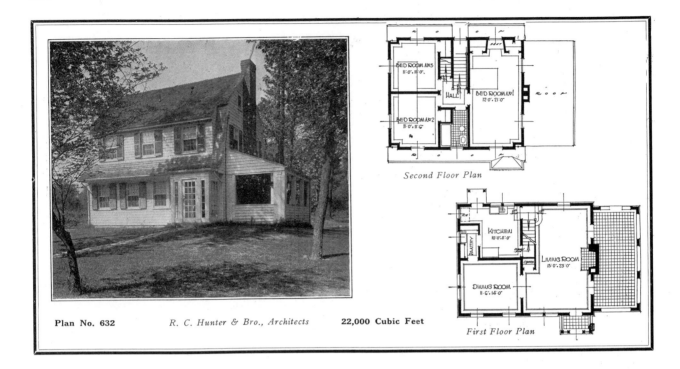

Plan No. 632   *R. C. Hunter & Bro., Architects*   **22,000 Cubic Feet**

Second Floor Plan

First Floor Plan

(Description of house shown in above plans)

THIS attractive seven-room Colonial house is particularly well suited for an environment such as that shown in the photograph. The house is of frame construction throughout, with an exterior of wide siding painted white. The large living porch which extends across one end of the house may be closed if desired. Two doors open on to this porch from the living room. The front entrance is directly into the living room, and stairs lead up from one corner.

(Description of house shown in plans below)

THERE is an old-fashioned simplicity about this house of face brick that makes it look like a comfortable home. It has full, square rooms and big windows, after the manner of the houses of the late Georgian period in England. It would look well set back from the road, with a drive at the left leading to a garage. The breakfast nook, if not desired, could be turned into a pantry; and similarly, on the second floor the trunk storage could be added to the bedroom.

Full directions for obtaining complete working drawings and specifications for these plans will be found on page 281

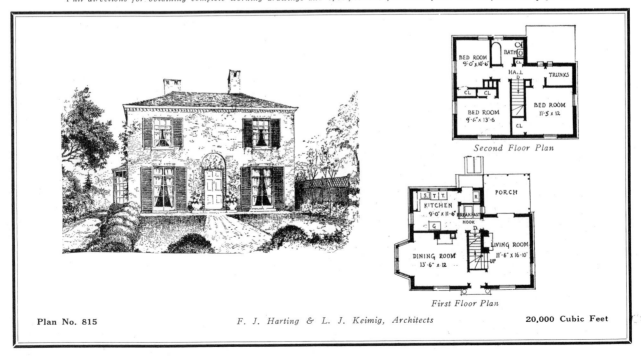

Second Floor Plan

First Floor Plan

Plan No. 815   *F. J. Harting & L. J. Keimig, Architects*   **20,000 Cubic Feet**

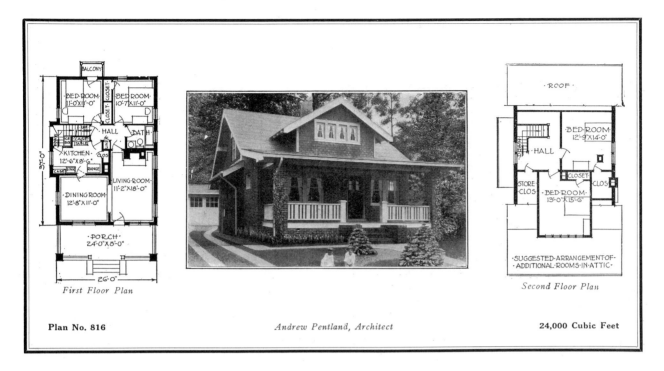

First Floor Plan

Second Floor Plan

Plan No. 816   *Andrew Pentland, Architect*   **24,000 Cubic Feet**

(Description of house shown in above plans)

IN the design of this house full advantage is taken of wide overhanging eaves, broken roof lines and the broad dormer to provide an interesting appearance. The exterior walls are of common brick construction and the same material has been used for porch columns. The front entrance is directly into the living room and a central hall is provided in an interesting manner, giving access to the stairs and to two bedrooms at the rear on the ground floor. On the second floor there are two large bedrooms.

(Description of house shown in plans below)

HERE is a pretty house of stucco with shingled second story. Overhanging eaves shade the bedroom windows and the single chimney is placed at the peak of the hip roof. The bay in the living room is unusual and interesting. A pleasant corner porch affords a view in all directions. The main stair rises from a small reception hall and a coat closet is conveniently located on the landing. There is a splendid wall space in the living room for the placing of furniture opposite the hearth.

Full directions for obtaining complete working drawings and specifications for these plans will be found on page 281

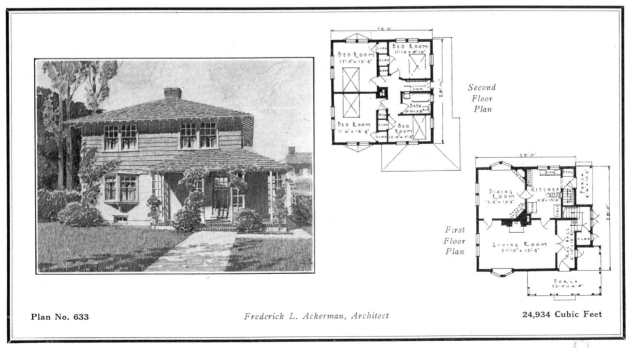

Second Floor Plan

First Floor Plan

Plan No. 633   *Frederick L. Ackerman, Architect*   **24,934 Cubic Feet**

First Floor Plan

Second Floor Plan

Plan No. 833   *Andrew Pentland, Architect*   **21,983 Cubic Feet**

(Description of house shown in above plans)

THIS well-planned six-room home has exterior walls of common brick construction. From the porch one enters directly into the living room, which has a fireplace at one end, with built-in bookcase on one side and entrance to the hall on the other. The entrance at the side of the house is into a small hall, where the stair to the second floor is located. The kitchen is well arranged and there is a splendid porch on which meals may be served during the hot weather.

(Description of house shown in plans below)

HERE is a popular plan for a six-room home of brick construction. From the entrance at the side of the house one may go into the living room, dining room or kitchen. There is also an entrance from the porch into the living room, which extends across the entire front of the house and has an open fireplace flanked by built-in bookcases with small windows over. The rear porch is large enough for a dining porch and above this is a sleeping porch.

Full directions for obtaining complete working drawings and specifications for these plans will be found on page 281

First Floor Plan

Second Floor Plan

Plan No. 834   *Olsen & Urbain, Architects*   **22,844 Cubic Feet**

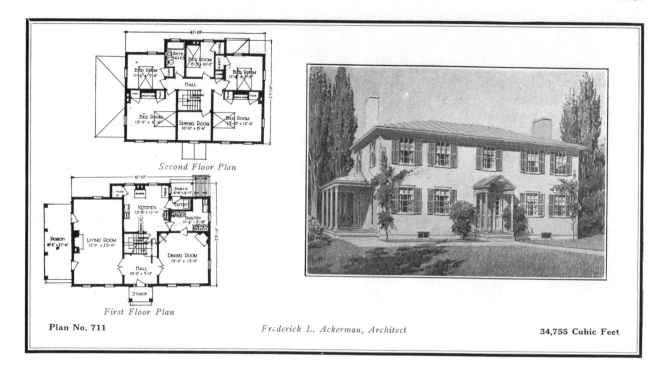

Second Floor Plan

First Floor Plan

Plan No. 711   *Frederick L. Ackerman, Architect*   **34,755 Cubic Feet**

(Description of house shown in above plans)

HERE is an example of Colonial architecture at its best. It is shown here carried out in stucco, with composition roofing on the flat hip roof. The central hall does not go entirely through the building, the kitchen being at the rear of the reception hall. This makes it possible to have direct access from the kitchen to the stair landing, doing away with the necessity for a separate rear stair. There are many built-in features which make for the convenient operation of the house.

(Description of house shown in plans below)

A PLAN with an entrance and stair hall at one corner gives a maximum of living room on the front, with unobstructed front windows. This is such a plan. A noticeable feature of the interior development is the symmetrical placing of the important architectural features in each room, French doors, fireplaces, bay, interior doors, windows, permanent furniture, long wall spaces. This shows expert skill in the handling of the plan.

Full directions for obtaining complete working drawings and specifications for these plans will be found on page 281

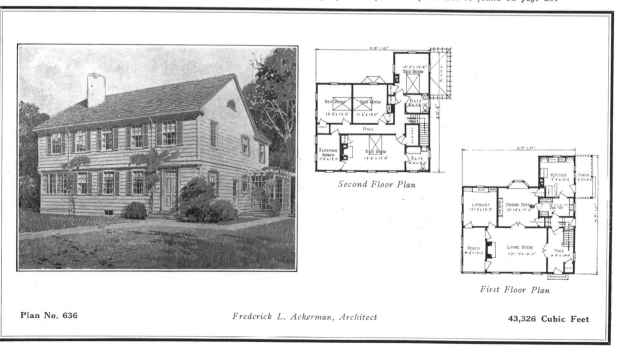

Second Floor Plan

First Floor Plan

Plan No. 636   *Frederick L. Ackerman, Architect*   **43,326 Cubic Feet**

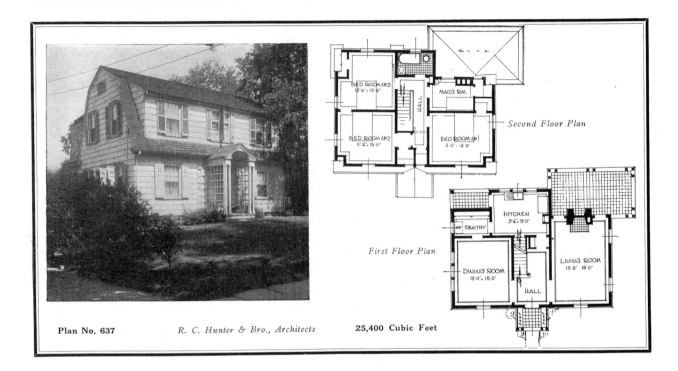

Second Floor Plan

First Floor Plan

Plan No. 637   *R. C. Hunter & Bro., Architects*   **25,400 Cubic Feet**

(*Description of house shown in above plans*)

HERE is a typical Dutch Colonial dwelling which is planned with a view to efficiency and comfort. A small covered entry leads to a central hall, in which the staircase is located. To the right and left broad inter-openings lead respectively into the living room with its sun porch and to the dining room which is served through a large pantry from the kitchen. Upstairs there are three master's bedrooms and one maid's room. House is frame construction throughout.

(*Description of house shown in plans below*)

ALTHOUGH the dimensions of this house are only 28 feet by 27 feet, there is an excellent arrangement of the seven rooms. Even the porch is included within these dimensions. By placing the entrance door across a corner, space has been gained for a vestibule and coat closet. One may go directly to the living or dining room, and it is only a step to the kitchen. The four corner bedrooms are provided with a good closet and all are cross-ventilated.

Full directions for obtaining complete working drawings and specifications for these plans will be found on page 281

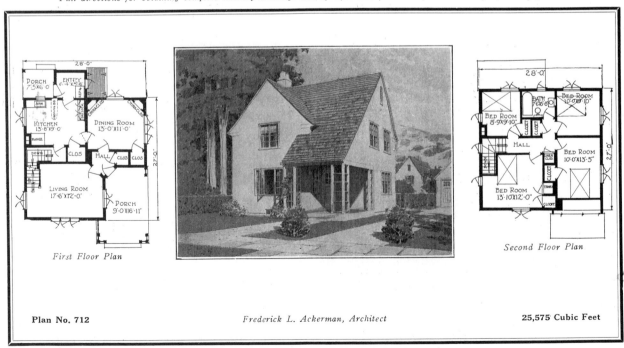

First Floor Plan

Second Floor Plan

Plan No. 712   *Frederick L. Ackerman, Architect*   **25,575 Cubic Feet**

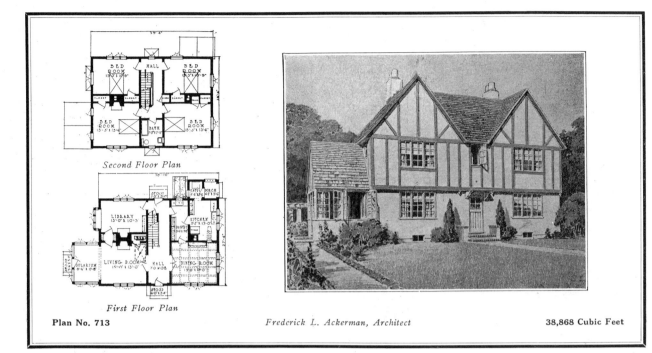

Second Floor Plan

First Floor Plan

Plan No. 713   *Frederick L. Ackerman, Architect*   **38,868 Cubic Feet**

(Description of house shown in above plans)   *(Description of house shown in plans below)*

HERE is another popular half-timbered house, having twin gables. The sun parlor, in the one-story addition at the left, is a most attractive exterior detail. The floor plans incorporate a maximum number of convenient features in the allotted space, and do so without a foot of waste room. There is a central hall extending through the house, with a front and a garden entrance, and an impressive stairway. At the left is the oak-paneled living room with the solarium adjoining through a cased opening.

THIS house of English type seems to have been designed for a family who love sunshine. The beauty of the house is due to the use of small-paned casements and half-timber construction, so that it does not lose its substantial appearance. The entrance hall is at the right and here there is a coat closet and a handsome stair. Near the foot of the stair is a door which communicates with the grade entrance, basement steps and kitchen; this is a most convenient arrangement.

Full directions for obtaining complete working drawings and specifications for these plans will be found on page 281

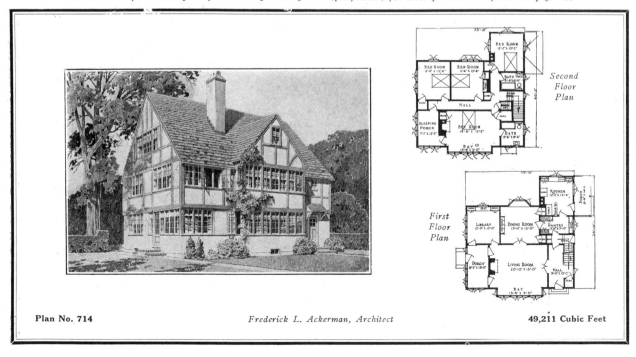

Second Floor Plan

First Floor Plan

Plan No. 714   *Frederick L. Ackerman, Architect*   **49,211 Cubic Feet**

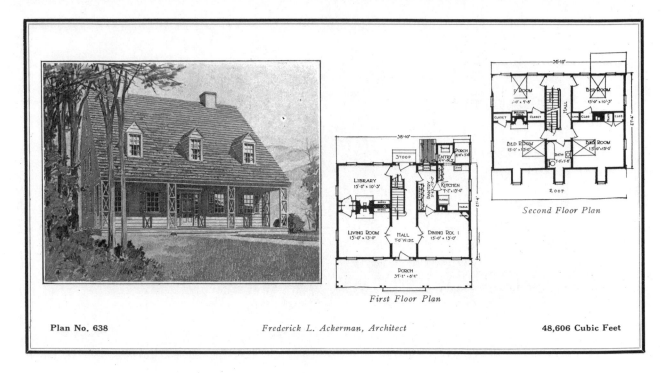

Plan No. 638   *Frederick L. Ackerman, Architect*   **48,606 Cubic Feet**

First Floor Plan

Second Floor Plan

(Description of house shown in above plans)

H ERE is an interesting variation of the Colonial type. It has eight rooms and two and a half stories, but seems much smaller because the eaves are only one story above the ground. The plan is excellent, from the basement with its five divisions and outside and inside steps, to the attic which may be used for additional rooms if necessary. The central hall runs straight through the house, and has a typical Colonial straight flight of stairs.

(Description of house shown in plans below)

S TUCCO and shingles laid eight inches to the weather are the exterior materials suggested for this splendid eight-room house of two stories and attic. It is an excellent example of the Western type, and is a home that is in good taste in any neighborhood. Every room in the house is large and well-lighted. The first floor includes a living room, dining room, kitchen and secluded library, in addition to the hall, coat closet, pantry, refrigerator entry and two small porches.

Full directions for obtaining complete working drawings and specifications for these plans will be found on page 281

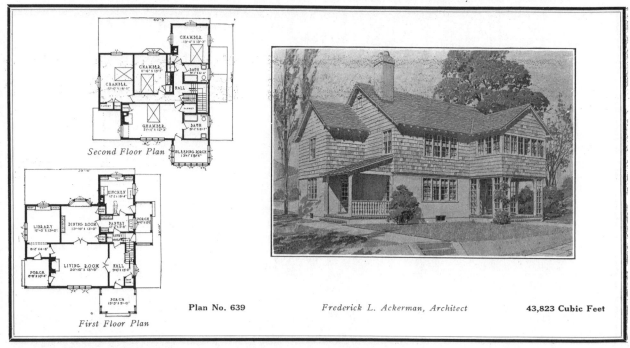

Second Floor Plan

First Floor Plan

Plan No. 639   *Frederick L. Ackerman, Architect*   **43,823 Cubic Feet**

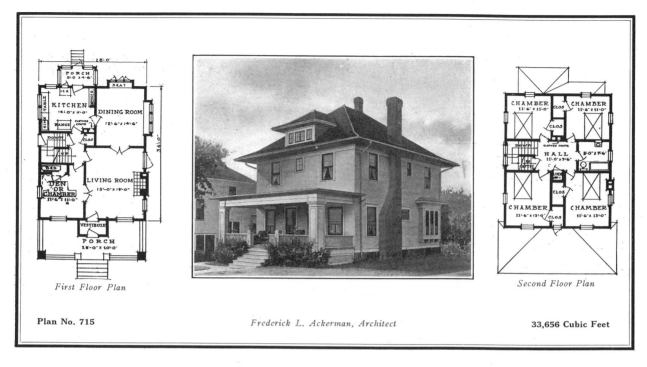

First Floor Plan   *Second Floor Plan*

Plan No. 715   *Frederick L. Ackerman, Architect*   **33,656 Cubic Feet**

(Description of house shown in above plans)

(Description of house shown in plans below)

THIS house is of the economical "square" type, and is built of stucco; it has eight large rooms besides bathroom and vestibule; a splendid basement; an attic which makes additional rooms possible, and an abundance of closet space as well as built-in features of convenience. The vestibule is built out on to the porch, and is lighted by the large glass in the front door. The living room has a brick fireplace with a simple wood mantel shelf. On two sides are French doors connecting with den and dining room.

THIS interesting Colonial dwelling was designed originally for the Superintendent of the Amawalk Nurseries. The photograph indicates the value of simple but attractive planting to set off the design of a moderate cost house. The house is of frame construction throughout with wide siding. The plan indicates an extension which is used as an office on the first floor and having a bedroom above. This extension may easily be omitted if desired or it provides additional rooms if required.

Full directions for obtaining complete working drawings and specifications for these plans will be found on page 281

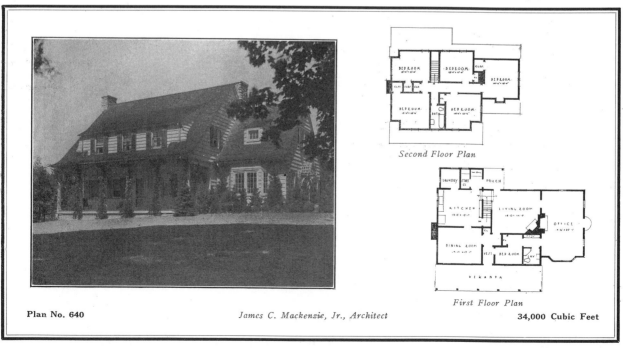

Second Floor Plan

First Floor Plan

Plan No. 640   *James C. Mackenzie, Jr., Architect*   **34,000 Cubic Feet**

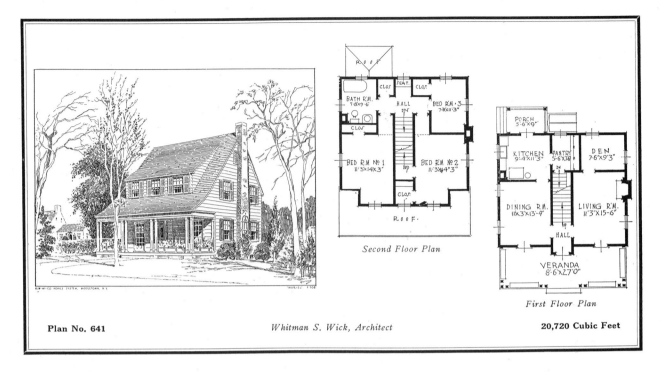

Plan No. 641   *Whitman S. Wick, Architect*   **20,720 Cubic Feet**

Second Floor Plan

First Floor Plan

(Description of house shown in above plans)

THIS type of simple, economical Colonial home is greatly favored where it is necessary to conserve the original investment. The house is of frame construction throughout, with wide siding and chimney of brick. A broad porch extends the entire width of the front, and entrance is into a small hall from which central staircase leads upward. Doors open to the right and left into living room and dining room. An open fireplace is provided in living room, with the additional feature of a small den.

(Description of house shown in plans below)

THIS is a popular type of dwelling which is simple and economical to construct. The exterior is of common brick. Entrance is directly into a large living room. Stairs are located at the rear of the house, where they occupy the least valuable space. The square design of the house allows an arrangement of four bedrooms on the second floor, each entered from a central hall in which is located a large linen closet. Each bedroom is provided with a closet, and is well lighted.

Full directions for obtaining complete working drawings and specifications for these plans will be found on page 281

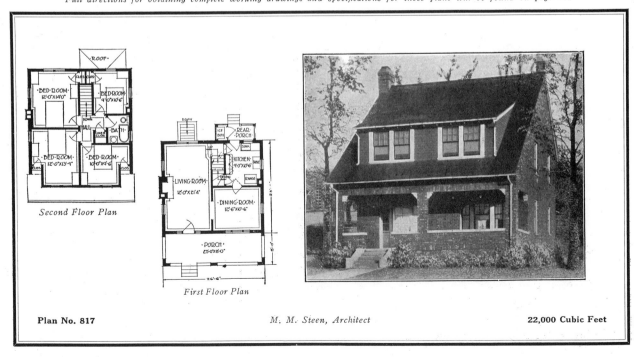

Second Floor Plan

First Floor Plan

Plan No. 817   *M. M. Steen, Architect*   **22,000 Cubic Feet**

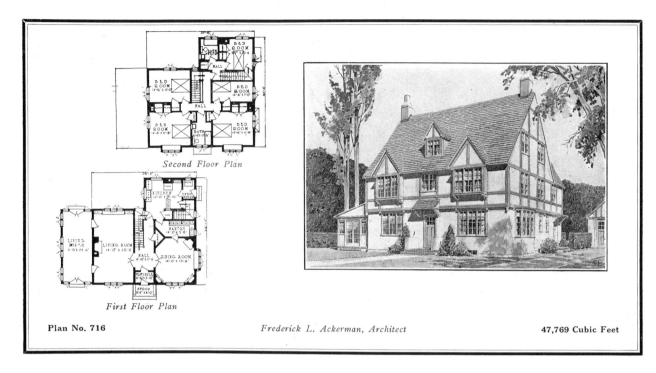

Second Floor Plan

First Floor Plan

Plan No. 716   *Frederick L. Ackerman, Architect*   **47,769 Cubic Feet**

(Description of house shown in above plans)

IT would be hard to find an eight-room home of more distinctive appearance than this half-timbered English house with its hooded formal entrance and outjutting second-story bays. The steep roof, the grouped casements and tiled chimneys are characteristic of the type. The huge sun parlor at the side is an American idea which has been cleverly handled. In fact, the entire floor plan is strictly in accord with American ideals. In the living room there is a fireplace, flanked by glazed doors leading to the sun porch.

(Description of house shown in plans below)

THERE is a flavor of the Colonial in the exterior of this dignified home of eight rooms, solarium and sleeping porch. Its simplicity focuses the attention upon the effective formal entrance. Its shuttered windows are very attractive. Brick is appropriate for houses of this type, although other materials can be used, as stucco, shingles, wide siding or a combination of them. The open porch and the solarium provide for both summer and winter comfort, and both are equally accessible to the long living room.

Full directions for obtaining complete working drawings and specifications for these plans will be found on page 281

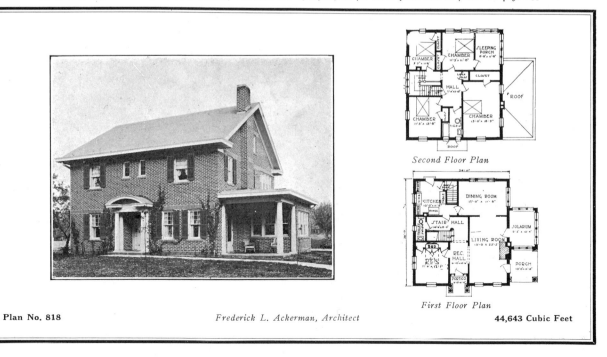

Second Floor Plan

First Floor Plan

Plan No. 818   *Frederick L. Ackerman, Architect*   **44,643 Cubic Feet**

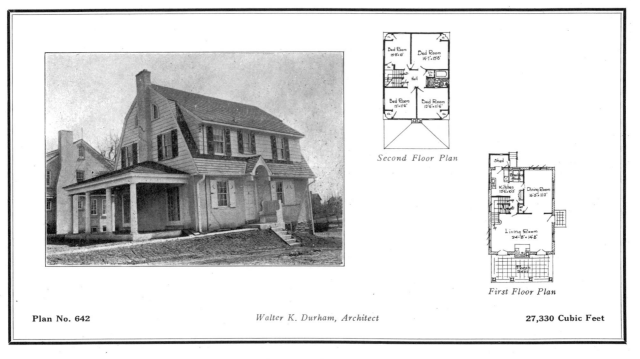

Second Floor Plan

First Floor Plan

Plan No. 642   *Walter K. Durham, Architect*   **27,330 Cubic Feet**

(Description of house shown in above plans)   *(Description of house shown in plans below)*

THIS house is a carefully planned Dutch Colonial type with exterior walls on the first floor constructed of Portland cement stucco on concrete blocks. Gables and dormers have wide Colonial siding, and chimney is of concrete. There is a large porch with floor of red cement marked off in tile sizes. The living room extends across the entire front of the house and has two French doors forming entrance from the porch and flanking the large fireplace. An attractive staircase ascends from the living room.

WIDE eaves and open cornice, as well as frank simplicity of both exterior and interior details, characterize houses of this Western type. There is much latitude for choice of materials and of designs of doors, windows, porches, chimneys and other architectural details. Little touches that distinguish this seven-room house from its neighbors are its chimneys, the lattice-and-stucco porch columns of the large living porch at the side, and sturdy batten shutters. It is not an expensive house to build, due to its simplicity.

Full directions for obtaining complete working drawings and specifications for these plans will be found on page 281

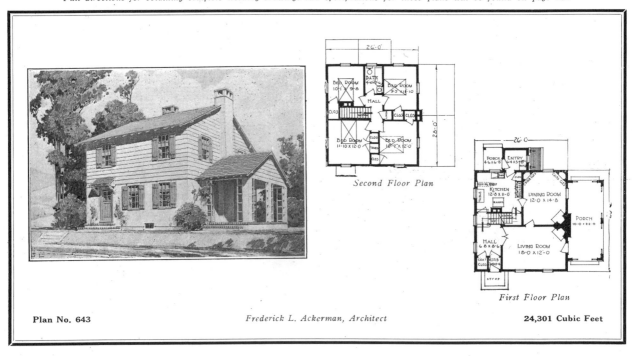

Second Floor Plan

First Floor Plan

Plan No. 643   *Frederick L. Ackerman, Architect*   **24,301 Cubic Feet**

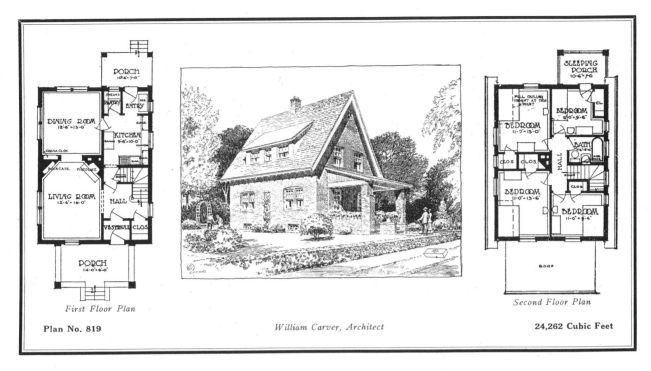

First Floor Plan

Second Floor Plan

Plan No. 819   *William Carver, Architect*   **24,262 Cubic Feet**

(Description of house shown in above plans)   *(Description of house shown in plans below)*

THIS attractive seven-room house has exterior walls of common brick. The plan includes two roomy porches—the one in the rear being large enough to be used as a dining porch. The entrance to the house is through a vestibule into a stair hall, in which there is a coat closet. The living room is large and well lighted, and the fireplace and built-in bookcase form a very artistic treatment of the end of the room. The dining room has two groups of double windows and the built-in china closet is an attractive feature.

HERE is an example of the pure Georgian Colonial in a modern home. No amount of ornament could be so effective as this six-panel door, surrounded by sidelights and fanlights transom, and sheltered by an arched hood, supported by correctly-proportioned columns. The usual symmetrical placing of all the openings is observed with excellent effect. One of the pleasantest features of this plan is the large open porch reached from the living room. The construction is of frame with exterior walls of wide siding.

Full directions for obtaining complete working drawings and specifications for these plans will be found on page 281

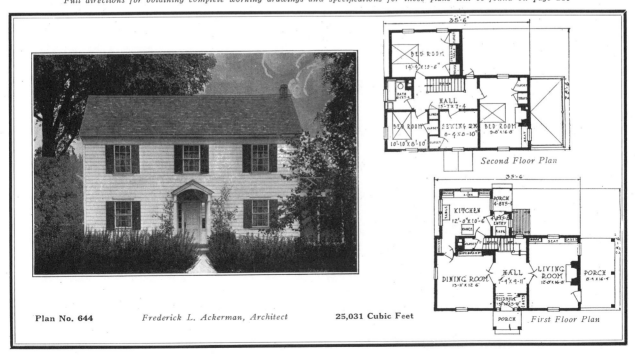

Second Floor Plan

First Floor Plan

Plan No. 644   *Frederick L. Ackerman, Architect*   **25,031 Cubic Feet**

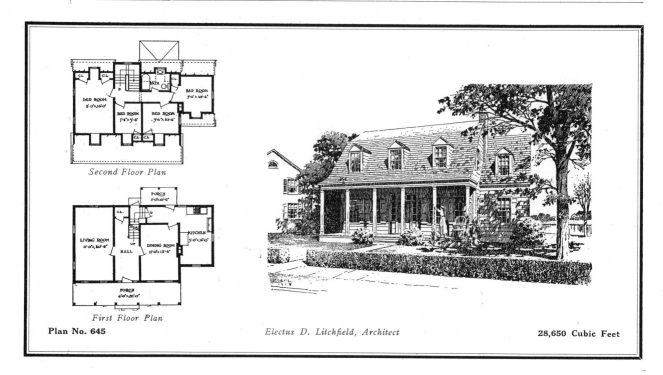

Second Floor Plan

First Floor Plan

Plan No. 645   *Electus D. Litchfield, Architect*   28,650 Cubic Feet

---

(Description of house shown in above plans)

THIS attractive home of Dutch-Colonial type is built entirely of frame construction, with exterior of wide siding. The architectural design is carefully studied to provide interest and balanced proportions. The living room extends across one entire end of the house. There is a very large, light kitchen, with ample space for shelving and pantry purposes. On the second floor there is one large bedroom lighted on the side by two windows and by dormer windows.

(Description of house shown in plans below)

HERE is a dwelling of comfortable, rambling type, having broad eaves and broken roof lines to lend interest to the design. From the large front porch, entrance is into a small vestibule and on into a large living room, from which stairs lead upward. There is an open brick fireplace in the living room which is flanked by small high windows. Here two of the bedrooms are located on the first floor, and bath is provided. On the second floor there are two bedrooms.

Full directions for obtaining complete working drawings and specifications for these plans will be found on page 281

First Floor Plan

Second Floor Plan

Plan No. 820   *William Carver, Supervising Architect*   33,628 Cubic Feet

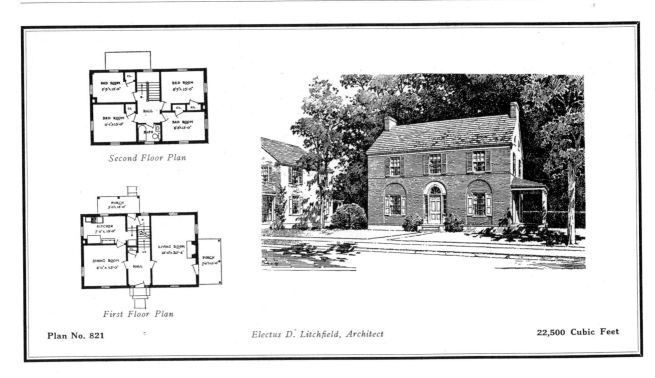

Second Floor Plan

First Floor Plan

Plan No. 821   *Electus D. Litchfield, Architect*   **22,500 Cubic Feet**

(Description of house shown in above plans)

THIS dwelling is of simple Colonial brick type, in the design of which the architect has provided an added note of attractiveness by setting the entrance door and first floor windows in arched recesses. The result is a perfectly balanced facade. The first floor plan is of the usual Colonial type, with central entrance hall from which stairs lead up. The living room has an open fireplace and a door to an open porch. The dining room and kitchen have a connecting door.

(Description of house shown in plans below)

THIS home charms by its very simplicity. The contrast of white-painted clapboards and green blinds, and the shingled roof, ending in a narrow cornice, are characteristics of the Colonial type. The entrance through the portico leads to an enclosed porch or solarium, and the main living room is at the rear of the solarium. This is a rectangular room with bookcases and window seat facing the fireplace that is well located in the center of a narrow hall. The kitchen has the feature of a service entry.

Full directions for obtaining complete working drawings and specifications for these plans will be found on page 281

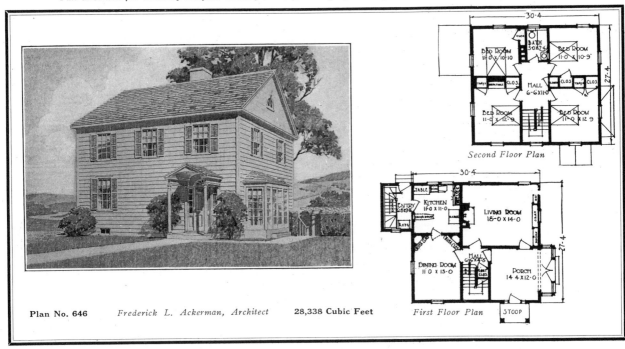

Second Floor Plan

First Floor Plan

Plan No. 646   *Frederick L. Ackerman, Architect*   **28,338 Cubic Feet**

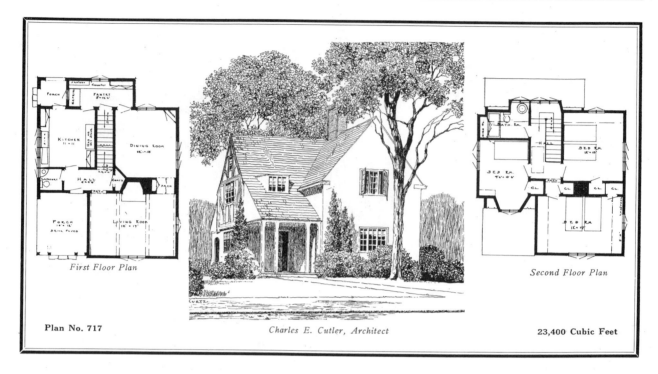

First Floor Plan

Second Floor Plan

Plan No. 717   *Charles E. Cutler, Architect*   **23,400 Cubic Feet**

(Description of house shown in above plans)

THIS stucco house is designed with a particularly attractive exterior, made interesting by broken roof lines and by the use of half-timber work in the gable ends. From the entrance porch one passes into the hall, where a lavatory and coat closet are located and from which stairs lead upward. The large living room is provided with an open fireplace and a double arched entrance into the dining room. The kitchen is large and well equipped with an entry porch and a butler's pantry.

(Description of house shown in plans below)

HERE is a house of the Western type that is distinguished by its roof, the overhang of the second story, and the combination of building materials used. The porch is unusual and pretty with its exposed rafters and lattice-covered stucco columns. This porch could be screened or glazed at little expense. The living room fireplace has a simple wood mantel and occupies an inside wall space, which many consider best for fireplaces. The space opposite the fireplace is occupied by a window seat with bookcases flanking.

Full directions for obtaining complete working drawings and specifications for these plans will be found on page 281

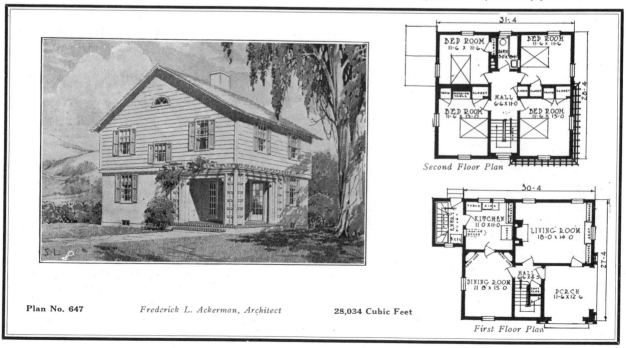

Second Floor Plan

First Floor Plan

Plan No. 647   *Frederick L. Ackerman, Architect*   **28,034 Cubic Feet**

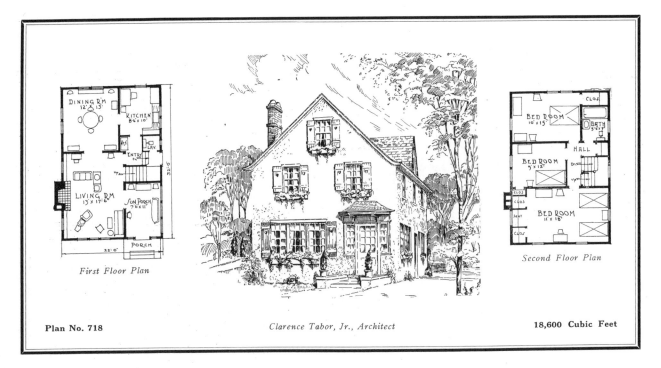

First Floor Plan

Second Floor Plan

Plan No. 718   *Clarence Tabor, Jr., Architect*   **18,600 Cubic Feet**

(Description of house shown in above plans)

THE plan of this stucco house is quite unusual, and is rendered even more interesting by the location of principal pieces of furniture. One enters directly into a large sun porch, and thence into the living room. This room has an open brick fireplace with tiled hearth and is flanked by high casements. From the living room the stairs lead upward. The kitchen has the added feature of a lavatory and a service entrance located at the side of the house. On the second floor there are three bedrooms.

(Description of house shown in plans below)

THIS type of Colonial frame dwelling is particularly well suited for location on gently sloping, wooded property such as that indicated in the photograph. The hooded entrance porch opens into a small vestibule which is provided with clothes closet and forms part of a large central hall at the rear of which staircase is located and lighted by a rear window. From the central hall wide inter-room openings provide access to the living room and dining room. The living room has a large brick and tile fireplace.

Full directions for obtaining complete working drawings and specifications for these plans will be found on page 281

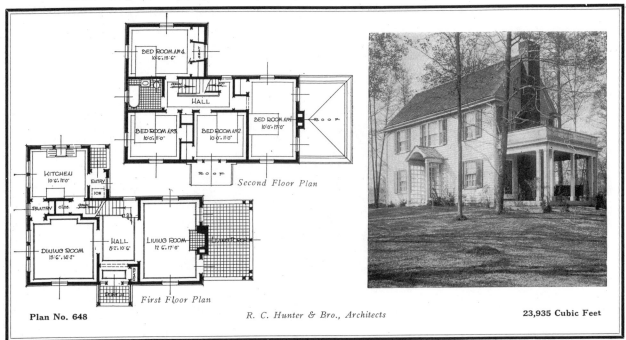

Second Floor Plan

First Floor Plan

Plan No. 648   *R. C. Hunter & Bro., Architects*   **23,935 Cubic Feet**

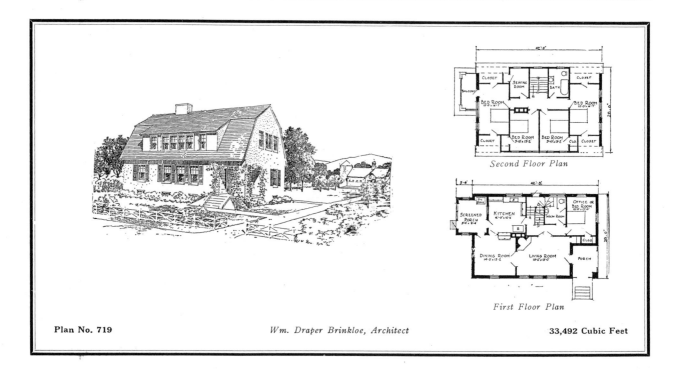

Plan No. 719   *Wm. Draper Brinkloe, Architect*   **33,492 Cubic Feet**

Second Floor Plan

First Floor Plan

(Description of house shown in above plans)

HERE is a design with exterior walls of stucco that is particularly suitable for the up-to-date farm. The front porch is a part of the house; the roof runs over it and is supported at the corner by a massive pier. The kitchen, connecting by swinging doors with the dining room, contains large closets and a china closet which can also be opened on the dining room side. There is a wash room conveniently located near the kitchen and entered from the rear.

(Description of house shown in plans below)

WITH such an unassuming exterior one is scarcely prepared to find this house has such a carefully planned, roomy interior. There are eight large rooms besides the reception hall. The entrance is a six-panel door of Colonial design, with sidelights. At the right an inter-room opening with paneled door cabinets invites into the living room, with its fireplace, bookcase and window seat. On the other side of the hall French doors lead to the dining room.

Full directions for obtaining complete working drawings and specifications for these plans will be found on page 281

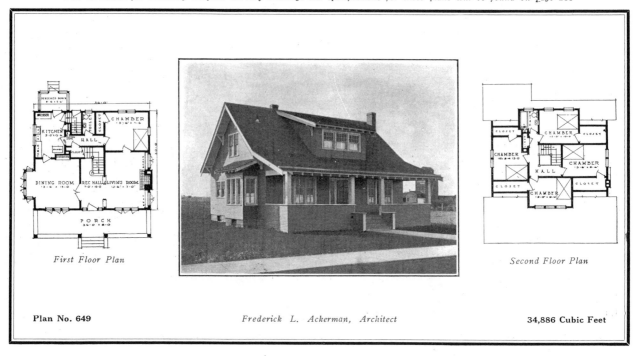

First Floor Plan

Second Floor Plan

Plan No. 649   *Frederick L. Ackerman, Architect*   **34,886 Cubic Feet**

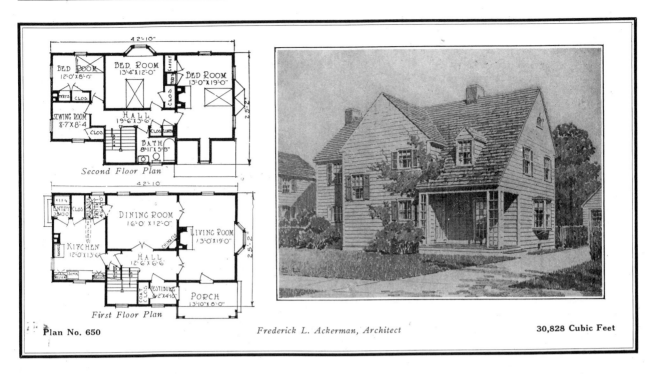

Second Floor Plan

First Floor Plan

Plan No. 650   *Frederick L. Ackerman, Architect*   30,828 Cubic Feet

(*Description of house shown in above plans*)

HERE is a splendidly planned seven-room house that is only twenty-five feet two inches wide. From either the narrow or the wide side it presents an interesting front. A bay like that in the living room is a feature of one of the upstairs bedrooms also. The dormer provides ventilation from a third side in another bedroom. At the right of the vestibule is the hall which brings living room, dining room, kitchen, main stair and basement stair into intercommunication. Construction is frame.

(*Description of house shown in plans below*)

THE main entrance to this frame house opens directly into a small hall, from which doors lead to the living room and dining room. The stairs open upward from the rear of the living room. A special feature of the living room is the interesting fireplace and large ingle-nook provided with seats. The kitchen and dining room arrangement is excellent from the service viewpoint, and a service entry is provided at the rear of the house with place for refrigerator and cellar stairs.

Full directions for obtaining complete working drawings and specifications for these plans will be found on page 281

First Floor Plan

Second Floor Plan

Plan No. 651   *Harry C. Starr, Architect*   23,200 Cubic Feet

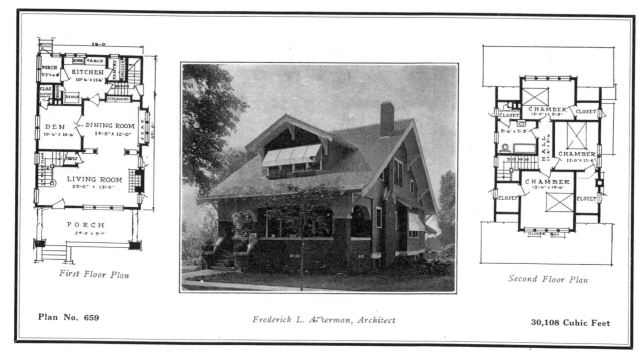

First Floor Plan

Second Floor Plan

Plan No. 659　　　　　*Frederick L. Ackerman, Architect*　　　　　**30,108 Cubic Feet**

(Description of house shown in above plans)

THE graceful roof lines and the combination of materials make this a very attractive home, and the floor plans include many desirable features. There is a long living room across the front of the house, with a beautiful open stair at one narrow side, and a homelike fireplace, flanked by high casements on the other. An inter-room opening with bookcases affords a vista toward the built-in sideboard in the dining room. The den, connected by French doors with the dining room, is an attractive feature.

(Description of house shown in plans below)

FOR the construction of this semi-bungalow type of seven-room dwelling common brick has been used throughout the exterior walls and for porch columns. A broad porch extends across the front of the house with a small vestibule opening into the living room. The living room has a large brick fireplace and a wide arched opening into the dining room. The dining room is equipped with built-in china closets, and has doors into the small rear hall and into the kitchen. This small hall provides entrance to two bedrooms.

Full directions for obtaining complete working drawings and specifications for these plans will be found on page 281

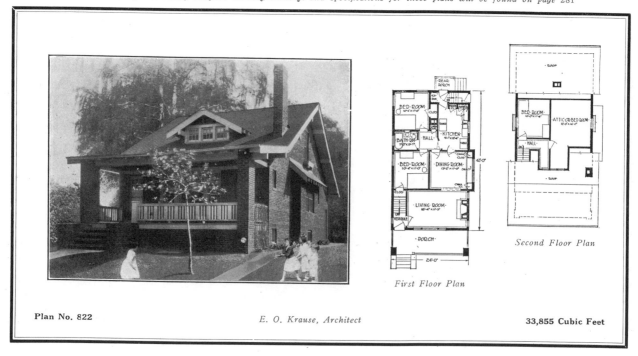

First Floor Plan

Second Floor Plan

Plan No. 822　　　　　*E. O. Krause, Architect*　　　　　**33,855 Cubic Feet**

Plan No. 652   *Frederick L. Ackerman, Architect*   36,296 Cubic Feet

Second Floor Plan

First Floor Plan

(Description of house shown in above plans)

THIS dwelling, with first floor of stucco and second floor of wide siding, shows an interesting arrangement of seven rooms. The recessed entrance opens into a good-sized hall with an open stair at the rear. French doors on each side connect it with dining room and living room. The living room has a fireplace, and doors on each side of it open onto the brick porch. The kitchen is efficiently arranged and a large pantry is an added feature. Four large bedrooms are well supplied with tray cases and closets.

(Description of house shown in plans below)

HERE is an interesting type of brick dwelling in which every effort has been made to develop economy of plan. There are but few partitions and all rooms are square. On the first floor a large living room, lighted on three sides, extends across the entire end of the house. There is a central hall and staircase, and the balance of the first floor consists of dining room and kitchen. On the second floor the plan lends itself to a division of four bedrooms of approximately equal size, each having a large closet.

Full directions for obtaining complete working drawings and specifications for these plans will be found on page 281

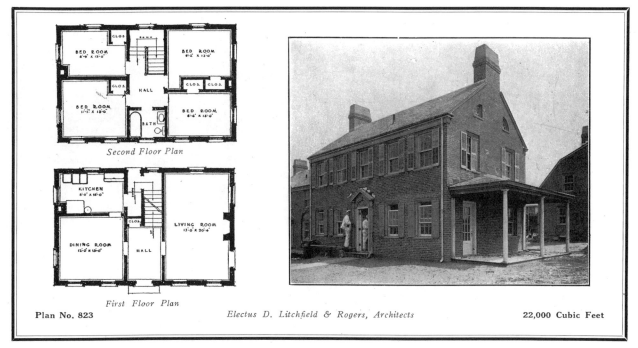

Second Floor Plan

First Floor Plan

Plan No. 823   *Electus D. Litchfield & Rogers, Architects*   22,000 Cubic Feet

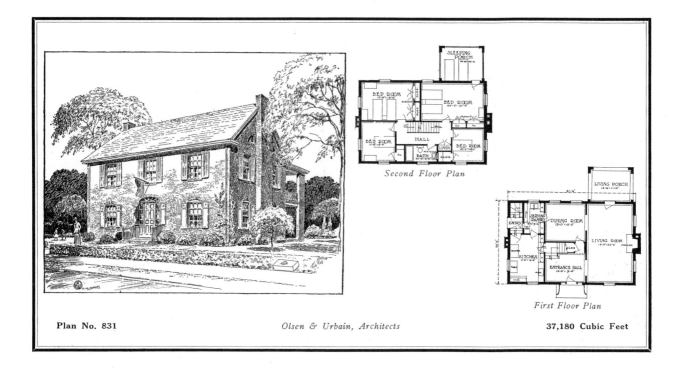

Plan No. 831   *Olsen & Urbain, Architects*   **37,180 Cubic Feet**

Second Floor Plan

First Floor Plan

(Description of house shown in above plans)

THIS attractive eight-room house has exterior walls of common brick. The house is entered through an interesting Colonial doorway opening into the entrance hall, which is 13 x 9 feet. A formal Colonial stair leads from this hall, and under the stair is a convenient coat closet. The living room extends the width of the house and has an open fireplace flanked by windows. There is also a door to the living porch. The serving pantry is an excellent feature.

(Description of house shown in plans below)

HERE is a splendid two-story house, with exterior walls of brick, which is very popular in the South. The first floor has the splendid feature of a bedroom and bath. Entrance from the pergola is into a hall, where the stair is located, and containing a coat closet. One may also enter directly into the living room, which is well lighted on three sides and has an open fireplace. On the second floor there are three large bedrooms and another bathroom.

Full directions for obtaining complete working drawings and specifications for these plans will be found on page 281

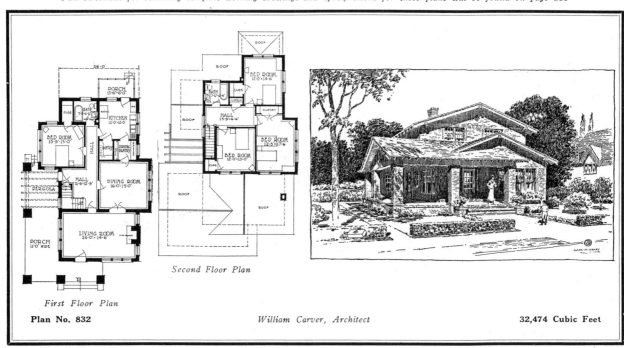

Second Floor Plan

First Floor Plan

Plan No. 832   *William Carver, Architect*   **32,474 Cubic Feet**

Plans and Service Approved by the Press

PRESIDENT HARDING, at the dedication of the "Home, Sweet Home" at Washington, stated:

"The home is at last not merely the center, but truly the aim, the object and the purpose of all human organization. We do not seek to improve society in order that from better homes we may bring forth better servants of the state, more efficient cannon fodder for its armed forces; rather we seek to make better homes in order that we may avoid the necessity for conflict and turmoil in our world.

"The home is the apex and the aim, the end rather than the means of our whole social system. So far as this world knows or can vision, there is no attainment more desirable than the happy and contented home."

The aim of the Home Owners Service Institute, the object and purpose of this volume and other books published by the Institute, is to create the desire for and to educate the prospective home owner to build better homes, where happiness and contentment will reign. The Institute is endeavoring to give the widest possible circulation of its service features so that its aim, object and purpose will become even more generally known.

For more than a year, tens of thousands of persons each week have been receiving a Home Owners Service Institute architectural plan as a feature on the "Small House Page" of the Sunday *New York Tribune.* During the next year, it is anticipated that over a million readers of newspapers each week will have presented for their consideration, in selecting their new home, the cream of the house plans published in this volume.

That famous newspaper—the *New York Tribune,* founded by Horace Greeley—has found the plan service rendered by the Home Owners Service Institute an entirely practical one, appreciated by its readers. The Institute has supervised the construction of a series of model demonstration homes in and near New York for the *New York Tribune,* built from these plans.

Other newspapers have requested the service. In an effort to aid the movement for better homes throughout America, the New York Tribune Syndicate has secured from the Institute the rights to contract with other newspapers throughout the United States and Canada to publish this feature educational page for the benefit of the prospective home owner. The Institute will continue to edit the syndicated "Small House Page" weekly.

No similarly edited or distributed page of interest to the home builder or buyer exists. There are a few syndicated plan services, but that is all.

Nationally known authorities, organizations and the Co-operating Members of the Institute will contribute the best articles obtainable, many illustrated, to aid and advise the prospective home owner. Many of the informative articles published in the Institute "Own Your Home" Service Library—sent free with any set of house plans ordered through the Home Owners Service Institute—will be reprinted through the newspaper syndicate. This

library of 14 text books (copyrighted by the Institute) is the text material for the United Y. M. C. A. Schools "Own Your Home" educational course.

With the support of its Co-operating Members and others, the Institute will supervise the building of one or more model demonstration houses—similar to the *New York Tribune* demonstration homes that have been so beneficial and popular—for educational exhibition in each city (when and where desired) under the auspices of the newspaper publishing the syndicated "Small House Page."

Of such work Theodore Roosevelt, Assistant Secretary of the Navy, says (reprinted from the *Tribune* "Small House Page"):

"Articles on improvement in household economy are good, but they do not accomplish nearly as much as visual demonstrations of those improvements. In the better homes work this is actually what is done.

"For all over the United States committees have arranged model houses where the fathers and mothers can come and see what may be done. It is in the family circle that the individual gets the slant on life that lasts. We get our ideals and character from the

family breakfast and dinner and from the group around the reading lamp in the family living room in the evening. Underlying every country and every civilization is the home. By the quality of our homes we stand or fall, for the home is the 'power-house of the line.' Anything we can do to help our homes we should do."

In the *Buffalo Commercial* appeared the following statement with reference to the "Home, Sweet Home" model demonstration house:

"The thought behind this home is this: The earning power of the average American has increased rapidly in the last few years. He and his family are better fed, better clothed, and (with the auto and radio and movie) better entertained. But they are not better housed.

"The standard of living has increased, but the standard of housing has not kept pace. He still builds houses that have to be constantly renewed. He has not learned in housebuilding the lesson of good materials that his wife learned long ago in the buying of clothes and foods. His house, as soon as complete, begins to decay and at once takes on a third mortgage of replacements.

"The lesson taught by 'Home, Sweet Home' is that better buildings mean better materials. The women of America deserve the best and at the same time the most economical construction to house that most vital element in future Americanism, the home."

Of the man's part in the building of a home—again in reference to the "Home, Sweet Home" dedication — the *Napa Register* (California) published the following editorially:

"All that the normal man does in the struggle for life is really that he may have a happy home, where he can rear a family, give them such advantages as his means can afford, and start them in their own lives with such aid as will best help them. The crowning joy of the typical man is in the home, to which he can repair when his day's work is done.

"But whatever the joy which the man gets from a happy home, it pales into insignificance when compared with the radiance which it brings to the soul of the gracious personage who, by her own competence, her own self-sacrifice, and out of the depths of such love as is beyond the comprehension of any man, makes the home what it is, and where she reigns supreme.

"No other ideal has the beauty of the ideal home. No other purpose can be nobler than increasing their number and their comfort. No other theme could be more inspiring."

Dr. Charles Fleischer, writing for the *New York American*, said, regarding the model demonstration house campaign:

"It would be beautiful if the nation could freely avail itself of the labors of the Home Owners Service Institute, that built the model Washington home in five weeks. But nowhere need you be homeless, if you really want a home—and have a heart."

A number of national magazines also are using the service of the Home Owners Service Institute. Thus this co-operative effort is going forward to aid these forces endeavoring to elevate the standards of small house construction, to the end that better homes will be built today and in the days to come.

From Plan Book to Finished Home

A practical manual of instruction for the prospective homebuilder which explains in detail the correct methods of analyzing sketch plans; obtaining working drawings and specifications; estimating costs and completing all arrangements for the actual construction of the dwelling.

ONE of the most practical forms of service which can ever be made available to the prospective builder of a moderate cost home is the provision at low cost of dependable plans and specifications complete and practical for actual construction.

During the past few years the imperative public demand for good house plans has been shown by the fact that over one million plan books of various types have been marketed to those who have wished to obtain definite ideas and suggestions when studying the problem of moderate cost homebuilding.

In the majority of instances the information which has been made available in book form has been incomplete from a service viewpoint. Often only sketch plans were presented, without making available the necessary working drawings and specifications. The majority of plans presented have been impractical from the viewpoint of utility and economy of construction. Few attempts have been made to thoroughly explain the use of such plans, the range of selection has been limited and advice on the

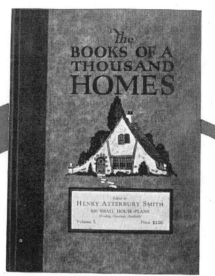

many problems of homebuilding has been general rather than specific.

It has been with a realization of these conditions that after many months of careful study this first volume of the Books of a Thousand Homes, with the parallel advisory service of The Home Owners Service Institute, is presented as the most practical service ever developed to meet the needs of the homebuilding public.

Every effort has been made to produce in this first volume of 500 practical dwelling plans not only the widest possible range for selection but to make certain that every plan should meet the test of actual construction economy. These plans have been selected as the best from various sources. A large proportion of

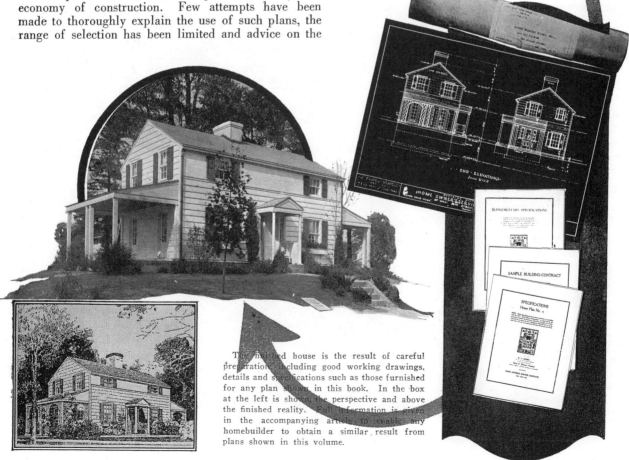

This finished house is the result of careful preparation including good working drawings, details and specifications such as those furnished for any plan shown in this book. In the box at the left is shown the perspective and above the finished reality. Full information is given in the accompanying article to enable any homebuilder to obtain a similar result from plans shown in this volume.

them are presented for the first time as original work of well known architects who have co-operated in creating this practical service. Others have been selected from prize winning groups of architectural competitions held within the past few years under the direction of building material manufacturers and their associations.

Each plan in this book is completely presented and offers not only a suggestion but a practical means of providing for actual construction because for each plan there is immediately available at low cost complete working drawings, details and specifications together with full advisory service as explained in later paragraphs.

Following will be found a complete description of the proper use of this plan book and the service which is made available to provide all necessary data and information in a true service from plan book to the finished home.

The Practical Use of This Plan Book

The first step is to select from this wide range of plans one which approximately meets the requirements of the homebuilder. With each plan the number of cubic feet contained in the house is clearly stated and costs can be estimated as explained later. After floor plans and perspective have been clearly visualized and cost determined approximately, complete working drawings, details and specifications can

be ordered for a modest fee from the Home Owners Service Institute.

It is important to realize that this service is made complete by the additional feature of a one-year membership in the Institute which is included with each set of working drawings. Under this membership the homebuilder is entitled to receive the 14 books of practical information and instruction described herewith—the "Own Your Home" Service Library—and full consulting service of a group of experts who during the year will answer any question pertaining to homebuilding methods, material and equipment.

Visualizing Houses From Floor Plans

The first essential in a careful study of the plans presented in this book is that the homebuilder shall be able thoroughly to visualize the suggested structure. For the exterior this is not difficult because the photograph or perspective drawing accompanying the plans indicates to the eye all that is necessary, except texture and color of materials used. Imagination will supply these, or actual desired color may be applied with crayon to be certain of the actual effect.

Visualizing interiors is more difficult and can be most easily accomplished by laying out the room size in some clear space and then building up an eye picture of each wall. Floor plans indicate types and sizes of windows and doors, size and location of fireplaces and built-in features, and serve

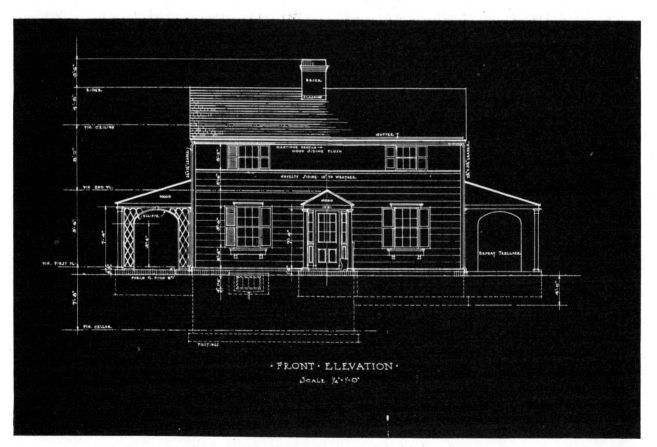

TYPICAL SHEET FROM WORKING DRAWINGS SUPPLIED FOR ANY PLAN IN THIS BOOK

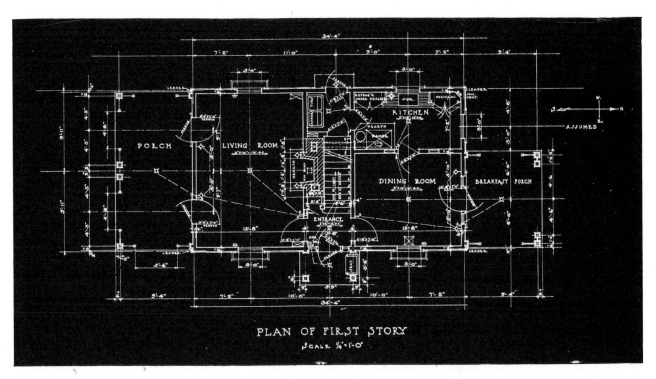

PLAN OF FIRST STORY
SCALE ¼"=1'-0"

DETAILED FLOOR PLANS AS PROVIDED IN WORKING DRAWINGS

to indicate vistas through door and window openings.

The actual finish of woodwork, walls and floors is left to the selection of the owner and can be added to the visual picture developed by this study of major factors in the plan.

Thus the exterior and room by room the house can be carefully built up in the mind until a real picture presents itself.

Careful attention should be given to room sizes in order that there be no disappointment when the house is actually built. It is not sufficient to have a general impression of dimensions. Room sizes and furniture arrangement should be carefully compared with existing rooms. The effects of lighting, daylight and artificial, should receive serious thought.

In visualizing a house from plans two other factors should receive consideration: first, convenience of room and service arrangements to suit *your* method of living but introducing no freakish arrangement which would adversely affect the sales value of the house; and second, *visualization of exterior to fit properly in the surroundings of the building site which you have selected.*

How cubic footage should be estimated

In order to provide additional service, the cubic footage of each house in this book is shown with the plan—

but if you wish to estimate other plans, here is the method:

(1) Determine the area by multiplying over-all dimensions of house, 36'x25'= 900 sq. ft. area.

(2) Multiply by full height from cellar bottom to top of wall plus ½ height of roof-peak above top of wall (roof-plate) 7'6"+1' +9'+1'+8'6"+3'6"=30'6" 900 x 30½=27,450 cu. ft.

(3) Add for porches ½ of cubical contents — 7 x 14=98 sq. ft. x hgt. 8 ft.= 784' x ½=   392

Total cubic footage   27,842

If house has wings, estimate separately as above

Estimating Costs by Cubic Footage

With a complete understanding of the cubic method of cost estimating, together with some local information which is not difficult to obtain if you know what to ask for, it is quite possible to make a reasonably close estimate of the probable cost of any given house built on the site which you have selected.

Each plan presented in this book carries with it a figure indicating the number of cubic feet. This has been worked out as a direct service for the convenience of the home-builder. In order that the method of estimating cubic footage may be understood, however, there will be found at the bottom of this page a graphic description showing a typical calculation of this nature.

It must be understood that cubic foot costs vary

Ready to Build—

How to Obtain Complete Working Drawings and Specifications for Any Plan Shown in This Book

Send your order to Plan Department, Home Owners Service Institute. The price of complete working drawings, details and specifications ready to build any house in this book is $25. This price includes a one year membership in the Institute with full advisory service. Plans and service are described in the accompanying article.

Total Cost, $25.00

HOME OWNERS SERVICE INSTITUTE
37 West 39th Street, New York

considerably with the materials of construction which are employed and with the general quality of fixtures and installations. In any locality the approximate cubic foot cost of any type of house may be

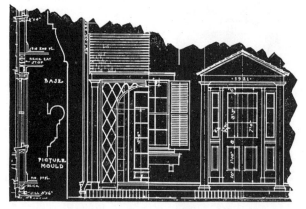

PORCH AND ENTRANCE DOOR DETAILS

obtained from a local building contractor, architect or from owners who have recently had houses constructed.

All small houses fall into general classifications of which those more often used are: frame finished in shingle or wide siding; stucco on frame, brick or hollow tile; hollow and solid brick walls finished in common or face brick; brick veneer and similar general divisions. Stucco is also applied on various patented bases.

The house in which you are interested will fall in one of these classes. After determining this, make inquiry locally as to costs of this particular class of construction. You may learn, for instance, that the cubic foot cost of shingle finished frame construction

is running approximately forty-seven cents (47c) per cubic foot in your vicinity. The house which you have selected from the plan book may contain 17,200 cubic feet. Multiply these and you have a base cost of $8,084. If your plumbing, lighting fixtures, hardware or other materials and equipment are to be better than the average, add three or four hundred dollars and know that your house will cost from $8,400 to $8,600.

Similarly, for each class of construction, you may obtain the local indication of cost and work out a conservative figure by adding a reasonable cost for special features. It must be realized that building costs vary greatly in different localities and sections of the country. This is why cost quotations are left out of this book and it is important to obtain local figures.

Making Simple Changes in Plans and Specifications

While the range of plan selection offered in this book is five times as wide as in any ever before presented to the public it will be quite true that after an individual plan has been selected the owner will in many instances desire to make certain changes in the plans and specifications. Usually these will be but minor changes. The working drawings and specifications received from the Home Owners Service Institute are definite in every detail. Every item of the construction is specifically described in plan and description.

Where it is found desirable to make changes in the plan, such as adding a sun porch, widening a room or similar revision, it will be found that a local architect or the building contractor can do this by changing the section of the plan in question. This change can be drawn out to the same scale and pasted over the affected part.

If more detailed changes are required it is best to take the plan to a local architect who will do this work at reasonable cost and may also be employed to inspect and supervise the construction work for the benefit and protection of the owner if desired. This can be arranged on a basis of reasonable charge per day or per visit to the job and constitutes an admirable safeguard for the owner. Such work is termed "architectural supervision."

Changes in specifications may be made by substituting desired materials and equipment. Details of specifications may be found in descriptive literature issued by manufacturers or will be supplied by the building contractor or consulting architect. Commencing on Page 289 there will be found a section devoted to a careful description of basic building materials and equipment and their proper use. This information will be found valuable if changes in specifications are desired. The specifications for each plan ordered from the Home Owners Service Institute are accompanied by a special book of "Supplementary Specifications" covering various materials and equipment which the owner may find desirable for substitution.

In making changes in the plan it is important to remember that the architectural effect must be retained and if room sizes are increased it may be necessary to relocate exterior openings, such as windows.

How Building Contractor and Material Dealer Will Help You

Several references have already been made to the possibility of obtaining information and co-operation from the contractor and material dealer. These men above all others are closely in touch with actual local building conditions, and, moreover, have a definite in-

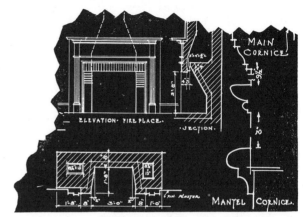

DETAIL OF FIREPLACE

terest in co-operating with homebuilders who are prospective clients.

From these sources information may be obtained as to prevailing building costs and material prices.

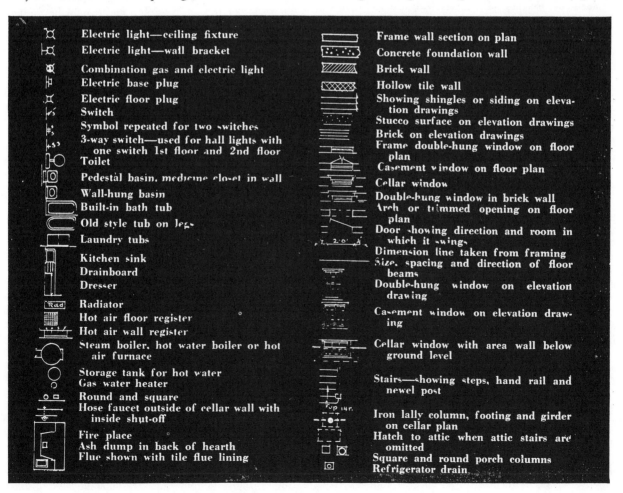

⊠	Electric light—ceiling fixture
⊢⊠	Electric light—wall bracket
⊗	Combination gas and electric light
⊞	Electric base plug
⊠	Electric floor plug
⊢S	Switch
⊢S₂	Symbol repeated for two switches
⊢S₃	3-way switch—used for hall lights with one switch 1st floor and 2nd floor
	Toilet
	Pedestal basin, medicine closet in wall
	Wall-hung basin
	Built-in bath tub
	Old style tub on legs
	Laundry tubs
	Kitchen sink
	Drainboard
	Dresser
Rad	Radiator
	Hot air floor register
	Hot air wall register
	Steam boiler, hot water boiler or hot air furnace
	Storage tank for hot water
	Gas water heater
	Round and square
	Hose faucet outside of cellar wall with inside shut-off
	Fire place
	Ash dump in back of hearth
	Flue shown with tile flue lining

	Frame wall section on plan
	Concrete foundation wall
	Brick wall
	Hollow tile wall
	Showing shingles or siding on elevation drawings
	Stucco surface on elevation drawings
	Brick on elevation drawings
	Frame double-hung window on floor plan
	Casement window on floor plan
	Cellar window
	Double-hung window in brick wall
	Arch or trimmed opening on floor plan
	Door showing direction and room in which it swings
	Dimension line taken from framing
	Size, spacing and direction of floor beams
	Double-hung window on elevation drawing
	Casement window on elevation drawing
	Cellar window with area wall below ground level
	Stairs—showing steps, hand rail and newel post
	Iron lally column, footing and girder on cellar plan
	Hatch to attic when attic stairs are omitted
	Square and round porch columns
	Refrigerator drain

They are conversant with the qualifications of various building materials and can make valuable suggestions for substitution demanded by economy or shortage. Be sure that you select individuals of proven reliability and known for good service.

Obtaining Working Drawings and Specifications

After a plan has been finally selected from this book the complete working drawings, details, specifications and membership advisory service and literature may be obtained for the nominal sum of $25. An order should be sent to the Home Owners Service Institute, 37 West 39th Street, New York City, describing the plan by the Plan Number shown with each plan in the book.

By return mail you will receive your membership certificate and the complete service literature—the "Own Your Home" Service Library—followed within one or two days by the four documents comprising each set of plans:

(1) Working drawings and details (5 to 12 blueprint sheets), (2) "Architect's Specifications," typewritten and bound for practical use, (3) "Supplementary Specifications," printed and bound information regarding various materials and equipment for better home construction, and (4) a "Sample Building Contract," the basic form for contract between owner and builder.

Duplicate sets of any one plan purchased by an individual can be obtained at $5 per set, which merely pays the cost of production, handling and mailing. Original sets on linen, if required, are $27.50 for the first set, and $7.50 for duplicate sets.

Money order or check may be enclosed with order, or payment can be made to postman on delivery at your door.

After this complete service has been received you are ready to take estimates on the construction of your house; you have advisory information covering practically every question which may arise; and you are entitled to the consulting service of the Institute for a period of one year to answer any specific question which you may care to ask.

How to Read Plans

Years ago a dwelling or building was designed in perspective by the architect and simple floor plans and measurements were drawn. The actual work was immediately undertaken in the field with the architect as the master builder directing a group of major and minor craftsmen. Gradually, however, the institution of working drawings and specifications developed until now every detail of measurement and material is carefully indicated in the working drawings and specifications. Sample sheets of the working drawings are shown on preceding pages. In designing a house the architect occasionally wishes to use a specially designed door, fireplace, moulding or built-in feature. The working drawings for these are often provided in more specific form on a larger scale and are known as "details." Illustrations of typical details which accompany working drawings for these houses will be found on the preceding pages.

After you have obtained working drawings and specifications you will undoubtedly wish to make a detailed analysis of them in order to determine exactly what is called for and to make any changes which you may deem desirable.

In the illustration will be found a tabulation of the more important symbols used in making working drawings. This will help you to interpret exactly what the architect has indicated in designing the house. In the Service Library which you receive as a member of the Home Owners Service Institute (which accompanies the working drawings) you will find a chapter on plan reading which will aid materially in your interpretation of the working drawings.

You will note that the exact types of windows, doors and all architectural details are clearly indicated so that you can easily visualize the result of construction. All dimensions are clearly given, including wall and partition thickness, room sizes and similar data. The actual construction of every part of the house is indicated. All installations of plumbing, heating and electric wiring are shown on the plans and carefully described in the specifications.

In general, insistence should be placed on specific carrying out of all requirements indicated by the working drawings and specifications. Occasionally, as a matter of expediency or economy, the contractor or sub-contractor will wish to deviate from these requirements. Judgment in this matter is largely a matter of common sense. If the explanation is clear and reasonable the owner can recognize it as such and agree accordingly.

Certain important information depends upon the character of the building site and cannot be included in the working drawings but must be determined by the owner. This is the establishment of grades and height of the first floor of the house.

The contractor is usually called upon to carry out the rough and finished grading of the site. The finished grade lines must be established; and before excavation for cellar is commenced and footings placed, it must be determined just how high the first floor is to be above the finished grade or ground level.

This is a very important question and has a strong bearing on the architectural effect of the finished house. If it is placed too high or too low the appearance may be much less attractive. The advice of an architect is important in this matter or the homebuilder must consider it carefully in accordance with the type of design and character of surrounding land and make the decision himself.

Materials and Equipment

A general discussion of materials and equipment used in homebuilding will be found in the next section of this book and more extensively in various sections of the "Own Your Home" Service Library which accompany working drawings and specifications.

There are certain fundamental considerations to which the homebuilder should give serious thought in making his selections. There are many grades of building materials on the market, some cheap and some comparatively high in cost. It is well to remember that such materials and equipment will give satisfaction almost in direct ratio to cost.

In considering the first cost of the house the fundamental idea should be to limit the size of the house rather than its quality. Value should be built in

—included with each set of working drawings and specifications

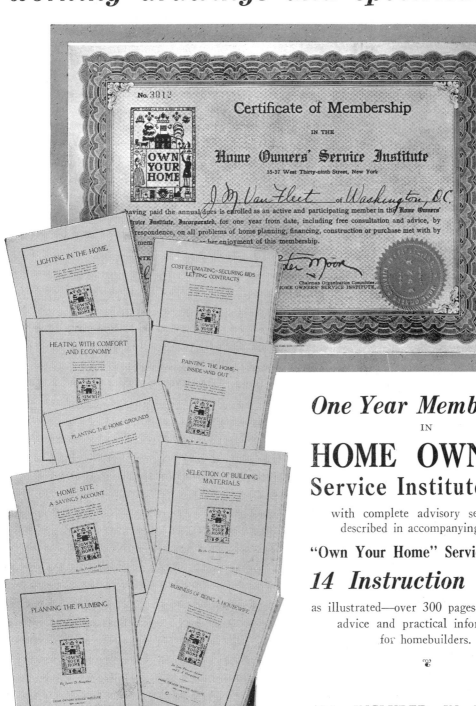

One Year Membership
IN

HOME OWNERS
Service Institute, Inc.

with complete advisory service as described in accompanying pages

"Own Your Home" Service Library

14 Instruction Books

as illustrated—over 300 pages of valuable advice and practical information for homebuilders.

ALL INCLUDED IN REGULAR FEE OF $25.00 FOR COMPLETE PLANS AND SPECIFICATIONS

when the house is constructed. If cheap materials and equipment are employed it is certain that the increased cost of maintenance and replacement within a very few years will bring the total cost much higher than to have built well originally. If the house has been cheaply built it will not maintain its intrinsic realty valuation. It cannot well compete with better built houses when offered for sale.

Considering homebuilding expenditure in the light of an investment, the best form of insurance for protection of the principal is the use of good materials, equipment and workmanship. Cheapness may be false economy in all things, but certainly it is an invitation to disaster and disappointment in homebuilding.

Interpretation of Specifications

The descriptive word "interpretation" is used advisedly above because it is customary for the homebuilder to feel that specifications are not understandable. While it is true that a certain degree of technicality must invade specific descriptive matter of this nature, it is equally true that with careful reading specifications will, for the most part, be found simple and understandable.

The "Architect's" Specifications which accompany these working drawings are in two divisions, the first being known as "General Conditions." As the title implies, these are the conditions under which the contractor undertakes the work and serves to fix equally his responsibility to the owner and the owner's responsibility to him.

The second division of the document, the actual specifications, is simply a detailed description of the materials, equipment and workmanship on the entire job. The various divisions of this section cover excavation, grading, etc.; masonry work including foundations, footings, piers, walls, chimneys, fireplaces and other stone, brick, concrete, tile and cement work. Sizes and quality of materials are definitely fixed. The carpentry division covers sizes, quality and workmanship on all lumber, trim and millwork in the house. Similar divisions are arranged for metal work, painting, plumbing, heating and electrical work.

It is customary to make specific cash allowances for such items which are left to the final selection of the owner, such as electrical fixtures, finish hardware and sometimes plumbing fixtures. Specifications must clearly indicate such allowances.

It is highly important that the owner should understand clearly all facts indicated in specifications, because these become an integral part of the building contract and as such are clearly open to question and misunderstanding when ultimate disputes arise between the owner and the contractor. When the contract is drawn up it is important that each sheet of the working drawings and each page of the specifications shall be separately initialed by both contractor and owner as specific evidence of mutual understanding of all facts and conditions indicated.

There are certain elements of the specifications which the homeowner cannot be expected to understand or appreciate. These are particularly the dimensions of framing lumber and other definitely technical items. The important elements from his viewpoint of the descriptions and indicated quality of materials and workmanship, the specific understanding of the type of equipment which he is to receive, the number and kind of paint coats, the understanding as to extra costs and similar definite items involving quality and good structural practice.

Impatience should never prevent the careful analysis of working drawings and specifications. The owner will find that time spent in this manner before the contract is signed will save money and misunderstanding at a later date.

One Year Advisory Service

It has already been noted that with each set of working drawings and specifications the purchaser becomes a member of the Home Owners Service Institute with full privilege. This organization has been developed by a group of experts in the building field to render a constructive advisory service to those interested in the building of moderate cost homes. Each member receives the following service: (a) The fourteen books of instruction—the "Own Your Home" Service Library—as described and listed on the preceding page; (b) The privilege, planning, construction, furnishing and land improvements for the home (with engraved membership certificate).

The consulting staff of the Institute is composed of leading experts in the various fields indicated. Architects, engineers, interior decorators, landscape architects and officials of loaning institutions co-operate to render this a practical service to provide specific information in answer to the question of members. This organization is not new but has been active in the homebuilding field for several years.

Under the direction of the Home Owners Service Institute the homebuilders' extension courses of the Y. M. C. A. have been developed. Similarly the Homebuilding Page of the New York *Tribune* and its syndicated service to newspapers throughout the country is edited through the Institute staff. These are but indications of the dependability of the organization and the value and sincerity of the advisory service which accompanies all working drawings and specifications issued from the Institute's Plan Department.

A service so complete as this, which carries through from plan book to finished home at the low cost of $25 has never before been offered to the homebuilding public and can now be offered only through the general support of leading manufacturers of building materials and their association, through the sympathetic co-operation of broad-minded architects in assisting to develop the plan service, and through official recognition and encouragement of many service organizations.

The result of this development is the unusually complete advisory service which can now be offered with all plans provided by the Institute.

If architects could afford to work in the moderate cost home field for little or nothing; if the prospective owner of a house ranging in cost from $6,000 to $15,000 could afford to spend hundreds of dollars for the valuable services of the architect—then indeed there would be no reason for the existence of the Home Owners Service Institute, and it would not exist.

The fact is that the moderate cost homebuilding field needs good architecture, for which it cannot afford to pay full value. It needs dependable advice toward the selection and use of good building materials and equipment. It needs legal advice, financing advice, in fact, as much building knowledge as may be required in fields of larger construction. For all this service the average moderate cost homebuilder cannot be called upon to bear the full expense if such expert advice were called upon, at regular fees, for counsel in regard to his individual project. A cooperative institution such as the Institute is the only logical form of service which can meet this economic demand.

The service which is offered through the Books of a Thousand Homes and membership in the Home Owners Service Institute is complete, dependable and serious of purpose. There is no phase of planning or construction in the homebuilding field which is not covered in some manner by this service.

Most of the mistakes and disappointments which have been the lot of homebuilders are due primarily to lack of proper preparedness, and carelessness in making business arrangements relative to financing and contracts. The elements of false economy should be definitely eliminated. No longer are there reasons why the small homes of this country should be lacking in attractiveness which is the result of architectural merit, nor should they lack any reasonable comfort and utility features.

Brief Business Facts for Homebuilders

FOLLOWING are a few facts and conditions which should receive consideration as practical business factors in relation to any homebuilding project. This brief discussion may present ideas of value to the homebuilder.

It is a generally established rule that the balanced relationship in the valuation of house and lot is one to five. That is, land cost should not exceed 20% of the cost of the house built thereon. Any excess cost is a luxury deliberately purchased for the enjoyment of a larger plot or as a premium for location in a highly developed residential district where land costs are unusually high. Remember this rule when you buy or build and that land improvements should be included in its cost.

Architectural Service at Fractional Cost   An interesting feature of the complete plan service and advisory service offered through the Books of a Thousand Homes is that this complete schedule purchased for $25 would cost several hundred dollars as an individual architectural fee.

It is not the purpose of this book and service to displace the architect, but to make available an improved plan service in a field where normally the owner cannot afford to increase his investment by the direct payment of a large fee. Architects recognize this condition as evidenced by the co-operation of a number of leaders in the field in the preparation of this book.

Because of improper planning many of the small houses built during past years are unattractive and impractical. The availability of a service of this nature is a direct contribution toward the improvement of American housing conditions and as such is offered to the individual homebuilder.

This definite saving without sacrifice of good planning adds considerably to the investment and sales value of any house.

Making Building Contracts   In arranging your contracts with builders and sub-contractors do not be misled by low bids. Sometimes the highest bidder is cheapest. Select a contractor on a basis of his reputation and experience in the field. Ask some one for whom he has built as to the advisability of placing a contract with him. Be sure that working drawings and specifications are made a definite part of the contract and all pages and drawings initialed by each party. Arrange to pay at definite periods during the progress of the work and when payments are due make them promptly. Do not order any extra work or changes verbally. If you really want them, get estimates and order in writing. Keep a careful account of all such orders and all payments. Keep a diary of progress according to your own inspections.

Estimating Annual Cost of Home-Owning   Avoid the misleading idea that once you own a home you do not pay rent. You do, in amended form, which might be termed the "owner's rental." This consists of interest, taxes, repairs and other maintenance costs. Estimate these before you build and make certain that you are not undertaking too great a load in comparison to your income.

Home-owning is a wise investment and pays dividends in several attractive forms, but business consideration should be given to the form and amount of this investment just as carefully as though you were buying stocks or bonds. This can be made a sound or a foolish investment in accordance with the amount of good judgment employed.

How to Obtain Complete Plans and Specifications

FOR ANY HOUSE SHOWN IN THIS BOOK

Complete working drawings, details and specifications ready to build any house shown in this book may be obtained for $25. This price also includes membership in the Home Owners Service Institute with full advisory service as described on preceding pages.

Send check or money order with your order or you may pay the postman when he makes delivery. Address Plan Department.

HOME OWNERS SERVICE INSTITUTE

35-37 West 39th Street, New York City

Better Homes

An Editorial Reprinted from "THE DELINEATOR" *Magazine of July,* 1923

*A*CKNOWLEDGMENT *of the co-operation of Associations, Manufacturers and Dealers that made possible the "Home, Sweet Home" permanent demonstration model house **at** Washington, D. C., this card having been framed and hung in the entrance.*

*N*OTE — *As Secretary of the National Advisory Council, Better Homes in America campaign, Mrs. William Brown Meloney (also Editor of "The Delineator") has been the guiding spirit and actual active organizer of the two Better Homes Week demonstrations observed nationally October 9 to 14, 1922, and June 4 to 10, 1923.*

AMERICA is a home-loving nation. The second year of the Better Homes in America Campaign gives proof of this. Two years ago the movement was only a dream in the minds of a few far-seeing, public-spirited men and women. A year and a half ago THE DELINEATOR crystallized the thought into action. We helped to organize the first Better Homes program as a noncommercial, educational movement.

In this second year of the campaign the scope of the work has broadened. Model small homes have been furnished, organized, equipped and budgeted. Millions of Americans have had an opportunity to visit these living examples of what an American home should be. In some cities these houses will be maintained permanently as demonstration homes for the teaching of home-making.

A national demonstration home was built in Washington for the General Federation of Women's Clubs. This house is a modernized version of John Howard Payne's birthplace at Easthampton, Long Island,

around which he wrote his immortal song, "Home, Sweet Home." Donn Barber, one of the foremost architects of America, made the plans for this demonstration house. Manufacturing associations contributed the material and labor, and the house was built by the Home Owners Service Institute in five weeks.

Experts who are supporting the Better Homes movement are studying all the problems of the home-maker —zoning, budgeting and building, as well as the cultural and spiritual interests of the home.

All great and fine things have their beginnings in thought. Every great movement, every work of art, every scientific discovery and industrial development lives first in the dream of some man or woman. Those elements in us which science can neither weigh nor measure nor analyze—the mind and the soul— are the forces behind every forward step civilization takes. So it has been in the movement for Better Homes in America.—MRS. WILLIAM BROWN MELONEY, *Editor.*

Materials and Equipment for Homebuilding

The following pages contain practical information regarding basic materials and general types of equipment used in homebuilding. Here will be found a valuable fund of data for the prospective homebuilder, including definite information as to the proper methods of using such materials and equipment.

Good Hardware for the Small Home

THE selection of hardware for the small house should be given careful thought and consideration. Perhaps no other home equipment comes into such intimate contact with the occupants as the locks and trim on the doors and windows. By their proper functioning the daily life of the home dweller is made more pleasant and comfortable. If doors and windows fail to respond to the devices designed to control them, then to a corresponding degree life may be made irritatingly disagreeable.

Hardware receives hard and constant usage every day in the year. It is expected to do its work faithfully as a matter of course. Very seldom is even a passing thought given to its operation. How many times during the day are doors opened and closed? We don't think of it. And it will not be necessary to think of it if the better grade of locks and hardware is installed when the house is built. Everyone likes the "feel" of good hardware, and the easy and smooth operation of locks satisfies and appeals to both owner and guests.

Why should not the selection of locks and hardware for the small house receive serious consideration? Not only does the general comfort and happiness of the occupants depend in a large measure on good locks and hardware, but actual safety to life and property is also an important factor. What is more essential than positive protection against forcible entry? All entrance doors of the home should be protected by the best locks obtainable, and the high-grade pin-tumbler cylinder lock should be the choice, as it offers the utmost in security and substantial construction.

And there are other doors in the house which should be securely locked. Closet doors where personal property and valuables are kept should be protected against those not authorized to enter. Basement doors should be guarded against intrusion, as it is the out-of-the-way places of this character which are often forcibly attacked. And remember always, the hardware is supposed to be a permanent installation. When the house is built it is not with the expectation that the locks will be replaced within a few years. They are expected to function as long as the house is habitable—and that may mean a lifetime.

The additional cost of good hardware for the small home is infinitesimal considering the returns received. The relative cost of hardware to the cost of the whole house is very small. It is unwise to economize on such an important detail. Cheap and inferior hardware is expensive at any price. It is very apt to give annoyance to the occupants from the time the house is first occupied, and it will require considerable attention and probably frequent replacement. The better grade of hardware calls for only the one original cost. There will be practically no upkeep. And the dividends which are received in carefree functioning of the locks and trim will make the investment a sound one.

The better grade of hardware is made of brass or bronze. These metals are the most durable and are unaffected by the weather. They do not deteriorate; they resist rust. Hardware made of brass and bronze will last a lifetime.

The use of iron and steel hardware should not be considered. While such hardware may be attractive in appearance when new, the plating will soon wear off, and the base metal will then be exposed to the action of the atmosphere and will quickly rust.

In selecting hardware for the home, care should be taken to see that it harmonizes minutely with the architectural *motif* of the house. It should be attractive to the eye and still it must be unobtrusive. It should enhance the beauty of the home in a quiet and dignified manner. The home is one's castle—even though it be a small one—and the best hardware obtainable should be selected. The environment in the home should be made as attractive as possible. Good hardware helps to add an air of distinction. The hardware on a house is a sure expression of the personal taste of the owner.

Entrance door hardware is the first object greeting one at the threshold. Whether it be a Door Handle or a Knob and Escutcheon, it should be simple in design and in close harmony with the other details.

The hardware for the interior doors also should be chosen with the same thought and care. These doors are constantly being opened and closed, and while the hardware is not exposed to the elements, as are the outside doors, it is, nevertheless, handled more frequently. Brass or bronze trim likewise should be selected for these doors. Then there will be no discoloration of metal to mar their beauty.

Good hardware on the small house makes it a more comfortable place in which to live. Good locks make it a safe place in which to abide. The feeling of security is of inestimable value. Good locks and hardware means economy in the long run, since they obviate the necessity of frequent repairs and replacements. Good hardware on the house will enable the owner to dispose of it much more advantageously should he desire. Summed up, the small house equipped with good locks and hardware is a better house in which to live. And that tells the whole story.

Information on Varnish and Enamels

On this page will be found practical information relative to the waste involved in purchasing inferior varnishes and enamels or allowing poor workmanship to impose its ultimately high cost. The importance of buying favorably known brands of these materials is indicated as the home-owner's insurance against disappointment.

THE well-known motto of the painting industry, "Save the Surface and You Save All," contains a wonderful sermon on true economy which home-builders may study with profit when the time comes to consider painting materials, paint, varnish, enamel.

The new house and all it contains from cellar to chimneytop begins to perish before the owner moves in. Moth and rust are far more certain to consume than thieves are to break in and steal.

The economy of fine quality materials, advertised materials, standard materials, is becoming axiomatic. Perhaps it is not so generally recognized that paint and varnish and enamel are needed to *preserve* the fine quality of practically everything that goes into the modern house.

The house that is well painted periodically, will live in its perfection for centuries, whether it be built of wood or brick or stone or cement.

The interior woodwork, the floors, the furniture of the house will live in their integrity and beauty as long as the frame work, if they are properly finished with varnish or enamel.

The average coat of varnish is much less than a thousandth of an inch thick. Perhaps this fact is the best of all arguments for the use of good varnish. If you are going to put three coats of varnish on your interior woodwork and the three coats together make a film much thinner than a thin sheet of letter paper, how absolutely essential it is that a tough, water-and-soap-and-steam-and-sunlight-resisting varnish be used.

A good durable varnish will wear on interior woodwork, at least twice as long as "pretty good varnish," which usually means poor varnish. If the wear is severe, as on baseboards or in the kitchen or bathroom, the poor varnish perishes beyond all beauty and all protective integrity within a few months.

Fine enamels are as necessary to economy as fine varnishes. Moreover, while the difference in appearance between poor varnish and good varnish in the beginning is not great, the difference in beauty between poor enamel and fine enamel is noticeable as soon as they are put on.

Good paint, good varnish, good enamel cost a little more by the gallon than inferior grades do. The minute the painter dips his brush in the first can on the house, this extra cost per gallon begins to justify itself.

Good materials cover more surface. They are easier to apply. The job may be done more quickly with them. Fewer gallons of good materials are required and the labor of the painter will cost less.

This is not all of the argument for good painting materials. The labor cost in the painting job is three or four times the material cost. When the interior woodwork has to be varnished or enameled once every two years, three-fourths of the cost is for labor. When good materials are used and the job lasts six years,

two labor costs are saved as well as two varnish or enamel costs, which is an economical investment.

The prospective home-owner, studying the question of the finishing materials to be used, may well consider the fact that while builders' hardware, for instance, or shingles or plumbing fixtures are definite, easily recognizable articles which show their merits to the trained eye, varnish and enamel all *look* much alike in the can. They are only a means to an end; a step in the production of an article. Moreover the manufacturer of a bath tub or a lighting fixture can put his trade-mark on the article as a further ineradicable symbol of quality. The varnish manufacturer can put his name on his can, but once the varnish leaves the can it is no longer recognizable. These are important reasons why standard, well-known, nationally advertised varnishes and enamels should be specified by name by the architect and owner, and why their use should be insisted upon and why the architect or the owner or both should not be satisfied with insisting upon their being used but should personally see that they are used.

Good Reputation Is Your Insurance

A good name—a good reputation—is of vital importance in a varnish or an enamel; because in large measure the architect and the owner must take the word of the manufacturer that the material is right.

It is an interesting fact in this connection that it is impossible to analyze a varnish chemically in the way that iron or steel can be analyzed. Oils, which may give the same reaction chemically are vastly different in quality when it comes to their suitability for varnish making. The same is true of gums. In the same way, it is a pretty difficult matter to determine by any test whether a varnish has been aged a year or shipped out the day it was made, and yet for some grades of varnish, aging is imperative if quality is to be obtained.

These notes on good varnishes and enamels have dealt chiefly with the matter of durability. It should be remembered that painting materials are used for two purposes—to "save the surface" and to beautify.

It might be argued that saving the surface is a purely utilitarian matter, but surely this is a narrow point of view. A poorly painted house, a piece of furniture, from which the paint or varnish is disappearing, can only be beautiful as decay is beautiful.

On the other hand, the dollars and cents value of a handsome job of paint upon a house is great. The worth of beauty here could almost be accurately measured.

The manufacturers of good varnishes are as keenly alive to the æsthetic value of their product as they are to its protective qualities. If you want a beautifully varnished living room floor or a beautifully enameled bathroom or kitchen, the way to secure it is to have high grade, nationally advertised varnish or enamel.

Painting the Exterior of Your Home

The homebuilder will find here a number of practical suggestions regarding the selection and use of paint for the exterior of the house. Included is information as to what constitutes good paint; how it is mixed; how many coats to apply; and which colors wear best.

THE homebuilder usually gives careful thought to the selection of an appropriate and pleasing color scheme for the exterior of his or her new house. All too frequently, however, no precautions are taken to make sure that the paint used is such as to give permanency to the color scheme chosen and adequate protection to the surface underneath. The most important point, particularly from the money standpoint, is thus neglected. You will find that it pays well to know what constitutes good paint and to learn a few cardinal principles about painting.

The right prescription for exterior wood surfaces is an old one—simply pure white-lead thinned to painting consistency with pure linseed oil. Nothing has yet been found to match this combination. It gives the best protection and decoration at the least outlay.

Pure white-lead is sold in paste form, that is, mixed with a small percentage of linseed oil. The painter simply thins this paste white-lead by stirring in more linseed oil which makes white paint. A small quantity of turpentine is usually added to induce better penetration and a little drier to make the paint dry more quickly. To make colored paint, merely the addition of the proper tinting colors is necessary. These colors are also sold in paste form and are called colors-in-oil.

A little lampblack, for example, added to the white paint produces gray, chrome yellow makes cream or any yellow tint, chrome green makes green tints, Chinese blue makes blue tints, etc.

In mixing paint to order as described above, the painter is able to control it absolutely. He can mix it thick or thin and vary the proportions of ingredients to meet any surface condition. He is able to match *exactly* any desirable color, many of which are obtainable in no other way. And, what is especially important, he is absolutely sure of the composition of his paint.

Paint made of pure white-lead and linseed oil forms a tough, elastic film which accommodates itself to all surface changes. Consequently, there is no cracking and scaling as with a hard, unyielding paint. The white-lead paint wears down uniformly, leaving a perfect surface for repainting. This means a saving on the next painting bill, for it is a well-known fact that a painter oftentimes has to charge more for burning and scraping off an old splotched surface than for applying the new paint when once the surface is ready for it.

Some Painting Pointers

The cost per gallon of lead-in-oil paint always compares favorably with the price per gallon of other paints, but the price per gallon of any paint is a minor consideration. Of far more importance is the price *per year*. A paint job is about three-fourths labor and only one-fourth paint. You have to spend the same for spreading the paint whether it be good or bad. If it is going to cost $75 to put the paint on, it makes little difference whether the balance is $25 or $20 or $30, but it makes a lot of difference whether your selection of the $20 paint or the $30 paint wastes the expenditure of the $75 for labor or protects it. The important consideration is not what you pay for the paint, but how long it will last. That determines the cost per year not only of the paint but of the labor. When property-owners learn this one little lesson, they will save money on their property.

Three coats should always be applied to a surface which has never before been painted—a thin priming coat and two heavier coats. Two coats only are sometimes used on new work, for the sake of economy, but it is not true economy. A third coat would cost only one-third more and would make the job last twice as long.

Instruct your painter to brush the paint well into the pores of the wood and not simply to flow it on. In the old days when round brushes were used more than now, the paint was brushed in more thoroughly and better jobs were the result.

Never have painting done while wood is wet or while rain or snow is falling, or immediately after a frost, however light. The pores of wet wood are then filled with moisture and the paint film, therefore, does not get the anchor hold in them which is necessary to make it stick.

If you would have the utmost wear out of your paint, choose warm tints rather than cold ones for exteriors. Tints based on the reds, browns and black are, as a rule, the most durable. Thus the grays, the slates, the browns and richer yellows etc., are excellent for wear and at the same time, are the most pleasing on the house. It has been found that grass greens, blues and cool shades of yellow hasten the deterioration of the paint film. This is due to the fact that they do not reflect or turn back the heat rays of the sun but allow them to penetrate the film.

Finally, employ a good painter. It is not economy to set unskilled labor at a job of painting just because anyone can spread paint on in some sort of fashion. The skilled painter's experience in diagnosing the needs of the surface and his knowledge of just the right proportions of lead, oil, turpentine and drier to fit the case make him a good investment. Like good materials, a good painter pays for himself.

On the following page will be found a number of practical points of importance in connection with the painting of home interiors.

Painting the Interior of Your Home

Because it is not exposed to the weather, paint for interiors is mixed and used differently than for exteriors. Important points to be considered are beauty, cleanliness and economy. Some interesting facts are presented for the homebuilder together with definite color suggestions for rooms.

THE decoration of home interiors presents a problem quite different from the painting of exteriors. Paint used inside is not exposed to the weather; consequently it is mixed differently from paint intended for outside use. Glossy paint is invariably used on exteriors; the decoration of interiors sometimes calls for a variety of finishes (lustreless or flat, semi-gloss, full gloss, etc.) and a range of color effects which includes those more delicate and elusive tints unsuitable for exterior use.

Points to consider in the treatment of interior surfaces are beauty, cleanliness and economy. Beauty involves color and style of finish. Cleanliness depends upon washability and consequent freedom from dirt and other impurities. Economy has to do with cost and years of wear. These three results are best reached by the use of paint made with pure white-lead.

While semi-gloss and gloss finishes are still used to some extent on certain interior surfaces, most interiors are done nowadays in glossless or flat effects. A flat finish is obtained by the painter with white-lead by mixing it with flatting oil. This gives a white paint which he colors to any desirable tint by the addition of the proper colors-in-oil. Such a paint produces a durable, washable flat finish of unusual beauty—one suggestive of the soft, rich, matt finish of an eggshell. It will stand frequent washing with warm water, mild soap and a soft cloth or a sponge, and can thus be kept absolutely clean and sanitary. The durability of the paint is not affected in any way and there is no unsightly streaking as often occurs when a less stable paint is washed.

You cannot get an idea of a beautiful, flat, white-leaded wall if you have never seen one done as the real decorator does it. There is no gloss. There are no brush-marks. As for tints, you can secure those which will harmonize perfectly with your rugs and draperies. There is a character and a distinction to white-leaded interiors which can be had with no other medium.

Good decorators have always known how to get these effects and, in homes where cost has been no drawback, white-leaded walls as well as woodwork have been enjoyed for years. With the coming of flatting oil, the daintily tinted white-lead can be applied more rapidly and cheaply and the washability has been increased. Three coats now give the most beautiful effects, whereas in the old days it was quite common to put on from six to ten.

There is perhaps no decorative medium which lends itself to so many artistic and beautiful wall treatments as white-lead paint. It not only enables you to secure the charming, one-tone, flat effects which are always in good taste, but it places at your disposal a large variety of interesting treatments. If other than a smooth finish is desired, the paint may readily be "stippled," which imparts to it a rough or pebbled texture. You have recourse to stenciling, striping and panel work to add a touch of individuality to your walls. Quite a number of pleasing blended and mottled effects are obtainable at no great added expense. It is also possible to secure, simply with two coats of paint, the most delightful figured or patterned effects in two tones. A good painter can produce any of these treatments.

Suggestions for Interior Color Schemes

The use to which a room is put determines to a considerable extent the color scheme which is suitable. Is it a living room, dining room or sleeping room? Each serves a different purpose and is accordingly treated somewhat differently.

Living Room

The living room is the place of family intercourse and rest. Friends and callers are entertained and made happy there. It should be comfortable and express refinement. Tan, medium brown, warm gray, old blue, gray-green, blue-green and other soft colors are excellent for living rooms.

Hall

Guests are welcomed in the hall. It should be inviting and suggest hospitality. In general, the color tone should be close to that of the living room.

Dining Room

This room exists not alone for the purpose of stoking the human furnace with fuel. The daily meals are made a pleasant function if china and linen and conversation are agreeable. So, too, may proper room decoration add to or mar the hours spent here. Soft old blue, dull orange, gray-green, dark tans and rich browns are suitable if the dining room is not too dark.

Kitchen

The kitchen should be bright, cheerful and clean-looking. An all-white kitchen is preferred by many, but a color just off the white, such as cream, is more satisfactory. It is less glaring and does not soil so readily. Light grays, greens and yellows may be used to good advantage.

Bedrooms

Bedrooms are for rest and sleep. Everything about them should make for tranquility. Consequently quiet tones should prevail. As bedrooms are shut off from each other, each room may be considered independently. Creams, soft yellows, delicate blues and light grays are restful colors and appropriate for bedrooms.

Bathroom

The bathroom is shut off from the rest of the house. It may be treated as a separate unit, but preferably in light tints to give an atmosphere of cleanliness. Ivory, creams, light grays and buff are suitable.

The Advantages of Architecturally Designed Stock Woodwork

"This is my home . . . a place for
work and dreams, and love and rest."

BECAUSE it *is* so essentially "a place of rest," all of us seek to have comfort in our homes. Bodily ease is not sufficient—we must have mental rest, too. Mental rest requires beauty; without beauty, no mental rest is possible. This isn't mere sentimental theory, but proven psychology. The Arabs have an old proverb, "If you have two loaves of bread, sell one and buy a flower, for the soul, too, must be fed."

So when we have provided mere physical comfort in this Castle in Spain of ours, we must look to its beauty. Two sorts of things make up the beauty of any house: those that are part of the structure itself, the architectural elements; and those which may be added to it, outside or in, the decorative elements. The two are complementary. Neither can be completely successful without the other. Trees and shrubs, rugs, furniture, lamps, fabrics, pictures—these, though necessities, are decorative elements. Much can be accomplished with them to bring beauty to the home. But if a house is to be truly restful, there must be beauty in the structural background that forms the setting for these things: porches, roof, walls, windows and entrances on the exterior; floors, walls, woodwork and the built-in things of various sorts on the interior.

Careful Selection of Woodwork Desirable

Woodwork, you see, is the chief element in this structural background. Everywhere that your eyes travel, they rest upon woodwork, always a background and sometimes a dominating feature. Shut your eyes, if you will, and try to picture a house without woodwork. There would be walls pierced by unfilled openings—a skeleton structure with no doors or windows, stairs, baseboards, moldings or paneling; with no mantel, china closets, kitchen dressers, or bookcases; with no bay or dormers or floors—and perhaps no porches or columns or roof or cornice. From ten to twenty per cent of the total cost of your house is its woodwork. Because there is so much of it, there is nothing which can do so much to make or to mar the beauty of your home. Someone has said that you cannot make a beautiful home with an ugly house as a starting point. Lovely furnishings can no more make up for ugly, jerry-built woodwork than a pretty dress can make up for ill-breeding in its wearer.

Not so many years ago, homebuilders who wished to have in their homes a background of beautiful woodwork that had any claim to architectural merit, could obtain it only by having it specially made, at necessarily great cost. Many people still think that the only way to get really well-designed woodwork is to have it made laboriously by hand, piece by piece, on the job. The only alternative open to homebuilders whose good taste exceeded their pocketbooks, was to make their selections from the catalogs of "stock millwork"—which meant, in almost every case, to content ourselves with hideous designs of pseudo-Mission style.

"The common problem," says Browning, "yours, mine, everyone's, is not to fancy what were fair in life provided it could be, but finding first what may be, then find out how to make it fair up to our means."

Along with higher standards of living in general, and education in better homes and interior furnishing, there has come a constantly increasing demand for woodwork of better proportions and patterns than are found in ordinary "millwork," for woodwork that could take its place without apology alongside period furniture and the newer furnishings.

The quality of good design itself adds nothing to cost of production of any article. It is just as cheap to make a good design as a poor one, and often involves less material rather than more, and simpler forms rather than more ornate ones. But in order to supply these good designs at a price the average homebuilder can afford certain manufacturers have gone a step further, and, with the help of architects, produced them in stock quantities. The woodwork items pictured in most "millwork" catalogs as *stock* are seldom actually on hand; they are, usually, a collection of suggested designs, which have been produced in the past, and which can be made up promptly, from details already on hand. It will pay you to investigate and know that the designs you select for your home are good architecturally and really available for immediate delivery.

Better Woodwork Available for Homebuilders

One large company, at least, is using the very modern methods of this machine-production age, not only to give homebuilders better designed woodwork, but to give it to them at lower cost. The needed architect's "details," since they are to be used not once but hundreds of times, have been worked out with the utmost care to save materials and labor and attain perfect design and construction. Intricate, highly specialized machines that require hours to set and adjust for each operation are used for a hundred pieces instead of only one, and this cost distributed over the greater quantity. Workmen making many pieces alike, instead of individual special designs, learn better ways of doing their work. Stock woodwork is therefore almost sure to be of better quality than "special" designs.

Consciously or unconsciously, you notice the maker's name on food containers or in garments before making your selections. You feel that certain names relieve you of the responsibility of carefully looking into the below-surface qualities, allowing you free choice in the selection of articles that gratify your own individuality and taste. The trade-mark assures you at a glance that the material you are purchasing is of the best material, made in the best known way. It is interesting to know that trade-marked woodwork of the highest quality of manufacture and design is available for prospective homebuilders.

See Illustrations on Page 140

Wallpaper: the Background in Home Decoration

During the past few years there has been a remarkable development in the designing of attractive wallpapers which have been placed on the market at reasonable costs. By creating an interesting background, well-selected wallpaper aids materially in furnishing a room and forms a valuable decorative element.

THERE are three standards by which to judge the value of the small house—commercial, artistic and sentimental. The commercial and artistic value may be estimated in dollars; the sentimental or the moral in feeling. A house is both a structure and a home. As a structure it gives shelter and protection; as a home it is an interpretation of the characters and personalities of those living within its walls.

The interior decorations of the house are outstanding influences in determining all of these values. A bare room has little merit of its own except from the structural point of view. Its value is increased by certain intangible qualities based on the taste of those who decorate and furnish it. Good taste pays material as well as æsthetic dividends. When character is shown in the interior of a house the value of that house is increased by every standard of estimation.

Nothing else, unless it is her clothing, is so pronounced an index to a woman's breeding and refinement as the interior decorations and furnishings of her home. In creating decorative effects wall treatment is the most important influence. It is the *motif* of interior decoration; the setting on which every other attribute must be based.

That is why wallpapers of good design and coloring are the hallmarks of taste and quality. For hundreds of years hostesses have taken pride in their wallpapers and been judged by them. Your wallpaper tells who you are, for it is a part of you, an index of your personality.

The selection of wallpaper, therefore, should be made with the greatest care and thought. Quality, coloring and design are of supreme importance, for they are influences on the commercial, artistic and sentimental values of your home.

Perhaps Beauty is the key to wallpaper value. Beauty combines quality, coloring, design and judgment in utilization. Through the working out of true beauty in the wallpaper of a home will come rest, comfort and contentment. No other decorative treatment allows such latitude for personal selection and effects.

Form, line and color are readily manipulated by the interior decorator, professional or amateur. When imagination and taste are used to secure the attractiveness of superior effects, tangible and intangible values have been added to the home—value measured by sentiment as well as by pocketbook.

In estimating values let us first consider the commercial. No other expenditure that you may make within your home is likely to pay better dividends than the cost of good interior decorative treatment. Good decorative treatment has an intrinsic value in estimating mortgage value and resalability. Many a house has been sold at top price because its walls reflected beauty, warmth, genial hospitality and home

atmosphere of the kind that only refinement in taste can breed. Good wallpaper adds a money value to any home far in excess of first cost.

Unfortunately the decorating cost is the final cost in home building and too often decorations suffer because of this. Roofs, basements, floors are house essentials—structural costs—but quality in wall treatment and house furnishings are likely to be considered of non-essential importance; something that may be developed to the heart's content later.

Yet the interior of the home is the most important of the many influences by which the acquaintance, casual visitor or possible purchaser will judge you and your property. Good interiors are assets; poorly furnished, poorly decorated interiors are liabilities. Well papered walls with coloring, design and texture of a quality that means taste, and shows harmonious treatment, give satisfaction and rest to all.

The cost of material and of labor in decorating walls with paper is so low in comparison with the effect produced and the possible influence on the owners, their guests and possible purchasers, that from a purely commercial standpoint it would seem poor business to neglect or stint this phase of house building and maintenance.

Taking up the artistic value of wallpaper and general interior treatment we would point out that virtually everybody is attracted by the beautiful and artistic.

There is, however, a style element in both beauty and art that should not be overlooked or underestimated. It is not always safe to go on taste alone if the house is to be judged by standards other than the desire of the owner for use as a home. If the owner builds with the idea that if opportunity arises he will sell, then it is advisable to study the trend of style carefully. If, on the other hand, outside influences such as resalability are of no consequence, the style influence may be ignored to any extent desired.

The artistic value of a house is expressed by creating the right atmosphere. A house without atmosphere cannot be artistic. The right wallpaper will help in creating an atmosphere and charm which will be felt by all who cross the threshold. Without proper decorative wall treatment warmth, charm, and atmosphere are unobtainable. Artistic value, therefore, can be estimated as a material asset—it adds dollars to the estimate of a structure's worth.

The sentimental value of a home is based largely on things personal, but only time can bring a sentimental value to a house that is not intrinsically beautiful and filled with atmosphere. Looked at through time's softening influences, almost any home may win some sentiment. Beautiful homes, homes filled with warmth and taste, homes of which we are proud, have a sentimental value from the first day we call them

(Continued on page 300)

Quality, Capacity and Completeness in Electrical Equipment

One of the most important features relative to the installation of electrical equipment is to be certain that the wiring system is adequate for present and future needs. Many home owners regret the lack of a sufficient number of electrical outlets after the new home is completed.

THE importance of quality and completeness in the electrical equipment of a modern home should be quite apparent to anyone with an appreciation of the part electrical service plays in our daily lives—the dependence, rapidly becoming general, upon the turning of a switch for the performance of the many household tasks so ably performed electrically. This appreciation necessitates, however, some little understanding of the demands placed on a residential electrical system; some consideration of the economics involved and the needs of safety and economy in making effective use of this great modern servant. For example:

The electrical equipment of the home, if not in continual use, is liable to be called into operation any minute, day or night. Some portion of it is in actual service a greater number of hours during the year than the water system, kitchen equipment or any other single service. It is rarely idle. Hence, reliability of the electrical service is essential in the modern home, and this important attribute can best be assured through a careful choice in the selection of the materials employed—of the wire, wiring devices, fittings and fixtures. The quality of the materials used and the competence of the contractor making the installation should be of high order, for skimping on the electrical work is simply an invitation for subsequent remodeling of the installation at an expense many times as great as the trivial additional cost which would have guaranteed a satisfactory installation in the first place.

The difference in investment entailed between a first-class installation and the poorest which could pass even the most cursory examination by the local building department and by the insurance inspector, is really quite negligible. The principal item of expense lies in the actual labor cost, and there no possible reduction can be made through the use of sub-standard material and equipment—in fact, there is more apt to be an increase. When apportioning the amount of money to be expended for the different services, it should be borne in mind that the electrical system is at least as important as an acceptable water system, heating plant, etc.

This does not mean that the plumbing of the home should be slighted or that any saving should be attempted by economizing on the heating system, but it does mean that proper provisions should be made to make the electrical installations comparable in quality and completeness. This should be done, if for no other reason than the effect upon the sales value of the residence, a consideration which no home owner can afford to disregard. The suitably electrified home not only finds a much readier market, but it commands an increase in price far in excess of the added investment made in electrical equipment. The more complete the electrical equipment, the greater will be the enhancement in property value.

And what are the visible evidences of completeness?

In general, a switch at every entrance to every room, a convenience outlet for every eight running feet of wall space, and lights so distributed that an even illumination, free from shadows or glare, may be had in any room. Plenty of well distributed light—complete and immediate control of these lights—accessible and convenient sources of power for appliances, and current for portable lamps—these are the objects of complete electrification which every home owner should seek.

The invisible evidences of completeness are also of prime importance, inasmuch as they affect the capacity of the system. This deals chiefly with the number of branch circuits and the size of the wire. The *minimum requirements* are laid down by the Electrical Code of the National Board of Underwriters, upon which are based virtually all local building requirements. Builders, however, should not be misled in the belief that the approval of the Underwriters is an assurance of complete service. The Underwriters and local inspectors are merely electrical policemen who patrol the border line between dangerous wiring and wiring which is not dangerous, so it will be seen that their approval, although important in itself, can be only an insurance against hazard. An automobile which will run without "blowing up" is not necessarily a good automobile—and the same logic applies to an electrical installation. Because home builders so frequently accept the approval of the Underwriters as an approval of the *serviceability* of the system, it is deemed wise to emphasize that they consider the *safety* of the system only.

Wiring, quite adequate for the lighting practice of the first century, could not handle with safety and efficiency the demands placed on the circuits of the modern home by the use of present day household appliances. Today's user of a flat-iron may be tomorrow's user of a washing machine, dish washer, refrigerator, etc. The difference in cost between complete and incomplete wiring is very little and unless the former is chosen today's saving may be tomorrow's regret.

Without a plentiful, almost lavish, use of convenience outlets for the accommodation of appliances and supplementary lighting by means of portable lamps, the home is almost certain to lack something in the way of comfort, which is to be secured only electrically. Quality and completeness in electrical provisions should be insisted upon by every home-owner.

The quality of electrical materials and workmanship virtually insures the avoidance of accidents or replacements.

The completeness of the electrical installation permits the realization of the many benefits electrical service affords, and insures economy in its use.

Each requirement in itself represents an investment which is certain to prove well justified, and together they go far to insure satisfaction and contentment.

Heating With Comfort and Economy

One of the most important problems in equipping the home is the provision of the right kind of heating apparatus.

IF your home is located where rapid changes of temperature occur in a few hours, you should provide a heating system that will respond quickly to your demands. Vapor and vacuum systems, steam and hot air furnaces meet such requirements equally well. Hot water requires slightly longer time to heat but conversely the radiators remain warm for a longer period of time after the fire is turned off.

Suppose your home is located where it receives broad sweeps of cold wind, being exposed to the weather on all sides. You must distribute heat properly and control it in all portions of your home, independent of outside conditions. This is very difficult to do with hot air in a house so situated.

The maintenance of the different heats vary according to climatic conditions, but in general a hot air furnace will burn a little more fuel than a steam system. Hot water and vapor systems should consume from a tenth to a quarter less fuel than steam.

Cover the heat pipes with a good air cell covering. Warm air pipes should not be covered with asbestos paper because by so doing, contrary to general belief, more heat is given off in the cellar than where the pipes are left bright tin. Air cell covering is the only satisfactory type of covering, and should be used not only to cover the warm air pipes in a warm air system but to cover all pipes of steam, vapor or hot water systems.

Before proceeding, it will be well to emphasize that all systems, to give thorough satisfaction, must have a good flue draft. A chimney should be straight, without any offsets where the soot can accumulate, and without any other openings than from the furnace or boiler.

You can install a combination warm air and hot water system. This is the principle of the vapor-vacuum-pressure or "Combination" system of heating which is economical for all seasons of the year.

The elimination of the effect of atmospheric pressure within the system allows vapor to rise as quickly as the water is warmed and benefits are equal throughout the house.

This is a radiator system, and each radiator may be controlled separately; installation and operation are simple; and the circulation is noiseless. Its flexibility makes it adaptable to almost any conditions, and it is particularly economical in the South and on the Pacific Coast, where many mild days occur during the heating season.

If your home is small and compact a pipeless furnace may give you just the kind of heat you require. It is a cheap, popular, and satisfactory way to heat small homes. The furnaces are extremely simple in construction, easily installed, burn either wood or coal, and there is little to get out of order.

The principle of operation is as follows: Cold air is taken through separate openings which surround the larger register to the fire chamber in the furnace, is heated and ascends through the one and only register opening provided for heat distribution. This opening is usually in the center of the main floor. The hot air rises to the ceiling, cools, falls to the floor, is again taken to the furnace for re-heating.

In order to heat all rooms, the room doors must be *opened* and registers placed in the second story floors. Grills or transoms must be put in the doors. These will permit the heat to enter naturally and next to the ceiling.

A warm air heating system is said to be the most healthful when the fresh air is taken into the house from out-of-doors, though some warm air heating systems take air in from the cellar. The air is heated thoroughly by contact with large heated surfaces and is easily humidified before it ascends in pipes to the rooms. Warm air heaters can be had that will burn most any kind of coal and are so constructed that the majority of gases are utilized instead of being blown through the chimney, as in times past. Water pans are always provided in the furnace and should be kept clean and filled; the air throughout your home will then be properly moistened.

Steam is the least expensive to install of all forms of radiator heat. It requires but a single set of piping whereas hot water requires two sets—one to carry the water to the radiators and the other to bring it back to the boiler. A hot water system costs more than steam to install.

Steam is a satisfactory heat and is used in both large and small buildings quite generally.

Some people complain because radiators knock and sizzle, but if they would insist upon well-made, non-adjustable air valves, properly installed, and that their pipes should be large enough with the proper pitch, the trouble would be eliminated. A boiler generates steam which ascends through pipes to the radiators. It gives off heat, condenses in the radiators and flows back usually by gravity to the boiler. It is again evaporated and completes the circuit.

Once heated, hot water will remain so for a number of hours. The fire may get low, but still the water remains warm, and gives off heat. Ordinarily hot water plants, that is to say, the boiler and mains, are placed in the cellar of your home. Suppose, however, you desire hot water heat and have no cellar. It is then possible to install both radiators and a special boiler on the same floor level. The mains, which carry the heated water to the radiators can be suspended from the ceiling, or carried in the attic. The water will pass to the radiators and be taken back to the boiler through pipes placed along the baseboard of the room, or below the floor.

Hot water operates like hot air. The water is first heated in the boiler. Next, it expands, grows lighter and passes through the piping system to the radiators. Here it cools and is returned through a separate set of pipes to the boiler for reheating and circulation.

It is best to have the pipes in a hot water system in partitions rather than in an outside wall. If it is necessary to have them in the outside wall care should be taken to have them well protected from freezing by insulating with asbestos air cell covering.

Selecting the Plumbing Fixtures For Your Home

The homebuilder is learning to give much more serious consideration to the question of good plumbing, fixtures and bathroom equipment. This is not only a question of convenience and comfort in daily home life, but involves the avoidance of expensive repairs and alterations by the selection and installation of a good system when the house is built.

THE sanitary equipment of the house includes many items. They are: drain pipes which carry off the waste, supply pipes which conduct the water to the various fixtures, shut-off valves in the basement or concealed in the walls, as well as all plumbing fixtures and bathroom accessories. These should all be selected with even more care, if anything, than the furnishings. When furniture wears out it can be replaced for the mere cost of buying new pieces. However, when the plumbing fixtures wear out replacement must cover the cost of the equipment, plus the cost of labor, taking out the old and putting in the new fixtures.

Quality and service should be the prime factors in selecting the sanitary equipment.

The selection of the lavatory, closet and bath depends primarily on the type of home, the amount of money that is to be spent and the space to be devoted to the bathroom. Whether the housewife is to do her own work or whether the work is to be handled by servants determines in large degree what additional plumbing may or may not be necessary.

Modern plumbing fixtures have been developed with the idea in mind of reducing to the minimum the labor involved in keeping them clean and in a sanitary condition.

Baths

Baths, for instance, of the built-in type not only reduce the floor space to be kept clean, but also the amount of floor space that must be tiled as well.

The porcelain built-in bath (a clay product) recommends itself highly because of cleanliness, the heavyweight type with sloping end for the more elaborate homes. The enameled iron built-in bath is generally used in the less pretentious home. It has become very popular, owing to its fine appearance and moderate cost. The weight being less than that of the porcelain tub makes it adaptable for homes of lighter construction.

Showers

The built-in bath is admirably adapted to the use of showers, the walls very often being tiled up to about six feet, although in some cases waterproof cement is used. In case of a recessed bath a curtain can be used across the front, while with a corner tub, the curtain can be extended along the front and one end, leaving the two walls to complete the shower inclosure.

Shower Valves

The modern shower is fitted with a mixing valve rather than with two separate valves. Experience has proven that shower mixing valves are time savers and water savers compared with the two-valve type of shower.

Mixing valves should be of a single lever handle, double compression type, of heavy construction, with generous-sized supply ports. Where the construction of the building will permit, the mixing valves should be built in the wall with, possibly, a china face plate. The construction should be such that the valve and all working parts can be removed from the front for re-washering and repairing.

The shower over the bath is becoming very popular because the busy man can take his morning shower more quickly than is possible with the bathtub. The shower will, however, never replace the bath for the warm plunge in the evening. Nothing is quite so soothing to the tired body and woos sleep quite so successfully as does the warm tub bath.

In the more ornate bathroom, where there is plenty of space, a separate compartment for the shower may be provided with a series of sprays along three side walls or four corners of a compartment with the pipes concealed within the wall. The shower head sprays and valve, which are exposed, may be of white sanitoure finish if desired. The door can be of plate glass with nickel-plated brass with white sanitoure finish or white metal frame and jamb. The receptor can be of porcelain, tile or marble to match the color scheme of the bathroom. In these more ornate bathrooms there is usually also provided a solid porcelain tub, of a built-in recess or corner type. The lavatory can be of the pedestal type of two-fired vitroware with the combination fittings with china mountings, and dressing table to match. Or they may be finished to order, to suit individual taste, with marble lavatories and dressing table to match. The marble lavatory may be made of Blanc "P" white, Egyptian black and gold, Breche violet or any other imported or domestic marble which may be selected by the architect or the owner. When marble is used it is usually selected to blend with the general color scheme of the room and surroundings. In such bathrooms the metal mountings for metal lavatories and dressing tables are usually white metal or brass, finished with colors to blend in with the general color scheme. There is usually provided a Sitz or footbath and dental lavatory. The bathroom may be finished with colored tile of several textures in keeping with the general color scheme.

Lavatories

Two-fired vitreous china lavatories have become very popular, having a smooth glass surface which is easily kept clean. A quick-draining waste with unobstructed outlet and removable outlet plug makes the most satisfactory waste. Enameled iron lavatories are used where cost is an important consideration, and prove very satisfactory. The enamel on cast-iron lavatories is not fired to as high a temperature as the two-fired vitreous ware and the surface is somewhat softer and requires a little more effort to keep clean. The smaller lavatories are usually fitted with two single faucets of the compression type where the pressure is fairly high and with quick compression of Fuller type where the water pressure is comparatively low. The larger lavatories are usually fitted with a combination hot and cold supply fixture and in some cases with all china handles and china escutcheons. This combination faucet enables the user, like in the case of the shower temperature adjusting valve, to wash in running temperate water. The combination faucet, whether for lavatory, bath or sink should be of heavy construction with generous ports for filling, encased composition seat washers with swivel disks, which lessen the wear on the washers and valve seats, renewable seats and standardized interchangeable parts.

Sinks

For the average home the kitchen sink answers for scullery, pantry, vegetable and baking sink. The most popular design is the double drainboard apron type with sink, back, drainboards and aprons all cast in one piece and covered with white porcelain enamel. It is quite usual to find them fitted with combination hot and cold swinging spout faucet, and china soap dish.

In the more pretentious homes the kitchen is very often tiled and fitted with a large solid porcelain kitchen sink, with separate drainboards, large solid vegetable sink, porcelain scullery sink, and white metal or pantry sink. These may be fitted with in-

tegral back or set flush against the wall. Or they may be finished without back, but tiled along the wall, or as some prefer them, may be set away from the wall, which permits of cleaning back of the sink and along the wall. In all cases the walls should be of tile. The fittings can be of white metal or nickel-plated brass, the faucets are usually combination type with tempered water supplied through a single swinging spout.

Closets

Low tank combinations are now almost universally used for the home, the noiseless all-white combination being the latest word in closet construction. The closet bowl, tank and flush connection are made of two-fired vitreous china, and the seat of wood, with white sheet celluloid covering.

Closets for the home are of three different types, known as the syphon jet, reverse trapway spyhon action and washdown syphon action. The syphon jets are in turn furnished in two types, the noiseless and the regular. The syphon jet closet carries a large water surface and deep water seat in the trap, reducing the liability of fouling and escape of sewer gas. The reverse trap closet has the general appearance of the syphon jet with the water surface and seat of a washdown closet, and are used where it is desired to keep the cost at a minimum.

Wallpaper: the Background in Home Decoration

(*Continued from page* 296)

"home." Here again wallpaper, the vehicle for the expression of beauty and warmth—the setting within which interior decoration creates atmosphere—has a value purely sentimental.

In order to obtain the best results in decorative treatment of a home one should plan the entire scheme in advance. To start without a definite *motif* and fairly clear visualization of the effect sought is almost certain to produce unsatisfactory results.

The following main points relating to the individual rooms and to the house as a unit should be taken into consideration in working out the wall treatment.

1. The use and purpose of the room.

2. The size, lines and contents of the room.

3. The personality of the occupant or occupants.

4. The lighting conditions—source and results desired—subdued, natural, artificial, direct, or reflected light.

5. Relation of the room to other rooms in the house.

6. Location and external surroundings of the house —city, suburban, country, etc.

7. The *motif*—a house is a harmonious whole. Let wall treatment blend with architecture, general decorative effect and furnishings.

Wallpaper will accomplish many things. The careful decorator may put wallpaper to work in the interest of beauty and utility. For instance:

Color has a definite effect on people. It is a pronounced influence in our lives. Wallpaper is the most natural, accessible and acceptable means of dis-

tributing color properly throughout the home. Red excites, yellow cheers and blue quiets.

Color may also be used to influence the proportions of a room. Red makes a room seem small, blue increases its size. Simple vertical stripes will increase height. Tapestry effects will give width. Proper utilization of wallpaper will emphasize the horizontal lines, reducing height. Warm colors decrease and cool ones enlarge the apparent size of a room.

Wallpaper solves the secrets of texture. There are papers which reproduce the feeling of damask, chintz, satin, leather, burlap, etc. It is difficult to distinguish between the actual fabric and the paper. Texture is an important influence in wallpaper selection; oak and mahogany, maple and walnut, each appear to better advantage when utilized with the proper texture of wallpaper.

Wallpaper possesses super-sanitary qualities. Disease-breeding germs cannot propagate on a porous and well-ventilated wall, and air passes freely through brick and plaster walls. Wallpaper itself is porous and in no way retards ventilation.

When you build a home remember that for centuries the leading authorities and most particular hostesses have utilized wallpaper as the setting for interior decoration. Such men as Sheraton laid great emphasis on the papering of rooms. Such hostesses as Martha Washington personally supervised the treatment of their walls. Your wallpaper is the greatest single influence in the interior decorative scheme of your home. Your wallpaper tells who you are.

Copper Products for Homebuilding

A significant statement on this page is that America can raise its standard of living by building time-defying houses for its people. The term "time-defying" in this sense implies the use of materials and equipment which do not show rapid depreciation or deterioration. Among these the products of copper, such as copper shingles, flashings, gutters, brass piping and brass and bronze hardware are particularly valuable in homebuilding because of their lasting qualities.

LABOR-SAVING devices, improved methods of production and modern transportation have been the means whereby that great aggregation of farms, mines, railroads and manufactories we call America has afforded its people a constantly rising standard of living. The earning power of the average American has, especially in the past two decades, increased at a truly remarkable rate.

The moving picture, the automobile, the radio, all making for the more advantageous use of leisure, are absorbing a growing proportion of our enlarged incomes. We are, in addition, better clothed and better fed than ever before.

But we are not better housed. While our standards of living have constantly improved in almost every other direction, the character and quality of our dwellings have shown but little improvement during the last twenty years.

The reason is not far to seek. Our attention has not, at least until very recently, been centered on our buildings. Little effort has been made to build for permanence. We build, and then rebuild bit by bit, and our repair bill is twice or thrice our original investment.

Yet, if we used the same care in selecting the materials which go, let us say, into our roofs, our plumbing, our sheet metal work and our hardware, as we do in picking out a new suit of clothes, a set of furs, or a player piano, we would assure ourselves not only of greater satisfaction but also of complete freedom from upkeep expense.

The "Third Mortgage" of Repairs

The lack of care in selecting materials in homebuilding, and more especially in the parts just named —which are called upon to withstand the greatest amount of exposure and wear-and-tear—means the creation of the costliest of all obligations, the "third mortgage" of excessive repairs.

Why has the cord tire crowded the fabric off the market? The cord costs a little more at first, but everybody knows it is worth the difference, because the cord gives a great deal more mileage, and therefore saves money in the long run. It is precisely the same with your roof, your sheet metal work, flashings, valleys, plumbing pipe, hardware.

Copper and brass cost a little more at first, but they give you infinitely more "mileage" than the substitute metals. An example familiar to everybody is found in the well-known fact that over a period of twenty-five or thirty years copper leaders and gutters actually cost only about one-sixth as much as galvanized iron. Metal mileage is what counts. Because you want most years for the dollar, it will repay you to make sure you get copper, the cord tire of metals.

The added carrying and amortization charges on a house equipped to withstand time, with a copper roof,

leaders, gutters and flashings, brass plumbing pipe, and real solid brass or bronze hardware and lighting fixtures, is very small—perhaps $25 a year on a ten-thousand-dollar dwelling.

You save several times that much every year, because you are protected against a leaky roof, with its costly chain of repairs, renewals and redecorations; and you are forever rid of that "hardy perennial" expense of rusted leaders and gutters which have to be renewed with seasonal regularity, and plumbing pipe that is constantly annoying you with rusty water and makes the plumber a regular visitor.

Labor is high these days; and while initially the labor required to install brass or copper is the same as the labor required to install substitute metals, in the long run it takes a great deal more labor to install these quick-rusting substitutes for brass and copper— because one has to keep renewing them.

The Value of "Rust Insurance"

Copper and brass will serve you as long as the house stands, because they do not rust.

And the importance of the rustproof service of copper and brass is evidenced by the fact that year after year home-owners in this country are spending more than $600,000,000 annually to repair and replace rusted metal work. The rust loss of home-owners is actually six times greater than the fire loss.

From the aspect of money loss, rustproofing a building is obviously of greater importance than fireproofing. While no one, and rightly, ever thinks of going without insurance against loss by fire, the need of rust insurance is too frequently lost sight of. Yet, it costs less to carry the one certain means of rust insurance—brass and copper—than it does to carry fire insurance.

There is another consideration. The unsightliness of rusted metal, an all too familiar object to need further description, not only spoils the appearance of the building, but also decreases materially the chance of an advantageous sale in case the owner wishes to dispose of the property.

By using copper and brass the owner not only assures himself of the greater satisfaction that comes from building for permanence, but he actually saves money every year the building stands. The man who builds his house with a copper roof, copper leaders, gutters and flashings, with brass pipe plumbing, and real brass or bronze hardware, not only has a more attractive place in which to live, but he can help maintain an automobile or keep himself in clothes with the actual savings in upkeep afforded by the repair-proof service of the everlasting metals.

America can raise its standard of living higher than it is by building time-defying houses for its people.

Advantages and Methods of Obtaining Crackproof Plaster

Home building has overnight become a fascinating topic for informal discussion wherever people meet. This is to be expected, because Americans are known universally as a nation of home lovers, and home ownership has come to the fore now that high rents have seemingly come to stay.

MANY details about building construction concerning which the inexperienced builder needs advice and reassurance are comparatively simple and readily understood by him when once the surface is scratched, so to speak.

Comparatively few, however, even of the well-informed, really know enough about plastering, for instance, to discuss the subject with assurance. Plastering is naturally a grimy and splashy operation, and it is difficult to approach close enough to the busy plasterer without coming away with evidence showing one's investigating turn of mind. Therefore, observations of the plastering art, and it really and truly is one, are usually made after the mechanics have completed their work, and when all that can be seen is the gleaming white surface ready for the decorator. Naturally we wonder how long this surface will retain its unmarred pristine beauty before it exhibits those seemingly inevitable plaster cracks that are the blight of the housewife's peace of mind, that focus the visitor's critical gaze and are the cause of a continual draft on the family pocketbook to pay for decorator's expense.

The question then arises: "Isn't there some way of building the house and plastering the walls so that cracks won't form? The answer is that there is and that it can be done easily and economically.

How Plaster Cracks Originate

In the first place plaster cracks may originate from:

(1) Unequal settlement of the foundation of the building.

(2) Drying out, shinkage, and subsequent settlement of the lumber used in the walls, partitions and floors.

(3) Absorption of moisture by ordinary lath in rooms such as bathrooms, kitchens and laundries, where extremes of temperature cause condensation (drops of water) to form on the walls and ceiling, and elsewhere where artificial heat is used.

(4) Unusual loads on ceilings, caused by grouping heavy furniture in the middle of the room, by dancing, romping children, falling objects, etc.

Each condition described above can be remedied, and by so doing, cracking of plaster can be nearly, if not entirely, eliminated.

For the first, the mason contractor must be specially instructed to carefully proportion the footings for the foundation, making them of ample size, depending on the size of the building and the character and bearing power of the foundation soil. The foundation is the last place to practice economy, because so very little of the first cost can be saved by skimping. On the other hand it is manifestly extremely unwise to save these few dollars by decreasing the size of the footing or foundations and then spend many times as much in patching countless cracks in the walls and plaster as the building settles unevenly with the course of time.

The formation of plaster cracks due to shrinkage (Cause No. 2) can probably best be counteracted by using expanded metal lath on the wood bearing partitions and load carrying plastered walls. The overlapping metal lath sheets, each about 2 ft. wide and 8 ft. long "bridge" across from stud to stud by means of their network of strands. This prevents the slight settlement of individual studs due to shrinkage. It is said that the expanded metal lath performs in a manner similar to the lattice truss commonly used for long spans in roof trusses and bridges.

Although expanded metal lath will help, it cannot entirely prevent cracks due to large settlements caused by faulty foundations, and for this the remedy suggested in a previous paragraph should be used. On the other hand small settlements can be counteracted and plaster cracks prevented by using twelve-inch strips of metal lath bent into the form of an "L," 6 inches on each side, and nailed into the corners of walls and ceilings. This narrow strip, "cornerite," is nailed directly over wood lath or plaster-board in corners from floor to ceiling where walls join, and for the length or breadth of the room where walls and ceilings come together. Many architects and builders use it, as experience and laboratory tests have shown it to be a very inexpensive yet effective method by which to eliminate corner cracks, especially in new houses.

Metal Lath Does Not Swell

Cracks caused by absorption of moisture and subsequent swelling of lath can be avoided by using metal lath which is non-absorptive. This lath does not "draw" water, therefore it cannot swell and crack the plaster. For a similar reason the streaking of ceilings, especially in furnace-heated houses can be avoided; and much costly re-decoration avoided.

Unusual floor loads, such as can easily be brought about by grouping the furniture in the center of a room for Spring housecleaning, re-decorating, laying a new rug, etc., by the falling of a heavy object, or children at play, cause plaster cracks on ceilings, because the "key" by which the plaster grips ordinary lath and in turn hangs on to the ceiling is not strong enough—rather there are insufficient numbers of them to resist the bending of the joist in the one case, and the sudden impact in the other. The mesh of metal lath automatically supplies thousands of "keys" and, besides, acts as a steel reinforcement for the plaster to resist bending strains in the sagging floor. It therefore holds the plaster in place and prevents cracking long after it would have cracked and possibly fallen off of other plastering bases.

For the average home it is not necessary that metal lath be used throughout the building. Cracks are most objectionable in prominent places, such as the dining room, living room and entry hall, and it would undoubtedly be advantageous to use this material on the ceilings of such rooms. For bedrooms and small rooms ordinary lath can be employed, using metal lath "cornerite" in the corners, and thus all the advan-

(Continued on page 310)

Face Brick—the Material That Meets All the Requirements for Home-Building—Beauty, Durability, Fire-Safety and Economy

IN building a home there are three chief considerations of equal importance: First, *utility*, or such arrangement of the interior parts as to meet the needs of the family that is to occupy it; secondly, *strength*, or such durability as justifies the care and the expense involved; thirdly, *beauty*, or such attractiveness as delights the eye and satisfies the artistic requirements of harmonious color and form. Utility depends entirely on skill and genius in laying plans, while strength and beauty depend largely on the nature of the materials chosen.

For these three basic requirements face brick is an ideal material. In strength, in durability, it is surpassed by none, and in varied beauty, charm of appearance, it presents a varied possibility of appealing value.

People, as a rule, would like to use Face Brick, but regard it as too expensive. The fact is that its structural durability and artistic beauty create economic advantages that save you money, and in the end actually reduce the cost of your brick house below that of the less substantial structures. The items that enter into this reduction are (1) maintenance or upkeep, (2) depreciation, (3) fire-safety and lower insurance rates, and (4) comfort with resulting advantages to health.

It is well to bear in mind that two sets of costs enter into home-owning; the initial cost of the building and depreciation and upkeep. Based upon figures gathered in various parts of the country it has been found that it costs six per cent more to build a house with solid brick walls than to build a frame house. Appraisal engineers figure that a frame house depreciates two or three per cent annually from the day it is built, while a brick house shows no depreciation for the first five years and after that period at the rate of only one per cent per year.

These factors of building economy have been more completely presented in carefully prepared literature which is available through the Home Owners Service Institute. Here will be found definite facts and figures which clearly indicate the economic value of the use of face brick, and demonstrate how the slight excess cost of this material may prove to be a valuable investment not alone from the æsthetic viewpoint but from the purely practical business viewpoint.

Other information which is available in printed form includes data and illustrations of the various types of brick bonds and data as to the selection of color and texture in purchasing face brick. It can be well understood that the artistic possibilities of this material are almost of unlimited range. In the first place there is a complete selection of colors which may be used in one or two combinations or in attractive variations. In addition to color there is the question of texture of the material which may be rough or smooth, fine or coarse, and may be selected as a suitable component in the creation of an artistic surface. Similarly, the question of brick bonding is highly important because it involves depth and width of the bond, the arrangement and placing of the brick and also the use of colored cement mortar.

No expenditure is so important as that which you make for a home. You are to live in it for a period of years, you will see it every day, and every day your neighbors will see it. It must have the quality of strength and durability, that is, it must *wear*; and it must have *style*. The quality you want for the comfort, safety, and welfare of yourself and family; the style you want to satisfy your own and their taste. Both you want for your neighbors and even passing strangers to judge you by. The manner of the house indicates the manner of the man within. It indicates, as it were, your standing in the community; and certainly, if circumstances lead you to move elsewhere, you want in your house, as a commercial asset, both strength and beauty, for these are sure to get a better return in rent or sale. That is, from every point of view, an attractive Face Brick home will prove to be a wise investment.

In conclusion it may be said that face brick is as durable as the eternal hills, it is proof against the corrosion of the seasons and the ravages of fire, thus reducing the cost of maintenance and depreciation to a minimum; and, beautiful in its varied colors and textures as the finest fabrics, it offers to the eye an artistic charm that meets the most refined and discriminating taste.

Your brick house costs you from a twentieth to a tenth more than the less substantial structures, but it lasts more than twice as long and remains in a better condition. The same brick house costs far less than the heavier and more pretentious structures, and yet lasts as long, rivals them in substantial appearance and dignity, and excels them in the range of artistic effects. Brick has unique characteristics of plasticity. The size and form of brick not only offer pleasing proportions to the eye, but easily lend themselves to the skill of the mason craftsman; and either their uniformity or variety of texture and color affords the utmost possibilities in designing the wall surface.

Brick has equal value for the poor man's cottage or the rich man's palace, or for the cobbler's shop or the city hall, the wayside chapel or the metropolitan temple, and yet combines that strength and beauty which meet the requirements of both good taste and a thrifty purse. In conclusion, we beg to repeat that there is no other building material that will combine any more merit of quality and style, strength and beauty, in your home as face brick.

These matters of building economy have been more thoroughly presented in "The Story of Brick," an attractively illustrated booklet that every homebuilder should read before he determines definitely on his building project, and one that he will find exceedingly interesting. A copy will be sent without charge to anyone contemplating building.

Using Common Brick for Homebuilding

The vast majority of people who build or buy homes would prefer to have a home of brick.
The home is an institution that deserves to be permanent. The walls should be as lasting as
the home sentiment itself. It should become the "old homestead," a place that lives not only
in the memory, but a place to go back to.

THIS country is renewing its acquaintance with brick. Although those who founded America came from countries where brick was almost exclusively the medium of construction, the prevalence of timber in the new country forced its use upon the builder. Until brick plants could be established in this land some quantities of brick were imported from Europe, and there are throughout the Colonial states today many examples of buildings erected with material brought over in the holds of the ancient ships. Although clay from which brick could be made abounds in nearly every part of this country, lumber was thought to be the cheaper material, and the country has grown up largely in lumber, as far as home building is concerned. Until quite recent years even New England and the Northern Atlantic coast states could build of local timber, but today the country faces a new situation. Even the supply of lumber in the South is nearly exhausted, and the Northern states, like Michigan and Wisconsin, are no longer able to provide timber for their own use. Much of the lumber today used throughout the country comes from the Northwest and Canada, and from the disappearing forests of the South.

With the excessive freight charges, the difference in cost of construction between frame and the permanent materials has been practically wiped out. It may reasonably be argued that in almost any part of the country today the ultimate cost of the more permanent construction is less than for timber construction. This, of course, takes into account the cost of maintenance and upkeep, the chief item of which is painting. The arguments for the use of brick are so well known that they hardly need repetition here.

Dwelling Exteriors of Common Brick

One needs to read no further than the advertising and literature of the lumber industry itself to learn that there is much criticism of the modern methods of timber construction. There has been a race for cheapness. The speculative builder has endeavored to leave out as much material as possibly could be omitted and have the house stand long enough to be sold. It will be freely admitted that a wide variance in quality is possible in timber construction, and that there is a wide difference in cost, in comfort and in wearing quality between a good and a poor frame house. There is no such opportunity for cutting in masonry construction. It has been so clearly proven that there is no economy in the veneers and other sham forms of construction, which pretend to be something that they are not, that today the line is fairly definitely drawn as between good, honest masonry construction and frame construction.

The most revolutionary development in home building in the past few years has been the wide and growing popularity of common brick. Common brick may be roughly defined as the ordinary, low priced brick produced in almost every community in the United

States. A beautiful and artistic product has been developed by the manufacturers who make brick exclusively for facing purposes. A wide variety of color and texture may be had in this product and it may always be argued that the investment in face brick is a profitable one.

Where economy is a foremost consideration, common brick makes a strong appeal to the builder. The general expression from some may be that common brick is fairly presented in factory walls and the back walls of commercial and apartment buildings. This is an injustice to common brick. It would be difficult for the average person to be able to tell what is a common brick and what is not a common brick when it is properly used.

The attention of some of the leading architects in the country has been brought to common brick with the result that the material is found today not only in the homes of modest and low cost, but in some of the most elaborate residences in the high priced districts of great cities. There is a strong feeling among many architects that no material can exceed in art and beauty a native material. A prominent example of this is the wide use of native stone in the residences of Philadelphia. It is equally true that the common, ordinary brick produced in any locality, when used with architect's skill, produces effects that need no apology. As far as quality is concerned, one brick is practically as good as another, and the poorest brick is sufficiently strong and enduring to last for hundreds of years.

Common brick are ordinarily manufactured without any design to make them beautiful. The intense heat to which they are subjected in the course of manufacture produces a variety of shades in the different units. They are never exactly uniform in size, there being a very slight variation in the shrinkage which takes place in burning. These features of common brick, which in the past may have been thought of as objections, now turn out to be advantages of the most pronounced sort. The architect finds that this variation of line and color when the brick are placed in the wall gives just the "vibration" that pleases the eye. Home builders in every part of the United States, before deciding upon the use of what they believe to be a cheaper material, owe it to themselves to investigate the use of common brick. If they go to a reliable architect or mason contractor they will learn that the home of their dreams may be worked out in this practically everlasting material at a cost well within their reach, and that they may have not a more or less temporary home, but a home that will become a greater comfort to them with each added day it is occupied; a home that does not discourage them with its cost of maintenance; a home which their grandchildren will be glad to inherit, and a home which will prove invariably a good investment, because its values are permanent. This new development in the use of common brick has smashed the fallacy that brick homes are expensive.

Concrete Masonry Construction

On this and the following page will be found practical information regarding qualities and use of concrete block and building tile. This information is presented with definite facts and figures so that the homebuilder may be thoroughly conversant with the qualifications and requirements of the material when discussing its use with his architect or contractor.

EVERLASTING beauty is the keynote of the concrete house. Its charm endures. Outside, the stucco finish produces a warm and pleasing effect. Inside, the cellular walls of concrete block make the house cozy and comfortable. The concrete house is fire-safe. It is cool in summer, easy to heat in winter and economical to maintain at all times. The first cost of the concrete house is little if any more than for a house of less enduring type. Its total cost during its term of life is always less than the corresponding cost for any other type.

Reliable estimates show that no less than 175,000,-000 concrete block and concrete building tile were used in the United States during the year 1921, while for 1922 the total reached the vicinity of 300 million. This tremendous increase impressively reflects the popularity of precast concrete units for residences, schools, garages, churches and a wide variety of industrial and public buildings. New uses are appearing continually, while the demand for concrete block and concrete building tile for the well established older uses continues to grow rapidly.

Widely distributed factories and building material dealers carrying concrete structural products in stock insure ready availability of these materials in almost every local community. Most manufacturers make guaranteed products, the quality of which is governed by the standards of the American Concrete Institute.

Similar rapid expansion is found in the concrete brick industry. While concrete common brick are extensively used in plain masonry, the development of variously colored surface textures have extended their use as face brick to the best types of architectural design.

Concrete Block and Building Tile

The use of concrete block and concrete building tile simplifies the work of both designer and builder, and gives the owner the advantages of rigid, permanent and maintenance-free construction at a saving in both the cost and the time required to build. The excess cost of houses built of concrete masonry units over frame construction seldom runs higher than three or five per cent. The wall dimensions of available units lend themselves conveniently to any desired design, and make calculations simple. The block run true to size and shape so that figured dimensions are easily adhered to. Concrete block and building tile lay up rapidly and bed firmly in the mortar; mortar and stucco adhere to them with greater tenacity than to other masonry units.

In both the hollow block and the two-piece block the amount of air space varies from twenty to forty per cent of their volume, but it usually approximates thirty-three per cent. The tendency of modern plants is to increase the amount of air space to about forty per cent, producing a lighter, more economical unit. Block are made in various sizes. The eight by eight by sixteen-inch block is the most common. It makes a wall eight inches thick and courses eight inches high. Block are also made regularly for building walls ten and twelve inches thick, and with variations in height from six to twelve inches and in length from sixteen to 30 inches; the eight and nine-inch heights and the sixteen and twenty-four-inch lengths predominating. Veneer and partition block are made six and four inches thick and in common heights and lengths.

Concrete building tile are smaller in size and lighter in structure than block, the standard size being five by eight by twelve inches. They are suitable for constructing walls either eight or twelve inches thick, according to the way the unit is turned in the wall. The height of five inches is equivalent to two courses of brick. The air space in tile amounts to fifty per cent or more of its total volume.

The sizes mentioned are nominal. A block of eight by eight by sixteen-inch size usually measures seven and three-quarter inches by eight inches by fifteen and three-quarter inches, allowance being made for one-quarter inch vertical and horizontal mortar joints. Most block are designed for one-quarter inch joints, although thicker joints may be used if desired, and some block molds provide adjustments to permit varying the joint thicknesses.

For economy of construction, it is well to make as general use as possible of "normal" or full size block of standard dimensions. Considerable saving can be effected by keeping wall lengths and door and window openings as nearly as possible in multiples of whole and half block. Corner block, joist block, sills, lintels and other special shapes should be made to course with the standard wall block.

Surface Finish for Concrete Masonry Construction

Portland cement stucco meets the popular demand for surface finish not only because of the variety of artistic color and texture treatments available, but because it needs no periodic painting or repair and remains permanently fresh and clear and undamaged by time or weather. Concrete block and tile provide the ideal backing for Portland cement stucco. The surfaces of these units are sufficiently rough to produce a strong mechanical key and their density may be regulated to give uniform, effective suction. The rigidity of concrete masonry construction insures against movement of the wall and consequent cracking of the stucco. Since concrete block and tile and the cement mortar in which they are laid are of the same general composition and have practically the same absorption, the stucco hardens to a uniform color throughout.

Most concrete products plants carry in stock rough, flat-faced block for stucco covering and in addition, one or two popular types of surfaced block suitable for the exterior faces of buildings to be finished without the stucco. Many plants are prepared to submit specimen faces in several textures and colors, and will make up block of special facing for individual jobs.

Concrete Masonry Walls

Thickness of walls is usually regulated by state or local building codes. Eight inches is the minimum thickness for exterior or load-bearing walls recommended by the Building Code Committee of the U. S. Department of Commerce. Partition and curtain walls are often made four or six inches thick, which is amply sufficient for supporting their own weight and lightly loaded floors with ordinary ceiling heights.

When concrete block and tile are used as a backing for brick veneer, the brick wall is usually bonded to the backing by means of suitable metal strips or ties, or cross bond may be obtained by using header courses of brick. Eight-inch courses of concrete block equal in height three ordinary brick courses; five-inch concrete tile courses equal in height two ordinary brick courses.

Portland cement mortar is recommended for laying concrete building units because of its great bonding power, compressive strength, density and resistance to weather.

Portland cement mortar should be made with clean, graded sand and clean water. A small amount of well slaked or commercially hydrated lime is sometimes added to make the mortar more plastic, or "flat," but the maximum quantity admissible is twenty-five per cent by volume of the cement in the mixture (about ten pounds of lime to each sack of cement). Mortar mixed in the proportion of one sack (one cubic foot) of Portland cement to three cubic feet of sand is best. It should be mixed thoroughly with just enough water to give maximum plasticity. The batches should be only of such size that they can be used within thirty minutes after water is added. Retempered mortar should not be used.

Mortar joints should break at the midjoint as nearly as possible, even in masonry which is to be covered with stucco. Irregularities may be permitted in stucco construction for the sake of economy, since they will not appear in the finished work. In block work which is exposed (without covering of stucco), careful attention must be given to regularity of the joints. When the wall thickness (block thickness) is equal to half the block length, the corner block are of the same dimensions as standard block. But if the block thickness is greater or less than half the block length, the corner should be constructed with special block.

Making Basement Walls Watertight

A dry basement is a positive essential of good construction. For well drained soils the only precaution needed in building concrete block walls below grade is to see that joints are well filled with cement mortar and carefully pointed. If the subsoil does not have good drainage, a line of drain tile should be placed around the outside of the footing below the cellar floor level and connected to a suitable outlet to carry off subsoil water. The excavation above the tile should be filled for a depth of one or two feet with gravel or cinders. If for any reason it is impossible to run a line of tile around the outside, the tile may be placed with the fill on the inside of the footing.

If the soil is very wet or the water table is likely to rise much above the footing, the exterior wall should be plastered with Portland cement mortar mixed in the proportion of one sack of cement to two cubic feet of clean, well graded sand. And an additional safeguard is to coat the exterior surface with hot tar. The wall must be clean and absolutely dry when this tar coating is applied or it may not adhere perfectly.

Basement Partitions

Basement partitions of concrete block or tile are recommended for carrying the weight of the floors and interior partitions as preferable to beams and columns. The rigid support afforded by interior masonry walls insures that there will be no settlement of floors or interior partitions and consequently no cracking of plaster or loosening of interior trim. Such walls afford fireproof enclosures for heating equipment and fuel, confine steam and moisture within the laundry and provide insulation for fruit, vegetables or other perishables.

Setting Door and Window Frames

Door and window frames are usually built into the walls as the latter are laid. The frames should be well bedded and pointed in mortar. In high-class work they are often caulked with oakum before pointing. Outside staff heads should not be fixed until stucco work is finished.

Door and window jamb block and tile are supplied to fit plank and box frames of all common designs and constitute one of the many convenient features of concrete masonry construction. By using these jamb blocks it is possible to make absolutely tight connections around the frames, excluding wind and water.

Outside Fixtures

At the time concrete block or tile are laid, provision should be made for attaching down-spout brackets, telephone and electric service wires and other house fixtures on the outside of the masonry walls. If the location of these fixtures cannot be determined as the walls are being built, it will be necessary to drill holes later.

Lintels and Sills

Precast lintels are generally more convenient and economical than lintels cast in place. Lintels should be made the same height as the block courses. These lintels may be larger and stronger than required to carry the load in most cases, but the standardization of lintel sizes is a very great convenience in ordering and saves the time and the labor otherwise required to fit block around lintels of special dimensions. Lintels spanning openings of more than three feet should be reinforced, the steel bars being located about one inch above the bottom. Two half-inch bars are needed for a four-foot span and three for a five-foot span.

For use in connection with hollow block walls to be furred and lathed on the inside, one-piece lintels having the same thickness as the wall are used. Walls with a continuous air space for insulation, where in-

(*Continued on page* 308)

Stucco Made With White Portland Cement Is Dependable and Economical

The homebuilder who is interested in facts regarding stucco exteriors will find valuable information on this page, including the important subjects of stucco finishes and colors.

THE use of stucco for surfacing walls dates back for centuries, and through these years has proved its value. With the steady advance in chemical science and engineering skill, the material has been refined and improved in quality far beyond that possessed by the stucco used in earlier generations, so that today stucco made from Portland cement and sand, or other aggregates, mixed with water, hardens into a stone-like substance known as concrete, the material used to build the Panama Canal, the Keokuk Dam, and many other great construction projects.

The modern method in the application of stucco made with Portland cement is to use the regular gray cement for the base or first two coats and white Portland cement for the final coat, to secure beauty in the finish, as described in the paragraphs below.

A house with walls of stucco made with Portland cement is literally sheathed in concrete, a time-defying, fire-safe, weather-proof wall containing nothing that can rust or rot, that will neither deteriorate nor disintegrate, furnishing insulating properties that make the house warmer in winter and cooler in summer, that needs no paint except for the trim, and requires no miscellaneous repairs year after year. It actually grows stronger with age, and proves to be a truly permanent wall.

And with all these advantages, stucco made with Portland cement is cheap in first cost. The lowest cost and least durable home is built of wood frame covered with wood siding, such as clapboards or shingles. If the wood siding were replaced with this stucco on metal lath, the cost in most localities would be the same; the result would be a durable, fire-resisting house.

Perhaps a more surprising fact, one that is of vital importance to every prospective homebuilder, is that for only about two per cent more than the cost of all-frame construction, he can secure a house made of concrete building units covered with stucco made from Portland cement, providing in effect a fire-proof home, permanently insuring against fire the safety of his loved ones and the various cherished possessions that go to make a home. And this concrete house costs about ten per cent less than all brick construction.

To build for protection against fire is of vital importance. Man has an hereditary fear of fire, and rightfully so. In the middle of the night, or during his absence, it may rob him of home, his family, and a lifetime's treasures. Every prospective homebuilder should know that according to figures published by the National Board of Fire Underwriters, the fire losses in the United States in 1921 reached the amazing figure of $495,000,000.

Beyond its great value to the home owner through insuring a permanent fire-safe home at low first cost, the use of stucco made with Portland cement insures definite yearly savings that are just as certain as interest on an investment. There will be a big saving on paint, for the stucco house needs no paint except on the trim. Tests conducted by the Armour Institute of Technology show that stucco houses provided a saving on coal as high as 13½% per year. There is also a saving on depreciation; and after a few years, a very material saving on the miscellaneous upkeep and repairs that are always necessary to a house of less durable construction. These savings multiply to the benefit of the house owner year after year.

For proof as to the dependability and desirability of stucco made with Portland cement, one has ample evidence in the countless fine country homes and in such monumental buildings as the twenty-story Fifth Avenue Hospital in New York, in the construction of which the materials were selected for their dependability, beauty and permanence, and these valuable features were supplied with economy.

In addition to the economy in first cost and the savings that the house owner accumulates year after year through the use of white Portland cement for stucco, he has also a material that provides him with endless possibilities of beauty in texture and tint not obtainable from any other material.

White Portland cement, when mixed with pure white sand or marble dust and water, yields a pure white finish of lasting beauty. If a tint is desired, such as cream or light buff, colored sand in the mixture will yield a pleasing tint.

Then, if more pronounced shades are preferred, such as dark buff, light brown, dark brown or red, a small amount of mineral pigment of the desired shade added to the mixture will give true color value, because the white cement readily lends itself to any shade or tint, and the color will be uniform over the entire wall surface, as well as permanent.

Stucco made from white Portland cement, when ready to be applied, is a plastic substance, like a heavy batter, that can be worked up with an ordinary trowel into any textural effect or finish which may suit the ideas of the owner of the house. Finishes of varying gradations of roughness or a spatterdash effect may be given, or the stucco may be applied in broad, featherlike sweeps, and these effects become permanent as the stucco hardens. The surface has then an attractive irregularity instead of a monotonous sameness, and this, combined with the color effects that are made possible through the use of white Portland cement, will give the house an individuality and character that lift it out of the commonplace.

If the builder desires, he can have the finish known as rock dash or pebble dash, for this can be readily applied to stucco made with Portland cement, the same as it can be applied to any other stucco; but the stucco made with Portland cement needs no rock dash for protection, because it is permanent in itself.

(Continued on following page)

The house builder who seeks the picturesque and home-like atmosphere provided through climbing vines on the house, will find stucco made with white Portland cement the ideal background. Its rough texture provides a surface to which vines readily cling, and since stucco surfaces need no paint, the vines need never be disturbed from their natural position and are thus permitted to retain permanently their appealing beauty. No matter how luxuriant the growth of vines on the house, the interior will not be damp, because stucco made with white Portland cement is impervious to water.

Homes covered with stucco made from white Portland cement have a tendency to increase community values, for, being beautiful themselves, they naturally attract similar beautiful homes. This attraction is made stronger when the construction is of a type that increases local fire-safeness.

Finally, the wise homebuilder looks forward to the possible time when he may want to sell his house. Will it show heavy depreciation with the passing years, or will it show increased value? The homes covered with stucco made with white Portland cement, will, as a rule, show increased value as the years go by, because they are permanent in construction and their appearance improves with age.

To sum up its value to the prospective homebuilder, stucco made with white Portland cement is economical in first cost and continuously economical. Its use provides fire-safety, dependability, lasting beauty, and permanence in construction.

Concrete Masonry Construction

(*Continued from page* 306)

terior plaster is to be applied directly to the masonry, lintels are made in two pieces to provide an air space between inner and outer sections. As a precaution, metal flashing may be placed over window heads in continuous air space walls, to guide condensed water, if any, away from the opening.

Window sills are usually precast like lintels. They should have a steep "wash" or slope to the weather. They should project at least two inches from the face of the wall and have a groove on the underside to form a "drip" to keep water from flowing over on to the face of the wall. They are often set at the time the wall is built; a better practice is to insert "slip sills" after the wall has been laid up. If built in, the joint below the sill should be left open and pointed up or filled after the wall has had a chance to settle, as otherwise the slightest movement will crack the sill.

Attachment of Sills and Plates

The usual method of attaching wood sills and plates to concrete unit walls is to bolt them down at intervals, six feet apart or less, to the top courses. Bolts should be about ten inches long with nuts and large washers inserted in the air cells of the block and filled around with concrete to insure firm anchorage. This method is much more satisfactory than spiking sills or plates to wall through mortar joints.

Furring and Lathing

It is customary to "fur out" before applying plaster to the walls of buildings of all masonry materials, and this should ordinarily be done where concrete block are used. A continuous air space usually affords sufficient insulation so that plaster is about the same temperature as the inside air, preventing condensation.

In types of concrete block construction which provide a continuous air space in the wall and where split sills and lintels are used, plaster usually may be applied directly to inner surfaces of exterior walls. For all other types of concrete block construction, plaster should be furred out where placed on the walls of residences and other buildings to be continually occupied.

Gypsum Plaster and Products for Dwellings

This is a very carefully prepared article which provides the homebuilder with definite and valuable information on the use of gypsum plaster and other gypsum products suitable for dwelling construction.   The use of such products is a subject with which the homebuilder is not sufficiently familiar.

IN the case of the walls and ceilings, the selection of the best suited plastering materials is of the greatest importance.   Upon these interior surfaces, which are constantly before one's vision, the expensive but perishable decorations are applied.   The wall surfaces have to resist the abuse of furniture that is frequently moved, the wear and tear of permanent or changing occupancy, the removal of old wall paper, calcimine or decorations and the application of the new.   Pictures and the necessary fastenings are dependent on the walls as often as upon the moldings usually provided for hanging.   Ceilings are subjected to severe cleaning, repeated decorating and the shocks due to vibrations from floors or the construction above.   Because of these deteriorating influences of occupancy, wear and time, the ideal plastering material must embody the following essentials:

1. It must be of such character as to provide a strong, firm key or clinch, or perfect adhesion, to the base or background upon which it is applied.
2. It must mix easily and must be sufficiently plastic to permit easy working and application, making possible smooth true plane surfaces.
3. When set and dry, it must be tough and hard throughout from face to back, so as to provide for a surface with appreciable wearing properties and uniform density for the entire thickness.
4. It must set and dry quickly in order to permit the progress of other work, such as the erection of the wood trim, etc.   Also, the quicker the building is completed the sooner it can be made to earn revenue.
5. It should be of such character as to resist for appreciable periods of time, the action of fire. Fires within a building which are not confined to the place of origin will, in a short time, destroy the entire structure.   Hollow partitions act as flues and contribute to the spread of fire.   The plastered surface, whether wall or ceiling, will or will not prevent the spread of fire.   The degree of fire protection afforded depends upon the character of base or background (lath) upon which the plaster is applied and, most important of all, the kind and thickness of the plaster coats.
6. It should be a poor conductor of heat or cold. This physical property will assure warmer interiors in the winter months and more uniform temperature conditions during the heat of summer.
7. It should be within the reach of all building projects.   In other words, the plastering material should be easily procured throughout the country in amounts to satisfy large or small operations, no matter where located.

All of the itemized and desired properties are found in gypsum and are vouched for in United States Government and other authentic publications. The United States Department of Interior, Technical Paper 155, entitled "Gypsum Products—Their Preparation and Uses" refers to the light weight, toughness, insulating and fire-resisting properties of gypsum plasters.   United States Bureau of Standards, Circular No. 108, entitled "Gypsum-Properties, Definitions and Uses," when referring to gypsum plasters states:

> "Wall plasters and other building materials made of gypsum have a remarkable ability to resist fire. The reason for this is due to the chemically combined water of crystallization, which, as stated, is about 20 per cent by weight.   The heat breaks up these crystals and liberates the water, the process being slower as the heat penetrates farther into the gypsum.   As long as there are any water crystals in the gypsum to be broken up the material will not warm appreciably above the temperature of boiling water."

There are many other similar evidences on record, all of which have added to our knowledge of gypsum plasters and products and have made possible a demand for gypsum in the construction of buildings which, at the present time, is more than three million tons annually.   A more recent illustration of the adaptability, low heat conductivity and fire-resisting properties of gypsum plasters is found in fire and water test report of the Underwriters' Laboratories, Inc., bearing date of August 10, 1922, and published as Retardant No. 1,355.   This report grants to gypsum plaster, upon metal lath, a fire resistance rating of one hour for the fire protection of the partitions and ceilings of ordinary (wood joisted and studded) buildings.   No other plastering material has obtained a similar approval.

The space of this article will not permit quoting from other authentic sources.   The reader and prospective home owner is naturally interested in knowing just what the mineral gypsum is, where it is obtained and to what other uses it may be employed (besides plaster) in the construction of buildings.

What Is Gypsum?

Gypsum is one of the most ancient of building materials.   The Greeks used gypsum in Pliny's time. The writings of this naturalist of ancient history (23-79 A.D.) are included in thirty-six, book XXXVI, dealing with the different kinds of stones and marble, including lime, sand and gypsum.   He also minutely describes the removal of a beautiful gypsum plaster frieze from Lacedaemon to adorn a public building in Rome.   Going further back, the Temple of Apollo at Bassae, built four hundred and seventy years before Christ, affords an excellent example of the use and permanent structural qualities of gypsum.   The great pyramids of Egypt contain plaster work of gypsum.

(Continued on following page)

The common name, Plaster of Paris, is often applied to all calcined gypsum because of the large quantities of gypsum rock beds found near Paris, France. In France and Germany, gypsum is used for many building purposes, including inside and outside plastering, walls, floors and roofs. In the United States and Canada, gypsum has for years been the predominating interior plastering material. In proper form gypsum is also used structurally for floors, roofs and outside walls. The United States Government, in its war building operations, used many million square feet of reinforced gypsum roofs.

Gypsum Ready-Sanded Plaster

This plaster (sometimes called Prepared or Ready-Mixed Plaster) is a plastering material in which the predominating cementitious material is calcined gypsum, and which is mixed by the manufacturer with sand and other necessary constituent parts in their proper proportion. It requires only the addition of water to make it ready for use. It is advantageous to use this material in cases where good clean sand is hard to procure. Where good sand is procurable and the freight rates do not amount to more than the cost of the sand, the use of ready-mixed gypsum plaster is not economical.

Gypsum Wood-Fibered Plaster

This is a plastering material in which not less than 80% by weight is calcined gypsum and not less than 1% consists of a non-staining wood fiber. The remainder may consist of materials, mixed in the required proportions by the manufacturer, to control the working quality and setting time. This plaster is used with or without the admixture of sand, and is in demand where lightweight, tough, insulating and highly fire-resistive surfaces are required.

Neat Gypsum Plaster

Neat Gypsum Plaster (sometimes termed Gypsum Cement Plaster) is a plastering material in which not less than 85% by weight of the cementitious material is calcined gypsum. The remainder may consist of materials mixed in the required proportions by the manufacturer, to control the working quality, setting time, etc. This plaster is identical with "Gypsum Ready-Sanded Plaster," but requires the addition of from two to three parts, by weight, of sand before mixing in water and applying.

Other Gypsum Plasters

It is not necessary, in this article, to enter into the details of other gypsum plasters which are manufactured and sold in large quantities for specific purposes; such as "Gauging Plasters," "Keene's Cements," "Bond Plasters," "Molding Plasters," "Trowel Finishing Plasters," etc., except to state that in practically all building operations there is a demand for some or all of the plasters named.

Where, for reasons of greater fire protection, an incombustible lath is required, gypsum plaster board is used to a great extent. This form of lath consists of sheets or slabs of gypsum reinforced with fibrous material on the surfaces. This form of lath is made in sheets thirty-two by thirty-six inches and three-eighths inch thick, which are quickly and easily nailed

to the supports. The gypsum plaster is then easily and quickly applied, the peculiar affinity for gypsum to gypsum providing a firm, strong bond to this lath and a tough and strong finished wall or ceiling surface.

To meet the demands of rapid construction, consistent with permanency, fire-protection and similar desired properties, the interior finish of walls and ceilings can be accomplished by using gypsum wall boards which are manufactured to take the place of other types of wall boards that introduce a hazard into the construction because of their inflammability and susceptibility to moisture and changes of temperature. The fire-resisting properties of gypsum wall boards are attested to in the strength, fire and water tests conducted by the Underwriters' Laboratories, Inc., and reported by them as Retardant Nos. 1,006 and 1,319.

Gypsum wall boards are made in sheets or slabs thirty-two or forty-eight inches wide, three-eighths inch thick and ten to twelve feet in length. They are nailed direct to the wall or ceiling supports and in such a manner that all joints and nail holes can be obliterated by the use of a filler applied with a decorator's putty knife.

This character of interior finish does not require the subsequent application of plaster. It is complete when erected and can be covered with wall paper, paint or otherwise decorated to suit.

METHODS OF OBTAINING CRACKPROOF PLASTER

(*Continued from page* 302)

tages of crackproof plaster can be obtained at minimum expense, where it is most needed.

Back-Plastered Metal Lath Stucco Construction

Back-Plastered Metal Lath Stucco construction has been in use for over fifteen years.

The type of better stucco house has successfully passed strength and endurance tests made by the U. S. Bureau of Standards and other authorities. At Armour Institute in trials it clearly showed itself to be much warmer than many common forms of construction. At the Underwriters' Laboratories after exhaustive tests, a preliminary report was issued, indicating a one-hour rating.

Back-Plastered Metal Lath Stucco construction combines the economies of good frame construction with both permanence and fire-resistive qualities.

Read Carefully the Practical Information Contained in Pages 281 to 289!

*T*HE *homebuilder will find on the pages referred to a carefully prepared explanation of the logical use of this plan service together with an advised course of procedure in determining his individual problems and their practical solution.*

The Selection and Use of Door Beds

One of the most practical installations which has yet been developed for the moderate cost home is the door bed, by the use of which the facilities of another bedroom are provided without a large investment cost. A number of the plans in this book indicate the use of door beds, and it is not difficult to rearrange any plan to provide for a door bed, as explained on this page.

ECONOMY in construction of small houses is one of the great objectives.

Not only is this to be accomplished by a better selection of materials, but also by the better organization of the entire job of construction and financing; in addition to a careful examination of every avenue of saving is the securing of modern devices for providing extra convenience without increasing the size of the house.

The door bed provides additional sleeping accommodations without increasing the number of rooms in a house. It is installed in any ordinary closet of medium size, swings on vertical bearings outward when the door is opened, and is pulled down to the floor with very little effort, and is then in appearance and in reality an ordinary bed with the bedding in place, held by suitable devices.

When not in use, the bed is lifted up to a vertical position counterbalanced by strong springs so it moves without difficulty and retains its position, and is then revolved on its vertical bearings back into the closet. The door is closed and the room restored to normal.

Where the closet is large enough, accommodations can be provided, even when the bed is in place, for dressing facilities and also room for the hanging of additional clothing back of the bed. These devices permit of the installation of an additional single bed, three-quarter bed, or double bed in a closet off the living room for use when guests arrive. They can be used either by members of the family or by guests, and obviate the necessity of carrying expense of an additional guest chamber.

The best types of these beds are strongly constructed of the best material, and when properly installed are almost incapable of being broken or getting out of working order. They are sanitary and can readily be cleaned. When the bed is lifted up from the floor to a vertical position, the under side is readily wiped free from dust, and every nook and corner can be reached for easy cleaning. When revolved back into the closet and the door closed, it is out of the dust of the room and that which is blown in through open windows. The closets can be easily ventilated and where adjacent to an outside wall can have a small window opening out for light and ventilation.

This bed can be installed in a half a dozen different ways. It can be used in any room in the house without interfering with the decorations.

This is because it is concealed by ordinary stock doors, matching the other doors in the room. More important still, when the closet door is closed, no one knows that a bed is provided in that room.

These door beds are especially adapted to use for sleeping porches where the design of the house is made with due reference to this use. The closet can be planned as a part of the original construction. It should be large enough to permit of space for dressing. Where necessary a door can be provided from the closet into the adjacent living room or bedroom. This makes a sleeping porch most easily accessible, obviating all the difficulty of special couches and cots which have to be carried in and out.

The door bed can be installed also in connection with sun rooms, either at the front or back of the house, whether on the first or second story. They are one of the greatest advantages that can be provided in connection with nurseries and children's play rooms. As these beds are made of metal throughout, and are hung entirely independent of the door, there is no wood about them to collect vermin. The bed clothing is held in place by friction clamps at the foot, and when the bed is upright in the closet, the mattress and linen hang loosely from the top, receiving perfect ventilation. The bed is attached to the door jamb on one side of the door opening, through which it revolves. The bed does not hang on the door but rests securely in a socket on the floor. The operation of the bed is not affected in any way by the settling of floors or the shrinkage or warping of woodwork. The bed is so constructed that when in a position for use, it cannot possibly close up accidentally. It has no weights, but is controlled by balancing springs. To swing the door bed out of a closet is just as simple as opening a door, and the bed is controlled so perfectly that it is managed without any special exertion to anyone; even a child can handle it with ease and safety.

In bungalow construction these beds are coming into use very generally. They have made the rooms of the bungalow otherwise reserved for sleeping rooms available for general use as well as practically doubling the accommodations of a four- or five-room bungalow. Every room in the bungalow which otherwise would be entirely devoted to sleeping purposes can be utilized for the living room, library, reception room or sewing room, as found most desirable. The installation of these beds is accomplished easily and without much expense, and the beds themselves cost a very moderate sum. Where they can be properly utilized in a suitably designed closet, they will save probably the cost of an entire additional room, amounting to $1,000 or more. The use of these beds in homes is extending rapidly throughout the country, although they have been most popular on the Pacific Coast and, in fact, throughout the West. They are used very generally in apartment houses and hotels in the Middle West, especially in the large cities where the tests have been of the most thorough and practical character and have extended over a considerable period of time. Even where plans have been drawn which do not provide a closet for this purpose, the bed can frequently be installed in a recess with French doors to close over the bed, or in a wardrobe built into the room for the purpose.

Hollow Building Tile in Residential Construction

MANY points must be deeply considered when taking up the question of homebuilding. The home should be speedily constructed; it must be economical, yet permanent and attractive; it must be dry and sanitary and it must, at the same time, represent the minimum in upkeep and depreciation. In order to adhere strictly to these requirements, the material used in the construction of a home must be fireproof and permanent, strong in bearing, yet light in weight, impervious to moisture, a non-conductor to the passage of heat and cold and pleasing enough in appearance to lend an attractive touch to the finished project. Such a material is hollow building tile.

Hollow building tile, an incombustible product of burned clay, was originally used as a fireproofing cover on steel beams. When it became apparent that the huge spans of steel could not withstand the ravages of fire, a light fireproofing material was sought for. Hollow tile was adopted, and successfully performed its duty in this capacity. Its use, however, was not long confined to this respect, as it soon found its place in the construction of foundations, walls, partitions and floors, and is now extensively used in the construction of homes, churches, hospitals, schools, factories and farm buildings, in which case it successfully fulfills every requirement of a permanent form of construction at the minimum upkeep and depreciation. Its many qualities and versatility have earned for it the universal recognition of a material whose use represents the most economical form of permanent construction.

These qualities were recognized by the United States Government's building program during the War, in which hollow tile played a very important part. In the construction of warehouses, arsenals, hospitals and homes included in the housing project, hollow tile was used throughout. The Government fully realized the necessity of permanent fireproof buildings which required the minimum of upkeep, and which had practically no depreciation. Though many of these homes were built as cheaply as similar homes could be built of wood, they will stand for all time, with little attention, silent tributes to just a little better form of permanent construction.

People have long harbored the false illusion that permanent construction was far above the average pocketbook, but it has been conclusively proved that a home of hollow tile costs, at the most, but five per cent over a similar frame construction. As hollow tile comes in larger units, the speed of construction is materially increased, and the cost of labor is proportionately decreased. In addition, a home of hollow tile needs no painting. When one figures the five per cent difference between a frame home and a similar home built of hollow tile, it can readily be seen that the small difference will not pay for many paint jobs. In a few years, the frame home will be more expensive and the expense will keep on increasing as the years go by. A brick home will cost from ten to fifteen per cent more than a home of hollow tile and has none of the many advantages and assets. One

of these, its insulating quality, combines both economy and health.

The voids in a hollow tile block, when constructed in a wall, form several layers of dead air, which effectively insulates the interior from the elements without. It has long been known that dead air is the best form of insulation and with this in mind, hollow tile manufacturers have worked on the various designs with the result that the hollow building tile of today represents the acme in wall insulation to the passage of heat, cold and moisture. A home built of hollow tile is a virtual thermos bottle, a home within a home, the air wall between them standing as a silent guardian to the passage of all objectionable. This quality has many inestimable assets to the comfort of the family within its shielded walls.

The tile home is cooler in summer and warmer in winter. A test made covering a period of one year disclosed the summer temperature twelve degrees less in the tile home than that of the exterior reading, while the following winter showed a ten to fifteen per cent saving in coal. In addition the walls of a hollow tile home are dry, rendering the inside sanitary and healthful. Germs and bacteria cannot thrive in a dry home; vermin cannot penetrate the hard burned walls. Summed up, a tile home is not only an economical project, but it is a builder of health, a safe and sanitary playground for growing children, a source of pleasure to the meticulous housewife, and a home of pride and beauty to the owner.

Exterior finish on a home of hollow tile may be left to the discretion of the owner, as the versatility of this material offers several kinds of outside appearances from which to choose. It may be left bare, or covered with stucco or brick. For the sake of economy, the walls need not be covered either inside or out, as the tile wall needs no further protective material to aid it in its shielding properties. Many homes built by the government were constructed in this way, proving warm and dry at a considerable saving.

Stucco applied to a wall of hollow tile will not peel, chip or crack off. The small absorption value of this material draws in a certain minute amount of the cement mixture which, when set, results in a perfect bond. In addition, a mechanical bond is formed by the use of the deep scoring on the face of the tile. No water can penetrate its way between the stucco and the tile wall to freeze and crack the finish, as the cement and tile form a homogeneous mass and leave no line of separation. In addition, tile walls will not shrink, bulge or sag, and the stucco once applied is permanent. Brick may also be used as an exterior covering by bonding it into the course of tile.

For a housing proposition, hollow building tile represents the acme of building materials. Most economical from all standpoints, fireproof and permanent, sanitary and healthful, the homes of hollow tile stand as an inspiration of progress in any community, and uplift to the standards of living, permanent testimonials to sound judgment, of contentment and of joy; symbols of satisfaction in the most economical form of permanent construction.